D1158327

PERFECTING
THE
FAMILY

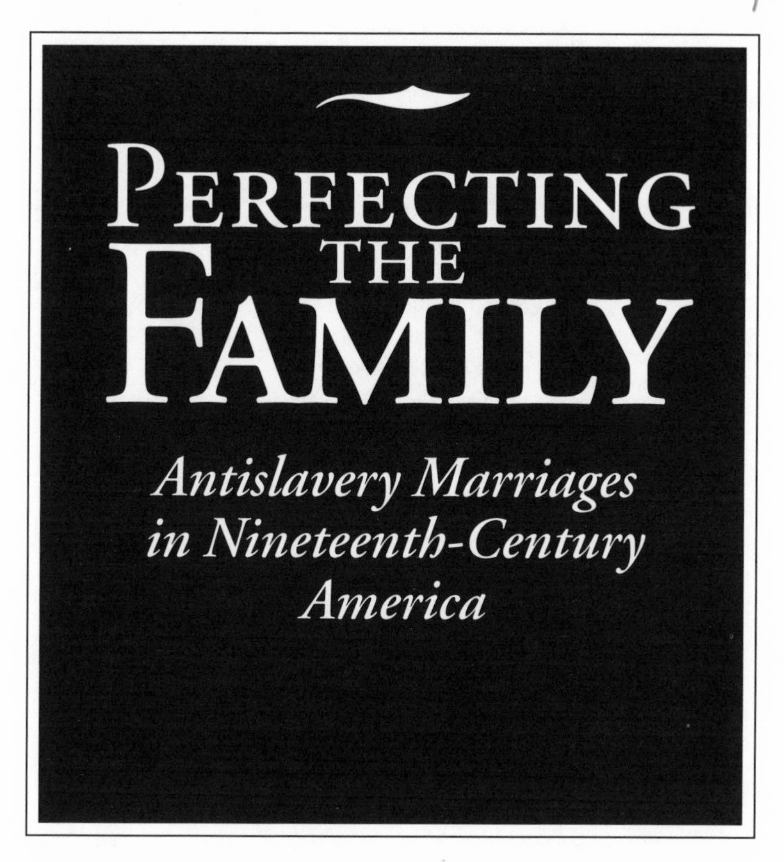

Chris Dixon

UNIVERSITY OF MASSACHUSETTS PRESS
AMHERST

Printed in the United States of America
LC 96-47627
ISBN 1-55849-068-x
Designed by Sally Nichols
Set in Adobe Garamond
Printed and bound by Braun-Brumfield, Inc.
Library of Congress Cataloging-in-Publication Data

Dixon, Chris, 1960–
Perfecting the family : antislavery marriages in nineteenth-century America / Chris Dixon.
p. cm.
Originally presented as the author's thesis—University of New South Wales, Australia.
Includes bibliographical references and index.
ISBN 1-55849-068-X (cloth : alk. paper)
1. Abolitionists—United States—Family relationships—History—19th century. 2. Man-woman relationships—United States—History—19th century. 3. Marriage—United States—History—19th century. 4. Family—United States—History—19th century. 5. Sex role—United States—History—19th century. I. Title.
E449.D6 1997
306.8′0973′09034—dc21 96-47627
CIP

British Library Cataloguing in Publication data are available.

For Jonk, Max, and Lorna

Contents

Preface

Of the many issues that have occupied the attention of American reformers, none have been more contentious than race and gender relations. Seeking to bring together these two aspects of the antebellum sisterhood of reforms, this study examines the connections between the family and antislavery in nineteenth-century America. Between the early 1830s and the Emancipation Proclamation of 1863, many Americans expressed their opposition to slavery. Most did so believing that slavery was the underlying flaw in a basically satisfactory society. A smaller group perceived additional blemishes, such as intemperance and the complicity of the churches in slave-holding. While their controversial demands for the immediate abolition of slavery could seem radical, these people remained conservative in their attitudes to the basic institutions of society, including marriage. The real radicals were those who regarded antislavery as an essential part of a concerted effort to effect fundamental reform of the whole society. The most comprehensively radical members of this group tended to be Garrisonian abolitionists. It is from this circle of abolitionists that most of the subjects of this study are drawn. By placing their ideas about family, sexuality, and gender within the context of their familial experiences, and by examining the domestic values and ideals that underpinned the theory and practice of radical abolitionism, I have used abolitionist attitudes and lifestyles as examples of the ways in which cultural abstractions were played out in individual lives. These abolitionists were few in number, but they were social and intellectual pioneers who had a profound influence on nineteenth-century social thought and reform practice.

Abolitionists believed that the violations of domestic life that occurred in slave society provided the sharpest contrast to the ideal. But not all were content to simply criticize Southern slavery. Applying the insights they drew from the oppression of the slaves to other social relationships, radical abolitionists set out to correct the imbalances they believed debased familial and gender relations throughout the Union. Central to their efforts to overcome gender and racial inequality were their attempts to perfect their own family lives. Believing that "marriage should be an equal and permanent relationship," radical abolitionists' concept of the ideal family was wide-ranging. In some cases this entailed dramatic experimentation with gender roles as they were commonly defined. By seeking to become ideal husbands and wives, parents, and lovers, radical abolitionists challenged prevailing cultural orthodoxies concerning masculinity and femininity, domesticity, and separate spheres. Endeavoring to place reciprocal affection, not power, at the heart of marriage, these abolitionists sought to make the most private of human institutions into a public statement—a contrast to the oppressive domestic environment that existed in slave society. Abolitionists respected privacy, and they regarded marriage and the family as distinct from public life. But in a period when the prescribed division between public and private life was in flux, abolitionists understood that their marriages were public symbols of their reformism. In striving for "true marriage," radical abolitionists placed great value on family life, and their attempts to improve domestic relations reflected their connections with the prevailing culture of the republic. Yet while radical abolitionists articulated and defended many of the ideals of the emergent Northern bourgeois society, their assault on racism and sexism cast them as radical dissenters, whose activism denoted the possibilities, and the limitations, of middle-class reformism during a period of dramatic social, economic, and political transformation. Consequently, by connecting race reform to gender and family relations, and by challenging white patriarchy in free as well as slave society, radical abolitionists were accused of seeking to undermine the entire social order.

I began this work during my graduate studies in the School of History at the University of New South Wales, Australia. In revising the manuscript for publication, I have incurred numerous debts. Ian Tyrrell has not only been a perceptive and challenging critic; he has provided immeasurable support in helping me embark on an academic career. I am deeply grateful for his help. I would like also to acknowledge Lorna Davin's contribution: Lorna has been a partner through every stage of this project, and her companionship and support—emotional, intellectual, and at times material—have sustained me in inestimable ways.

During the long process of transforming thesis into book, I have received assistance from many people. In particular, my thanks go to Michael Fellman for his incisive critique of earlier drafts of the manuscript, and for his ongoing enthusiasm for the project. Tony Barker's keen insights into antebellum reform, and his support and friendship over many years, are warmly appreciated. My thanks also to Margot Melia, for sharing with me her extensive knowledge of black Garrisonian women. Several other people have read sections of the manuscript and offered helpful critiques; thanks go to Shane White, Steve Piott, and Mary Gillingham. I wish also to acknowledge the contributions of the anonymous readers who reviewed the manuscript for the University of Massachusetts Press. I am grateful for their suggestions for revision. For their encouragement and efficiency, my thanks go to Bruce Wilcox, Janet Benton, and the rest of the team at the University of Massachusetts Press.

Researching and writing American history from Australia presents particular logistical difficulties. The Faculty of Arts and Social Sciences at the University of New South Wales provided financial support that enabled me to travel to the United States to complete the research for this work. I am also grateful to the Research Management Committee at the University of Newcastle for awarding me a New Staff Research Grant, which helped in bringing the project to completion. Librarians and archivists in Australia and the United States have provided invaluable assistance. The staff in the

Social Sciences and Humanities Library at the University of New South Wales and in the Auchmuty Library at the University of Newcastle have demonstrated inexhaustible patience in the face of innumerable requests for material on interlibrary loan. In the United States, particular thanks go to archivists in the Rare Book and Manuscript Room at the Boston Public Library; the William L. Clements Library at the University of Michigan; the Houghton Library at Harvard University; the Library of Congress; the Sterling Memorial Library at Yale University; the Massachusetts Historical Society; the Schlesinger Library at Radcliffe College; the Friends Historical Library, Swarthmore College, Pennsylvania; the New York Public Library; and the Butler Library, Columbia University. Other libraries provided material on microfilm, or photocopied documents and manuscripts: I am grateful to staff at the American Antiquarian Society, the Division of Rare and Manuscript Collections at Cornell University Library, and the Historical Society of Pennsylvania.

The School of History at the University of New South Wales provided social as well as academic companionship; my thanks to Sean Brawley, Malcolm Campbell, Leanne Comer, Keith Beattie, Roger Bell, and Nick Doumanis. Thanks also to my colleagues in the History Department at the University of Newcastle, particularly Claire Walker and David Lemmings. I am also grateful to Eric Andrews, whose support during the last three years is very much appreciated. For their good humor and friendship, my thanks go to Paul Bird and Louise Slavin. Others who have helped along the way include Chris Shanahan, Patrick Bonsworth Davin, Keith Eldershaw, Kerry Howe, and Ian Hoskins. I am also indebted to several people in the United States. Louise and Bob Gold, Keith Lowe, and Thomas Hague offered kind hospitality and friendship during my visits to Washington. In San Francisco, Mark Boissy and Stu McGregor reminded me there is life outside the archives.

Finally, I wish to acknowledge the contributions of several people in Perth. My sister, Louise, and her husband, David, were supportive and encouraging. For their assistance at an early, crucial stage of my postgraduate education, and on a number of occasions since, I am grateful to Don and Joanna Box. Wayne Constable has been friend, teacher, and mentor for twenty years—thanks, Max. My greatest debt is to my mother, whose support and encouragement has never wavered, and whose persistence in the face of considerable adversities remains an ongoing inspiration.

ABBREVIATIONS

AASS	American Anti-Slavery Society
ACS	American Colonization Society
ASC–BPL	Anti-Slavery Collection, Boston Public Library
ASP–CUL	Anti-Slavery Papers, Division of Rare and Manuscript Collections, Cornell University Library
BFASS	Boston Female Anti-Slavery Society
BFASSL–MHS	Boston Female Anti-Slavery Society Letterbook, Massachusetts Historical Society
BFP–SLRC	Blackwell Family Papers, Schlesinger Library, Radcliffe College
BP–LC	Blackwell Papers, Library of Congress
CBC–HL	Crawford Blagden Collection, Houghton Library, Harvard University
HSP	Historical Society of Pennsylvania
HWS	History of Woman Suffrage
KFC–WHM	Abigail Kelley Foster Correspondence, Worcester Historical Museum
KFP–AAS	Abby Kelley Foster Papers, American Antiquarian Society
LMCP	Lydia Maria Child Papers
LSP–LC	Lucy Stone Papers, Library of Congress
MGP–NYPL	McKim-Garrison Papers, New York Public Library
MP–FHL	Lucretia Mott Papers, Friends Historical Library, Swarthmore College
PFASS	Philadelphia Female Anti-Slavery Society
SHGP–CU	Sydney Howard Gay Papers, Rare Book and Manuscript Library, Columbia University
SP–SU	Gerrit Smith Papers, Syracuse University Library, Department of Special Collections
VP–HL	Oswald G. Villard Papers, Houghton Library, Harvard University
WGL	Weld-Grimké Letters
WGP–UM	Weld-Grimké Papers, University of Michigan
WLGL	William Lloyd Garrison Letters

Introduction

In the transformation from an agrarian society, marked by profound sectional differences over slavery, to an industrializing, nominally free nation, nineteenth-century America experienced tensions that divided North from South, blacks from whites, and men from women. Abolitionists were concerned with all of these divisions. As deeply committed opponents of slavery, their intimate involvement in the contest between free and slave societies—culminating in 1861 with the bloodiest test of American nationhood—has ensured them a lasting place in the American historical consciousness. But some abolitionists were also engaged in another, more subtle contest, concerning the precise meaning of freedom within Northern society. These radical abolitionists were not only interested in the public fight against slavery; they were also concerned with gender and family relations, and the advancement and emendation of marriage were central to their reforming mission.

The idea of an antislavery family is not a new one, and was well recognized by the abolitionists themselves. Reflecting the pervasive significance attached to the family in nineteenth-century America, much of the immediate post–Civil War commentary on abolitionism was shaped by an awareness of the importance of the family. The belief, however, that the public sphere was more significant than the domestic subordinated the study of the abolitionists' private lives.[1] Interpretations of abolitionism have shifted dramatically over succeeding decades. Initially revered, north of the Mason-Dixon line at least, as epitomes of the victorious North, abolitionists were subsequently held responsible for the Civil War, which some believed could have been avoided. Later they were disparaged as psychologically unbalanced, and, in the post–World War II period, abolitionists were hailed as harbingers of the modern civil rights movement. Studies of abolitionism have also been influenced by the new social history. Not only is it now recognized that African Americans, women, and other "minorities" have histories that warrant attention—and that they were more than just passive victims of conditions imposed upon them—but also that they went a long way toward shaping their own lives, particularly within the context of their families. Ronald Walters, and others, have recognized that the family was an important component of antislavery, and a number of recent studies have focused on women's abolitionism. Noticeably absent, however, from abolitionist historiography has been a comprehensive assessment of gender and familial relations among radical abolitionists.[2] Such a study provides a framework for integrating abolitionists' public reformism with their private concerns, and for delineating the impact of abolitionism upon the demarcation of the sexes into distinct social, economic, and political spheres.

Besides disputing the abolitionists' place in American history, historians have argued over the internecine quarrels within abolitionism. Much of the focus has been upon William Lloyd Garrison (the most famous of the abolitionists) and his followers. Garrisonians were criticized for "promoting all sorts of ideas," including "militant feminism." Yet it is erroneous to regard these as frivolous or tangential matters, as each was connected to radical abolitionists' family lives. Sharing Lucy Stone's belief that "all reforms are fractions of a unit, and what helps one aids all," these abolitionists identified a range of factors, apart from slavery, threatening family life;

hence their interest in reforms such as temperance, peace, and moral reform. Indeed, during a period in which thousands of Americans supported social reformism, there was a symbiotic relationship—in terms of tactics, personnel, and ideologies—within the "sisterhood of reforms."[3] And not only was the interrelatedness of the various reforms clear to the Garrisonians, but their struggle to free the slaves was also a struggle to liberate themselves. For radical abolitionists, all of these reform objectives were connected to the idea of the family.

The family thus became an integral aspect of the antebellum struggle over slavery. The issue of what constituted the *ideal* family was contentious in nineteenth-century America; even abolitionists expressed a range of ideas on the subject. They could agree, however, that family life and gender relations in slave society were the antithesis of the ideal. It is only by appreciating that radical abolitionists sought gender and familial, as well as racial reform, that their movement—and the responses it generated—can be understood. Not only did radical abolitionists' search for "true marriage" represent the essential difference between their view of the marital relationship, with its emphasis on intimacy and affection, and the patriarchal ideal that dominated social relations in the slave states; it also connected their private and public reformism, and occupied a central position in their ideology.[4]

For radical abolitionists, the goal of combining public activism with domestic responsibilities, along with their efforts to establish and maintain personal relationships, and sustain marital intimacy, entailed challenges to the social, cultural, and political bases upon which antebellum gender relations and ideologies were premised. Abolitionism thus holds valuable clues to the construction of gender during a period of dramatic social, economic, and political upheaval. Debates over familial and gender relations were connected with antebellum America's "market revolution."[5] Despite a steadily declining birth rate, the market revolution was associated with a rapidly growing population that was youthful, mobile, and increasingly urbanized. Significant, too, was the geographical expansion of the United States—a process of particular concern to abolitionists, as the addition of each new state or territory to the Union prompted renewed debate over the future of slavery.[6] Bringing with it the decline of the household economy, the market revolution not only increased the levels of production and consumption but also affected familial and gender relations. For abolitionists, as for other Americans, while family life was affected by these transformations, the family was also expected to be a site of stability and moral guidance. Yet there were significant differences regarding the consequences of the changes taking place in antebellum America. After traveling through the United States during the 1830s, Alexis de Tocqueville referred to the "democratic family." But radical abolitionists, convinced that in practice the family was often a site of oppression, believed that family and gender relations reflected patriarchal, rather than democratic principles.[7]

Antebellum observers commonly conceptualized these matters in terms of gendered "spheres" that distinguished a competitive masculine public sphere from a nurturing feminine private sphere. Amid the "ongoing chaos of a changing society," women became "central actors" within the family.[8] According much of the responsibility for maintaining domestic life to women, and commonly excluding them from public life, the dominant ideology was predicated on widely shared assumptions regarding gender differences. Besides examining the degree to which abolitionists rejected, as well as adhered to prevailing gender prescriptions, this study assesses the utility of the notions of separate spheres and domesticity in light of radical abolitionists' beliefs and behavior. As the ideology and practice of radical abolitionism reveal, the separate spheres of the nineteenth century were never absolute. Instead, they were the subject of constant argument and negotiation. These deliberations had important implications for women. While there is much truth in the claim that the aspirations and efforts of women to improve their condition were "at odds" with their role in the family, it is also true, as Marilyn Ferris Motz has noted, that women's "power base" stemmed from their position within the family.[9] Motz's theory is especially helpful in the case of female abolitionists, whose efforts to project elements of women's domestic power into public life undermined the division of men and women into distinct spheres. By explaining that women's and men's worlds intersected in ways hitherto ignored by historians mesmerized by the "trope" of separate spheres, a study of family life and gender relations among abolitionists casts doubt on the paradigm that has exerted such a powerful influence over the historiography of nineteenth-century America.[10]

Analyzing familial and gender relations among radical abolitionists provides an opportunity to examine afresh the particular meanings that were ascribed to notions of "male" and "female" in antebellum culture. During the nineteenth century, as in later times, those who sought gender reform encountered a host of "paradoxes," stemming in large measure from the fact that while men and women "are alike as human beings," they are "categorically different from each other." As Nancy Cott has put it, the "samenesses and differences" between men and women are derived from "nature *and* culture."[11] Both in public and domestic life, radical abolitionists confronted these issues. Simultaneously challenging and endorsing the culture that supported sexual inequality, radical abolitionists' familial experiences and ideologies hold valuable clues to the relationship between antebellum reform and contemporary ideals and values. Far from "an insignificant social challenge to the prevailing arrangements of the day," radical abolitionists' family lives, coupled with their efforts to expand women's public role, constituted a serious challenge to the status quo—in both free and slave society.[12]

Aileen Kraditor has argued that "to understand" movements for social, economic, and political change, "we must focus on the points of contact between the movements and the limits imposed by their societies, and see the circumstances not as negative limits of their freedom but as positive determinants of their activity and to a certain extent of their thinking." Drawing particular attention to the oft-unacknowledged significance of ideology in American history, she has suggested that many of the conflicts historians have addressed "took place not only despite but because of a deeper consensus about all the values and beliefs that really matter to the maintenance of the social order." Kraditor's theory is helpful for understanding the nature and function of radical reformism in nineteenth-century America. As a foundation stone of the American ideology, the family provides an excellent reference point for historians interested in analyzing reformism and radicalism in the United States. Besides being an obstacle to gender reform, the American family also provided the ideological and practical parameters within which abolitionism functioned. Kraditor's comments are apposite: as "useful delineators of their societies," radical and reform movements—and the responses they evoked—reveal a great deal about "the hegemonic ideas and values" of a particular society.[13] In addition to signifying the possibilities and limitations of reformism, radical abolitionists' racial and gender ideologies said much about the environment in which they operated.

Abolitionism in general, and Garrisonian abolitionism in particular, was a "movement" in only the loosest sense of the word. Yet while abolitionists argued over ends and means, they did agree that certain issues—including gender and family relations—would be the ones over which they would argue. To these issues radical abolitionists brought an immediatist energy. Refusing to accept the given, they set out to perfect social relations at home as well as abroad in the land. This project entailed a dramatic revision of the goals and tactics of earlier antislavery movements. Prior to the 1830s, opponents of slavery had advocated a gradualist approach to the issue. Garrisonians, asserting that slavery was a sin that befouled all aspects of American life, unequivocally rejected compromise and gradualism. Beginning with their provocative demands for the immediate and unconditional emancipation of the slaves, Garrisonians articulated a comprehensive critique of gender and race relations that many Americans—Northerners and Southerners alike—regarded as nothing less than a radical attempt to subvert social relations throughout the nation. But the Garrisonians' goals were not the only cause of alarm; the rhetoric they employed, and the means they embraced to effect reform were equally contentious. Disavowing violence, radical abolitionists espoused nonresistance as both a tactic and a goal. In the process they rejected not only the tyranny and violence associated with slavery, but also the coercion they believed underpinned most human relationships throughout the nation. Garrisonians were convinced that such coercion was evident in both the public and private realms. The Jacksonian period has been described as the "era of the common man" but for radical abolitionists the repressive nature of public life was graphically represented by the slaveocracy's successful attempt to "gag" congressional discussion of the antislavery petitions that abolitionists of both sexes had labored to compile. Eschewing organized politics as incurably corrupt and ineffectual, Garrisonians instead sought reform through the moral suasion of the individual. Enunciating a reform model that rested on individual perfectionism, and seeking to liberate Americans "from all coercive forces and institutions," immediatist abolitionists thus challenged many of the structures of antebellum society—including the family.[14]

For radical abolitionists, these concerns shaped the public and private imperatives of reformism. As Henry Blackwell's 1853 reference to a desire for an "equality of Progress, of Development, not of Decay" implied, abolitionist marriages, like all human relationships, were neither static nor perfect, and should not be viewed in terms of an inevitable progression toward emancipation and independence for women. Theodore Weld spoke for many of his abolitionist colleagues when he noted in 1838 that "among the dislocations of the age marriage and the relations of husband and wife are perhaps as they now are the most horrible perversions of all." Radical abolitionists' perceptions of slavery shaped their public efforts to reform marriage as a key institution in civil society; for some—like Lucy Stone who declared in 1854 that marriage was a "state of slavery"—there were explicit parallels between marriage and slavery. Yet abolitionists did not seek to abolish marriage, as they did slavery. Instead, admitting the imperfections of their own household relationships, some sought to create the ideal family.[15] Radical abolitionists discovered, however, that overcoming the gender inequalities of nineteenth-century America was a complex mission. In idealizing familial and gender relations, and striving to cleanse them to a probably impossible degree, they did not entirely transcend the attitudes and beliefs of their time. Indeed, the class, gender, and racial values that radical abolitionists betrayed were in many ways characteristic of the emergent bourgeois culture of nineteenth-century America. While abolitionists rejected many of the premises of racism and sought to act upon egalitarian principles, they failed to understand how they misused their own domestic servants, and they treated African Americans—slave and free—with condescension. Besides shaping both the public and private aspects of abolitionism, these limitations suggested much about the boundaries of social reform in the United States.

Radical abolitionism was premised on the interdependence between domestic life and the outside world. Garrisonians believed that meaningful reform began with the self, and their conversion model of reform commitment differentiated them from subsequent generations of reformers. Moreover, they respected privacy, and regarded marriage and family life as distinct from public life. Yet, as Nancy Cott has noted, perhaps "no institution is simultaneously so private and so public as marriage." Accordingly, radical abolitionists were certain that their marriages were symbols of their reformism; indeed, they were public statements. Accordingly, their mission of reforming the world began, quite literally, at home. Lucy Stone's future husband eloquently enunciated these connections. Convinced that the "true mode of protest is to assume the natural relation," Henry Blackwell asserted in 1854 that to "reform others we must try to reform ourselves, by assuming the natural relations of humanity & acting our part well therein. . . . How can we speak of what we do not know?"[16] This nexus between the public and private aspects of equality in marriage—and by extension in reformism—was encapsulated in the "Protest" against prevailing marriage laws and practices signed by Blackwell and Stone, upon their wedding in 1855: "While acknowledging our mutual affection by publicly assuming the relation of husband and wife, yet in justice to ourselves and a great principle, we deem it a duty to declare that this act on our part implies no sanction of, nor promise of voluntary obedience to such of the present laws of marriage, as refuse to recognize the wife as an independent, rational being." Marriage, Stone and Blackwell declared, "should be an equal and permanent relationship."[17]

Radical abolitionists, determined to overcome gender as well as racial inequalities, had opponents within and beyond the antislavery movement. The debate over women's role was a major factor behind the 1840 schism in the American Anti-Slavery Society (AASS).[18] That division can be viewed as the formal divergence among abolitionists over the meaning of family reform, particularly the part that women should play within that process. On one side were the Garrisonians. Conceiving family reform in terms of a reordering of gender roles, and believing that women should be liberated from the confines of the domestic sphere, they attributed an important role to women in the reform process. The Garrisonians' radical vision of family reform, and their desire to "rise up to purify the domestic altar, now so polluted and defiled," contrasted with other abolitionists' fears that attempts to expand the boundaries of women's sphere threatened the success of the movement to emancipate the slaves. These "political" abolitionists did not seek to exclude women from reform; however, reflecting and reinforcing the dominant ideology, they did contend that women should be limited to a subsidiary role, working in the private sphere commonly allocated to women.[19] The abolitionists' division over women's place in the movement was one aspect of the much larger nineteenth-century contest over women's role. Historians have often approached the woman question in abolitionism by focusing on its relationship to the emergence of feminism. But this issue was also significant for family life. This book establishes that through their efforts to restructure familial and gender relations, radical abolitionists were early proponents of what would later be labeled companionate marriage.

Companionate marriage entailed consideration of the individual desires and needs of both sexes. One of the principal themes of twentieth-century feminism, and of feminist historiography, has been an emphasis on women's right to find individual self-satisfaction in all aspects of their lives. While individualism has long been recognized as a goal of social reform movements, the meanings attached to that term have always been contentious. Radical abolitionists valued individualism both as a means and as an end. Their focus on individualism as an ideal, shaping their perceptions of gender and race relations, contrasted with the Southern perspective. But radical abolitionists also believed that reform was largely dependent on individual improvement, especially within the domestic circle. If we are to understand abolitionism properly, these connections must be kept in mind—particularly since individualism was relevant in both public and private life. In the case of the private sphere, because the institution of the family demanded mutual, though usually unequal, obligations, the abolitionists' belief that "marriage transforms character" was riddled with tensions. And as L. Maria Child's 1842 reference to the "old entanglement between man's *social* responsibility, and his *individual* responsibility" revealed, balancing individualism with the public good was no less complex. Radical abolitionists were certain, however, that proper marriage and individualism were compatible. Describing the requisites for a "true marriage," Lucretia Mott insisted that "the independence of the husband and wife is equal, their dependence mutual, and their obligations reciprocal."[20] For Mott, and other abolitionists committed to gender reform, women could achieve their rights within the context of marriages where domestic relations were underpinned by affection and equality.

Individualism was closely connected to the capitalist ethos. The relationship between the demise of slavery and the evolution of commercial capitalism has provoked considerable historiographical debate. Aware of the apparently concurrent evolution of capitalism and humanitarianism, historians have questioned whether there was a common thread between the two phenomena. Thomas Haskell's theory that the "market reinforced the long-term drift of Western culture toward *vigorous self-surveillance and far-flung causal horizons*" is useful for understanding changes in gender relations.[21] For abolitionists, the development of commercial capitalism simultaneously altered family life and shaped their perception of slavery. These changes, and the rise of the market, stimulated their concern with both family and slavery.

Concomitant with the rise of commercial capitalism was a growing confidence that people could influence the world around them. Increasingly committed, like other members of the emergent middle class, to the principles of organization and efficiency, nineteenth-century reformers realized that the evils of the world could no longer be ignored as inevitable consequences of God's will. In the case of the abolitionists, the conviction that humanity's destiny was in its own hands was reinforced by the changes in religious practices and beliefs of the early nineteenth century. The notion that the future was not predetermined, and that people's actions would affect the world, merged with a rejection of what William L. Garrison denounced as the "absurd" and "monstrous" Calvinist doctrine concerning the innate sinfulness of mankind.[22]

Abolitionists were not unique in asserting the benefits of individualism. This raises the issue of the relationship between abolitionism and the rest of American society. For many decades, historians emphasized the differences between abolitionists and their nonabolitionist peers. More recently, the emphasis has been on assessing the movement's connections to the society of which it was a part. Examining the abolitionists' family lives indicates that this is not a debate that can be answered one way or the other. Garrisonian abolitionists were radical reformers. But like their contemporaries, their lives were shaped by the economic, political, social, and religious changes of the post-Revolutionary period. Moreover, an interest in reformism was not uncommon in the antebellum period. Through its involvement in moral reform, temperance, and benevolent societies, the abolitionist leadership communicated with people who were often concerned with slavery, but whose lives were not defined by their abolitionism. More specifically, while the formal, organized abolitionist movement must not be confused with the larger, more broadly based antislavery movement, tens of thousands of Americans were interested in antislavery. Through the antislavery societies, which by 1840 represented a combined membership of one hundred and fifty thousand people, abolitionists interacted with the society around them.[23]

While those connections provide a context for understanding abolitionism, this study adopts a more specific approach toward abolitionists' gender and familial relations. By placing detailed analyses of eight marriages among radical white abolitionists within the wider context of abolitionist attitudes toward domestic relations, new light can be thrown both on abolitionism, and on nineteenth-century constructions of gender. The focus herein is on white abolitionists, but reference is also made to African American reformers, whose domestic ideologies and experiences reveal contrasts, as well as similarities, with those of white abolitionists.[24] To varying degrees, all abolitionists were interested in gender reform, and there were always connections between the different abolitionist factions. Nevertheless, as the 1840 split suggests, it was the Garrisonians who more clearly perceived the connections between gender and racial oppression. It is from this group of abolitionists—who displayed reformist attitudes to gender relations—that most of the subjects of this study are derived. Because these reformers represent a spectrum of those abolitionists interested in familial and gender reform, their marital experiences and ideologies reveal much about the range of possibilities for domestic reform in nineteenth-century America. In some cases, their radical public views were matched by dramatic efforts to reshape family life; in others, radical public pronouncements coexisted with domestic arrangements that owed much to prevailing notions of a masculine public sphere and a feminine private sphere. It is significant, too, that several members of the coterie assessed herein were also directly engaged in the public struggle for women's rights.

Lucretia and James Mott were icons of the antislavery movement. The Motts were considerably older than many of their abolitionist contemporaries, which is just one reason why they were so well regarded within reform circles. Their reputation derived not just from their public contributions to reform, but also from their much-lauded domestic environment. Yet while the Motts' Philadelphia home was both a center of abolitionist activity and symbol of domestic harmony, Lucretia Mott understood all too well the rigors of domesticity. She knew that for many American women domestic life was far from perfect, and alongside her labors on the slaves' behalf, she was an early proponent of women's rights. Historians have debated the influence of abolitionism upon the nineteenth-century women's rights movement, but Mott's presence at the December 1833 meeting in Philadelphia which led to the establishment of the AASS was an early sign of abolitionism's role in challenging popular notions of women's capacities and roles. James Mott's contribution to antislavery has often been overshadowed by his wife's role in reformism, but he too was an active member of the abolitionist community.[25]

Lucretia Mott was an important influence on Elizabeth Cady Stanton, who became a key advocate of women's rights. But Stanton, a cousin of the prominent New York abolitionist Gerrit Smith, was also an opponent of slavery, and her efforts to reform familial relationships reflected the rhetorical and ideological associations that radical reformers drew between the institutions of marriage and slavery. For Stanton, as for other abolitionist women, the personal was most certainly political, and much of her interest in gender reform reflected the experiences of her marriage to Henry Brewster Stanton. Variously regarded by other abolitionists as both a "villain" and a "giant in the cause," Henry Stanton was one of the original Lane Rebels who spurned the Lane Theological Seminary after its board of trustees voted in 1834 to expel a group of students for refusing to desist from their antislavery activities. Although he was a founding member of the AASS, Stanton broke from the Garrisonian wing of the movement during the 1830s, and his advocacy of political abolitionism (with its more conservative view of gender and familial relations) distinguished him from most of the other abolitionists analyzed here.[26]

Angelina Grimké, a Southerner, achieved notoriety during the 1830s for her public attacks on slavery. Indeed, she was one of the first female reformers to breach the walls of domesticity.[27] But Grimké's refusal to be bound by conventions concerning gender roles is only one reason why she remains a compelling figure in the abolition movement. During 1837–38, Grimké engaged in a very public quarrel with Catharine Beecher, the best-known advocate of domestic ideology. At the center of that debate were fundamental differences regarding the nature of true womanhood. Grimké's public activities were curtailed after her marriage in 1838 to Theodore Dwight Weld and their relationship says much about radical abolitionists' public and private efforts to reform social relations. For his part, Weld occupied a crucial role in the abolition movement during the 1830s, but he did not regard his subsequent retreat to the private realm as an abrogation of his responsibility to the slaves. The Weld-Grimké relationship is also significant as any analysis of their domestic life must also include Angelina's elder sister, Sarah. Because she spent much of her adult life in her younger sister's home, because she remained single, and because she was a significant contributor to both the abolitionist and women's rights movements, it is appropriate to include Sarah Grimké in this analysis.[28]

L. Maria Child's marriage, and her wide-ranging reform career, offer fascinating insights into the tensions between public and private life in antebellum America. Since her interest in domesticity complemented her abolitionism, there were occasions when Child's reformism merged radicalism with values congruent with popular notions of womanhood. In this way she typified the ambiguities and contradictions confronting reformers of all persuasions. A public woman whose private life was marked by frustration, L. Maria Child's marriage in 1828 to David Lee Child not only played a part in shaping her reform career, but also came to reflect many of the strains of married life during the nineteenth century. One of the most prolific female authors in antebellum American, Child's early writings dealt with topics that fell into the sphere deemed suitable for women. Nevertheless, as a female writer, she was testing the boundaries of "women's sphere." "When I published my first book," Child recalled in 1869, "I was gravely warned by some of my female acquaintances that no woman could expect to be regarded as a lady after she had written a book." Child, however, was not deterred, and like women who took a public stand against slavery, she refused to be constrained by prevailing assumptions regarding women's sphere. Child's interest in abolition can be attributed in part to the influence of her husband, who had been present at the formation of the AASS. David Lee Child's abolitionism took a variety of forms. In addition to his editorial and lecturing work, Child sought to turn his scant entrepreneurial and agricultural skills to the struggle to liberate the slaves. Those endeavors led on occasions to lengthy separations between L. Maria and David Lee Child, separations that revealed both the strengths and weaknesses of their marriage.[29]

Abby Kelley and Stephen Foster were also compelled to deal with long absences from each other. Their marriage in 1845 came only after they had carefully negotiated the terms under which it would function. Kelley, well aware that for many women marriage amounted to a form of domestic entrapment, was determined to maintain her public endeavors on the slaves' behalf. Kelley's abolitionism earned her praise from her radical colleagues, but even their tolerance of individuality was sometimes tested by the actions of her husband. Stephen Foster was a radical in both words and deeds. Beginning in 1841, his habit of interrupting church services to denounce slavery earned him considerable notoriety. This reputation was enhanced by his 1843 tract, wherein he labeled the clergy "a brotherhood of thieves." Like so much abolitionist propaganda, Foster's pamphlet explicated connections between slavery and domestic life, particularly the marriage relationship. As Foster put it, by "converting woman into a commodity, to be bought and sold, and used by her claimant as his avarice or lust may dictate," the slaveholder "totally annihilates the marriage institution." Foster's reputation for extremism prompted the poet-abolitionist James Russell Lowell to depict him as "*A kind of maddened John the Baptist/To whom the harshest word comes aptest.*" Whilst some abolitionists regarded Foster's extreme behavior as a threat to the success of the movement, not all his coadjutors were antagonistic to his methods. Indeed, there was considerable respect for what David Lee Child tactfully described as Foster's "peculiar zeal."[30]

Lucy Stone shared many of Abby Kelley's concerns about marriage. Despite her subsequent prominence as an advocate of women's rights, Stone initially achieved public status in the abolition movement, where her lecturing skills were acclaimed by reformers during the late 1840s and early 1850s. As one observer commented in 1850, while Wendell Phillips, Frederick Douglass, and others, had done well in their antislavery lectures, "none have given better satisfaction" than Lucy Stone. It was perhaps only predictable that such a public and feisty woman would approach marriage cautiously, and Stone's relationship with the British-born abolitionist Henry Browne Blackwell—both preceding and following their wedding in 1855—evinces many of the tensions confronting women who sought to merge public reform with family life. For his part, Blackwell's earnest efforts to overcome stereotypical assumptions regarding gender roles were paralleled by his public commitment to women's rights.[31]

Not all female members of abolitionist marriages were public advocates of antislavery, or of a more expansive role for women. But even those women who were not public figures affected their husbands' commitment to abolitionism. Helen Garrison and Ann Phillips were two such women. As the wife of the best-known abolitionist, Helen Garrison's contribution to reform was better-recognized by her contemporaries than it has been by historians. William Lloyd Garrison has been the subject of several biographies, and much of his reputation as a radical reformer derived from his support for gender reform. Garrison did seek radical change. But by placing his public activities, and his views on women's rights, within the context of his own family life, this study suggests that Garrison's commitment to gender reform was bounded by many of the very same cultural precepts that he was accused of undermining.[32] The marriage of Wendell Phillips and Ann Terry Greene, a cousin of the well-known Boston abolitionist Maria Weston Chapman, is also of interest. Following her marriage in 1837, Ann Phillips fell victim to a debilitating illness that prevented her from participating publicly in the abolition movement. Yet her role was not insignificant. Unlike Helen Garrison's confinement to the private sphere, where domestic management remained largely in female hands, many of the roles of husband and wife were inverted in the Phillipses' marriage.[33] As with the Garrisons' marriage, the relationship between Ann and Wendell Phillips reveals much about radical abolitionists' commitment to gender and familial reform.

Concentrating on eight marriages provides an opportunity to personalize and contextualize specific individual experiences. It is useful, nonetheless, to compare these relationships with the broader contours of women abolitionists studied by Donald Kennon, Blanche Hersh, and Nancy Hewitt. These historians have compiled demographic and social profiles of abolitionist women; with some qualifications, the individuals studied herein fit the profiles of the wider abolitionist community described by Kennon and Hersh.[34] Abolitionist women generally enjoyed a comfortable class position, and most could point to what Hersh described as "a solid ancestry." With regard to geographical origins, Hersh found that thirty-three of her fifty-one women could claim ancestry from New England. Of the seventeen abolitionists considered in the study that follows, twelve were born in New England; two were from New York State; the Grimké sisters were from Charleston, South Carolina; and Henry Blackwell was British.[35]

Religious experiences and affiliations played a critical role in antislavery, with the Second Great Awakening of the early nineteenth century shaping several leading abolitionists' commitment to reformism.[36] A number of the abolitionists surveyed here were Unitarians, and just as Hersh and Kennon noted the numerical significance of Quakerism in their samples, several of those assessed herein were brought up in, or later joined, the Society of Friends. Religious conversion was an ongoing process, however; in addition to those who converted to Quakerism, some reformers found the Friends' relatively liberal attitude toward women's role in society too restrictive, and either left, or were expelled from the Society. Despite the powerful religious impulse behind antebellum reform, and the abolitionists' strong Christian faith, they had a range of experiences with the churches, and many shared Stephen Foster's conviction that the clergy and churches played a part in the subjugation of women and African Americans.[37]

Like the women in Hersh and Kennon's groups, the women chosen for this study tended to marry later than their nonabolitionist peers. This indicates that their reform interests preceded their marriage.[38] Several women remained single until they were assured that marriage would not interfere with their reformism, although tensions within certain marriages indicate the dynamic nature of these relationships. The age at which women married affected the number of children they bore. Including L. Maria Child and Ann Phillips, who had no children, the women assessed here bore an average of 3.1 children—slightly lower than the figures of 3.7 and 3.4 for Hersh and Kennon's groups. What is most notable about these statistics, however, is that abolitionist families were typically smaller than those of their contemporaries. In 1800 the average number of children born per married woman in the United States was 6.4, and fifty years later the figure had fallen to 4.9. Having married later than their contemporaries, abolitionist women were less likely to have large families, but their commitment to reform, and their determination to retain their independence, were also significant factors.[39]

Abolitionism was a wide-ranging social movement with connections to many disparate causes. Yet because abolitionists were distinguished, above all else, by their unrelenting opposition to chattel slavery, and because their indictment of slavery contained such a forceful critique of Southern gender relations, it is appropriate to begin this study by examining how the plantation family was represented in abolitionist thought and practice. Regarding the violation of domestic values that occurred under slavery as the most extreme manifestation of the abuses associated with unbridled power, abolitionists were particularly appalled by the exploitation of female slaves. But, echoing many of the tenets of antebellum moral reformism, radical abolitionists' denunciation of slavery's assault of gender relations was more than a catalogue of the sexual and social abuses of African American women: they were also concerned with the ramifications of those abuses for Southern family life—in white as well as black families.

Realizing that the family, like the Southern plantation, could be oppressive, radical abolitionists were not content merely to chronicle the evils of slavery; they also set out to reform their own family lives. Their comprehensive denunciation of Southern society, and their controversial efforts to overcome slavery, put them at odds with many of the values of their society. Yet there was a tension here; in condemning slavery, abolitionists articulated views that accorded with widely held beliefs, at least in the

Northern states. This tension is especially evident when domestic ideology, which prescribed strict limits on women's appropriate role and function, is placed alongside abolitionism. Domestic writers and abolitionists agreed that through a systematic application of principles of morality, men and women could be shielded from the corrupting imperfections of the outside world. Similarly, the redemptive powers abolitionists attributed to women were representative of the broader antebellum culture. But the Garrisonians' conviction that women should actively change society, rather than effect reform through the polite persuasion of their husbands, fathers, brothers and sons, was more controversial. Radical abolitionists, believing that females had a special role to play in reform, suggested that women were especially qualified—indeed, obliged—to comment on the sufferings of slave families.[40] Chapter 2 reveals that even while abolitionism underscored the prevailing domestic values, it challenged the division of women and men into distinct spheres. And while many abolitionists repudiated the formal political structures and systems of nineteenth-century America, their vigorous discussions of gender roles, and their insistence upon women's right to engage in reform, were important contributions to antebellum political culture and to debates regarding the nature and responsibilities of citizenship in the American republic.

Like their peers, abolitionists exalted the home, and regarded it as a refuge from the pressures of the public sphere. Nonetheless, recognizing that the reality of family life rarely corresponded to the idealized visions that resonated through public discourse, radical abolitionists demonstrated their dissatisfactions with prevailing patterns of gender relations. They addressed these dissatisfactions in all aspects of the complex network of individual and institutional relationships they forged. Chapters 3 through 6 assess that network. Because radical abolitionists' marriages stood at the core of their elaborate web of affectionate relationships, and because they established and maintained their marriages in the context of the gender spheres ideology that did so much to prescribe domestic relations, it is appropriate to explore their efforts to reshape their domestic arrangements. As Chapter 3 explains, some abolitionists went to considerable lengths to ensure that household obligations did not preclude women from making a public contribution to reformism. In so doing, these abolitionists forged domestic arrangements in which familial responsibilities were shared between men and women. By seeking to resolve the tensions between individuality and responsibility to the collective unit of the family, radical abolitionists confronted an enduring tension in American culture. And all the while, they were conscious that their efforts to transform their family lives stood in opposition to what they depicted as the Southern antifamily.

Since abolitionists were committed to improving all human relationships, consideration must be given to their friendships outside marriage. Relationships between nineteenth-century women, including reforming women, have attracted a good deal of interest from historians. Chapter 4 reveals that while female friendships were an important source of companionship and support, abolitionist sorority was not only limited by considerations of class, race, and ethnicity, but must also be seen in the context of abolitionist women's abiding commitment to marriage and family. This suggests the limits of abolitionist sorority, and evinces the conflict between collectivity and individuality—and points also to the contradictions and limitations of abolitionism as a social reform movement.

Historians have belatedly turned their attention to fraternal bonding in nineteenth-century America. Chapter 5 establishes that while abolitionist men freely expressed their attachment to each other, their sense of fraternity was just one aspect of their deeply felt commitment to public and private reform. That reformism promoted individual and institutional friendships among abolitionists; by working alongside women in the antislavery societies, and by sometimes forging friendships with those women, radical abolitionist men tested gender prescriptions concerning the distinctions between masculinity and femininity. Masculine responsibility for others was not a new phenomenon, but as men came to be regarded as sole providers for their families, they also assumed new public responsibilities. Men's involvement in social reformism was one expression of that process. Radical abolitionists' construction of masculine responsibilities and characteristics must be located within a wider context. There were competing versions of masculinity developing in the United States in the nineteenth century. Abolitionists, shunning domination and power, favored a version of masculinity that emphasized cooperation and equality. Viewing slavery's abuse of the masculine role as one of the most evil aspects of the peculiar institution, these men sought to be considerate husbands, fathers, and lovers. By challenging the social and cultural bases of existing patterns of familial and gender relations, radical abolitionists renounced the enormous power that American law accorded to husbands. Contrary to the ideology of separate spheres, male abolitionists demonstrated that there was a place for men in the private world of home and family. Many of the values they projected in their reformism paralleled those that were prized by female abolitionists and advocates of domesticity. Yet as the sectional conflict over slavery intensified into increasingly violent confrontations during the 1850s, there was a reluctant "masculinization" of abolitionism.

Chapter 6 explores intimacy and affection between abolitionist wives and husbands. The delineation and exercise of power have always been at the heart of every human relationship. Radical abolitionists, however, fought to change power relations within marriage, and to place reciprocal affection, not power, at the heart of such relationships. Despite the emphasis on women's right to exercise the nebulous concept of influence within the family, the prevailing ideology of the nineteenth century suggested that for women, marriage usually entailed the submission to the will of their husbands. Indeed, the statement "man and wife" is suggestive of that imbalance.[41] Affection and romance became increasingly significant aspects of marriage during the nineteenth century, and abolitionists' relationships reflected this shift. The final chapter also assesses aspects of the abolitionists' sexual relationships. While radical abolitionists were determined to prevent the abuse of women, they believed a balanced and equitable sexuality was an essential aspect of marriage. In each of these ways, radical abolitionists sought to forge a new—or companionate—type of marriage, one that took account of individual aspirations, abilities, and desires. For some abolitionists, this was to occur within the context of a public career for both husband and wife, while for others the gendered boundaries between public and private life remained distinct. But in each case, by bringing the "private" matters of love and marriage into public discourse, abolitionists played a significant part in shaping the "public" sphere.

Striving to reform themselves, as well as the South, radical abolitionists confronted issues that transcended their own social milieu, and that reveal much about the boundaries of middle-class reformism in nineteenth-century America. The broader "problems" that resulted from the presence of African Americans in the United States were not solved by the Civil War. But in linking family, gender, and race reform, abolitionists aroused anxieties that struck at the core of white patriarchy in both the North and the South. Realizing that the difficulties confronting women could not be redressed in isolation, radical abolitionists' marital experiences shaped their efforts to elevate women. Companionate marriage was ultimately not possible in a society where legal, economic, and political inequalities precluded genuine sexual equality. Nonetheless, while the questions of gender roles that were of concern to radical abolitionists remain largely unanswered, they established an agenda for subsequent debate, and contributed to the ongoing movements for purity, temperance, and women's rights. Before exploring gender relations among the abolitionists, we begin by surveying their understanding of slavery's deleterious impact on family life.

ONE

"The Dreadful Immorality":

Slavery and Family Life in Abolitionist Discourse

A CONCERN FOR FAMILY LIFE AND gender relations stood at the center of the antebellum contest over slavery. Writing in 1857, the proslavery ideologue George Fitzhugh insisted that slavery "leaves but little of the world without family." Abolitionists, too, portrayed slave society in familial terms, but they condemned the Southern family as an antifamily, a den of domestic devilishness. With characteristic eloquence, Wendell Phillips captured succinctly the abolitionists' revulsion toward slavery. The South, Phillips declared in 1853, was "one great brothel, where half a million of women are flogged to prostitution, or, worse still, are degraded to believe it honorable. The public squares of half our cities echo to the wail of families torn asunder at the auction block." For Phillips, and other abolitionists, the unrestrained sexuality of slave society was indisputable evidence of the pervasive corruption associated with the breakdown of domestic relations that occurred under slavery.[1] By conjoining sexual, familial, and racial concerns—and by denouncing slavery as an institution that defiled both public and private life—radical abolitionists raised their opponents' ire in free as well as slave society. Proslavery theorists, censuring abolitionists as radical fanatics intent on the destruction of family life, defended values that abolitionists of both sexes considered antithetical to human progress. Because the abolitionists' critique of slavery included a sustained indictment of Southern familial and gender relations, their understanding and representations of slave society reveal much about their views on home and family throughout the nation. Radical abolitionists challenged the gender roles prescribed by separate spheres ideology, but domestic values remained a powerful influence on their reformism: by linking the absence of domestic bliss in the Southern states with the depravities of slavery, they contributed to wider discourses of family and gender relations. While abolitionists shared many of the concerns expressed by moral reformers—whose activities and ideology provoked little controversy—everything radical abolitionists said and did during the 1830s proved contentious. By the 1850s, however, when Harriet Beecher Stowe's *Uncle Tom's Cabin* brought the horrors of slavery home to millions of Americans, many of the domestic concerns of radical abolitionists had coalesced with those of the culture that had earlier spurned them.

Lamenting what Orlando Patterson has described as the "secular excommunication" of the slaves, and convinced that family life in the South was the antithesis of the companionate ideal, radical abolitionists were equally sure that slavery's polluting effect transcended the Mason-Dixon line. This belief had direct consequences for their endeavors to promote true marriage. Writing in 1835, Angelina Grimké linked slavery with domestic conditions in the Northern states. Certain that the multifarious interactions between the North and the South corrupted "the very heart's blood of the nation," she asked whether Northern men who visited the South returned "uncontaminated to their homes?" Believing that these corrupting interactions occurred in institutions vital to the moral development of the nation, and signifying the connections between moral reform and abolitionism, she contended that the admission of Southerners to "theological and academic institutions" endangered "the purity of the morals" of Northern sons. As Grimké explained, women in the North were ineluctably involved in the slavery issue. Have "Northern women then, nothing to do with slavery," she asked in terms foreshadowing the concerns of the postbellum social purity movement, "when its demoralizing influence is polluting their domestic circles and blasting the fair character of *their* sons and brothers[?]"[2] Linking family life to the public sphere, radical abolitionists argued that slavery's domestic corruptions were undermining the republic. As David Lee Child's 1843 remark that "slavery has determined, (and by means so foul and corrupt that they cry to Heaven) every question of any importance both of domestic and foreign policy" revealed, radical abolitionists had long regarded political life as tainted by the slaveocracy. During the turbulent 1850s, however, they argued slavery was poisoning the nation's political culture in ever more alarming ways. Explaining the effects of the notorious 1850 Fugitive Slave Act (which acknowledged Southerners' right to reclaim escapees from slavery) L. Maria Child expressed concern for the future of the republic. Reiterating that Northerners were intimately involved with slavery, she noted that conflicts "harden the heart by familiarity with violence." Radical abolitionism accorded a great deal of moral agency to women, but abolitionist men were equally explicit in their depictions of the corruptions associated with the "great system of licentiousness." As one male opponent of slavery put it, "the disgusting pollution of slavery . . . covers with moral filth every thing it touches."[3] The conflict over slavery was thus part of a larger contest of values concerning human progress and American democracy.

There were several forms of antislavery propaganda; each betrayed differences in style as well as content. Reaching out to the American public through speeches, newspapers, and tracts, abolitionists went to great lengths to assure their audience that they were providing authentic depictions of slave society. But there were also occasions when, confident of the righteousness of their cause, and understanding the value of fictional depictions of slavery, abolitionists were willing to use fiction to portray what they considered the essential *truth* of slavery. Resplendent with domestic and sentimental imagery, antislavery fiction—of which *Uncle Tom's Cabin* was the best-known example—was one component of a wider literary genre of the antebellum period, when sentimentalist novels poured forth from improved printing presses, to be assiduously read by an increasingly literate American population. Ex-slaves made important contributions to antislavery discourse. By providing firsthand accounts of Southern life, the "slave narrative" became an important literary genre in the antebellum period. White abolitionists, whose own depictions of love and sex among those in thraldom were informed by their reading of slaves' narratives, encouraged ex-slaves to reveal those aspects of Southern life most likely to affect the public—including slavery's impact on African American families, and the abuse of slave women. Significant, too, were powerful visual images designed to provoke horror at the abuses endemic to slave society.[4] Because each type of antislavery material informed and reflected other forms of abolitionist propaganda, and because the similarities (particularly the common appeal to domestic values) between the varieties of antislavery material signified the connections between abolitionism and the wider culture of antebellum America, it is appropriate to consider them together.

These connections are well illustrated by comparing Theodore Weld and the Grimké sisters' 1839 *American Slavery As It Is,* with the case of Harriet Beecher Stowe. Prior to the publication of *Uncle Tom's Cabin* in 1851, Stowe did not have a reputation as an abolitionist, and she never embraced Garrisonian immediatism. On the surface, Stowe's novel differed markedly from *American Slavery As It Is.* Weld and the Grimkés had used the testimony of Southerners to provide a "factual" indictment of slavery—a common tactic within abolitionist circles. The Weld-Grimké compilation was significant for its role in alerting Stowe to the slaves' plight, and *Uncle Tom's Cabin,* like *American Slavery As it Is,* detailed slavery's effect on Southern families. In *The Key to Uncle Tom's Cabin*—wherein Stowe specifically cited *American Slavery As It Is*—she sought to legitimate her novel as a true representation of the horrors of slavery, by demonstrating that it was based on factual reports from the South.[5] And by placing feminine and domestic values at the center of the public fight against slavery, Stowe was continuing a well-established tradition in abolitionist discourse.

When they denounced the "dreadful immorality" of family life under slavery, abolitionists walked a fine line.[6] On the one hand, they accused cruel Southerners of failing to recognize the vitality of slave family ties; on the other, they sometimes failed to emphasize these ties themselves. Angelina Grimké, for one, asserted in 1837 that slaves lacked the right of marriage. Yet her insistence that under slavery there was no "sacredness attached to the marriage contract," and her claim that for slaves the marriage relationship was "entered into for the most without established forms, and is dissolved at the will of the parties," failed to accord due recognition to marriages between slaves. Brutalized by slavery, those in bondage allegedly stood little chance of developing the peaceful aspect of their nature, or of expressing themselves in a loving manner to those around them. Here we are concerned with the discourse surrounding, rather than the reality of, familial and gender relations in the South. But the slave family was an important defense against the horrors of the peculiar institution, and the brutalities of slavery did not prevent slaves from maintaining social bonds and ties of affection. Abolitionists identified these bonds of affection, and they accepted the reality of slave marriages. Indeed, for their propaganda regarding the breakup of slaves' families to be effective, abolitionists had to convince their audience that slaves had constructed domestic environments and family structures that were of sufficient importance to cause anguish if they were broken. Moreover, abolitionists reasoned that given equal opportunities, African Americans could construct a proper domestic environment. L. Maria Child presented the abolitionists' mixed feelings on this issue in 1836. "There is no doubt that their [the slaves'] degraded situation," she wrote, "tends to blunt their feelings, as well as to stultify their intellect. . . . But there are numerous instances to prove that the poor creatures do often suffer the most agonizing sensations when torn from those they love."[7]

Former slaves affirmed the strength of their familial ties. Infusing abolitionism with a sense of immediacy, slave narratives provided compelling evidence that the rigors of slavery had not prevented African Americans from forming meaningful familial relations. The prominent black orator and clergyman J. W. Loguen stressed that slave marriages were formed primarily to serve the purposes of slave owners. Yet he did concede that despite the "law to the contrary," the "strongest affections grow up between male and female slaves." Henry Bibb, who like many escapees from slavery found sanctuary in Canada, was more emphatic regarding the significance of slave marriages. Alongside his assertion that he considered the "circumstances" of his "courtship and marriage" to be "among the most remarkable events of his life as a slave," the strength of Bibb's marriage was proved by his repeated attempts, despite the ensuing punishments, to rescue his wife. Noting that his "little family" was "the only object of attraction" strong enough to induce him to return to the South, Bibb revealed that the lack of legal sanction did not diminish the significance of slave marriages.[8]

White abolitionists need have looked no further than their statements regarding their own marriages to better appreciate slave marriages. True marriage, they agreed, was based on mutual affection, rather than legal formalities. Writing to his fiancée in 1834, William L. Garrison distinguished between the formal ritual attached to marriage, and the true union of man and woman. "I know that to be legally one," he wrote, "the law properly requires us to go through a certain process; but we are now really and truly one." As L. Maria Child remarked the following year, there was no legal demand to have a marriage performed by a clergyman. For white abolitionists, whose marriage ceremonies often reflected their sense of individualism, the informality of slave weddings should not have undermined their importance. Compare the marriage ceremonies of white abolitionists who protested publicly against the legal and social inequalities that women suffered under marriage, with Henry Bibb's description of his own wedding. Bibb conceded that although there was "no legal marriage among the slaves of the South," his wedding ceremony—whereby he and his bride clasped "each other by the hand" and "pledged their sacred honor" that they "would be true"—was significant. Bibb pointed out that his own wedding included a call on "high heaven to witness" the "rectitude of their purpose," but perhaps because slaves were often denied access to religious instruction, he also admitted that slave weddings were different from marriages performed by clergymen. Determined to demonstrate the slaves' piety, Bibb was "happy to state" that upon reaching freedom "many fugitive slaves" sought the services of an "anti-slavery clergyman." Further proof of Bibb's perception of the links between marriage and religion, so important to domestic writers and white abolitionists, was his disappointment at discovering that "according to the law of God and man," his wife was living in a state of adultery.[9]

The abolitionists' appreciation of familial structures among slaves was evident on many levels. In recounting the mistreatment of slaves he witnessed during his travels in the South in 1819, one commentator recalled the reply given by one slave trader when questioned why he manacled his slaves. Explaining that his slaves had wives in the neighborhood, the slave trader worried that the proximity of those women would prompt his slaves to escape. Abolitionists also realized that slave partners were denied their fundamental human rights, even the right to physical contact with each other. Angelina Grimké described the "*great* hardship" endured by chambermaids and seamstresses who were forced to sleep in their "mistresses' apartments." Referring to one female slave "who had been married eleven years," but who had not been permitted to "sleep out of her mistresses' chamber," Grimké denounced the "barbarity" involved in not allowing slaves to enjoy "social intercourse."[10] For Grimké, and other abolitionists, such practices placed Southern society at odds with civilized values.

These concerns were also evident in antislavery novels. *Uncle Tom's Cabin* became the most famous piece of abolitionist propaganda, but it was not the first antislavery novel. Fifteen years prior to the publication of *Uncle Tom's Cabin,* Richard Hildreth's *Archy Moore* had made a similar appeal to the Northern conscience. Outside abolitionist circles, however, Hildreth's novel received none of the acclaim that was to greet Stowe's narrative, and following the publication of *Archy Moore* in 1836 Hildreth turned to nonfiction to press his case against slavery. *Archy Moore* differed from *Uncle Tom's Cabin,* both stylistically and thematically. Most obviously, Hildreth's narrator did not use the slaves' vernacular language, and unlike the central character in Stowe's novel, Archy employed violent means to achieve his objective. Yet there were common threads between the two novels. Like Stowe, Hildreth's fictional approach did not preclude him from presenting the "stern reality of actual woe" associated with slavery. Both authors posited their appeals on the domestic values that had so effectively penetrated antebellum culture. Premising *Archy Moore* on the assumption that slavery was "fatal to domestic love," Hildreth's reference to "the most affectionate of mothers"—like his remark that when Archy "clasped the dear girl" to his "bosom," he "seemed to have reached the very height of human fruition"—betrayed a belief in the universality of love and affection—typical themes of domestic writers.[11]

Archy Moore was well known among radical abolitionists, who praised its antislavery message. William L. Garrison published excerpts from *Archy Moore* in the *Liberator,* and one correspondent to the *Herald of Freedom* optimistically claimed the publication of Hildreth's novel would "form an era in the overthrow of slavery."[12] Recognizing the potential impact of antislavery fiction, abolitionists and their opponents debated whether novels could accurately represent slave society. Abolitionists, convinced that they had been reborn into the *Truth,* were certain that fiction could provide honest depictions of slavery's sins. L. Maria Child, whose own novels were imbued with moral lessons, argued that Hildreth's "*wonderful* book" showed an "intimate knowledge of the local peculiarities of the South."[13] Another observer, acknowledging the connections between antislavery fiction and the wider literary culture of antebellum America, remarked that fictional representations of slavery such as *Archy Moore* served an important function in transmitting the abolitionist message: "It is a fashionable romance, though founded on real life, and will find its way into the hearts of thousands of fashionable females, who would read nothing relating to slavery in any other form." The specific relationship between fictionalized representations of slavery, and the reality of the peculiar institution also concerned "an accomplished lady in Worcester County." "It is doubtless a fiction," she wrote, "but 'fiction may throw as fair a light on truth,' and its beams are often permitted to penetrate those recesses from which Truth is carefully excluded."[14] Predictably, antislavery novels elicited a different response from defenders of the peculiar institution. Belittling *Uncle Tom's Cabin* as "a fiction throughout," George Frederick Holmes—defender of slavery and teacher of the classics at several Southern colleges—criticized Stowe's motives: "It is a fiction, not for the sake of more effectively communicating truth; but for the purpose of more effectively disseminating a slander. It is a fictitious or fanciful representation for the sake of producing fictitious or false impressions. Fiction is its form and falsehood its end."[15]

Despite, and possibly because of, the abolitionists' acclaim of *Archy Moore,* it failed to arouse widespread public indignation over the slavery issue. It was perhaps the increasing acceptance of domestic values, rather than, as abolitionists claimed, that they had inculcated antislavery values in the North, that accounted for the subsequent success of *Uncle Tom's Cabin.* Evan Brandstadter, emphasizing the superior literary credentials of Stowe's novel, and the more tactful manner in which she dealt with the horrors of slavery, has argued that Hildreth's portrayal of adultery and incest on the Southern plantations exceeded the taste of antebellum Northern sensibilities. Abolitionists, however, implored the public to recognize the depth of Southern depravity. L. Maria Child, implying that Hildreth's novel was in some respects more factual than the sentimentalized fiction characteristic of the period, alluded to the far-reaching corruptions associated with slavery. "Some are shocked because Archy Moore married his own sister," Child wrote in 1837, "but it must be remembered that the author is not attempting to describe a beau-ideal of human perfection; he is showing what a man of powerful character is likely to become under the degrading influence of slavery. It would be unnatural to suppose elevated purity of sentiment, or unimpaired moral strength, either in slaves or masters."[16]

Harriet Beecher Stowe, too, was interested in these corruptions. Since much of the impact of *Uncle Tom's Cabin* was predicated on the successful inculcation of domestic ideology, it was appropriate that it was the sister of Catharine Beecher, the most famous advocate of domesticity, who penned the work that best represented the nexus between domesticity and abolitionism. *Uncle Tom's Cabin* revealed as much about Stowe's idealized images of the family as it did about the institution it denounced. Ann Douglas has noted that *Uncle Tom's Cabin* was "a great book, not because it is a great novel, but because it is a great revival sermon, aimed directly at its readers." These characteristics were precisely those that abolitionists had long sought to instill into their reformism, but Stowe's novel reached a wider audience than the abolitionists' material. Antonio Gramsci's depiction of *Uncle Tom's Cabin* as "a book written to effect the shopkeepers of North America" was an accurate comment on Stowe's intended audience, and the novel's success suggested the ascendancy of middle-class values in mid-nineteenth-century America.[17]

Stowe's vehement literary condemnation of slavery sold more than three hundred thousand copies in its first year of publication, and initiated a series of far-reaching literary and journalistic exchanges that contributed significantly to the prominence of the slavery issue during the 1850s. Stowe was not a radical abolitionist, but her book went a long way toward undermining the hope that the Compromise of 1850 had permanently solved the problem of slavery. Horrified by slavery, Stowe was determined to fulfill what she considered her obligation to take positive steps to destroy the peculiar institution. It was her desire to write an account of slavery that was "graphic and true to nature in its details," rather than her support for black colonization, which shaped the abolitionists' responses to *Uncle Tom's Cabin.*[18] Consequently, despite Wendell Phillips's dismissal of *Uncle Tom's Cabin* as "mere sentimental excitement," and radical abolitionists' recognition that their demands for immediate emancipation differed from Stowe's more measured antislavery ideology, they appreciated the value of her novel to their cause. Praising *Uncle Tom's Cabin,* William L. Garrison argued that Stowe had "displayed rare descriptive powers, a familiar acquaintance with slavery under its best and its worst phases, uncommon moral and philosophical acumen, great facility and emotions of the strongest character." Referring to an illustrated edition of *Uncle Tom's Cabin,* a reviewer in the *Liberator* revealed the breadth of the abolitionists' perception of their reforming role: "Let it be circulated far and wide, till it shall have penetrated every 'log-house beyond the mountains,' and been perused by every individual who can read, from the child six years old to the aged veteran whose sight is not yet wholly extinct,—touching every heart and softening every eye, and swelling the tide of feeling and sentiment against the hideous system of slavery, until it becomes irresistible, giving freedom to all in bonds and peace and reconciliation to the whole land."[19] Alongside the diversity of their antislavery message, the abolitionists' recognition of the power of an appeal to domestic values—and the contrast between those values and slavery—was evident.

Uncle Tom's Cabin sanctified the family, and the emotionally charged depictions of the breakup of slave families were among the most effective sections of the novel. Elizabeth Cady Stanton, writing soon after the birth of her first daughter, described Stowe's novel as "the most affecting book" she had ever read. It was this quality that explained Stowe's significance: couching her message in terms of sacrosanct values and attitudes, she had linked abolitionism to familial experiences and emotions that were valued throughout the nation. Indeed, domestic values, and the celebration of maternal figures and responsibilities, were at the heart of *Uncle Tom's Cabin.*[20] Stowe's appeal to maternal sentiments mirrored a wider pattern, and abolitionist appeals to women were based on the premise that given the opportunity, all females would construct a domestic environment that replicated the model abolitionists sought to create in their own homes. White abolitionist women betrayed a patronizing attitude toward African American women, but they did assert that aspects of women's experiences were common to females, regardless of their physical location, race, or class. As "sufferers in a common calamity," abolitionists (black as well as white) reasoned that "every woman in the community should raise her voice against the sin, that crying evil that is degrading her sex."[21] Just as slavery degraded womanhood, it degraded motherhood. Radical abolitionists challenged gender-specific aspects of parental responsibilities, but from the development of Garrisonian immediatism in the early 1830s they attributed great significance to the maternal role, and portrayed motherhood as a universal phenomenon to which all women could similarly relate. A poem published in the *Liberator* in 1831 singled out maternal love as an influential force: "*Of all things on earth, next those above / I value most my mother's love.*" The belief that there was "no class of women to whom the anti-slavery cause makes so direct and powerful appeal as to mothers" was a persistent theme in abolitionism. Subsequent chapters explore radical abolitionists' emphasis on maternal responsibilities in more depth; suffice it to say here that these responsibilities were based on deeply felt appeals to the plight of slave mothers.[22]

The abolitionists' emphasis on motherhood complemented their despair over slavery's impact upon children. Rejecting proslavery theorists' claims that "slavery protects the infants," abolitionists' descriptions of the death of slave children reflected their personal experiences, as well as their awareness of what was likely to affect the conscience of the Northern public. Abolitionists were sure that these issues—accentuated by the high rate of infant mortality amongst slave children—became important even before the birth of slave children. Juxtaposing the violent sexuality of Southern society with the violence inflicted on slaves, one former slave noted that slave babies were "the offspring of brute passion and the subject of brute neglect and suffering." Abolitionists also contended that slave owners' disregard for the hallowed role of motherhood was manifested by their treatment of pregnant women, who besides being forced to perform arduous manual tasks, were subjected to violence unimaginable in civilized society. Viewed in the context of radical abolitionists' endeavors to maintain harmonious domestic environments, their references to maternal sympathies constituted one of the most telling aspects of their appeal to the nation's conscience. Angelina Grimké, imploring her audience to empathize with those in bondage, asked her readers whether they would reduce their own children to slavery. Harriet Beecher Stowe articulated a similar appeal in 1854. "I do not think there is a mother among us all," she argued, "who clasps her child to her breast, who could ever be made to feel it right that the child should be a slave; not a mother among us all who would not rather lay that child in its grave."[23]

Female abolitionists explicated the connections between the suffering of women within their own coterie, and the horrors inflicted upon slave mothers. This connection was well illustrated in the case of Harriet Beecher Stowe. Profoundly affected by the loss of one of her own children, Stowe laid great emphasis on the death of slave children in *Uncle Tom's Cabin.*[24] This theme was evident too in a letter of condolence from the well-known Philadelphia abolitionist Mary Grew to Helen Garrison, written shortly after the death of one of the Garrisons' children. Grew's comments were representative of the empathy abolitionist women felt for enslaved African American mothers. Grew described how she was in an antislavery meeting where she compared the Garrisons' "affliction and sorrow with that of the slave parent, child, husband, wife, who are torn from their dear ones, not by the gentle hand of the death-angel, but by the merciless grasp of the traffickers in human souls; and it seemed almost a contrast, rather than comparison, for the one became almost joy and blessedness beside the deeper bitterer woe of the other. And I told the audience that it seemed to me that in our sorrow, better than in our joy, we can sympathize with our enslaved brothers and sisters."[25] Grew's comments touched many themes of abolitionism. Specifically listing the suffering of slave parents, children, husbands, and wives, she affirmed that all members of the slave community were affected by the separation of families. By contrasting the "gentle hand of the death-angel" with the actions of the slave traders, Grew implied that the disruption of slave families was more painful than the death of loved ones. And her reference to slave traders as "traffickers in human souls" signified a recognition of the slaves' spiritual as well as physical torment. Grew was certain that suffering on the part of abolitionists would enable them to better empathize with slaves. But her remarks point ultimately to the limits of that empathy; abolitionists knew their own family lives, even with their imperfections, were not subject to the savage separations that occurred under slavery.

Abolitionists understood that slave children were abused in many ways. Besides suffering physical abuse, slave children were victims of emotional and psychic pain, ranging from separation from their families, to the denial of education and religious instruction. Radical abolitionists also believed slavery precluded the inculcation of appropriate values in children. Insisting that slave women were denied the opportunity to fulfill their maternal functions properly, they contended that the plight of slave children was typified by the mistreatment they were forced to endure during their early years. Radical abolitionists' belief that children were not exempt from moral responsibilities merged with their perceptions of slaveowners forcing slave mothers to take their infant children into the fields. Abolitionists contrasted the abuses inflicted upon slave children with the moral atmosphere of Northern—particularly New England—society. Introducing one of her instructional tracts, L. Maria Child referred to those who had the "good fortune to be born in New England, where the moral atmosphere stimulates intellect, and the stream of knowledge flows free and full to all the people." Southern children, denied the benefits of a proper education, grew up in an environment abolitionists considered antithetical to the development of those values. Unlike children in the North, slave children were not exposed to the virtues of "Gentleness, patience, and love"—values praised by Child as "almost every thing in education." Abolitionists' exhaustive condemnations of slavery's impact on Southern children—white and black—were congruent with domestic writers' thesis that a peaceful environment was essential for the correct education of children.[26]

Abolitionists' depictions of slavery's impact on Southern children merged with their efforts to make antislavery a family activity. Urging families to make spiritual and physical contributions to help the slaves, radical abolitionists fostered a reforming spirit among their own children. Mary Grew praised Lucretia and James Mott for working alongside their children at antislavery fairs; Abby Kelley, seeking to instill empathy for the suffering of slave children, hoped her daughter Paulina (Alla) would become a reformer. Implying that she held men responsible for slavery, and explaining her absences from home by referring to her duty to "preach to those wicked men," Kelley was perhaps seeking to assuage her own guilt when she asked the four-year-old Alla whether she often thought "of the little slave girls who can never see their dear mothers again?" To the chagrin of their opponents, abolitionists hoped that children in all American families would take an interest in antislavery. As William L. Garrison remarked in 1852, the impact of *Uncle Tom's Cabin* would be especially valuable "upon the rising generation in its plastic condition."[27]

Echoing the beliefs of domestic writers, radical abolitionists attributed considerable redemptive power to children. Children were expected to be more than passive recipients of abolitionist ideology: properly educated in the correct domestic environment, they were to play their part in the moral stewardship of the nation. Antislavery material produced for children raised similar concerns as that directed toward adults.[28] During the early 1830s "The Juvenile Department" was a regular feature in the *Liberator.* While some of the stories included therein appeared to have little immediate relevance to antislavery, their didactic presentations of an idealized vision of "The Family Circle" rested on the inculcation of widely shared values such as morality, Christianity, love, and rationality. Predictably, these were all characteristics lauded by black and white reformers who counseled self-elevation for African Americans.[29]

Children's antislavery societies operated in two complementary ways. At the same time as they enabled young people to contribute to abolitionism, they were to act as an educative forum, where proper values—including those concerning racial and familial relations—could be instilled. Boys as well as girls were expected to play a part in reform, but certain gender-specific assumptions, including the notion of sexual difference, underlay the abolitionists' efforts. Although the technical aspects of the correct ordering of the home and family had to be explicitly taught to young women, it was agreed that women's potential power as a moralizing influence, and their moral nature, were inherent qualities. Consequently, girls had similar powers to women, and were accorded their own field of moral influence. Children also served the abolitionists' argument that racial prejudice was neither natural nor inevitable. L. Maria Child's contention that white children felt "no repugnance to black nurses" signified the abolitionists' belief that until they were taught otherwise, black and white children harbored no ill-will toward each other.[30] Accordingly, abolitionists believed that since racial prejudice was a product of environmental and cultural influences, race relations—like gender inequalities—were susceptible to reform. Convinced that the task of promoting meaningful reform required an assault on the cultural, as well as political bases of racism and sexism, radical abolitionists were certain that the task of instilling suitable values should begin with children.

Radical abolitionists' attitudes toward parental duties informed other aspects of their reformism, including the relationship between white and African American abolitionists. In common with other antebellum reformers, abolitionists were imbued with many of the racial values characteristic of the nineteenth century. White abolitionists effusively congratulated each other for being able to feel "the wrongs of the slave as if they were inflicted upon" themselves. Similarly a determination to treat their "free colored sisters" as equals—underpinned by a sense of bonding with slave women—was a major force motivating abolitionist women to toil on behalf of African Americans. For Angelina Grimké, the sense of obligation to the slaves was predicated on the assumption of humanity's common origin. Invoking the parental function, and insisting that abolitionists "utterly deny" the mental inferiority of the African Americans, she asserted that there is "but *one race* of human beings, as they have all sprung from one common parentage."[31]

Yet white abolitionists' identification with enslaved blacks did not prevent them from behaving in a patronizing manner toward their African American colleagues. L. Maria Child emphasized in 1836 that she did not consider African Americans as inferior. But she also betrayed the condescension that was characteristic of the white abolitionist movement. "If I believed that the colored people were naturally inferior to the whites," she declared, "I should say that was an additional reason why we ought to protect, instruct, and encourage them. No consistent republican will say that a strong-minded man has a right to oppress those less gifted than himself." Reflecting the racial attitudes of the nineteenth century, and foreshadowing Harriet Beecher Stowe's assertion that blacks were more "childlike" than other races, radical abolitionists also used the analogy of blacks as children. Lucy Stone couched Theodore Weld and Angelina Grimké's withdrawal from the public sphere in patronizing terms that rested on the implicit assumption that while abolitionists were adults, slaves were children. Stone found it "entirely unaccountable how one who is struggling in the waves to rescue a drowning child, can leave it to contend alone, and feebly, with the devouring elements, quietly saying, 'there is a better life for me than this.' "[32]

If white abolitionists' rhetoric betrayed much about their attitude toward African Americans, so too did their actions, including their practice of adopting senior roles in the antislavery movement, and their attempts to confine their black co-workers to positions that confirmed their apparent inferiority. The racial assumptions of even the most ardent devotees of immediate emancipation, manifested by the initial exclusion of blacks from some antislavery societies in the early 1830s, suggested that white abolitionists carried the racial values of the wider community into their reformism. Early efforts to redress these attitudes were tempered by the desire to allay fears that abolitionists were advocating racial amalgamation.[33] White abolitionists' commitment to the slaves is beyond dispute, and the fact that they assumed senior positions within the movement does not impugn their motives. Rather, their attitudes and behavior are more accurately viewed as reflections of the influence of the wider antebellum culture.

There were, of course, many occasions when abolitionists confronted that culture. Again, the depiction of blacks as children served as a focus of their reformism. By denying the prevailing belief that blacks were like children, abolitionists were refuting an argument widely used to rationalize the unequal treatment of African Americans. This practice was evident throughout the nation, but the paternalism of slave society rested more explicitly on the assumption that blacks, like women and children, required protection. The 1857 abolitionist tract, *The Child's Book on Slavery,* contrasted the relationship between parent and child with that between master and slave. Asserting that there was "a *natural relation* between the child and the parent," the authors denied that a comparable relationship existed between slave and master. God charged parents with the responsibility for the "training and care of their children," but the slaveholder had "no such natural rights to the slave." Most important, every parent had a "peculiar love" for their children that "generally" led them to "try to do well for them." Conversely, since no such love existed in the "hearts of slave-masters toward their slaves," they could not properly care for them. Although the relationship between parent and child benefited the child, the opposite was true with regard to slave owners' relationship with the slave, who could never become "his own ruler."[34]

This matter of the slaves' environment was just one aspect of the abolitionists' racial ideology. In part, their portrayals of African Americans as different from whites might have been shaped by a desire to arouse sympathy for the slaves, rather than by any real conviction that blacks were the Sambo-like characters described in antislavery tracts. Believing perhaps that African Americans were less well equipped by nature to cope with the demands of the public sphere, some antislavery writers implied that blacks attached a greater importance to the domestic sphere than did whites. The common association of women with domestic values prompts the question of whether white abolitionists believed African Americans were more "feminine" than Anglo-Saxons. Writing in 1843, L. Maria Child compared women and blacks: "the African race are destined to a higher civilization than any the world has yet known; higher, because it will be more gentle and reverential. In comparison with the Caucasian race, I have often said that they were what women is in comparison to man. The comparison between women and the colored race as *classes* is striking. Both are characterized by affection more than intellect; both have a strong development of the religious sentiment; both are exceedingly adhesive in their attachments; both, comparatively speaking, have a tendency to submission; and hence, both have been kept in subjection by physical force, and considered rather in the light of property, than as individuals."[35] Perceiving both groups as victims of physical power, whose individuality was rarely recognized, Child identified several common traits between blacks and women: an affectionate and religious nature; a proclivity toward social bonding; and passivity. Sarah

Grimké suggested that if "Theodore Tilton's theory" was correct—"that the African race is the feminine race of the world"—then they could play an important part in improving the world. Yet Grimké assumed that the African race was not ready to fulfill that role. She believed that to carry out "those refining, elevating, & softening influences which woman sheds on the other sex," it was necessary to wait until "civilization has done for them [members of the African race] what it has done for the white race."[36] Abolitionists' views on civilization are explored in the next chapter; the pertinent point here is that some believed women and blacks shared certain "domestic" characteristics.

Harriet Beecher Stowe also pondered this question of African Americans' attachment to the domestic sphere. Privately at least, she believed that "the strength" of the slaves' "instinctive and domestic attachments" excelled those of "the anglo saxon." Referring to those feelings that "woman deepest feels," Stowe implied that African Americans were in some respects more "domestic" than whites. Publicly, Stowe was more guarded. But in asserting that blacks were more "affectionate than whites," and arguing they were "not naturally daring and enterprising, but home-loving," she inferred that dark-skinned people were endowed with traits widely attributed to females *and* that they lacked the characteristics deemed necessary for survival in the masculine sphere of public life.[37] From the point of view of the slaves' domestic environment, the implication of Stowe's statement was that African Americans suffered particularly adverse affects from the separation of their families.

The essentially racialist notions of many abolitionists and antislavery novelists were further evidenced by their differentiation between "full-blooded" blacks, and those of racially mixed parentage. Again, racial reform fused with questions of sexual behavior. Denouncing the "unbridled lusts" of the slaveowners, Stephen Foster noted that some of their victims did not have "even the tinge of African blood." Similarly, antislavery novelists often ascribed different characteristics to mulattoes, quadroons, or octoroons. The use of racially mixed figures in general, and the particular emphasis placed on the plight of the "tragic octoroon," was significant from several perspectives.[38] In the first instance, it might have represented the authors' deep-seated views regarding racial differences. Antislavery sentiments could coexist with such attitudes, and some authors may have genuinely believed that an octoroon's predicament *was* more tragic than that of a "black" slave.

Alternatively, it might have evinced a belief that the depiction of figures who were essentially "white" as enslaved would arouse greater feelings of sympathy and indignation than if the central figures were "black"—the implication being that the plight of the light-skinned slave could also be the plight of the reader. In the context of rising sectional tensions, whereby the Fugitive Slave Law of 1850 had made it easier for slave owners to reclaim their human property, these concerns became all the more urgent.

Depictions of racially mixed characters in antislavery discourse also betrayed abolitionist repulsion toward the sexual abuse of slave women. On this issue, abolitionists' attitudes reflected the wider concerns of nineteenth-century bourgeois culture, which "tended to see any woman who was sexually active outside of marriage as a prostitute." During a period in which much was made of women's "purity," abolitionists' vigorous condemnations of the "fearful havoc which slavery makes of female virtue" was an issue of serious concern. Sharing moral reformers' outrage at what Wendell Phillips described as the "hideous problem of modern civilized life," radical abolitionists' concern for sexual purity and virtue was not confined to the abuses that occurred in slave society. Characteristically, William Lloyd Garrison used familial imagery to evoke sympathy for the victims of sexual vice: "I thought of her as a sister—as *my* sister—seduced, it may be, by some villain, who had pledged to her eternal fidelity. I thought of her as a daughter,—as *my* daughter—once the hope, the pride, the ornament of the family circle—now a castaway, and forever shut out of civilized society." The implication from Garrison's remarks was clear: once a woman's sexuality had been corrupted, there was no chance for her to reclaim her purity. For radical abolitionists, the slaveholders' violations of slave women's sexuality were fundamental to the defilement of true womanhood in the South. Convinced that "the peculiar, the monstrous aggravations which attend the slavery of WOMAN" was both agent and symbol of slavery's destructive process, abolitionists juxtaposed images of white Northern women with the plight of Southern women. Most obviously, slavery's perniciousness was confirmed by the physical violence inflicted upon female slaves: incontrovertible proof that the "Southern women-whippers" were guilty of unconscionable crimes.[39] Although L. Maria Child stated that the "general licentiousness produced" by slavery could "never be described without using language too gross to be addressed to a civilized community," abolitionists of both sexes chronicled the abuses of sexuality that occurred under slavery. Angelina

Grimké, asking whether slaves were "generally married," or whether they lived "promiscuously," alluded to her concerns regarding slavery's abuse of black women's sexuality. Stephen Foster was more explicit. True to his uncompromising reputation, and foreshadowing Wendell Phillips's later denunciation of the Southern states as a brothel, Foster unambiguously denounced the slaveholders' sexual crimes. Claiming that slave women were "the lawful prey of every pale-faced libertine," who chose to "prostitute" them, he argued that the slaveholders' real crime was not adultery, but rape. Inevitably, abolitionists asserted, the slaves' sense of sexual propriety, and their ability to reach sound moral judgments, were flawed by the baneful impact of slavery. Abolitionists argued that for some slave women, the only means of survival was through resorting to what radical reformer Susan B. Anthony labeled as "the legalized *prostitution* of nearly *two* millions of the daughters of this proud republic."[40] Through all of these depictions of Southern life, radical abolitionists stressed that slavery contradicted the values they sought to achieve in their own marriages.

Realizing that black women were not the only victims of slavery, abolitionists regarded Southern white women's acceptance of slavery as both symptom and cause of the overall failure of domestic relations in the slave states. Abolitionists averred that the immoralities of slavery prevented white women in the South from exercising "the fearful responsibilities pressing upon" them. Invoking the notion of sorority, and imploring Southern women to fulfill their obligations, female abolitionists deplored slavery's affect upon free women in the slave states. The ambivalent relationship between African Americans and white women in the slave states defies easy characterization, but radical abolitionists—believing that Southern women's natural hostility to slavery was blunted over time—were certain that women in the slave states were abrogating their responsibilities. The failure and denial of female responsibility was shown by the testimony of Moses Roper, a former slave. Roper's 1838 description of a beating he received indicated that while domestic values were not entirely absent from the South, there were strict physical limits within which those values could be applied. Following an abortive escape attempt, Roper was being punished adjacent to a plantation household. Upon hearing what was occurring, the planter's wife "came out and begged them, not to *kill* me *so near the* house." This particular Southern woman disapproved of violence being perpetrated so near to her home. Yet there was no suggestion that she should step beyond her sphere and persuade Roper's attackers to cease their brutality. Angelina Grimké, horrified by the "most disgusting scenes of dissension" evident in Southern families, and recalling how one of Charleston's leading ladies punished her slaves, was particularly alarmed by the Southern mistress, who "acts out a part derogatory to her character as a woman." Portraying Southern women's failings as a partial consequence of the wider failure of sororal feelings in the slave states, and detailing the widespread miscegenation in the South, she asked her readers not to reject her "dreadful assertion" that women in the South "hold *their own sisters* and brothers in bondage." Female abolitionists, contending that the evils associated with the peculiar institution should be abhorrent to all women, assumed that under different circumstances white women in the South would be also be horrified by slavery. Believing that there was nothing natural about women's involvement in slavery, and resting their argument on the assumption of a common female nature, abolitionists asserted that slavery brutalized Southern women in the same way as it brutalized their fathers, brothers, and husbands. Yet even as they charged white women with complicity in the perpetuation of slavery, abolitionists suggested white Southern women were also victims of the peculiar institution. With neither institutional nor personal restrictions upon their power, slave masters were free to abuse all those around them—including their wives.[41]

Abolitionists believed slaveholders' crimes reflected the overall failure of Southern spiritual and intellectual development. Emphasizing that the Southern assault on morality included the abuse of those values glorified in domestic literature, abolitionists argued that slavery left no room for virtues such as honesty, piety, and education. In particular, it was widely agreed that honesty was essential for human relations. William Wells Brown's successful attempt to avoiding a flogging by deceiving a fellow slave was indicative of the horror of slavery. But it also signified the slaves' inability to live their lives truthfully; Brown's success in tricking that individual was illusory, for the corollary of his actions was that he could not trust others.[42] African Americans were not the only victims of slavery whose sense of honesty was corrupted by slavery. The abolitionist portrayal of the slaveowners amounted to a thorough critique of Southern willingness to profit from a system that depended on the greatest deception: that slavery was not an evil institution.

Abolitionists were convinced that the churches were intimately involved in the perpetuation of that deception. Their references to the "family altar"—suggestive of the connections they drew between religious practices and family life—coupled with their emphasis on their own spiritual regeneration (including their conversion to abolitionism), led them to attach great importance to the denial of religion to the slaves.[43] Perhaps placing too much emphasis on the slaves' inability to establish formal church organizations (which was incongruous given their own denunciations of religious institutions), abolitionists underestimated the extent to which slaves constructed their own religious values. Rejecting proslavery theorists' claims that the Bible sanctioned slavery, abolitionists such as Stephen Foster denounced the slaveowners' abuse of the slaves' religious freedom. Criticizing the fact that the Bible was a "sealed book" to the slaves, he condemned the slaveowners' practice of making "the public worship of God a crime." Abolitionists believed that Southerners had perverted religion; again, slavery corrupted everything it touched. Already convinced of the churches' complicity in the continuation of slavery, abolitionists rued that there were ministers and clergymen in the South who not only actively defended slavery, but who themselves owned slaves, a practice Angelina Grimké labeled a "wicked absurdity in a Republican country."[44]

The abolitionists' interest in gender relations, and their denunciations of slavery, raised the vexed issue of interracial sex. When they objected to laws prohibiting interracial marriage, radical abolitionists struck at deeply held fears, in both free and slave society. Their critique of such laws reflected their insistence that the government had no right to interfere with marriage. Responding to a debate in Massachusetts concerning the propriety of interracial marriage, the editors of the *Liberator* alluded to slaveholders' influence over slaves' marital relations, and to Northern legislation concerning interracial marriages. Neither individuals nor government, they insisted, had the right to interfere with the "indispensable union." Marriages should be based on mutual affection, and a common moral purpose. "An unnatural alliance is not that which joins in wedlock an African descendant with an American, or an Indian with a European, who are equal in moral worth," the editors of the *Liberator* wrote, "but that which unites virtue with vice, knowledge with ignorance, sobriety with drunkenness, and piety with profligacy. . . . To attempt to force or obstruct the flow of affections is ridiculous and cruel."[45]

Abolitionists' defenses of interracial marriages exacerbated fears that they were advocating racial amalgamation. During the mid-1830s, when anti-abolitionist sentiment was at its peak, this complaint was common. The fears aroused by the activities of white abolitionist women, who had not only stepped beyond the private sphere, but who also advocated racial equality, converged in the accusation that abolitionists favored racial amalgamation. Indeed, the theme of sexual relations was central to anti-abolitionist propaganda. Exploiting widespread fears regarding racial mixing, and appealing specifically to the "dear and refined relations of domestic life," one critic condemned abolitionists for their advocacy of miscegenation. Abolitionists were charged with "both openly and covertly endeavoring to lead" the nation into "that foul coalition" of a racially mixed society. Abolitionists' statements regarding interracial marriage were seen as further evidence that they were determined to revolutionize the prevailing pattern of family relations. Claiming that the abolitionists' goal was a thorough "social revolution," George Fitzhugh likened antislavery to "Communism," "Socialism," "Red Republicanism," and—in a thinly veiled allusion to the havoc wreaked in Haiti following the expulsion of the French in the late eighteenth century—"Black Republicanism." Inevitably, argued Fitzhugh, the abolitionists' formula for the United States would lead to the breakdown of law and order, and the "total overthrow of the Family and all other existing social, moral, religious and government institutions."[46]

The virulent response against the abolitionists disguised their ambivalence toward interracial marriage. This ambivalence was clear to African Americans, including the author and editor David Ruggles, who contended that abolitionists opposed racial amalgamation. White abolitionists defended individuals' right to marry people of a different complexion, but they also stressed that they were not advocating widespread racial mixing. L. Maria Child, assuring her readers that abolitionists had "not the slightest wish to do violence to the distinctions of society," remarked that "of all accusations" leveled against the opponents of slavery, "that concerning intermarriage" was "the most perfectly ridiculous and unfounded." No abolitionist, she asserted, considered "such a thing desirable." William Lloyd Garrison was equally emphatic on this issue. Writing in 1843, he explained why abolitionists had supported the repeal of a Massachusetts law prohibiting interracial marriages: "Our object has not been to promote 'amalgamation,' but to establish justice, and vindicate the equality of the human race."[47] Again, abolitionists might have been seeking to endear themselves to the public, but their treatment of African Americans betrayed a more ingrained sense of racial difference.

Abolitionists countered the accusation that they favored miscegenation with the irrefutable evidence that in practice it was the slaveholders who encouraged interracial unions: regardless of the slaveowners' rhetoric, slave women were constant victims of white men's licentiousness. White men's immorality was evidenced by the increasing numbers of slaves who were of racially mixed parentage. As the Massachusetts abolitionist Charles Whipple put it, "the formation of a new [family] tie" was an effective means of keeping the slaves "submissive," and preventing them from "running away." But not only did some slave owners hope to discourage slaves from fleeing by contriving familial attachments, they also exploited slave relationships as a means of increasing the value of their stock. Abolitionists abhorred this fusion of economic and social corruption. Insisting that a spouse should be selected on the basis of mutual affection and sound judgment, and believing "that it is wrong to have children unless people love each other," they regarded the slave owners' version of arranged marriages as a deliberate contravention of human nature and the antithesis of true marriage. Besides condemning the slaveholders' practice of selecting a female slave to be their mistress, abolitionists believed male slaves were also affected by their masters' desire to expand their slave population. These economic and social imperatives crossed racial lines; one observer described how a white man of his acquaintance was offered twenty dollars "for every one of his female slaves, whom he could get in the family way." Recognizing the pressure on slave women to breed—and betraying a belief in a racial hierarchy common among white Americans in the nineteenth century—the same commentator alleged that the offer was "no doubt made for the purpose of improving the stock, on the same principle that farmers endeavour to improve their cattle by crossing the breed."[48]

The theme of interracial sex figured prominently in antislavery literature. Richard Hildreth's *Archy Moore* established a scenario in which many of the sexual values of nineteenth-century America were destroyed by slavery. In Hildreth's novel, the contentious matter of interracial sex intersected with the equally controversial notion of incest. Not only was Archy's wife, Cassie, a daughter of Colonel Moore, but since Archy was also the result of one of Moore's liaisons with a slave woman, the relationship between Archy and Cassie was incestuous. Southerners may have been appalled by incest, but their horror was apparently confined to relations between white family members. Under the immorality of slavery, not only were black women forced to have sexual relations with white men, but when they did establish relationships with fellow slaves, there was always the possibility that the relationship was incestuous. It was not just antislavery novels that recounted the consequences of white men forcing themselves upon slave women. Writing in 1836, Angelina Grimké drew attention to the fact that when slaveholders sold their slaves, they were sometimes selling their own offspring. Grimké was careful in her language, but she suggested that "female slaves of the South" were "sold by their fathers." Abolitionists expressed continuing interest in the issue of slave owners disposing of the offspring of their own sexual sins. Elizabeth Cady Stanton, always sensitive to the particular problems faced by women, questioned in 1860 how "the beautiful daughter of a southern master" could "honor the father who with cold indifference expose her on the auction block to the coarse gaze of licentious bidders."[49]

The charge of amalgamation leveled against abolitionists was supported by the suggestion that they associated with African Americans in social life—a practice widely considered distasteful.[50] Such criticisms revealed the depth of the abolitionists' challenge to the sexual and racial status quo. The claim that abolitionists mixed socially and professionally with African Americans did have some effect. Denying that abolitionists wished to "force" people to relinquish their prejudices, L. Maria Child explained her decision regarding her choice of company in terms of social hierarchy. In so doing, she signified the boundaries of nineteenth-century middle-class reformism: "An educated person will not naturally like to associate with one who is grossly ignorant. . . . I would not select an ignorant man, of any complexion for my companion."[51]

Child's statement inferred that abolitionists and their opponents held similar assumptions regarding social hierarchy. Yet to focus on those points of agreement would be to mute the extent of radical abolitionists' challenge to prevailing patterns of familial and gender relations. Abolitionism deeply worried Southerners. Appropriating many of the domestic values that underpinned antebellum moral reformism, radical abolitionists assailed every aspect of the breakdown of family life in slave society. Their unrelenting assault on slavery, expressed in many forms from the early 1830s, but reaching its apogee in the 1850s, was both cause and effect of the clash of cultures that culminated in the Civil War. But this contest was not simply a matter of North versus South. While radical abolitionists' focus on the domestic corruptions of slavery struck an increasingly sympathetic chord with Northerners, their formula for the restructuring of social relations throughout the nation ensured they remained dissenters in free as well as slave society. The tension between Garrisonian abolitionism and the values of the free society of the North is most starkly evident when we appraise the relationship between abolitionism and domesticity—an ideology that prescribed strict limits on women's functions.

TWO

From Private to Public:

Domestic Values and Abolitionism

ABOLITIONIST ATTITUDES TOWARD gender reform evolved within the wider discourses and conventions concerning gender relations in nineteenth-century America. Here, radical abolitionists displayed complex, often contradictory views. Like domestic writers, they revered concepts such as "the home" and "the family," concepts central to antebellum culture and society. Radical abolitionists, however, brought different meanings to those terms than did proponents of domesticity. Consequently, although the relationship between abolitionism and domesticity was not entirely antagonistic, Garrisonian abolitionists were radical reformers, who dissented from many of the principles and practices of their society, and who violated prevailing models of true womanhood. At the heart of antebellum notions of true womanhood were gendered assumptions of women's moral superiority. As radical abolitionism revealed, these assumptions could have both radical and conservative connotations.[1] Garrisonians made much of women's moral virtues, but in defending women's right to agitate against slavery, and by linking slavery to the contentious issue of women's rights, they challenged the division of the sexes into separate spheres. Increasingly certain that the "greatest foe we have to contend against is our own household," radical abolitionists and advocates of women's rights understood the close relationship between the confinement of women to the domestic sphere and their subordinate status.[2] This threat to one of the central means of social organization provoked intense controversy, both within and beyond the antislavery movement. Many Americans, certain that the "order of the social state" demanded the subordination of wives to their husbands, believed that abolitionist women who moved beyond the private sphere were intent not only upon the destruction of slavery, but of the entire social order.[3] Since the family was widely regarded as the place in which republican values and principles were to be imparted to future generations, radical abolitionists' efforts to reshape domestic relations were commonly construed as attempts to undermine the foundations upon which the republic was based. Far from regarding themselves as threats to republicanism, however, radical abolitionists believed they were exemplars of the republican values that had been articulated, but not realized, during the Revolutionary era. Yet the Garrisonians' attempts to translate their republican vision into reality had indisputably radical consequences. By politicizing women's domestic role, and by connecting "domestic woman with the public world," radical abolitionists challenged the fusion of "masculinity and republicanism" that had underpinned notions of citizenship in post-Revolutionary America.[4]

The intricate relationship between abolitionist and domestic ideologies resonated through the practice of abolitionism, and held implications for women's engagement in the public sphere. The concept of "separate spheres," like the notions of "public" and "private," is as much an analytical tool as it is a description of the complexities of gender relations. Of course, the wide interest in the "cult of domesticity" cannot be dismissed as a mere historiographical fad; the cultural, social, and economic factors that shaped gender roles, and that distinguished between public and private life, were significant forces in the nineteenth century—and beyond.[5] Nonetheless, the separate spheres of the nineteenth century were far from absolute. Not only did domestic tracts prescribe, rather than describe, people's lives; familial and gender ideologies—including domesticity—were always matters of dispute. Domestic ideology, as Joan Scott has noted, was not "created whole." Rather, it was "the constant subject of great differences of opinion." Radical abolitionists were at the forefront of the antebellum contest over domesticity. Concurrently appropriating and disavowing domestic values, Garrisonian abolitionism must be seen in terms of the possibilities, as well as the limitations of the ideology that underpinned differentiated social, economic, and political roles for men and women. Since radical abolitionists' interest in gender relations was an important aspect of a broader contest over gender-based divisions of society, and because they realized that the contentious relationship between the problematic notions of "private" and "public" was, as feminist scholars have noted, "in itself a political issue," any understanding of nineteenth-century women's political culture requires an assessment of the links between abolitionism and domesticity. By linking the theory and practice of antislavery to domestic values, Garrisonian abolitionists simultaneously challenged male rule in two ways: besides asserting the value of the female sphere, they also attempted to enter the masculine sphere. In the process, abolitionist women forged new relationships with public activities and institutions. To borrow a phrase used by Paula Baker in her recent study of the relationship between gender and politics in the late nineteenth and early twentieth centuries, abolitionist women made an early contribution to the "moral frameworks of public life."[6] While there were significant differences between reformers in the antebellum and Progressive periods, the power inherent in the symbols of motherhood and feminine virtue, and the conviction that women were obliged to promulgate the moral values of domestic life, served to link reformers from different eras. Moreover, by actively shaping the priorities of public reformism, and by insisting on women's ability—and responsibility—to participate actively in the implementation of those objectives, abolitionist women presaged what Theda Skocpol has described as the "maternalist" social welfare policies of the Progressive Era.[7]

Abolitionist women were better placed than most to define their own life-course. Confident that they would be able to return to the public sphere after they had nurtured their children, and often able to afford domestic assistance, they regarded domesticity as a temporary interlude, rather than as a life sentence. That awareness altered their perceptions of domesticity. But their interest was more than voyeuristic, and the separate spheres of the nineteenth century were more than ideological constructs. Indicative of the impact of separate spheres ideology, and the way in which gender shaped an individual's life-course, was the statement of Judge Daniel Cady, upon the death of Eleazor, the only one of his five sons to survive into adulthood. Hoping to ease the sorrow of her grieving father, the eleven-year-old Elizabeth Cady assured him that she would devote herself to filling the void. Daniel Cady's insensitive reply, that he wished Elizabeth had been born male, not only left a deep impression on the mind of the ambitious young woman, but also reflected the pervasive belief that women could never assume men's roles in society.[8]

This case raises the matter of the extent to which abolitionists were representative of the wider community. It is tempting to view Stanton and other reforming women as somehow exceptional. True, their solutions to women's inequalities were radical, but the dilemmas they faced in trying to merge private and public labors were relevant for millions of women in the industrializing society of the nineteenth century. Abolitionists, in many respects, were atypical of their times, but prototypical of the future. Without completely discarding the "dissenting minority" thesis that some historians have proposed, more can be learned by viewing abolitionists within the context of American society rather than considering them solely as outsiders.[9] While female abolitionists expressed enthusiasm for certain domestic values, they were always operating within boundaries that had been prescribed for them, since the extent to which they could fulfill their ambitions was limited by the constraints of a patriarchal society. There are parallels here with the plight of Southern slaves. African American slaves were not just victims, but they did live in a world dominated by their masters. That analogy, of course, was not lost on female abolitionists, whose efforts to reconcile the demands of domesticity with a determination to participate in the public sphere resounded through abolitionism, and remained a telling impulse in the nineteenth-century women's rights movement.

Interpretations of men's and women's physical responsibilities reflected the alleged mental and physical differences between the sexes, and the emergence of "domestic economy" rested in part on "a thorough reconsideration of female nature." In questioning whether they should demand and exercise female influence on the basis of human equality, or as a function of their differences from men, domestic writers and radical abolitionists were confronting a feminist dilemma. Although Angelina Grimké, the most controversial of the women abolitionists during the 1830s, denounced the "fallacious doctrine of male and female virtues," abolitionists and other radical reformers were themselves unclear on this "age-old dilemma of equality versus difference."[10] On the one hand, radical reformers seemed to share domestic writers' assumption that women were spiritually and physically different from men. It was on this basis that many female abolitionists claimed the right to participate in public reform: by carrying the virtues of "true womanhood" into their abolitionism, women could make a unique contribution to public life. Conversely, the idea that women were entitled to be treated equally was also a telling impulse in nineteenth-century reformism. Indeed, abolitionist and feminist ideologies owed much to eighteenth-century and Enlightenment notions of natural rights. Black abolitionist women encountered these imperatives rather differently than white women. Encouraged by their menfolk to exert moral influence and provide a proper example, and constantly confronting stereotypes that judged all black women as degraded, African American women were commonly excluded from prevailing images of feminine virtue. Accordingly, while black women knew that gender roles as they were commonly defined served to banish women from public life, they also understood that the widespread denial of feminine virtue to African American women was a powerful impediment to their elevation. One potential means of overcoming that marginalization was to emphasize gender difference, and proclaim black women's feminine qualities. For both white and black abolitionist women this issue turned upon competing models of true womanhood. As Debra Gold Hansen has argued in reference to the Boston Female Anti-Slavery Society, one of these models was "based on woman's difference from men, the other on women's equality with men." Yet while Hansen was right to identify these competing views, her dichotomic depiction of Boston's white abolitionist women as being divided into two distinct "coalitions" requires modification. For example, Hansen represented L. Maria Child as one of those who believed that "women, by nature and predisposition, were different from men." But on this question, as on others, abolitionist women defy straightforward characterization. Their uncertainty on this issue was well summed up by Child in 1842. While she was insistent that there "is no inferiority or superiority," she argued that she was "not one of those who maintain there is no sex in souls." Expressing ambivalence on this question of gender differences, she asserted "that the nature of men and women are spiritually different, yet the same."[11]

The ambiguity inherent in Child's statement, characteristic of many reform movements, and evident in radical abolitionists' racial as well as sexual ideologies, was in part a reflection of the scientific advances of the nineteenth century. Yet opponents of gender and racial reform also betrayed their faith in science. Indeed, sexism and racism, reflecting cultural stereotypes rather than biological facts, were frequently predicated on scientific beliefs. Defenders of slavery used science to argue that African Americans were naturally suited to physical work, rather than intellectual development. Attempts to separate the sexes were similarly based on pseudoscientific and biological evidence that purportedly proved that women could not participate effectively in the public sphere, and that they would never be able to achieve equality with men. Physical differences between the sexes, highlighted in domestic literature, were often cited as evidence that women were incapable of performing the tasks assigned to men. Sustaining this view was the belief that women's role in the reproductive process was at the heart of their physical and intellectual "nature." A whole body of nineteenth-century literature, much of it invoking religious sanction, asserted that women were frail and incapable of sustained physical or intellectual exercise. That perception, besides being a base on which women were limited to the domestic sphere, was one of the factors behind the lack of recognition accorded to their domestic labor. Although radical abolitionists were certain that women were peculiarly able to empathize with the slaves, they were also sure that, as Elizabeth Cady Stanton put it, "sexuality in no way affects the individual manifestations of mind or body." Radical reformers believed that women's position, like that of the slaves, did not stem from innate biological characteristics, but was rather the result of the environmental conditions imposed on them by the society in which they lived. These issues were far more than intellectual meditations; radical abolitionism not only challenged prevailing views of "male" and "female," but also helped define and expand women's sphere in ways unanticipated by domestic writers.[12] Besides denoting the limits—and the possibilities—of domestic ideology, radical abolitionism suggested the fluidity of the separate spheres of antebellum America.

More than any other individual, L. Maria Child represented the connections between domesticity and public reformism. Her published writings covered many topics and genres, but the reform imperative was evident throughout. "In the simplest things I write," she remarked in 1856, "whether for children or grown people, I always *try* to sow *some* seeds for freedom, truth, and humanity." Child's domestic tracts, of which *The Frugal Housewife* was the best-known, betrayed this reformist impulse. Initially published in 1829, and reprinted regularly thereafter, *The Frugal Housewife* was a precursor to Catharine Beecher's better-known *Treatise on Domestic Economy,* which explicitly defined what many considered the proper boundaries for women in the antebellum period.[13] There were dissimilarities between *The Frugal Housewife* and *A Treatise on Domestic Economy.* Child's work lacked Beecher's more practical approach, and where Child's advice regarding illness and injuries reflected traditional practices, Beecher sought to scientifically explain the internal processes of the human body. Nor did the two books speak to the same audience. Child claimed her book was aimed at poor women, but it spoke more directly to women of the lower-middle class. Beecher's *Treatise,* however, addressed a different group again: whereas Child assumed her readers were unable to afford servants, Beecher specifically discussed the delicate subject of "The Care of Domestics."[14]

But it is the similarities between the two books that are most striking. Domestic ideology and abolitionism emerged amid profound changes in America's economic—and hence familial—structures. Ann Douglas's claim that Child's *Frugal Housewife* was "designed to ease the tensions of economic transformation by rationalizing the middle-class woman's new identity" applies equally to Beecher's *Treatise.* As Leonore Davidoff and Catherine Hall have remarked with reference to nineteenth-century Britain, one of the "strongest strands binding" various elements of the middle class together "was the commitment to an imperative moral code and the reworking of their domestic world into a proper setting for its practice." The success of that mission depended on the efficient and morally sound management of the domestic sphere; by advising women how they could most efficiently accomplish household tasks, domestic writers such as Child and Beecher endorsed the moral imperatives of the market economy. This commitment, particularly characteristic of the emergent middle class, and reflecting what Stuart Blumin has labeled an "organizational didactic," was concomitant with changing perceptions of gender roles. A profusion of domestic tracts, many of them penned by physicians, clergymen, and—in the words of Nathaniel Hawthorne—"scribbling women," elevated women's domestic role, and reinforced the division of the sexes into separate spheres. Women and men's roles had always differed, but the Industrial Revolution, bringing with it new modes of production, and a decline in the primacy of the family as the major economic unit, demanded a more precise demarcation of gender roles, and a consequent sharpening of the dichotomy between "public" and "private." To earn the wages necessary for their family's survival, men were increasingly compelled to find employment outside the home. According to the dominant ideology, behavior in the male/public sphere was based on the ideology of laissez-faire individualism. Only the strongest and most resourceful could survive in the world of business and politics, a world permeated by greed and self-interest. These characteristics, which radical abolitionists thought achieved their fullest expression in the institution of slavery, were widely regarded as male traits. On the other hand, the female/domestic sphere, through the institution of the family, provided a refuge for men, from the outside world of avarice and selfishness. Since women were allegedly "swayed more by the affections and moral sentiments" than by their intellect, it was widely believed that sound moral judgments predominated in the female world. From their protected position within the domestic sphere, women defended the morality of their families. In a period of rising literacy among women, domestic works reached wide audiences.[15]

Child and Beecher, concurring that the family was the most important social unit, carefully acknowledged women's role within the family. Yet they did not consider domesticity as symptomatic of the oppression of women. Nor was their advocacy of the division of men and women into separate spheres an admission of women's inability to play an important role in worldly matters. Rather, their vision of domesticity sought to elevate women's role. Seeking to give status to women's domestic function, domestic writers contended that the private sphere was as significant as the public realm. They claimed that women could play a significant, though indirect role in public affairs by shaping the domestic aspect of American life. Women were thus expected to influence, rather than enter public life. Domestic writers, arguing that the "safety and happiness of a free republic" was based largely upon the role of women in "family government," placed a high value on women's role in the regeneration of the nation. Referring to "this day of disorder and turmoil, when the foundations of the great deep seem fast breaking up, and the flood of desolation" was "threatening to roll over the whole face of society," Jonathan F. Stearns, a Massachusetts clergyman, asserted in 1837 that "the destiny of our country" depended "in a most important degree," on American women. Radical abolitionists, accepting that the "crisis *has* come when it would be sin for women to stay at home & remain silent," also ascribed an important role for women in the regeneration of the United States.[16] But in counseling women that duty demanded their participation outside the home, these abolitionists contradicted a canon of domestic ideology, and exposed flaws in the rigid conceptualization of distinct gender-based public and private worlds.

Beecher's pronouncements against women's direct participation outside the home are well known, but the significant points of agreement between domestic writers and those who advocated a more public role for women are less well understood. The celebration of the home and family was the most notable of these similarities, and it was widely agreed that the private sphere was more than a retreat; it was also the place where individual relationships could be reformed.[17] Beecher believed that proper domestic reorganization was essential for the reform of the private sphere. Radical abolitionists, too, valued domestic organization. Indeed, their faith in the related principles of organization and efficiency, and an awareness of their role in reform, were particularly significant in the domestic sphere.[18] This emphasis on household organization, linking values common to the public and private spheres, and revealing that women were affected by the prevailing faith in organization, was evident on several levels. For many women abolitionists, the successful organization of their domestic sphere was a prerequisite for their involvement in public reformism. In 1898, Elizabeth Cady Stanton recalled that her "love of order" was "carried throughout" her home. Lucretia Mott placed great emphasis on the proper organization of her household, and Theodore Weld and the Grimké sisters followed the system of domestic organization and task management prescribed by William Andrus Alcott in his 1838 work, *The Young Housekeeper; or Thoughts on Food and Cookery.* Less overtly, Sarah Grimké's advice to Sarah Wattles was also suggestive of the links between domesticity and abolitionism. Grimké asked in 1855 whether her young friend was familiar with the *Treatise on Domestic Economy.* Implying that Wattles would benefit from studying Beecher's book, Grimké's question reflected the influence of domestic values in nineteenth-century America.[19]

The principles of organization and efficiency resonated through the practice of abolitionism. Just as domestic writers advocated an efficient approach to household organization, abolitionists claimed that slavery was an inefficient mode of production—as William Lloyd Garrison's denunciation of "southern practices" as "disorganized" inferred. Not only was free labor fairer than slavery; abolitionists reasoned it was also a more efficient mode of production.[20] This emphasis on efficiency also sheds light on radical abolitionists' attitude toward institutions. Recognizing their proclivity toward organization—especially within the family—further discredits Stanley Elkins's emphasis on the abolitionists' "anti-institutionalism." There was an anti-institutional strain in abolitionism, represented most forcefully by the disunionist element of the movement, and by those who rejected clerical authority. But it would be misleading to exaggerate that attitude at the expense of abolitionist support for institutions; like individuals, institutions could be reformed. The duality of the abolitionists' relationship with public institutions was well represented by Stephen Foster's 1854 statement (phrased in characteristically hierarchical terms) that he was henceforth going to seek to teach "the masses how to re-model those institutions others were seeking to demolish." Despite protestations from some abolitionists regarding the time spent discussing the evils of slavery, formally organized antislavery societies remained an indispensable component of abolitionism. This faith in organization was evident in other nineteenth-century reform movements. "Organization," noted Anna Q. T. Parsons in the women's rights paper the *Una* "is a law of nature. True organization gives freedom and efficiency to all the parts."[21] All of this implied that women had a duty to manage domestic affairs efficiently.

The question of women's duty was also evident in reformers' attitude toward American exceptionalism. Embracing exceptionalist principles, abolitionists believed that the United States could be an exemplar for the rest of the world to emulate: "At every expansion of American influence, the older countries are destined to undergo new changes, and to receive a second character, from the colonies which they have planted, whose greatness is on so much larger a scale than that of the parent countries, and which will exhibit those improvements which exist in miniature in Europe, unfettered by ancient prejudices, and dilated over another continent."[22] Yet that potential was unfulfilled. The ideal of the republic was a central tenet of the American ideology; by declaring that "Abolitionism is Democracy," abolitionists framed their movement as the means by which the United States could reconcile the wide divergence between the rhetoric of American democratic and republican ideology, and the reality of slavery. Abolitionists believed that if the United States was to attain its rightful position as a model society among the family of nations the slaves had to be emancipated. Reiterating that "all men are created equal," the founding members of the American Anti-Slavery Society (AASS) presented their movement as an extension of the American Revolution. "We have met together," the delegates in Philadelphia declared in 1833, "for the achievement of an enterprise without which that of our founding fathers is not complete." In the same way as domestic writers explained their mission in terms of the preservation and projection of republican values, abolitionists insisted that they were only demanding that Americans abide by the principles that underlay the republic. Invoking the "example of our fathers," who had "proclaimed the inalienable rights of man," they traced their movement to the establishment of the American republic. L. Maria Child, telling Americans that "honest republicans" should work toward overcoming racial prejudice, used Thomas Jefferson's reference to the "boisterous passions of slavery" to strengthen the abolitionist case. Citing Jefferson's *Notes on Virginia,* Child chose not to discuss Jefferson's ownership of slaves, nor his advocacy of African colonization, but argued instead that abolitionists were ideological heirs to the Founding Fathers.[23]

Abolitionists juxtaposed their denunciations of slavery with affirmations of American superiority over other nations. Even African American abolitionists—who understood the contrast between American rhetoric and the reality of American racism more clearly than their white colleagues—reflected the assumptions inherent in exceptionalism. As the black abolitionist William Wells Brown put it in 1847: "Go to the capital of our country, the city of Washington; the capital of the freest government upon the face of the world. Only a few days since, an American mother and her daughter were sold upon the auction-block in that city, and the money put into the Treasury of the United States of America."[24] Brown's statement captured many aspects of the abolitionist ideology. Alongside his belief that women were commodified under slavery, and the notion that the American republic had been defiled by the peculiar institution, Brown's assertions regarding the role and corruptibility of government reflected deeply held abolitionist concerns. Besides focusing on the motherhood cult, Brown's reference to the slave woman as "an American mother" reflected the abolitionists' belief that slaves were entitled to the benefits of American citizenship.

Reformers of all persuasion connected exceptionalism to women's role.

Quoting generously from Alexis de Tocqueville, Catharine Beecher argued that the United States was a unique nation, with a far greater degree of social mobility than was evident in Europe. For radical abolitionists, slavery linked women's role as domestic reformer with the health of the American republic—particularly in the context of the South's increasingly assertive defenses of slavery. Slave owners had always had justifications for the ownership of slaves, but the deliberate effort to depict the peculiar institution as a "positive good" (with all its implications for the continuing oppression of women) was contemporaneous with the rise of immediatist abolitionism. As the delegates to first national convention of abolitionist women asserted in 1837, the "women of America" were "solemnly called upon by the spirit of the age and the signs of the times" to "discuss the subject of slavery." But not only were women morally bound to speak out against slavery: as managers of households and consumers of goods, they were also in a position to act according to their antislavery beliefs.[25]

Radical abolitionists' emphasis on the role of women in the regeneration of the nation reflected values prized by domestic writers—especially the emphasis on motherhood. But radical abolitionists' determination to arouse a sense of empathy in Northern women for enslaved African American mothers (paralleling a wider emphasis on the responsibilities of what Linda Kerber has labeled "republican motherhood") infused motherhood with a clear political function. This process was evident among black as well as white abolitionists.[26] Indeed, given that African American women were doubly marginalized from the polity, the links they drew between domestic reform and the public political culture of antebellum America were doubly significant. In large measure, these challenges were only possible because abolitionist appeals rested on widely shared precepts such as the value of motherhood. Abolitionists asserted that motherhood peculiarly qualified women to speak out against slavery: since women supposedly had a better understanding than males of the sins of slavery, they were morally bound to act against the peculiar institution. For Garrisonian abolitionists, the survival of slavery in the United States made American women's maternal and regenerative roles all the more important. In the aftermath of the ill-fated Compromise of 1850, Lucy Stone explicated the connections between the failure of motherhood and slavery's expansion. "Go to Washington," challenged Stone, "into the Capitol, and look at the deeds that are done there. See the oppression, and wickedness, and malice that are contained in the

Fugitive Slave enactment, and tell me if the men who passed such a law are the sons of worthy mothers!"[27]

Linking motherhood with the health of the republic was common among reformers. L. Maria Child, suggesting "perhaps there is no country in the world, where women, as wives, sisters, and daughters have more influence," urged American women to fulfill their particular responsibilities. These responsibilities were spelled out by Sarah Grimké in 1854: "Woman must live out the Life of love, if ever she is instrumental in bringing man out of the pit of moral degradation into which the exercise of irresponsible powers has cast him. When thro' her he is imbued with the Love Principle he will sit down in the prison with the terror stricken slave."[28] In this way, Grimké forcefully connected the values of womanhood associated with domestic ideology to men's irresponsible exercise of power, especially slavery. As Elizabeth Cady Stanton's 1898 recollection that the "life and well-being of the race seemed to hang on the slender thread of such traditions as were handed down by ignorant mothers and nurses" suggested, domestic values exerted an ongoing influence on nineteenth-century reformism.

There were other indications of radical abolitionists' faith in women's regenerative powers. "How many times have nations been saved by their women," asked the women of the Boston Female Anti-Slavery Society (BFASS), "when every other hope seemed extinct; and so it may be with America, if we will have it so." Abolitionists used the example of Britain to argue their case. American abolitionists took pride in their forebears' struggle for independence, but their criticism of Britain was tempered after the Emancipation Acts of 1833, particularly since, as one Vermont woman noted, "Our sisters of England have done nobly in the cause of Emancipation."[29] Abolitionist equivocation toward Britain was summed up by William L. Garrison, who like a number of his coadjutors, visited Europe. Typically, gender was a major concern. In reference to the exclusion of women delegates from the 1840 World's Anti-Slavery Convention, Garrison declared that while in "some matters of high civilization," Britain lagged behind the United States, "in this matter of courageous benevolence how far are you before us!" Yet Garrison also bemoaned the moral decay of British society. Implicitly presenting himself as an unwitting example of New World innocence thrust into Old World corruption, he expressed disgust at the blatant ways in which prostitutes plied their trade in London. The "immense number of prostitutes," Garrison told his wife in 1846, "was calculated to shock and overwhelm a good man from the United States."[30]

Abolitionists disagreed over revolutionary upheavals, and there were ambiguities in their rejection of European political and social traditions.[31] James Mott contrasted those traditions to slavery. Mott told Wendell Phillips in 1841 that to "every real lover of freedom," visiting Europe would "make him a truer democrat than he was before he witnessed the crushing effect of the aristocracy of that country." That statement implied that American social arrangements were superior to the European class system. At the same time, however, Mott argued that the "thraldom of kingcraft & priestcraft, is not quite as bad as slavecraft, but they are all too bad for humanity to submit to, and should be swept from the face of the earth, no more to oppress the soul of man." This rejection of European political and social structures, and condemnation of the immorality of the class system, did not preclude abolitionists from using the evidence of foreigners to endorse abolitionism—and to praise the virtues of the middle class. Abolitionists ridiculed the "feeble argument" that foreigners should not meddle with American institutions. L. Maria Child noted in 1834 that although foreigners "from monarchical countries are often rendered unfit, by their education and habits, to judge fairly of our institutions," they could still provide astute observations on the nature of American society. The abolitionists' consciousness of social hierarchy is discussed in a later chapter, but the links they perceived between social class and behavior were evident in their critique of the Old World. Arguing that a "great deal of vice prevails in England among the very fashionable, and the very low classes," Child implicitly endorsed the values of the expanding middle class, both in the United States and elsewhere.[32]

Middle-class reformers in the United States, seeking to avoid the social upheaval that they believed plagued Europe, embraced education as a means of instilling appropriate values in the minds of young Americans.[33] Particular emphasis was placed on the education of women. Convinced that the United States faced a social and political crisis, and agreeing that the education provided within American families was incomplete, radical abolitionists and domestic writers concurred that women's education was crucial for the future of the nation. If women were to wield their influence effectively they had to be properly educated. Again, exceptionalist assumptions were evident, and Catharine Beecher and L. Maria Child agreed that the education of young women was particularly important in the United States. Child, certain "that the situation and prospects of a country may be justly estimated by the character of its women," insisted that in the United States it was "peculiarly necessary that daughters should be educated" in such a way that prepared them to fulfill their obligations. She also emphasized the importance of feminine traits in the development of the nation, and reasoned that a "preponderance of selfish policy," would "destroy the republic." Alluding to Americans' predilection to travel, she argued that if they really were republicans, American mothers would "stay at home, to mind our business, and educate our children." Beecher, stressing American women's "Peculiar" duties and responsibilities in the "great moral enterprise" of American democracy, also encouraged American women to pursue an education. Indeed, she argued that the success of American democracy depended on women's influence over the moral character of the mass of the people. Not only did Beecher's emphasis on the role of moral rejuvenation correspond to the Garrisonians' policy of moral suasion, but her thesis also paralleled radical abolitionists' belief that the regeneration of the world was "to be achieved through the instrumentality of Woman."[34]

This faith in the regenerative potential of education was linked to the maternal role. Catharine Beecher thought that since the education of children was the responsibility of mothers, it was vital that women receive the correct education. Whereas the "proper education of a man" only decided the "welfare of an individual," she wrote, the education of a woman could secure "the interests of a whole family." Abolitionists—and other radical reformers—also linked education to the maternal role. Every mother, resolved the delegates to the 1838 women's antislavery convention, was "bound by imperative obligation to instruct her children in the principles of genuine abolition, by teaching them the nature and sanctity of human rights."[35] Abolitionists, both black and white, shared Beecher's belief that women should be given a proper domestic education. L. Maria Child, lamenting "the absence of *domestic education*" in the United States, claimed that "a knowledge of domestic duties" was "beyond all price to a woman." Child was sure that domestic life did not have to be miserable, but because women in the United States were "ignorant of the important duties of domestic life," the "great pleasures" associated with domestic duties soon became "tiresome." Abby Kelley (who, unlike Child, did not publish works directly concerning domesticity) agreed that young women should understand how to fulfill their domestic obligations. Women should not marry, Kelley maintained, until such time as they were able to "provide for the wants of a family."[36]

Yet while advocates of domesticity portrayed motherhood as the principal component of women's destiny, radical reformers insisted that women's education should also equip them to participate in the public sphere. In this way they defied "patriarchal gender definitions."[37] Rejecting Catharine Beecher's suggestion that the "more intelligent a woman becomes," the more she could "appreciate the wisdom of that ordinance that appointed her" to the "subordinate station, and the more her taste will conform to the graceful and dignified retirement and submission it involves," radical abolitionists vigorously criticized the inequalities of the American educational system. They understood the parallel between the slaveholders' desire to keep the slaves "brutally ignorant" and the gendering of education: both processes reflected and reinforced the subjugation of slaves and women. Sarah Grimké acknowledged that "a complete knowledge of household affairs" was "an indispensable requisite in a woman's education," but she objected to the fact that women's education "consists so exclusively in culinary and other manual operations." Grimké's awareness of the relationship between women's domestic responsibilities and their need for wider interests and opportunities left the way open for women's involvement in the public sphere. The ways by which the gendering of education disadvantaged women continued to interest reformers in the period after the Civil War. In 1866 L. Maria Child asserted that gender differences were not the result of any natural differences; rather, they stemmed from "the consistent education" people received "from the influences of their position in society." Signifying that postbellum women's rights ideology and tactics continued to be influenced by the experiences of abolitionism, Child countered suggestions that women were "insufficiently trained for a part in public affairs," by noting in 1873 that such claims were as fallacious as "the old pro-slavery argument that the slaves were not *fit* for freedom." Like slaves, she reasoned, women could never prepare themselves for higher obligations while they remained subjugated.[38]

Less obviously, Child had expressed similar sentiments in an 1852 children's story. As was the case with the slavery question, abolitionists recognized the value of presenting children with correct perspectives on gender issues. Far more than an innocuous tale for young people, *The Brother and Sister* revealed that while Child was less visibly involved in the public struggle for women's rights than a number of other women, she was acutely conscious of the continuing subjugation of women. Stressing that Esther, the young female character of her tale, was "as eager for information as her more vivacious brother," Child discussed the forces working against women acquiring a meaningful education. Following a recommendation from a minister who was typically portrayed as preserving sexual inequalities), efforts were made to secure an education for John, the young male character of her story. Due to the family's straitened financial position, the responsibility for providing the requisite material support fell upon Esther's young shoulders. With a selflessness typical of women characters, "the one absorbing thought" in Esther's life "was how to assist in sending John to college." Although the "spiritual distance" between John and "his honest parents" that resulted from his "superior culture" was lamented, he was in a position to travel and pursue a career. Child starkly juxtaposed John's options with the tedium faced by Esther: "The young man went forth to seek novelty and adventure; the young woman remained alone in the dull monotony of an uneventful life." Characteristically, however, the conclusion to Child's tale merged sadness with optimism. Esther's ill-health and premature death were regretted, but her life was not without meaning or purpose, since John vowed to help women receive the benefits of an education. Consequently, following his marriage to a young woman who had qualities similar to his late sister, he established a "Normal School for Young Women."[39]

Other female abolitionists were also interested in improving educational opportunities for women. In raising this issue, Elizabeth Cady Stanton touched on themes concerning gender roles and identity. On the one hand, in endorsing the value of women's education she articulated sentiments closer to the viewpoint of domestic writers than might be anticipated from a radical advocate of women's rights. Moving from the premise that the "only *lasting* distinctions in life are those that are the result of education," Stanton affirmed that motherhood was "the most important of all the professions." Asserting that if "any of the race need to be educated," it was mothers, she argued in 1856 that they required "the development of every power of body and soul." Yet Stanton disputed the notion that women's education should be fundamentally different from men's. Inferring that since the skills of motherhood were either apparently intrinsic to all women, or were too basic to require special training, she asserted that women did not need a "*particular* kind of education" to be wives and mothers any more than men required special preparation to be husbands and fathers. Since it had been widely assumed that whereas men achieve manhood, women are "naturally" women, Stanton thus simultaneously contradicted and reflected domestic ideology. This issue was raised in discussions about whether young men and women should be educated together. Stanton, describing American colleges as "sinks of iniquity," contended that placing young women in the same educational institutions as young men would provide graduates with a finer sense of their moral obligations and powers. Resting her argument for coeducational colleges on women's moralizing influence, and reiterating the significance of marriage, Stanton questioned where else "shall man prepare himself for the holy sacrament of marriage." Other radical reformers agreed that the full development of the individual required interaction with members of the opposite sex. This belief was evident on many levels. Theodore Weld and the Grimké sisters, distinguishing between the intellectual role of teachers and the nurturing role of mothers, hoped to ensure that the "place of mother" would be supplied by a "special individual not engaged in the intellectual instruction." But they also insisted on educating the sexes together, to "promote symmetrical development of the whole mind."[40]

While reformers agreed that the family was an essential aspect of the educational process, they also believed that there were benefits to be gained from exposing young people to wider influences. Catharine Beecher's attitude in this respect was tangibly demonstrated by her establishment of a female seminary. Angelina Grimké (who visited Beecher's Hartford school in 1831) shared Beecher's attitude toward education beyond the home. Although she admitted in 1849 that "home education" had "some advantages," Grimké believed it could never "expand the hearts" of their children as she and Theodore Weld wanted "to see them expanded." Typically, there were direct connections between education and reformism; Grimké also noted that their children's outlook had to be "expanded in order that they may be useful in developing the great principles of Love practically in their generation." Indeed, she explicitly connected education with abolitionism. The doctrines of abolition, she argued, "are preeminently calculated to qualify men and women to become faithful and efficient teachers. They alone teach fully the doctrine of human rights." Again, there was an ambivalent relationship between abolitionism and domesticity; while Beecher and Grimké agreed that children could benefit from education outside the family, Grimké's connection of abolitionism with education was anathema to Beecher.[41]

Abolitionists and domestic writers also disagreed on whether education was women's particular responsibility. Catharine Beecher endeavored to create a special niche for women as teachers, contending that as the value of education increased, women's value would increase commensurately. Thousands of women found employment as teachers during the nineteenth century, but radical abolitionists did not accept that it was women's destiny to be defined as educators. Accordingly, while Sarah Grimké sought to use the teaching function to advance women's cause, by arguing that "no avocation" was "more elevating" than that of the teacher, other abolitionist women agreed with the younger Grimké sister, who pointed out that once the rights of women were understood, men would "see and feel that it is their duty to cooperate with us, in this high and holy vocation." As Henry Blackwell attested after the birth of his daughter, certain abolitionists, at least, were able to put these values into practice. Rejecting the notion that the responsibility for raising children fell naturally on women, Blackwell's emphasis on "the sense of parentage" indicated that some male abolitionists took seriously their parental responsibilities.[42]

This shared sense of responsibility emerged when radical abolitionists discussed the obstacles standing in the way of the inculcation of sound values in children. They realized that young women—as objects of physical attraction—were particularly vulnerable to corrupting influences. Abolitionists of both sexes decried the fact that young women were encouraged to waste their time on frivolity and fashion. Echoing L. Maria Child's reference to the "foolish excitement" of "showing off the attention of somebody," James Mott expressed great satisfaction that his "dear children" recognized "the folly of soirees" and "such like nonsense." Confident that they were not "drawn away" by such distractions, Mott described the "gratitude" that was "carried in the heart of a parent at such manifestations of correct principle in children."[43] Sarah Grimké connected these matters to gender roles. Attesting to the reformers' hierarchical perspective, and reflecting a wider condemnation of what some regarded as the middle-class preoccupation with fashion, Grimké asked that not all women be judged by the "butterflies of ballrooms." There was a "multitude of women," she argued, who were eager to "elevate the sex above the paltry pursuits of vanity." These concerns—and an underlying distaste for the excesses of conspicuous consumption—were evident in the abolitionists' personal relationships. An 1834 letter from William L. Garrison to Helen Benson represented the fusion of the abolitionists' distaste for fashion with their own desires. "I cannot express to you how great was my satisfaction," Garrison remarked to his future bride, "on arriving at your house to meet you dressed in the same simple manner in which all my preceding visits I had seen you. It was fine proof of your good sense and sterling integrity, in rejecting all tawdry ornaments and artificial aids to the embellishment of your person."[44]

Radical abolitionists' condemnation of fashion accorded with the Reverend Adoniram Judson's belief that fashion and vanity not only prevented the construction of a "Church of Christ in this heathen land," but also stood in the way of the elevation of the minds of female converts. Writing in 1832, Judson sought the formation of "*Plain Dress Societies*" in "every city and village throughout the land." Radical abolitionists' and women's rights advocates' interest in the Bloomer costume (a skirt over long loose trousers that enabled women to move more freely) added a more obvious ideological imperative to the issue of dress reform. But as L. Maria Child revealed in *The Family Nurse,* there was a shared awareness among abolitionists of the damage caused by constricting clothing, and a common rejection of the underlying depiction of women as objects of physical attraction. Child's postbellum reference to the "capricious frivolities of fashion" in the columns of the *National Anti-Slavery Standard* revealed how abolitionism served as a locus for these interests. Women's rights advocates, too, recognized the destructive influence of fashion. Agreeing that women were "still frivolous," the delegates to the 1870 women's rights convention regretted—in language that signified how the abolitionists' condemnations of slavery affected the sensibilities of other nineteenth-century reform movements—that women were still "the slaves of prejudice, passion, folly, fashion, and petty ambition."[45]

Domestic values exerted an ambivalent influence over the practice of abolitionism. One area of common concern was the question of peace. Radical abolitionists, denouncing the violence associated with slavery, and sure that reform began at home, implored each other to promote peace and to live their lives according to peaceful principles. This objective owed much to domestic ideology, as did abolitionists' perceptions of the links between religion and individual peace. Sarah Grimké, alluding to the importance of personal serenity, emphasized that individual disharmony endangered the domestic circle. Suggesting that Theodore Weld allow himself "a little time to relax from the *positive* state," Grimké noted in 1855 that "to live a life of such tension" was not only likely to result in the breakup of "the family relation," but was "utterly antagonistic to the symmetrical development of the moral being." These comments do not prove that abolitionists suffered from stress any more than their contemporaries—as was once suggested by historians of the movement.[46] Rather, they indicate that abolitionists' efforts to seek refuge in the private sphere accorded with the prevailing domestic ideology, and suggest that the tensions commonly associated with "modern" living were manifested long before the twentieth century.

Domestic values, including a desire for peace, were evident in the institutional activities of antislavery women. Anne Warren Weston commented in 1835 on the activities of the BFASS: "we have distributed a number of Anti-Slavery tracts and publications and observing how useful children's handkerchiefs have been made in disseminating the truth on the subject of Temperance, the ladies of our Society have been induced to publish an Antislavery Handkerchief, which we hope may be a means of teaching to some of our New England children those truths of liberty they cannot learn too soon."[47] Besides affirming radical abolitionists' conviction that they were agents of the *truth,* Weston's letter signified female abolitionists' perception of women's particular role as reformers. Her remarks also showed that abolitionist women utilized the prevailing ideology of women's role as educators. By referring to the example of temperance workers, she inferred the links between nineteenth-century reform movements. One of the strongest connections between antebellum reforms was that women's role should be a peaceful one: the subject of slavery was controversial, but it is difficult to conceive a less aggressive means of furthering abolitionism than through the distribution of handkerchiefs to children. These efforts might appear naive, but by using women's everyday skills on behalf of public reform, abolitionism was the means through which women's private activities could intersect with public life.

The abolitionists' emphasis on peaceful persuasion was most eloquently demonstrated by their strategy of moral suasion. On this issue, Garrisonian abolitionism owed much to domestic ideology. An important aspect of this process was the distinction abolitionists drew between the institutional evil of slavery, and the individuals implicated in its practices. Despite their hatred of slavery, abolitionists refused to hate the slaveholders, and as the women of the BFASS noted, abolitionists must not only love their opponents, but must also pray for them. Rather than force Americans to convert to antislavery principles, abolitionists were initially determined to achieve their goals peacefully: aggression, violence, and impatience would only serve to undermine their appeal. During the 1830s, especially, the hope was that an appeal to the slave owners' consciences would convince them that slave-holding was sinful, and prompt them to emancipate their slaves. Angelina Grimké spoke for many abolitionists when she remarked that she had refused to involve herself in the antislavery crusade until she was convinced that the abolitionists' "principles were *entirely pacific* and their efforts *entirely moral.*" Placing particular responsibility on female abolitionists, and renouncing violence, Grimké asked her readers whether they could believe "for a moment" that she would "prove so recreant to the feelings of a daughter and a sister, as to join a society which was seeking to overthrow slavery by falsehood, bloodshed, and murder?"[48] Garrisonian abolitionists' insistence on peaceful persuasion led some to embrace nonresistance as an underlying philosophy. Sarah Grimké, for example, described the doctrine of nonresistance as "the greatest test" of the abolitionists' faith. Lauding peace as the "root of all reformations," she optimistically contended that if "the simple precept 'resist not evil' " could be "entrenched in the hearts and consciences of man, slavery & war & oppression & domestic tyranny & the usurping of authority over one another" would "wholly cease." But there was also a pragmatic consideration. Some abolitionists, believing that violence would further alienate an already hostile public, were convinced that nonresistance was the only possible means of converting Americans to the cause of abolitionism.[49]

The Garrisonians' frequently intemperate language, along with their demands for an immediate end to slavery, were widely construed as evidence of their uncompromising fanaticism. Yet immediatism was a more moderate strategy than many assumed, and reflected the Garrisonians' determination to achieve their objectives peacefully. Immediate emancipation was widely portrayed in terms of the instant, unconditional emancipation of the slaves. Certainly, this was the way slave owners perceived and portrayed immediatism. Abolitionists, however, generally interpreted the phrase to mean the immediate renunciation of the right to own slaves: the actual emancipation of the slaves did not necessarily have to be immediate. The parallels between the abolitionists' peace ethic and domesticity were manifested in radical abolitionists' reluctance to endorse slave revolts. Although they were accused of inciting violence among the slaves, abolitionists stressed that if the nation heeded their warnings, bloodshed could be avoided.[50] Often referring to religious duties and principles, white abolitionists generally discouraged African Americans from seeking a violent solution to their plight. Most white abolitionists argued that if the slaves were to act along truly Christian principles, they would wait patiently for freedom, rather than resort to bloodshed. This ethic persisted, even though, as a later chapter shows, they did increasingly accept the contention of most black abolitionists—even those aligned to the Garrisonian wing of the movement—that the slaves had a right to revolt.[51]

The emphasis on peace had other implications for the practice of abolitionism and for the wider political culture of antebellum America. Reformers of all persuasion contemplated the relationship between means and ends. Domestic writers, insisting that women seek to improve the world in a particular manner, emphasized the primacy of means over ends. Aileen Kraditor, characterizing the split in abolitionist ranks in terms of differences over "ends" and "means," has noted that for the Garrisonians, the means by which they achieved their objectives were as important as the ends.[52] For radical abolitionists this issue was linked to the question of gender roles. While they did not always treat women as equals, Garrisonians were determined to provide women with a platform to express their views on the slavery issue. And, like domestic writers, they did recognize the value of women as moral agents. Denying that they were deliberately causing controversy, female abolitionists actively contributed to the Garrisonians' emphasis on moral suasionism.[53] Abolitionists equivocated over the validity and morality of political antislavery, but even political abolitionists valued moral arguments. Echoing domestic writers' injunctions against women's public activities, Garrisonians maintained that their involvement in such immoral activities as politics would inevitably lead them to forfeit the moral advantage. Since politics was perceived as a masculine domain, not only could the Garrisonians' rejection of political abolitionism be construed as a rejection of a "masculine" solution to slavery, but their insistence upon moral suasionism can be interpreted as a projection of feminine, or domestic, values into the outside world.

Again, however, tensions were evident. Not only did the Garrisonians eventually retreat somewhat from their antipolitical stance, to the extent that they acknowledged other people's right to vote, but their controversial defense of women abolitionists' right to involve themselves in the antislavery petition campaign amounted to a defense of a form of political activism that transgressed what was widely considered appropriate for women. Indeed, while the Garrisonians have often been characterized as eschewing politics, abolitionist women's defense of the right to petition reveals the shortcomings of a dichotomic depiction of the Garrisonians as antipolitical, and other factions of the movement as pro-political.[54] By challenging the barriers between the private and public spheres (particularly through their insistence that they be entitled to engage in petitioning) abolitionist women introduced a peculiarly feminine contribution to the public and masculine world of politics. During a period in which increasing numbers of men were engaging in the rough-and-tumble of Jacksonian-era politics, abolitionist women thus played an important part in the "domestication" of American politics. Not only were they expanding upon the legacy of earlier women who had sought to influence the political process; antislavery women also prefigured subsequent generations of female reformers who more assertively demanded women's direct engagement in the political process.[55] In seeking to carry domestic values into the public sphere, abolitionists did not always fully appreciate the radical implications of their reformism, but they did sense—long before most other Americans—that the division of the sexes into separate spheres was, at least in part, a contrivance that reflected and reinforced imbalances in gender relations.

The political implications of women's abolitionism, symptomatic of the dynamic tensions between abolitionism and domesticity, were well represented by the experiences of Angelina Grimké. Grimké, vigorously claiming women's right to participate in the public sphere, embarked in 1837 on a controversial lecture tour that provoked the ire of many Americans. Yet the following year, she enthusiastically entered what some other abolitionists at the time, and historians since, considered an irreversible slide into domestic confinement. Underpinning these shifts in Grimké's attitude was an abiding commitment to the family, which she described in 1854 as "God's model school."[56] This commitment to family life united abolitionists, and linked them to values central to the wider culture of nineteenth-century America. But while abolitionists and their opponents shared a commitment to the *ideal* of the family, they envisaged that ideal in dramatically different terms. Radical abolitionists such as Grimké conceived the ideal family as an egalitarian one; domestic ideologues such as Catharine Beecher argued differently, endorsing what was in practice a patriarchal set of domestic arrangements. When the Grimké sisters began lecturing on behalf of the abolitionist cause, these issues were the subject of considerable public debate. Consequently, the ensuing dispute between the Grimkés and Beecher not only reveals much about the relationship between domesticity and abolitionism, but also points to the abolitionists' place in the broader culture of antebellum America.[57]

The quarrel between the Grimkés and Beecher, set against the backdrop of American women's increasing influence over religious affairs, was closely connected to the religious imperative behind women's reformism. Regardless of their position on the question of where women should seek to wield their influence, reformers of all types embraced a sense of Christian responsibility. Both domestic ideology and abolitionism were linked to the changes in religious beliefs and practices of the early nineteenth century. As Angelina Grimké's assertion that "it is as a religious question that we regard it [slavery] as most important" signified, women's involvement in the antislavery crusade stemmed from the same imperatives that determined their domestic role as moral guardians of the nation.[58] Yet there was a complex relationship between women's reformism and religion. Religion was both a source of power for American women, as well as a means of validating their confinement to the domestic sphere. Nineteenth-century women, assured that religion had "a peculiar sweetness, when it mingles with the modest softness of the female character," were actively encouraged to "promote the cause of true religion." Barbara Welter has referred to the "feminization" of American religion, and for some women at least, religion was an avenue through which they could transcend the domestic sphere without renouncing their feminine identity. The Second Great Awakening of the early nineteenth century played an integral part in that process: it not only "expressed, confirmed and legitimized" the increasing role of women in the Church, but also prepared them to expand their social role.[59]

Women's expanding role in religious affairs paved the way for their involvement in benevolent activities. These activities drew wide support, even among those like Hannah Mather Crocker, who argued that women's influence should be exerted by "reason and persuasion." She accepted that women had "an equal right, with the other sex, to form societies for promoting religious, charitable, and benevolent purposes." It was at this point, however, that strict boundaries were placed on women's reforming role. Women were warned that they should act on the "proper occasions," and then only "by example and persuasion." Such advice—like the clergy's admonition that women should confine themselves to "*the family circle*"—endorsed the separation of men's and women's spheres. Many people agreed that while it was proper for women to ameliorate social ills, by involving themselves in religious or charitable organizations, they should not challenge the fundamental principles or institutions of their society. Abolitionism was the catalyst that dramatically brought this issue to the public eye. Church authorities condemned the Grimkés' foray into the public sphere. Although the "Pastoral Letter of the General Association of Massachusetts to the Congregational Churches Under Their Care" (written by the Reverend Nemiah Adams) did not specifically name the Grimkés, it was clearly directed toward the Garrisonians. The Pastoral Letter, issued in July 1837, reiterated that women should confine themselves to the private sphere.[60] These themes shaped the debate between the Grimké sisters and Beecher.

Beecher's dispute with the Grimkés was prompted by the publication of a tract by Angelina Grimké, wherein she sought to persuade Southern women of the sinfulness of slavery, and by the sisters' decision to deliver abolitionist lectures in public. The Grimkés elicited considerable reaction when they lectured to female audiences, but it was their addresses to "promiscuous" audiences—consisting of men as well as women—that proved most controversial. Although they insisted that their primary motivation was to help emancipate the slaves, the sisters' entrance onto the public stage challenged the boundaries of women's sphere. Their critics, both within and beyond abolitionist circles, urged them to retreat to the domestic sphere. But, sensing the deeper significance of their public activities—and increasingly conscious that the division of the sexes into separate spheres served to subordinate women—the Grimkés refused to be silenced. Raising the issue of gender roles, Angelina condemned the division of the sexes. "This doctrine of men & women having *peculiar* duties & rights," she told fellow abolitionist Amos Phelps in 1837, "appears to me to have spread desolation over our moral being. Woman has been used as a drudge & caressed like a spoiled child." Radical abolitionists' recognition of women's right to work outside the home, albeit for voluntary reform, defied the dominant ideology of the early nineteenth century. Female abolitionists' efforts on the slaves' behalf were not in strict accordance with conventional definitions of "work," and were not particularly lucrative. Nevertheless, not only did they consider abolitionism as work; many women also regarded it as a "vocation."[61]

Underpinning female abolitionists' sense of duty was an abiding faith in the value of Christian ethics. This was clearly shown by Angelina Grimké's 1836 *Appeal to the Christian Women of the South.* Again, too, domestic values were evident. By endorsing the value of women's "influence," and by contending that the women of the South could overthrow "the horrible system of oppression and cruelty," Grimké reaffirmed women's capacity to exert moral influence in the public sphere. She suggested four means by which Southern women should fight slavery. The first two, "reading" and "praying," were uncontroversial. Similarly, her third tactic, wherein she urged Southern women to "persuade" their husbands, fathers, brothers, and sons of the inherent sinfulness of owning slaves, was congruent with domestic ideology. At that point she was prepared to place her faith in the efficacy of one of the principal aspects of the Garrisonian, and domestic, ideology: "there is something in the heart of man which *will bend under moral suasion.*" Grimké's optimistic portrayal of women's redemptive capacities paralleled the views of other abolitionists. Melania Ammidon, the Corresponding Secretary of the BFASS, merged domestic images with a religious imperative. Arguing that "feeble woman can do much towards cleansing her guilty nation from a sin that must look as black as midnight in the eyes of a holy God," Ammidon explicitly used domestic imagery to describe women's mission of purification.[62]

Catharine Beecher agreed that women should use their powers of persuasion to reform the world. But, in addition to inveighing against the Grimkés' increasingly public abolitionism, Beecher disputed one specific right that the sisters claimed for women. Objecting to the fourth tactic outlined by Angelina Grimké—a defense of women's right to petition on behalf of abolitionism—Beecher believed such behavior would exasperate and anger men. Maintaining that women should confine themselves to the private sphere, she reasoned that true womanhood did not include any of the traits she attributed to American abolitionists. Adamant that "Heaven has appointed one sex the superior, and to the other the subordinate station," she argued that women's acceptance of that subordinate position did not negate the significance of their role. Alleging that American abolitionists had not approached slaveholders "with the spirit of love, courtesy, and forbearance" that true Christianity demanded, she insisted that women should confine themselves to the "domestic social circle." Beecher worried that if women stepped beyond their sphere, and presented themselves in the corrupting world of politics and public life, they would not only surrender the basis on which they exercised disinterested and peaceful judgments, but would also sacrifice their ability and right to influence males. Paradoxically, however, by publicly rebuking the Grimkés for their abolitionist activities, Beecher unintentionally contradicted an underlying principle of domestic ideology: that women should not involve themselves in public controversies.[63] In this respect, Beecher mirrored a wider pattern. While her objections to abolitionist women's public activism were premised on widely shared assumptions regarding women's nature, the organized benevolent activities that derived from those assumptions, coupled with a political culture that prized widespread participation in the democratic process, eroded gendered beliefs concerning women's benevolent function. As Lori Ginzberg has put it, there were "inconsistencies between the ideological separation of morality and politics and their everyday interconnection."[64]

Female abolitionists, linking questions of morality and individuality to the issue of women's right to participate in public life, understood these inconsistencies as early as the 1830s. Angelina Grimké argued that abolitionism rested not only on such "womanly" principles as morality, but on a recognition of the slaves' individuality. It was the realization that such arguments were as applicable to the rights of women, as they were to the rights of the slaves, which underpinned much of the opposition to women's abolitionism. Turning to the precepts of domestic ideology, Grimké argued for the ascendancy of "moral" principles over intellectual "endowments," and suggested that Beecher's arguments were flawed because they ignored the aspirations of slaves and free blacks. Nor did Beecher's advocacy of gradual emancipation find favor with Grimké, who emphasized that as the daughter of a prominent slaveholder, she had "seen too much of slavery to be a gradualist." Sharing other abolitionists' view that slavery was "one of the greatest infringements of the law of peace and love," the Grimkés averred that the overwhelming evil of slavery must be brought to an immediate end, and insisted that any ideas of women's proper place be ignored for the sake of the slave. Similar priorities underlay the actions of the members of the

BFASS, who noted that "they were accused of 'sowing dissensions among brethren.' "[65]

On the surface, this suggested there were occasions when abolitionist women were prepared to forsake peaceful means. Yet the women abolitionists of Boston, believing they were remaining true to their principles, not only hoped to avoid bloodshed by the peaceful emancipation of the slaves, but also asserted they had not initiated any violence. Instead, they had been fulfilling their Christian duty. Appealing to the authority of religious precedents, the Boston women "remembered that Christ pronounced *peace* a secondary consideration, when the question is of repentance and its fruits." Angelina Grimké, replying to Beecher's argument that American abolitionism was neither peaceful nor Christian, contended that the same had been said of Christ. She thus betrayed, in the immodest manner characteristic of many reformers, the extent to which abolitionists believed they were doing God's bidding. Again, these connections were explicated in gender-specific terms by the women of the BFASS, who sought to utilize the special authority deriving from their womanhood to fulfill their responsibility "to labor to increase the knowledge and care of God." As "*wives* and *mothers,* as *sisters* and *daughters,*" they believed they were "deeply responsible for the influence" they had "on the human race." These beliefs rested on many of the same assumptions that underscored notions of true womanhood. But living and working amid a political culture that celebrated democratic principles, female abolitionists declared that the particular obligations that accompanied womanhood did not mean women could be denied their rights as American citizens. The consequences of these beliefs were clear: during the 1830s abolitionist women vigorously claimed the right of petition; a decade later, radical proponents of women's rights began calling for the vote.[66]

Part of the rationale for excluding women from political life was that they were ill-equipped to deal with such worldly issues. Domestic writers rationalized that exclusion by elevating women's domestic role. Radical abolitionists, realizing the sophistry of such arguments, understood that the issue of women's capacities was linked to the question of women's role. Certain that they were correctly interpreting God's will, abolitionist women implied that domestic writers such as Catharine Beecher did not fully understand the true Christian perspective on women's appropriate role. Angelina Grimké, rejecting Beecher's contention that the superiority of men, and the consequent subordination of women, did not reflect the "character or conduct of either," explained that the "*mere circumstance of sex*" did "not give to man higher rights and responsibilities than to woman." Yet while they disagreed with Beecher over the question of what constituted women's responsibilities, the Grimkés' pronouncements reflected the influence of the concept of separate spheres, even upon radical women. This practice of analyzing women's position and role in terms of their physical place was common in the nineteenth century—and beyond. For domestic reformers such as Beecher, the focus on the contrast between the domestic sphere and the outside world was the basis on which they sought to improve women's status. Radical abolitionists, however, believed that the limitations that the home imposed on women not only contrasted with the wider choices available to men, but also emphasized women's plight.[67] Sarah Grimké was determined "to depend solely on the Bible to designate the *sphere* of woman." She was emphatic that the prevailing boundaries of women's sphere, which she recognized as a telling factor behind the injustices suffered by women, had not been determined by God, but by man. "All I ask of our brethren," she wrote, is "that they will take their feet from off our necks." Yet Grimké expressed ambivalence about the notion of separate spheres. She was troubled by the question of women's proper role, and her public assertion that "God designed woman to be" a "help meet for man," implied that woman was an adjunct of man. Privately, however, she asserted that men and women were "Created in perfect equality," and maintained that God made women to be "*in all respects*" the equal of man.[68]

At the first convention of antislavery women, held in Philadelphia in 1837, Angelina Grimké assertively denounced the confinement of women to the private sphere. Perhaps emboldened by the company of like-minded women, she proposed a resolution that unambiguously claimed women's right to participate in public life. Grimké's proposal did not win unanimous support, but following an "animated and interesting debate," the delegates resolved that "the time has come for woman to move in that sphere which Providence has assigned her, and no longer remain satisfied in the circumscribed limits with which corrupt custom and a perverted application of Scripture have encircled her." Disputing Beecher's claim that men and women should occupy different spheres, Grimké charged that there was no proof that the Bible sanctioned the superiority of one sex over the other. Since they were "not the gifts of man," women should not be dependent on the largesse of men for their position. A decade and a half later, with her resolve strengthened by the experience of her own marriage, Grimké publicly reaffirmed that women's sphere was not limited to the home.[69]

Even the most radical advocates of women's rights acknowledged the strength of the notion of gender spheres. Elizabeth Cady Stanton's argument that "if God has assigned a sphere to man and one to woman, we claim the right ourselves to judge of His design in reference to us," implied a grudging acceptance of the notion of separate spheres. Yet while she continued to think in terms of "spheres," her spheres were determined on the basis of individualism, rather than on the basis of gender. "There is no such thing," she stated, "as a sphere for sex. Every man has a different sphere in which he may or may not shine, and it is the same with every woman." Angelina Grimké also implicitly raised the question of individuality when she pointed out that the division of the sexes into separate spheres had reduced women to underlings of men. Reflecting abolitionist doctrine, as well as her personal experiences, and returning to a tenet of Garrisonian abolitionism, she framed the consequence for women in terms of their transformation from an end to a means.[70]

Much of Catharine Beecher's argument against female abolitionists' public forays was predicated on the assumption that American households had been peaceful prior to women's entry onto the abolitionist stage. Radical reformers rejected this proposition. Elizabeth Cady Stanton recognized the divergence between the idealized rhetoric of domestic ideology, and the reality of women's lives. Contending that much of "this talk about domestic harmony," was "the sheerest humbug," she asked her colleagues to look around their "whole circle of friends." Stanton wondered "how many truly harmonious households" there really were in the United States. She knew that quietness should not be confused with real harmony: "Quiet households we may have, but submission and harmony produce very different states of quietness." As abolitionists rejected slaveholders' assertions that the lack of slave rebellions was evidence of the slaves' contentment, Stanton pointed out that there was "no true happiness where there is subjection—no harmony without freedom."[71]

Resonating through these debates was the question of who represented "real" American values. Here, the issue of women's political rights merged with the ideal of participatory democracy. Countering Catharine Beecher's claims to be defending the principles of the American Revolution, and arguing that women were entitled to have a voice in all the laws by which they were governed, Angelina Grimké's defense of petitioning foreshadowed women's rights activists' demands for the franchise. Employing the analogy of the War of Independence, where the principle of "taxation without representation" had been central to American rhetoric and ideology, Grimké defended women's right to petition as "the only political right" available to them. She declared that the denial of the vote to women was "but a poor reason" to deny them the right of petition, which they should be allowed to exercise whenever they felt "aggrieved." Moreover, in a resolution to the first women's antislavery convention, Grimké traced women's political rights to God and the American Constitution. The "right of petition," she said, "is natural and inalienable, derived from God and guaranteed by the Constitution of the United States."[72]

Given these beliefs, it was not surprising that female abolitionists were irked by Catharine Beecher's denial of women's right to petition. Again, women's involvement in abolitionism was inextricably linked to the conventions surrounding American political and social life. Recognizing that the "most formidable barrier that is presented before us is the *political bearing of slavery,*" radical abolitionists identified connections between the denial of women's political rights, the forces defending slavery, and the belief that women's nature rendered them suitable only for domestic duties.[73] These links were equally well understood by opponents of abolitionism, who expressed alarm at women's involvement in the antislavery struggle. Female abolitionists were warned that their public activities rendered them morally deficient and hence incapable of fulfilling their domestic role. George Frederick Holmes, commenting on Harriet Beecher Stowe's *Uncle Tom's Cabin,* expounded on women's sphere: "If she deliberately steps beyond the hallowed precincts—the enchanted circle—which encompasses her as with the halo of divinity, she has wantonly forfeited her privilege of immunity as she has irretrievably lost our regard, and the harshness she may provoke is invited by her own folly and impropriety."[74] Holmes was a Southerner, but such attitudes were not confined to the slave states. His view corresponded to domestic writers' belief that women's involvement in the public sphere entailed the loss of the redemptive and purifying qualities that distinguished women from men.

Other opponents of abolition identified deeper risks of women's abolitionism. In an 1835 admonition against the abolitionists, John Tyler, a future president, spelled out his particular objections to women's engagement in abolitionism. Drawing specific attention to an antislavery petition that had been signed by fifteen hundred women, Tyler outlined the threat that women's abolitionism posed to the political—as well as sexual and racial—order in the United States: "Woman is to be made one of the instruments to accomplish [the abolitionists'] mischievous purposes. . . . Yes, woman is to be made the instrument of destroying our political paradise, the Union of these States; she is to be made the presiding genius over the councils of insurrection and discord; she is to be converted into a fiend, to rejoice over the conflagration of our dwellings and the murder of our people."[75] Tyler's tirade painted a picture of abolitionist women as the antithesis of the feminine ideal. Instead of fulfilling their responsibilities by reigning over their own domestic spheres, abolitionist women were portrayed as threatening not just the domestic peace of American homes, but the political well-being of the whole nation. Recognizing the powers inherent in the notion of republican motherhood, Tyler was convinced that female abolitionists were abrogating their patriotic responsibilities, both at home, and in the wider world.

Abolitionists, defenders of slavery, and domestic writers thus shared an interest in domestic harmony. But this common desire for peace and order in American homes contrasted with the terror confronting some abolitionists. Radical abolitionists' sense of alienation from their northern culture—and their sense of persecution—were most starkly apparent when abolitionists faced the wrath of their opponents. Indeed, the violence to which abolitionists were subjected signified the depth of their challenge to prevailing social values and practices. Particularly during the 1830s, abolitionists encountered considerable mob violence. This violence—including the death in 1837 of antislavery editor Elijah Lovejoy at the hands of an anti-abolitionist mob in Alton, Illinois, and culminating the following year with the burning of Pennsylvania Hall by an enraged mob intent upon halting the second convention of antislavery women—terrorized abolitionists, and signified the depravities of the slaveocracy. The impact of slavery upon domestic harmony was summed up by Helen Garrison after an anti-abolitionist mob had vented its spleen against her husband. Contrasting Garrison's "calm and quiet state" with the violence of the throng, Helen rued the fact that their "domestic happiness" was disrupted "by a lawless mob." Abolitionists regarded the family, and the values of womanhood, as antitheses to the mayhem of mob rule. Not only did abolitionist families function as support mechanisms for those reformers who faced hostile mobs; women's role was specifically connected with social development. Invoking the ideal of women as civilizing influences, L. Maria Child characterized anti-abolition mobs in gender-specific terms. Confronted by one man in an anti-abolition mob who declared, "this is no place for women," Child replied: "They are needed here to teach civilization to man."[76] Abolitionists demonstrated fortitude in the face of hostile mobs, and they recognized the potential value that martyrdom could have for the movement. But the personal dangers they faced in the public sphere made a domestic retreat all the more valuable.

L. Maria Child's deliberate association of woman's public abolitionism with civilization touched another aspect of nineteenth-century thought. For radical abolitionists, and other reformers, women's apparently unique insights into the world's ills were related to their civilizing function. The American mission, expressed in many ways during the nineteenth century, from Manifest Destiny, to the reforming efforts of benevolent societies, was premised on assumptions concerning American civilization. Based in practice around the hegemony of patriarchy and racism, civilization was both an ideal, and an impediment to individualism for men *and* women. There were explicit contradictions between what Huck Finn, employing a metaphor of slavery, disparaged as the "shackles of civilization," and women's roles.[77] Abolitionism incorporated many of the tensions to which Samuel Clemens alluded; in a nation experiencing dynamic change, there was constant reevaluation and debate over the role of women as a civilizing impulse.

The notion of women as a civilizing influence was a complicated one. While the conquest of the frontier was widely regarded as evidence of the expansion of "civilization," the cultural association of woman with nature meant that women were both agents and victims of the civilizing process.[78] American territorial expansion in the nineteenth century reveals the confluence of these ideas; the expansion of slavery into the West not only provided the backdrop for the increasing sectional differences between the slave and free states, but also impelled women to engage in abolitionism. These differences reached a flash point in Kansas in 1856, when proslavery and antislavery settlers fought over the status of slavery in the region. Charles Sumner, the abolitionist senator from Massachusetts, linked slavery's expansion to the corruption of masculine and feminine sexual roles. Besides referring to "the harlot, Slavery," Sumner denounced the peculiar institution as an expression of unrestrained masculine sexual aggression. His depiction of the events in "Bleeding Kansas" as "the rape of a virgin territory, compelling it to the hateful embrace of slavery," was not only posited upon connections between women and nature, but specifically contrasted an unspoilt, apparently feminine landscape, with the destructive aggression and expansion associated with Southern slavery. Sumner's implicit association of womanhood with nature differed from the common abolitionist representation of femininity as a cultural construction. In both cases, however, the relationship between women and civilization was a matter of serious concern. Abolitionists were certain that the ideology and reality of slavery, unmistakably represented by the vicious assault on Sumner on the floor of the United States Senate, were antithetical to the forces of civilization, and hence to the values and interests of women as a sex.[79]

For abolitionists, civilization stood delicately balanced with individualism. Henry Blackwell inferred that unbridled individualism was the antithesis of civilization, but he also insisted that civilization was compatible with self interest. Soon after he advised Lucy Stone that one way to avoid the political injustice she suffered in the United States was by "retiring from civilization to some uninhabited and barbarous country where *individualism* is the only law," Blackwell associated the right of reformers to happiness with their ability to fulfill their reformist goals. "We have a right," he insisted, "to be happy *in & for ourselves.* If not what a stupid thing to try to make other people happy." As Blackwell's statement suggested, radical abolitionists associated civilization with the extension of marriage. Setting the scene for their enduring interest in the connections between marriage and reformism, an 1831 editorial in the *Liberator* portrayed the abolitionists' objectives in specifically familial terms: "As civilization, and knowledge, and republican feelings, and christianity prevail in the world, the wider will matrimonial connexions extend; and finally people of every tribe and kindred and tongue will freely intermarry. By the blissful operation of this divine institution, the earth is evidently to become one neighborhood of family."[80] The implications of the abolitionists' advocacy of interracial marriage have been mentioned, but linking civilization, education, republicanism, and Christianity with the marriage relation suggested the breadth of radical abolitionists' mission.

One aspect of the abolitionists' mission was a concern with children's domestic environment. This concern was evident in their condemnations of slavery's impact on Southern children, but anticipating postbellum temperance advocates' emphasis on "peace as a way of life," they also encouraged the creation of peaceful domestic spheres in Northern homes. Elizabeth Cady Stanton affirmed the significance of the connections between the circumstances of conception, a peaceful domestic environment, and a progressive and rational approach to childrearing: "a child conceived in the midst of hate, sin, & discord, nurtured in abuse & injustice, cannot do much to bless the world in himself. If we properly understand the science of life—it would be far easier to give to the world, harmonious, beautiful, noble, virtuous children."[81] By providing a peaceful and loving environment, parents could go a long way toward ensuring their children embraced proper reformist principles.

Agreeing that peaceful domestic environment required happy marriages, abolitionists and domestic writers sought to make marriage a rational and informed process rather than a random choice. L. Maria Child, reflecting the experience of her own marriage, criticized the emphasis that was placed on women marrying. She believed that women who entered marriage hastily were often inadequately prepared to discharge their own obligations, and were unaware of their husband's character. Single and married abolitionist women were interested in these matters. Sarah Grimké, contending that women should strive for the same objectives and goals as men, lamented that women who fail to marry "rarely rise above the disappointment." Reformers believed that one consequence of men and women entering marriage without a proper knowledge of each other, or of the responsibilities of the relationship, was the relative scarcity of happy and mutually satisfying "homes" in America. Utilizing images recurrent in nineteenth-century reformism, one contributor to the *Lily* graphically remarked in 1849 that "the marriage union" was thus "prostituted throughout the civilised world." The "terrible retribution," she continued, was "seen in the myriads of discordant and disordered households."[82]

This linkage of marriage and domestic harmony (and by extension, the well-being of the public sphere) was characteristic of nineteenth-century reformism. The theory and practice of abolitionism raised important questions pertaining to the division of men and women into public and private spheres. Abolitionism, especially women's role within abolitionism, reflected values pivotal to domestic ideology. In particular, domestic writers and abolitionists prized women's contribution to reformism. It was widely agreed that women had an obligation to participate in the improvement of the world, a task that was widely considered of particular importance for American women. Radical abolitionists and domestic writers also agreed that women should strive to improve their status, especially through education. This faith in education was as much a means as it was an ends; through their educational and maternal influence, women were expected to play an important role inculcating proper values—especially the peace ethic—into those around them. Yet while abolitionism reflected many of the values of domestic ideology, abolitionist women emphatically rejected the confinement of women to the domestic sphere. That rejection, one of the most controversial aspects of radical abolitionism, called into question the whole notion of separate spheres, and played a significant part in shaping the political culture of nineteenth-century America. Unable to participate directly in the political life of the public sphere, female abolitionists used the precepts of domestic ideology to advance their reform agenda. But in so doing they challenged the social, economic, and political divisions upon which domesticity—and republicanism—were predicated. The complex ideological relationship between radical abolitionism and domesticity was evident too in the abolitionists' private experiences. We shall take up this subject in the next chapter.

THREE

The Practice of Domesticity:

Radical Abolitionists' Experiences of Marriage

THE PICTURE OF IMMEDIATIST ABOLitionists that emerged in the previous chapter is that of reformers who were both radical dissenters, and heightened advocates of values central to their culture—traits equally evident in their domestic lives. Disillusioned with domesticity, a number of female abolitionists mounted a sustained critique of the confinement of women to the private sphere. Yet in rejecting the confining nature of domesticity, and articulating their grievances with the notion of separate spheres, radical abolitionists did not discard all of the values associated with domestic ideology. Garrisonian abolitionists claimed women's right to participate in the public sphere, but, like other middle-class Americans, they also viewed the family as a refuge from what Mary Ryan has described as an "alien public world." Indeed, anticipating a respite from the rigors of public reformism, and optimistic about the importance of reform in the private sphere, some abolitionist women expressed enthusiasm about a retreat, albeit temporary, into domesticity. As Elizabeth Cady Stanton's remark that "the same woman may have a different sphere at different times" suggested, individual circumstances, including the female life-cycle, were also significant factors.[1]

For Garrisonian abolitionists, marriage stood at the center of a complex web of affectionate relationships, a web that could facilitate reform careers, and promote marital bonds. At the same time, however, abolitionists' efforts to merge public and private reform were complicated by an underlying tension between individualism, and a responsibility to the family. Although they declared that it was within the family that individuality and collectivity should come together, these radical abolitionists also realized, long before most Americans, that the family could be an oppressive, rather than liberating institution. This tension—characteristic of a larger, enduring tension between individuality and collectivity in American culture—was experienced differently by women and men. The cultural assumptions that underpinned the gender spheres of the nineteenth century specifically excluded women from many aspects of public life, including the world of commerce. Through the free produce movement, which projected domestic values into the public sphere, and linked women's economic role with the expanding market economy, radical abolitionists challenged the exclusion of women from commercial life. Abolitionists did not speak with one voice on the question of gender roles, and they were unable to completely remodel gender relations within the household. Yet living and working in the context of a legal system that gave extensive authority—physical, sexual, and financial—to husbands, radical abolitionists did suggest new patterns of domestic organization that not only enabled them to engage more equitably in the public sphere, and that contrasted with the patriarchy of slave society, but that also signified the tensions inherent in merging public and private reformism. This chapter explores these issues by examining the ways in which abolitionists organized their households. In the process, it also provides an essential context for the ensuing analysis of other aspects of the Garrisonians' network of reformist relationships, including abolitionist women's sororal sentiments and friendships, the meanings applied to masculinity within abolitionist circles, and the ways in which abolitionist husbands and wives sought to establish and maintain marital intimacy.

Just as it is impossible to delineate one family "type," either across or within societies, there was no single type of abolitionist family. Nor was there a "typical" abolitionist marriage. Certain characteristics, however, were particularly valued by all abolitionists, black as well as white.[2] Widely praised as an example to which other wives and husbands should look to model their own relationships, the most celebrated abolitionist marriage was that between Lucretia and James Mott. Although Lucretia Mott entered the public sphere, she exhibited many of the characteristics idealized by domestic reformers, and preserved her feminine identity as it was commonly defined. The devoted mother of six children, Mott was not only an efficient housekeeper who could never be accused of neglecting the obligations of motherhood, but, in a tangible representation of radical abolitionists' connection of home life with the work of reform, her house was a locus of activity for the wider antislavery family. In their praise of Mott's "palace of a home," abolitionists attributed a religious importance to her domestic environment that paralleled the sentiments of domestic writers. William L. Garrison praised Mott's domestic environment: "your home—to borrow the language of Dr. Watts—seems 'like a little heaven below.'" Yet Mott was also an active participant in the public sphere, lobbying assiduously for both the emancipation of the slaves, and the elevation of women. Abolitionists praised the depth of Mott's reformist resolve, and—as Henry Blackwell's reference to her "matronly dignity & experience of her past life" implied—they also respected her success in combining the roles of public reformer with the demands of managing her domestic environment.[3] Typically for the Garrisonians, the means were inseparably linked to the ends.

According to the prevailing gender ideology of the nineteenth century, women's raison d'être was to provide for the needs and wants of others. Female abolitionists, despite their efforts to realize their own ambitions, were affected by this aspect of domestic ideology. Writing in the early 1830s, an unnamed friend of Lucretia Mott succinctly described how women's lives were constructed around the needs of others: "As a wife, Mrs. Mott is all her husband can desire; as a mother, she is more than her children have any right to ask. As a hostess, she is unsurpassed, her hospitality often exposing her to imposition from its excesses; and as friend she is ever faithful and true."[4]

Yet while Mott was proud of her domestic abilities, and was always prepared to offer hospitality to as many friends as her house would accommodate, these idyllic presentations of her life must be viewed alongside evidence suggesting her sense of tedium in the domestic sphere. This awareness was evident on several levels. Publicly, Mott's support for women's rights indicated that she understood the problems confronting women. But she also hinted that she was not absolutely satisfied with life in her own domestic sphere. Writing in 1828 to her mother-in-law (who was presumably thought to be sympathetic to Mott's predicament) Mott drew attention to the demands placed on her by her children, and noted that she "never had so many cares pressing" upon her. Twenty years later, although all but one of her children had married and left home, Mott's household remained full. Describing their home as a "general rendezvous" for husbands to "come and dine," she noted that she often counted "thirty a day," including family members who continued to visit frequently.[5] Mott provided an account of one evening's work in the same period: "If I did not iron twelve shirts like cousin Mary, I had forty other things which I accomplished; for we had a large wash, and hurried to get the ironing away before the people flocked in. Five came just before dinner. I prepared mince for forty pies, doing every part myself, even to meat chopping; picked over lots of apples, stewed a quantity, chopped some more, and made apple pudding; all of which kept me on my feet till almost two o'c., having to come into the parlor every now and then to receive guests. Now I should rest, as I sit and write after dinner, with all gone to the Assembly Building, if —— hadn't thought best to remain and be *agreeable!*" Clearly, Mott saw beyond the romanticized depictions of domestic labor. And as her 1859 remark that it was "a treat to have nothg to do" revealed, the demands of domestic work were unremitting.[6]

Mott's biographers, like contemporary observers, have largely ignored or played down these expressions of discontent. Their idealized depictions of Mott's ability to combine public reformism with the management of her domestic sphere signify a determination to present abolitionist women as models for other women. With the proper domestic training and an understanding of the social ills of the nation, all American women were encouraged to emulate Mott's successes. Otelia Cromwell noted in 1958 that Mott "seemed to find a certain satisfaction in the performance of household tasks." But that statement, like Homer T. Rosenberger's earlier assertion that "Mrs. Mott was a feminine type of woman rather than a 'mannish' sort," said as much about the continuing strength of the ideology confining women to the home in the twentieth century as it did about the reality of Mott's domestic obligations a hundred years earlier. It is more appropriate, perhaps, to link her reformism to a more radical strand of feminist thought, one that reemerged more forcefully in the period after Cromwell and Rosenberger's works were published. Indeed, Mott identified many of the woes described by Betty Friedan, whose *Feminine Mystique* was published five years after Cromwell's sanitized biography of Mott. Of course, as Margaret Hope Bacon's 1980 depiction of Mott as a "Sensible grandmother" whose "favorite task was laying down carpets" revealed, old stereotypes are remarkably durable.[7]

Lucretia Mott's ability to merge private labors with public reformism was dependent upon efficient domestic management. The management of the Mott household remained firmly in female hands, but Lucretia was aided by the encouragement she received from her husband, who shared his wife's interest in abolition and women's rights. Appending a note to one of his wife's letters, James remarked in 1838 that "L[ucretia] has not told you anything about her dear self,—what with house cleaning last week, convention this, she has had quite as much to attend as her health and strength are sufficient for." Besides suggesting Lucretia's self-deprecation, James Mott's acknowledgment of her difficulties proved that at least some abolitionist men appreciated women's domestic obligations. By juxtaposing reformism with the demands of domesticity, Mott's letter reflected a persistent dilemma for abolitionist women. Anna Davis Hallowell, in her account of her grandparents' marriage, has praised the support that James Mott provided to his wife. Hallowell's depiction of Mott as a "noble, loving husband" was predictably laudatory, but more interesting was her assessment of gender roles and traits. Claiming that James Mott's "disposition" was "gentler and more yielding" than Lucretia's, Hallowell maintained that "*his* life made hers a possibility."[8] This signified an apparently willing reversal of many of the roles of husband and wife. Not all abolitionist marriages involved such reversals, but other abolitionists' relationships (including those of Stephen

Foster and Abby Kelley, and Lucy Stone and Henry Blackwell) entailed even more radical changes in gender roles and responsibilities.

Lucretia Mott exerted an important influence over Elizabeth Cady Stanton, a foremost advocate of women's rights in the nineteenth century. Based partly on her own experiences, Stanton became an incisive critic of prevailing marriage practices. When she married in 1840, however, she not only expressed enthusiasm for domestic life, but also hoped her own marriage would be different from the norm. This confidence was reflected by her decision to retain her own name, although, like Angelina Grimké before her, she did add that of her husband.[9] The example of slavery was a telling influence in this practice. In addition to asking "why are the slaves nameless, unless they take that of their master?" Stanton noted the similarity between "calling woman Mrs. John This and Mrs. Tom That, and colored men Sambo and Zip Coon." Above all, the meaning of patriarchy was clear to Stanton, who asserted in 1847 that such practices were "founded on the principle that white men are lords of all." Another public affirmation of radical abolitionists' determination to demonstrate women's equality was the decision of some to omit from their marriage vows the traditional promise from the woman to obey her husband.[10] Both of these practices were significant. Women who decided to retain their own name were making a public declaration that they would preserve their individuality in marriage, a conviction that resonated through the women's rights movement. Equally, since the wedding ceremony is a public representation and affirmation of private feelings, the insistence of some abolitionists that women were not obliged to obey their husbands was a conspicuous example of the conjunction of private and public gender reform.

Elizabeth Cady Stanton's early enthusiasm for domestic life was encouraged by the circumstances of her marriage. Her family had not welcomed her decision to marry Henry Stanton; in response to their urgings, she temporarily broke off the engagement. Eventually, however, she decided to wed Stanton, and they were married shortly before they departed for London, where Henry was a delegate to the 1840 World's Anti-Slavery Convention. Elizabeth Cady's marriage to Henry Stanton, like other abolitionist women's decisions to marry men notorious for their public reformism, was not only an assertion of her independence from her family, but was all the more notable in a period when emotional or geographic breaks from the family were "neither expected nor condoned in women."[11] From a privileged background, Elizabeth had led a comfortable existence, but the prospect of achieving a degree of intellectual independence was appealing. Henry Stanton, by contrast, was not a part of the local elite, and although he sought to convince Elizabeth and her family otherwise, his income was neither large nor secure. Elizabeth's initial positive response to marriage and domestic life, eased by the presence of domestic assistance, was shaped in part by her belief that she was liberating herself from the restrictions of her life prior to marriage.[12] By contributing to the work of reform, her life took on a meaning that would not have been possible had she followed the path her parents preferred for her.

This process was encouraged by Stanton's experiences in 1840. In London that year Stanton first met Lucretia Mott. Against the backdrop of women's exclusion from active participation at the World's Anti-Slavery Convention, Stanton and Mott discussed the injustices faced by women, and formulated tentative plans to hold a convention to address the issue of women's rights.[13] Upon their return to the United States, the Stantons settled in Boston, where the attractions of living in close proximity to a circle of intelligent and busy reformers were not lost on Elizabeth. But her worldly experiences in Europe, and her contact with New England's reforming community, contrasted with the domestic duties in which she subsequently found herself embroiled.

These dissatisfactions emerged when Henry Stanton decided in 1847 that the family should move from Boston to the upstate New York town of Seneca Falls. This "somewhat depressing" change awakened Elizabeth to the demands of domestic life. With a succession of seven children, and the interminable drudgery of domestic chores, "the novelty of housekeeping" that Stanton had once enjoyed soon faded. Following the birth of her sixth child in January 1856, she lamented the "grievous interruption" to her plans. Six months later, while she was delighted in having two daughters, her domestic frustrations were even more evident. "Imagine me," she wrote to Susan B. Anthony, "day in and day out, watching, bathing, dressing, nursing and promenading the precious contents of a little crib in the corner of my room." Longing for an end to her housekeeping duties, she described how she would "pace up and down" her "two chambers," like a "caged lioness." Unlike the births of her first six children, the birth of Stanton's last child in March 1859 proved difficult. Noting that she had "never suffered so much before," Stanton expressed relief that she was "through the siege once more."[14]

Stanton's maternal efforts were acclaimed by other women reformers. During a period in which medical and other advice literature regularly implied that motherhood incapacitated women, Stanton earned the admiration of her peers for her rapid recovery from the rigors of childbirth. Lucretia Mott, who had continued to work as a teacher until six weeks before the birth of her daughter Maria, expressed pride in Stanton's physical resilience: "What a woman! I showed thy letter to some young mothers, as an example, or caution, as they might best receive it. We who live after the older school methods, cannot tell what the hardy reformers can bear. I rode out in less than a week after the birth of one of my children and was classed among the Indians for so rash an act."[15] Beyond affirming reformers' sense of optimism regarding the changing attitudes to gender roles, Mott realized that demonstrating that women were not so frail as many supposed served a valuable political function.

Although Elizabeth Cady Stanton remained interested in public matters, she felt increasingly confined by domestic obligations. This discontent was exacerbated by the lack of support her husband provided within the domestic sphere. As well as pursuing a legal career, Henry Stanton served in the New York state legislature, and remained active in the abolitionist movement. Writing to his wife in October 1856, the applause that Henry claimed one of his speeches received threw into sharp relief Elizabeth's confinement to the home.[16] The difference between the lack of support Stanton received from her husband, and the assistance provided by the husbands of some of her contemporaries, must have been apparent. In particular, Stanton would have been aware of the encouragement that Lucretia Mott received from her husband. Like other female reformers, Stanton was supported by a network of women friends, of which the friendship with Susan B. Anthony was especially valuable. Nonetheless, there was a contrast between the shared commitment of reforming couples such as Lucretia and James Mott, and Lucy Stone and Henry Blackwell, and the Stantons' case. Symptomatic of Henry Stanton's disengagement from the domestic sphere were his absences from home during the births of all his children. Even considering that births in nineteenth-century America were generally performed by midwives, and that childbirth was largely "a female ritual and rite," Henry Stanton's absences indicate that the burden of domestic management (if not labor, a considerable portion of which was performed by paid domestic helpers) rested almost exclusively on his wife's shoulders.[17]

Childrearing was perhaps the most onerous of Elizabeth Cady Stanton's domestic responsibilities. On this issue Stanton both reinforced and challenged popular beliefs and practices. Seeing beyond romanticized descriptions of maternal bliss, she understood the demands of motherhood. Of her experiences in Seneca Falls, Stanton recalled in 1898 that "much that was once attractive in domestic life was now irksome." This, of course, reveals her domestic unhappiness. But what is perhaps most revealing in Stanton's rejection of a domestic lifestyle is her admission that she *ever* found it attractive. Despite all her dissatisfactions, Stanton reflected the pervasive influence of the culture that sought to confine women to the home, particularly its emphasis on the maternal role. Accordingly, while she rejected many of the prevailing ideas about motherhood, Stanton embraced maternity.[18] Stanton's interest in improving the way in which children were raised was typical of the period. It was widely accepted that childrearing practices should be brought into line with the scientific and moral improvements of the nineteenth century, and radical abolitionists' interest in improving Americans' parenting skills was related to the notion that mothers' nurturing role required proper and specific training. Consequently, while radical reformers added their own ideas to this wider pattern of "scientific" childrearing, their interest was related to broader societal trends, especially the elevation of motherhood. It was no coincidence that Stanton "commenced the study of medicine" shortly before the birth of her first child. Many years later, she devoted a chapter of her memoirs to her experiences and ideas regarding "Motherhood." Acknowledging the influence of Theodore Weld and Angelina Grimké, Stanton explained how she had overturned longstanding notions concerning the care of infants. Abolitionists' concern for children's health reflected more than just parental anxieties. Typically, the reform impulse was evident, and physical well-being was considered an essential adjunct of intellectual and moral training. Private and public concerns merged in the mind of Stephen Foster. Linking good health with individual self-satisfaction and the ability to exert influence, Foster told his ten-year-old daughter in 1857: "I think it useful for young persons to make themselves as agile & graceful as possible in all their motions, as ease of motion & grace contribute both to health and personal influence." Foster's recommendation, like similar advice from other abolitionists, echoed Catharine Beecher's assertion "that exercise is indispensable to the health" of the body.[19]

These beliefs resonated through the abolitionist and women's rights movements. Physical well-being was considered essential if women were to fulfill their responsibilities to the human race, and play their part in the civilizing process. Elizabeth Cady Stanton, arguing that there was "little hope" for the "mass of women, with their shrivelled bodies and brains," looked specifically to "the young girls" for the "regeneration of the race." Noting in 1852 that women were "slaves to their rags," she emphasized the importance of dress reform, and asserted that it was "nonsense" to talk of the "minds and bodies" of young women "until their bodies" were "made whole." Besides inferring that it was time that "public thought" be given to the "physical condition of American girls," she linked public and private reform. Juxtaposing the potential virtues of home life against the reality of many people's domestic sphere, Stanton advocated the transformation of American homes from "mere hospitals for the diseased and dissatisfied" into "retreats of joy and rest." Reformers sought (albeit with a hint of reluctance) to follow their own pronouncements concerning the necessity of physical exercise. Commenting in the late 1850s on the practice of going to the "Bowling Alley," Angelina Grimké admitted to Theodore Weld: "I play for *your sake* my dearest T—because you think my lungs are weak."[20]

For Elizabeth Cady Stanton, the experience of domesticity was a telling factor motivating her toward an explicit and public stance on the issue of women's rights. Not all abolitionist women, however, shared Stanton's domestic experience. In the cases of Angelina Grimké, Abigail Kelley, and Lucy Stone, their feminist consciousness was refined prior to their marriages. Yet, while these women were careful to discuss the issue of women's responsibilities and rights within the marriage relationship before they wed, their varying domestic experiences—particularly in the period after the birth of their children—affirmed the links between public and private reform.

These links are particularly evident in the case of Angelina Grimké, who more than any other single individual brought the issue of women's abolitionism to the public eye. Paradoxically, although Grimké's marriage to Theodore Weld owed much to their shared commitment to abolitionism, her marriage was widely regarded by her contemporaries, and by historians, as the primary cause of her withdrawal from public reformism. Indeed,

Grimké's most recent biographer has depicted her life in terms of a lifelong struggle for emancipation, initially from her South Carolinian family, and then from the demands of her own family.[21] The Weld-Grimké marriage, however, is better viewed as an example of the constant tensions between the attractions of the domestic sphere and the belief that individual private reform was essential for the reform of the wider world on the one hand, and the limitations and frustrations of the confinement of women to the domestic sphere on the other. Despite her subsequent dissatisfactions, Grimké looked forward to her marriage, and expressed enthusiasm for certain aspects of domestic life. Exploring her initial response to marriage and domesticity does not invalidate the interpretation that she later became disillusioned with the restrictions she felt. Rather, it demonstrates that her ideas evolved over the course of her life, and that her subsequent discontent cannot be transposed to her entire marriage.

The Grimké sisters' quarrel with Catharine Beecher raised important questions concerning gender roles in antebellum America. In itself, this was demanding, but like Theodore Weld's, their health suffered as a consequence of their public abolitionism. As Sarah Grimké told Anne Warren Weston, the demands of lecturing greatly taxed her "vital energies." Furthermore, while they did not believe they were withdrawing from the task of reforming the world, Angelina drew a distinction between the public and private spheres when she praised "the release from public service." The Grimkés' itinerant lifestyle in the period of their public abolitionism, along with their alienation from the South Carolinian community and family in which they had grown up, increased their yearning for the stability and comfort of a more permanent home. Angelina discussed these concerns in her correspondence with Weld. Insinuating that the demands of the abolitionist community were stifling her individualism, Grimké not only remarked in 1838 that certain abolitionists believed she and Weld "had *no right* to enter into such an engagement, but noted that some were "almost *offended*" that she should "do such a thing as to get married." Grimké and Weld were regarded as valuable assets to the abolitionist cause, and by telling Weld that some of their colleagues considered them as "public property," Grimké explicated her concerns in terms that not only expressed an awareness of the demands of the public sphere, but that also implied that the practice of abolitionism was in itself a commodifying process. Reflecting her optimism in the regenerative function of the private sphere, Grimké insisted that she was making the correct decision: "I tho't yesterday, perhaps our marriage was to be my dismission from *public* service. O! how I should rejoice at it, if the Master should say '*It is enough.*' It is an increasing trial to me and most gladly would I retire from public view and sink down into *sweet obscurity.* Perhaps the slave needed my service in this way just when I was called out, but the crisis is rapidly passing away and he will need them *no longer.*"[22]

Initially, Angelina Grimké did not feel restricted by marriage; although she knew there would be less public reformism, she and Weld anticipated that their private efforts could contribute to abolitionism *and* to the quest for women's rights. Indeed, the confluence of abolitionism and women's rights was evident in Angelina's belief that "toiling in domestic life" was doing "*as much* for the cause of woman" as their public speaking had done. Stressing that it was "absolutely necessary" to "show that we are not ruined as domestic characters," she hoped that even their "enemies would rejoice," if they could "look in upon us from day to day & see us toiling in domestic life, instead of lecturing to *promiscuous* audiences." The task, as she saw it, was to demonstrate to a hostile public that lecturing had not rendered her unfit for marriage. As Abby Kelley indicated when she noted "how much" her own "influence was lessened" by reports that she had neglected her mother, other abolitionist women also identified a close connection between their reformism and the public suspicion that they had disregarded their domestic obligations.[23]

Affirming radical abolitionists' perception of the importance of domestic organization, as well as their belief of the impact of those values on the wider population, Angelina Grimké referred specifically to the efficient management of the domestic sphere. Emphasizing that "superintending" her "household affairs," was "proving that public lecturing does not make a woman unfit for private duties," she recognized the extent to which abolitionists' private lives were open to public scrutiny. Grimké hoped her private domestic arrangements would be not a liability to the movement but a practical demonstration of the abolitionists' commitment to family life. Henry Blackwell also attested to the abolitionists' understanding of the relationship between their private lives and their public reformism. Blackwell was determined not to offend public sensibilities prior to his marriage to Lucy Stone. "I do not think it would make any difference in the case of a lady unknown," he wrote in 1855, "but in *you,* to come a thousand miles to *me might* seem a violation of the customary etiquette of good taste, which might strengthen the many silly, or misinformed people (the last class a very large one) in the idea that you really are the migratory, unfeminine, ungraceful contemner of proprieties which newspaper critics & common gossip pronounce woman's rights ladies to be."[24] Blackwell's statement hinted at the duality of radical abolitionists' mission—and their self-perception. Coexistent with their sense of social hierarchy was a desire to be regarded as a part of American society.

Angelina Grimké's experiences prior to her marriage, and her awareness of women's subordinate status, did not detract from her initial enthusiasm for a domestic routine that in many ways reflected the gender spheres ideology. After her wedding, Grimké described the enjoyment she was deriving from her "new cares," and noted that she was "far prouder" of the bread she was baking than she ever was of her lectures. She also expressed pride in the way the household was organized, for although their "ignorance & inexperience often" led to "mistakes and failures in the cooking department," she remarked it was "very sweet to serve one another in love, each bearing a part of the burden." The "division of labor" within their home, with many of the domestic tasks shared between the sisters, made it "comparatively easy to get along." Weld's insistence that the household adhere strictly to the dietary regimen advocated by Sylvester Graham simplified the task of domestic management; despite the sisters' inexperience in the kitchen, they were soon able to prepare a week's food in advance. That disciplined approach to food preparation, coupled with the household's use of William Alcott's scheme for domestic organization, reflected radical abolitionists' faith in the principles of domestic arrangement and time management.[25]

Yet while Weld and the Grimkés believed they were following the correct path, some of their colleagues lamented the loss of three such valuable members of the abolitionist movement. Even Lucretia Mott, whose domestic virtues and values were universally acclaimed, bemoaned the apparent squandering of the Grimkés' abolitionist talents. Not all abolitionists, however, condemned Weld and the Grimké sisters. Referring to Weld's school at Belleville, Henry Stanton expressed satisfaction that after "so much groping," his friend had finally found his niche. Elizabeth Cady Stanton's praise for Weld's active role in the children's lives reflected her faith in the role of domestic peace and happiness—and raised questions concerning the impact of marriage on Weld's reformism. Weld's marriage did not so much terminate, as change, his reform activities, but he had always expressed disquiet about aspects of the public struggle to free the slaves. He had never regarded conventions (which he considered largely a waste of time) as a priority, and the damage he had incurred to his voice during his rigorous abolitionist tours compelled him to curb his speech-making activities.[26] In addition, the ruptures in the antislavery movement of the late 1830s and early 1840s left Weld in an awkward predicament. Ideologically, he was closer to the Garrisonians on the issue of women's rights, but friends such as Lewis Tappan and Henry Stanton were aligned with the New York faction. Uncertain of where his real loyalties lay, Weld's withdrawal from the public abolitionist circuit might have simply been the easiest option, particularly since Angelina and Sarah identified more closely with the Garrisonians.[27]

Sarah Grimké also reflected the uncertainties of public reformism. In retiring from the lecturing circuit, she not only looked forward to a respite from the rigors of public speaking, but also believed she was doing God's bidding by staying with Angelina and Theodore at Fort Lee, New Jersey. Both sisters rejected pleas to return to Massachusetts to renew their labors for the abolitionist movement. The tensions in Sarah's mind, and the extent to which she was acting from a religious impulse, were evident when she admitted that while she "really desired that the Lord might send me back" to New England, she had "not been able to see that he wills me to any where at present but at Fort Lee." Reformism, agreed Weld and the Grimkés, was a union of private and public activities; as Sarah's statement revealed, the fulfillment of the individual's responsibilities to God stood at the center of this reform imperative. Sarah also remarked in 1840 that "since Angelina's marriage," their time had "been occupied in a different way in the service of the slave." While they were not working publicly for abolition, she was insistent that their "hearts" were "true to the slaves." Arguing that they were doing "those things which in the ordering of providence we believe it is our duty to do," Grimké portrayed their actions in terms of Christian duty, just as she had done earlier when quarrelling with Catharine Beecher.[28]

This sense of duty was evident on several levels. One very tangible manifestation of an ongoing commitment to the slaves was the publication in 1839 of Weld and the Grimkés compilation of the horrors of slavery. Widely considered the magnum opus of the abolitionist movement, *Ameri-*

can Slavery As It Is chronicled those aspects of slavery—including the desecration of womanhood and family relations—that all abolitionists found so abhorrent.[29] Weld and the Grimkés' sense of self-involvement in reformism was also manifested in another, more subtle way. Complementing their continuing desire to contribute to reformism, the Weld-Grimké marriage demonstrated women's economic role in abolitionism. Concomitant with some male abolitionists' involvement in the domestic sphere was the entrance of certain abolitionist women into the outside world of business and politics. These concerns coalesced in the free produce movement, which by providing alternatives to slave-produced products, and by reducing the demand for goods produced in the Southern states, sought to undermine slavery. Although Wendell Phillips's declaration that "slavery comes to an end by the laws of trade" was an exaggeration, the abolitionists' interest in free produce revealed much about the role of women and the family in reformism in the context of the expanding market economy. Abolitionists, believing that "the riches of the North" were "the greatest supports" of slavery, understood that the economic relationship between the North and the South strengthened the peculiar institution. Indeed, in alleging that those in the North who consumed the "productions of slavery" were the "most efficient supporters of the horrid system," abolitionists phrased their advocacy of the free produce movement in terms that directly acknowledged the significance of the notion of efficiency. Characteristically, too, radical abolitionists' interest was expressed in familial terms. Arguing that "we should regard slave labor produce as the fruits of the labor of our own children, brothers, and sisters," they couched their arguments in favor of the free produce movement in a way that paid specific attention to family ties.[30]

Through the free produce movement, radical abolitionists linked the reform imperative with women's economic and familial roles. Women's struggle for political equality has received considerable attention from historians; less well recognized are individual women's efforts to control their own, and their families', financial affairs. Indeed, partly because women's work within the home lacks any exchange value, the role of women as laborers and managers within the domestic sphere has rarely been accorded due recognition. Yet that lack of recognition, underscored by the difficulty of placing an accurate financial value on women's work within the home, did not minimize the significance of women's domestic labor. Here, again, women's plight bore parallels to that of the slaves. Women's contribution in the private sphere, unlike the slaves' contribution to the Southern economy, was largely unacknowledged. Yet while the slaves' labor was valued by their owners, those in bondage received no payment for their labors. In this sense slaves were in a similar position to women, whose domestic labor was not a part of the market economy. Moreover, the idea that women were naturally suited to domestic duties echoed proslavery writers' claims regarding the capabilities of black people. Defenders of slavery, seeking to extract the maximum labor from the slaves, asserted that dark-skinned people were capable of greater physical exertion than were white men. Domestic writers argued differently, claiming that women were incapable of sustained or strenuous physical labor. Nonetheless, confining women to the home was an efficient way of extracting their social and physical labor.

This lack of recognition of domestic labor was a common problem for women in nineteenth-century reform movements. Phillida Bunkle's remark, made in reference to the middle-class urban women who constituted the leadership of the New Zealand women's movement in the 1890s, has a wider relevance. She has pinpointed the relationship of women reformers to the marketplace, both in a didactic and participatory sense. Bunkle argued that since women's labor in the domestic sphere lacked any exchange value, and they were "totally dependent on the family," the "end to domestic production posed an excruciating dilemma for such women." As women lost their role in production, she explained, they "became not just consumers, but commodities, objects of consumption."[31] Domestic ideology claimed to protect women from the corruptions of the commercial sphere. There is some evidence—such as L. Maria Child's 1841 declaration of a "plague on business! It leaves no room for the heart"—that abolitionists shunned the marketplace as tainted with commercial values.[32] This would confirm Bunkle's insights. But despite the changes in economic and social relations associated with the transition from domestic production, the boundaries between the "masculine" world of business, commerce, and production, and the "female" domestic sphere were less precisely demarcated than a reading of domestic tracts would suggest. Adapting to the changing economic structures of the antebellum period, the ideology and experiences of female abolitionists (particularly their involvement in the free produce movement) not only illustrates the reality of women's role in the economy, and suggests the diversity of their relationship to the marketplace; it also signifies their resistance to the process of objectification to which Bunkle referred.

The significance of the abolitionists' interest in free produce extended beyond the movement's ostensibly negligible achievements. As managers of the domestic sphere, women were charged with the responsibility for caring for their families, which required increasingly direct involvement in economic transactions. At first glance, the activities of antislavery women in their families' financial affairs bear little relevance to the wider struggle for economic liberation. Their real significance, however, derives from the relationship between individual private reform, and public activities. Again, radical abolitionists were challenging and redefining the division of men and women into separate spheres. If women could manage their own finances, and those of their families, they could also play a role in managing financial affairs beyond the home—as their success in managing their own female antislavery societies proved. Domestic ideology demanded that women confine themselves to the home, and delegated to them the responsibility of home management. It was in that capacity that many women initially exercised varying degrees of influence over the family economy.[33] Radical abolitionists' emphasis on the potential power of women as consumers to help undermine slavery was an extension of Catharine Beecher's belief that American families would benefit from the systematic organization of household finances. Beecher's recognition of women's role in financial management of the domestic sphere, coupled with her belief that domestic organization and harmony were essential for the welfare of the nation, was suggestive of radical abolitionists' more overt emphasis on women's role as agents of change.[34]

The free produce movement fused the abolitionists' commitment to antislavery in the domestic circle with their public reformism. But in addition to encouraging large-scale British and American merchants to use the products of free labor, free produce advocates sought to modify the domestic purchasing patterns of consumers at home and abroad. Many radical abolitionists conscientiously sought to abide by their own dictums regarding free produce. Having observed in 1837 that "multitudes of northern women are daily making use of the products of slave labor," it was only natural that Angelina Grimké (with the cooperation of Theodore Weld) felt "morally bound to use no other" but the fruits of free labor. David Lee Child, too, was interested in the free produce movement, and James and Lucretia Mott—building upon the example of other antislavery Quakers—were not only determined to avoid using slave-derived goods, but, at considerable personal cost, also opened a store that stocked only free-labor items.[35]

The free produce movement was suggestive of the complex relationship between reformism, the cult of domesticity, and the emergent liberal ideology of free labor as it evolved during the nineteenth century. Radical abolitionists' efforts to eliminate or modify the theory and reality of separate spheres amounted to an implicit, and perhaps unwitting challenge to a foundation of the emerging capitalist ethos, which rested in part on the demarcation of men and women into closely defined separate spheres. While there can be no questioning abolitionists' and women's rights advocates' adherence to many of the elements of the doctrine of economic individualism, their support was not unqualified. Like domestic writers, they recognized the dangers presented by the apparent ascendancy of unbridled capitalism. Their perception and depiction of the family, coupled with the projection of women's influence beyond the domestic sphere, were attempts to mitigate against the undesired, depersonalizing effects of the market economy.[36] At the same time, however, female abolitionists' adherence to aspects of the free market ideology could be construed as implicit acceptance that the home was, or should be, a refuge from the outside world of corrupting commercial values. Despite the accusation that radical abolitionists sought to undermine the prevailing social order, most endorsed the capitalist ethos, which was closely associated with the republican ideal they idealized. Moreover, abolitionists believed that the market could be an agent of reform. Predicated on a faith in the marketplace, the free produce movement attested to a belief that consumers had the power to influence the world around them. This recognition of the power of consumers presaged a more widespread faith in the potential of reform through the alteration of peoples' consumption patterns. Abolitionists' efforts in this regard played a role in alerting their successors to both the limitations faced by women and the opportunities that were available to them. Indeed, for some abolitionist women, an interest in economic affairs came to represent more a search for women's economic independence than a means of individual reform. During the postbellum period, by encouraging women to seek financial independence and establish their own business enterprises, women's rights advocates betrayed an abiding faith in the efficacy of the market as a means of achieving their social, political, and economic objectives. Ultimately convinced that the economic deprivation of women played a key role in their subjugation, postbellum feminists urged women to exercise more control over their own labor.[37]

Evidence of women abolitionists' role in the economy outside the domestic sphere comes from various sources. L. Maria Child and Lucy Stone made indispensable contributions to their families' income—as did many black Garrisonian women, whose economic circumstances were invariably more precarious than their white coadjutors.[38] And overt demands for improved pay and employment opportunities are obvious examples of women's increasing determination to involve themselves in the public sphere. More subtle were the actual interventions in the marketplace through fund-raising activities. Female antislavery societies channeled the profits derived from the sale of various articles of needlework, and other items, back into the antislavery societies. To facilitate selling these goods, abolitionist women organized annual antislavery fairs. In this way, women's domestic skills, carried into the public sphere, were contributing to the work of reform and giving women experience in the marketplace. These activities had implications for women's political and economic roles: in the process of providing a crucial source of income to the abolitionist movement, antislavery fairs enabled women to achieve power within the larger antislavery societies.[39] Not only were antislavery fairs important avenues for women's expanding role in public life; women's authority was deriving from their commercial acumen, as well as their moral virtue. And the fact that women were gathering together to conduct these activities fostered a sense of sisterly solidarity.

Like their British predecessors, American abolitionists accorded a particular role for women in the free produce movement. Angelina Grimké emphasized women's responsibilities: "Wives and mothers, sisters and daughters, can exert a very extensive influence in providing for the wants of a family; and those women whose fortunes have been accumulated by their husbands and fathers out of the manufacture and merchandize of such produce, ought to consider themselves deeply indebted to the slave, and be peculiarly anxious to bear a testimony against such participation in the gains of oppression."[40]

The notion of efficiency thus merged with women's moralizing influence. Yet this tangible expression of domestic values did not shield abolitionist women from criticism. Such was the emotional fervor that surrounded slavery, and particularly women's involvement in the issue, that anything they said or did relating to that broad issue was inherently controversial.[41] The tensions evident in Abby Kelley's mind when she referred to the "dreadful" business of raising money hinted at the real significance of abolitionist women's entrance into the marketplace.[42] An unintended consequence of female abolitionists' experiences in the marketplace was that they gained experience outside the domestic sphere. Having realized they could conduct financial transactions just as effectively as their husbands and male collaborators, abolitionist women refused to accept the notion that commercial matters should be reserved for men. This was made clear during the 1840s, when Boston's women abolitionists successfully resisted the encroachments of men into the organization and administration of the annual antislavery fairs. Men were welcomed as co-workers, but the Boston women were unwilling to allow their male coadjutors to assume control of the fairs.[43]

Within their households, too, abolitionist women claimed the right to participate in matters of finance. Abolitionist women were sometimes accorded a role in the usually male domain of selecting and purchasing property to be used for business purposes. During the 1840s, Angelina Grimké assumed responsibility for purchasing the land and buildings for a school she and Theodore were establishing. Here the ethics of business did not preclude the reform imperative; Weld and the Grimkés not only hoped their schools would provide them with an income, but would also contribute to the reform process. Seeking to translate rhetorical endorsements of education into meaningful action, Weld and the Grimkés labored to establish innovative schools where young women and men could receive a sound education. Again, public and private reform merged. Inculcating what they deemed to be correct values in their pupils, the Grimkés and Weld considered their involvement in education as an adjunct of their abolitionism. True to radical abolitionists' statements that men should share the obligations and responsibilities of educating children, Weld played an important role in their educational projects.[44] Moreover, in their educational endeavors, Weld and the Grimké sisters promoted their idealized vision of the family. This emphasis on family values was more than a daytime occupation; just as their commitment to abolitionism bore all the hallmarks of religious vocation, their commitment to education necessitated self-sacrifice. Onerous and demanding as it was, their responsibility to their pupils were lightened by their perception that their role as teachers was analogous to that of parents. Lamenting the domestic chores, Angelina Grimké's dissatisfactions were allayed by the fact that their twenty-five pupils constituted a "family."[45]

Weld and the Grimkés' long-standing devotion to education, like their commitment to antislavery, involved compromising their own individuality and domestic peace for the greater good. Individualism was a paramount concern in the Weld-Grimké marriage, but Angelina and Theodore's sacrifices in this regard were sustained by their religious faith. Indeed, their perception of individuality was closely linked to the individual's relationship to God. Explaining her decision to confine herself to the domestic field, Sarah Grimké noted in 1838 that neither Angelina nor Weld had "said one word to sway" her conclusion. Arguing that an individual's duty was "too sacred for us to touch," she stressed that they left "each other entirely free to follow the indications of God's providence."[46] Abolitionist attitudes in this regard reflected a wider pattern of the early decades of the nineteenth century, when religious revivals emphasized the individual's relationship to God, free of church intervention. For many abolitionists, doubts about organized religion were reinforced by a conviction that the churches were supporting slavery.

All of this implied that Weld and the Grimkés' religious faith enabled them to merge their individuality with a desire to serve the wider community. Nevertheless, there were disappointments. Angelina's statements on this point are instructive. While she found solace in the knowledge that she was doing God's bidding, she envied her friend Jane Smith's "nice comfortable little home where peace and quietness" reigned. The burden of being surrounded by nearly eighty children and youths took its toll, and Angelina regretted being unable to "enjoy privacy & quiet." Most revealing of her aspirations at that time was her disappointment at not having a home to call her own until late each evening, when the responsibilities of caring for the students finally abated.[47]

In one sense, this was suggestive of Grimké's domestic frustrations. In another way, however, Grimké sought to transcend the domestic ideal: while she and Theodore concurred that they should devote themselves to the domestic sphere, and to the family circle, they eventually sought to widen their horizons. Uncertainties over the duty of the family, and the role of the individuals within, gave way to a conviction that it was time to return to the public sphere. Although she achieved public notoriety prior to her marriage, Grimké's path resembled that of Elizabeth Cady Stanton. Grimké ultimately tired of domestic life, and longed to renew her public involvement in reform. Her responses to requests that she attend conventions and make speeches not only signified her determination to do as much as she could for reformism, but also revealed domestic pressures. "I will do the best I can," she told Jane Smith, "under the pressures which rest upon me."[48] It is also revealing that Angelina urged Theodore to involve himself in the public sphere. While Weld spent time in Washington in the early 1840s lobbying on behalf of abolitionism, he was also drawn to his family. Like the Grimké sisters, he felt a tension between the demands of public service, and the sanctuary of domestic life. By the late 1840s, Grimké was suggesting that Weld would be happier if he could move into his "proper sphere." Hoping he would "live for a community," rather than their "little *circle,*" Angelina argued they were living "too selfish a life to be happy in each other," or in their "professions." This indicated her desire to reenter the public fray. Yet there was an ongoing tension between Angelina's attachment to the attractions of a peaceful domestic environment, even with its obvious burdens, and the obligations of public reformism. Even as she longed to participate in the world beyond the home, she expressed an "indescribable sadness on leaving home." Returning to a common theme among reformers, she noted in 1852 that it was her sense of duty, rather than any inclination to leave home, which led her out.[49]

With the passage of time, Angelina's dissatisfactions became more explicit. Writing to Sarah in 1854, she asserted that she was well aware of what she needed: "if I ever can go away for a few weeks I shall gladly do so." Domestic obligations, however, remained a heavy burden. Angelina was often able to rely upon Sarah to help in the domestic circle, but this was not always the ideal solution. In 1854 she noted that on previous occasions when she had left Sarah in charge of domestic duties, she regretted having done so. The "severe attacks of illness" that Sarah incurred when she was left in control "entirely satisfied" Angelina that she had no right to leave her family in her elder sister's care again. Angelina felt her domestic duties heavily, but like other abolitionist women she was also proud of her ability to manage her family efficiently. Claiming that housekeeping affected Sarah much more than it did herself, Angelina noted that "somehow, things always seem to go wrong when I go." Despite mutual tensions and doubts, however, Angelina valued Sarah's role in the family.[50]

For her part, Sarah Grimké derived great pleasure from her sister's family. Living with Angelina and Theodore almost continually following their marriage, Sarah was in many ways a full member of their family. As she told Henry Clarke Wright in 1838, she was grateful that after "years of tossing & buffeting," God had provided a "sweet harbor of rest." Besides appreciating a stable domestic environment—even one marked by frustrations over the success of educational projects, and tensions concerning the union of private and public reformism—Sarah played an important role in co-parenting Angelina and Theodore's children. Here again, tensions were evident. In claiming that she knew "something" of both "the enjoyments of marriage and the barrenness of single life," Sarah noted that she had both "suffered for," and "delighted in Angelina's children as much almost as she has."[51]

The Weld-Grimké marriage illustrated many themes of nineteenth-century reformism. Alongside the tensions between public and private activities, the issue of the extent to which individual aspirations should be sacrificed for the goals of reformism—and for familial obligations—was also evident. Through all of their reformism, public and private, Weld and the Grimkés attested to the importance of religious faith as a reform imperative. And, as well as demonstrating the significance of education in reformism, the Weld-Grimké union signified women's growing role in the marketplace and the reform possibilities that derived from that role.

A number of abolitionists reacted with skepticism to Angelina Grimké's assertions that marriage had not led to her withdrawal from reformism. Abby Kelley and Lucy Stone's references to the Weld-Grimké marriage reveal their understanding that a precondition of women forsaking their own needs and wants for the sake of others, as demanded by domestic and separate spheres ideologies, was that females sacrifice their own individuality. Kelley's marriage to Stephen Foster was notable for the determination with which both sought to retain their individuality, and for their merging of private and public labors. As Joel Bernard has pointed out, "there was an essential and logical connection between" Kelley and Foster's "personal meaning of slavery and their radical commitment."[52] In different ways, Kelley and Stone's marriages offer insights into the ways in which they sought to retain their individuality, within the context of loving companionate relationships where wives as well as husbands could continue to engage in public reformism. For Kelley, the tension between the competing demands of public and private life was particularly evident in the period following the birth of her daughter.

Although Abby Kelley was vilified by opponents of abolitionism, she was acclaimed by her reformist colleagues.[53] Aside from their commendation of Kelley's housekeeping abilities, much of the praise of her public reformism from her coadjutors reflected the influence of domestic ideology. Writing in 1849, Lucretia Mott described Kelley as "our model for self-sacrifice & indomitable energy." Male abolitionists also lauded Kelley. The British abolitionist George Thompson specifically extolled her abolitionism in terms of a maternal role. Noting that Kelley had "wrought wonders in her day," he remarked in 1851 that "her children are found wherever she has laboured." The maternal theme was evident elsewhere in the praise accorded Kelley. Acclaiming Kelley's influence, one observer at an antislavery meeting described her role in domestic and gender-specific terms, which emphasized the maternal function: "I think she did much good, more than men in her place could do, for Woman feels more as being and reproducing—this brings the subject much more into home relations."[54]

These representations of abolitionism as the fulfillment of maternalism were echoed by Lucy Stone and Henry Blackwell's daughter. Praising her mother as "the most motherly of women," Alice Stone Blackwell asserted that Stone's "motherliness overflowed far beyond her own family." Given Stone Blackwell's long-term participation in the women's rights movement, her deliberate connection of women's maternal role in the private sphere with the work of public reformism not only signified the relationship between domestic values and radical abolitionism, but also attested to the ongoing influence of those ideas into the twentieth century. Yet even as women abolitionists' interest in maternal values connected them to the wider American culture, their response to questions of gender isolated them from many of their contemporaries. This tension was reflected within the public and private practices of abolitionism. Abby Kelley, following her controversial role in the 1840 rupture within the American Anti-Slavery Society (AASS), was subsequently associated with women's claim to equality. That notoriety may have been one of the factors attracting Stephen Foster to Kelley. Having already achieved notoriety for his own brand of radical abolitionism, Foster must have found her iconoclasm appealing. Equally, Kelley was impressed by Foster's radical approach to abolitionism.[55]

After meeting in 1841, Kelley and Foster's interest in each other became personal during the following year. Kelley's desire to continue to work for the abolitionist movement, coupled with her demand that she be allowed to retain her personal autonomy, made her reluctant to marry.[56] Here, the example of Angelina Grimké was important. But while Kelley resolved that marriage would not lead to the cessation of her labors in the abolitionist movement, she was conscious that other factors had played a part in Grimké's withdrawal from the public sphere. Writing in mid-1839, she conceded that Grimké's health was "truly very feeble," and feared that she would "never recover from the attack." Kelley, eventually persuaded that marriage would not interfere with her public reformism, acceded to Foster's marriage proposal. Yet the two-year passage between their engagement and their marriage in 1845 suggests Kelley's caution, as well as Foster's patience.[57] Like some of their abolitionist contemporaries, Kelley and Foster omitted the traditional promise of obedience from their wedding vows, and they sought to live out the ideals they had promulgated prior to their marriage.

For many women, the task of merging public and private roles was complicated by pregnancy and motherhood. Although women sought to control their fertility, contraception in the nineteenth century was unreliable.[58] Dorothy Sterling has noted that Abby Kelley "greeted her pregnancy with mixed emotions." There was pleasure at the prospect of having a child; but there was also a desire to remain publicly active in abolitionism. These activities were interrupted by the birth of Paulina (Alla) in May 1847, which severely curtailed Kelley's public role for the next two years. Nevertheless, like other abolitionist women, she did not disguise the pleasure she derived from motherhood. Acknowledging that Alla consumed "lots of time," Kelley was emphatic in her assertions of the pleasure of motherhood: "altho' I had always thought there was great pleasure in being a mother, I had not anticipated the half."[59]

That pleasure in maternalism complemented another area where radical abolitionists agreed with domestic writers. The domestic sphere afforded the same protective and peaceful role for abolitionists as it did for Catharine Beecher and other domestic writers. Inverting gender roles as they were espoused by domestic writers, the private sphere provided Kelley with refuge from the rigors of the outside world. These concerns had emerged even before she married. Kelley emphasized in 1843 that her "love of a home" was "very ardent," and that she was "yearning for a spot" she could call "*home! sweet, sweet home!*" This view was confirmed after her marriage. Like a number of other abolitionist women, however, Kelley also remained committed to public activism, and her marriage reflected this ambivalence. In part, Kelley's domestic arrangements reflected the importance of her role in the abolitionist movement. While Stephen Foster was widely considered one of the most radical of the abolitionists, Kelley was in greater demand as an antislavery lecturer. Hence, she spent more time directly engaged in the public sphere. When Kelley resumed lecturing, Foster spent a good deal of time at home, where he not only filled the traditional male role of farmer, but also the less-common role of manager of the domestic sphere.[60]

Kelley's confidence that she could leave Alla in the care of Stephen and other family members affected her outlook on motherhood. Marrying at thirty-five years of age, and comforted by the knowledge that her husband not only supported her reformism, but was prepared to co-parent their child, Kelley knew she was not going to be trapped by the demands of raising children for as long as most women. Nonetheless, the tensions between individual desires, the demands of public reformism, and familial obligations were evident in the Kelley-Foster marriage. Kelley's 1847 remarks to Sydney Howard Gay, editor of the *National Anti-Slavery Standard*, expressed this tension between the public and private realms. Writing just four months after the birth of her daughter, she outlined her plans to reenter the abolitionist fray. In so doing, she alluded to the conflicting demands of reformism and family duties in terms framed specifically around maternal obligations. For Kelley, the duty to the slaves, aided by a cooperative spouse and family, should have permitted an early return to public abolitionism: "But great as is my pleasure in the care of our daughter, I expect next year to consign her to the care of Stephen's sister Caroline, and engage in the field workforce again—This, at least, is my design if we should all be well—Stephen says I shall not be willing to leave her—We shall see whether I care too much for my baby as to forget the multitudes of broken hearted mothers."[61] Besides suggesting the depth of her friendship with Gay (a sign that some abolitionist women and men maintained working relationship that defied stereotypical depictions of gendered separate spheres) Kelley juxtaposed her own maternal feelings with those of slave women. Although she framed her prospective return to public life in terms of an obligation to the slaves, Kelley also hinted that she missed the hurly-burly of public abolitionism. As she made clear in late 1847, Kelley clearly relished at least some aspects of public life. Referring again to her wish to be involved in the public struggle against slavery, she expressed her desire to "be in New York, breaking the bridges between the true and the false." But she made it clear that for the moment at least, her responsibilities to her infant took precedence. And, as she had prior to her marriage, Kelley appreciated domestic peace. As she told Sydney Howard Gay in May 1849, " 'Tis good to get into the quiet."[62]

Just two months later, however, Kelley was expressing a rather different point of view. Expressing frustration with domestic life, and confident that two-year-old Alla could be well cared for by Foster and various relatives, Kelley's relative freedom was made clear in the advice she gave to Elizabeth Gay. Counseling Gay to spend more time outside the domestic circle, Kelley noted that she "used to go out about once in six months," but that she would "never stay at home so again—'Tis perfectly killing."[63] Kelley's marriage, however, was in many ways exceptional; most women, lacking the active support of their husbands, were unable to combine public activities and private concerns in this way. Equally, abolitionist women who were absent from home missed their families. Whenever she thought of home, Kelley explained to her six-year-old daughter in 1854, she felt "quite homesick." Contrasting a domestic vision of a family "sitting around the fire and having a delightful time," with her own movements "among strangers" who cared little for the slaves, Kelley's extended absences from home must have induced feelings of guilt, and of loneliness.[64]

Abolitionist women such as Abby Kelley knew that their public activities constituted a challenge to the ideological nexus between women and the domestic sphere. But in pointing out that women were able to contribute to public life, radical abolitionists were careful to stress that they had not forfeited the values commonly associated with women. Lucretia Mott, describing how Kelley "left her little girl of 20 months" to journey to Pennsylvania to raise much-needed monies for the antislavery movement, reiterated her pride in the achievements of those women able to merge motherhood with public reformism. Yet Mott was certain that women's assumption of an active role in reform did not detract from their womanhood, or undermine their ability to fulfill their familial role. Referring implicitly to the accusations leveled against abolitionist women's alleged evasion of their domestic responsibilities, Mott insisted in 1849 that Kelley "cherishes all a Mother's feelings."[65] Mott's approval of Kelley's actions was a statement that women's public reformism did not entail neglect of their children; abolitionist women were again being perceived and presented as role models for other women.

Not all abolitionist women agreed, however, that such role models were beneficial to the movement. Echoing the role assigned to women by domestic ideology, some contended that abolitionist mothers should not leave their children in the hands of others. Jane Elizabeth Jones, co-editor of the *Anti-Slavery Bugle,* couched her criticism of Abby Kelley leaving Alla in terms of an abrogation of maternal responsibilities. "For the sake of the slave," Jones wrote in 1848, "I am glad you are going to lecture in March, but for the sake of millions of suffering children whose mothers have thrown off the duties & responsibilities of mothers & left them in the care of aunts & sisters & hired nurses . . . I am sorry. Your influence on the course of human freedom will be good, but your influence on home duties & home virtues will be bad. If you would wait till your child is old enough to wean it would be less reprehensible." Reminding Kelley that the abolitionists' domestic behavior was closely scrutinized, Jones asserted that she would "set a better example" with the "little stranger" that she was expecting.[66]

Jones had raised the issue of abolitionist women leaving their children in the hands of hired helpers. Reflecting their hierarchical assumptions toward other women (a subject explored in the next chapter) abolitionists who left their children in the care of others were careful to choose women who could perform the task satisfactorily. Sarah Grimké broached this matter with reference to Theodore and Angelina's children. Signifying her own sense of self-involvement in the Weld-Grimké family, Sarah explained to Elizabeth Pease in 1842 "we are not willing to employ strangers to do what we believe God designs we should do ourselves." "We have thus far been unable to find a servant," she wrote, "to whose care we could conscientiously entrust the bodies and minds of our dear babes."[67] Grimké's statement revealed much about the pressure weighing on abolitionist women. Alongside the belief that parents were best equipped to care for their children—a view they believed was ordained by God—there were times when there was an obvious need to find an outsider of a suitable caliber to perform that very function. In many American homes, relatives often assumed some of the responsibilities of childcare. This was the case in the Kelley-Foster household, where relatives were occasionally persuaded to lend assistance in the domestic sphere.[68]

For his part, Stephen Foster's abolitionism has often been characterized as the product of an unstable mind; given that some of his contemporaries had questioned his sanity, it is not surprising that historians have commented on his eccentricities.[69] At first glance, Foster's behavior suggests he was psychologically unbalanced. But there has been insufficient analysis of his ideology and career to justify such accusations, which in any case are often culturally and socially determined. Designed perhaps to attract publicity to the cause, Foster's more notorious acts might be indicative of nothing more than an acute sense of what would draw attention to abolitionism. Indeed, his married life with Kelley indicates that both were well-adjusted individuals, whose mutual desire for love, support, and companionship merged with their emphasis on individualism to produce a marriage that was unconventional for its day, but that portended the subsequent stress on individual self-fulfillment. Moreover, like his contemporaries, Foster valued domestic stability. Writing to Abby in 1855, he declared: "You can hardly imagine what a dislike I have of this wandering mode of life. It is the next thing to being a slave."[70] Foster thus suggested the conjunction between radical abolitionists' appreciation of the significance of the domestic sphere and their perception of the uncertainties and horrors of slavery. For Kelley and Foster, like other abolitionists, a peaceful and secure home served as a reminder that slaves were denied what was a fundamental human right: the right to construct a stable domestic life.

As with the marriage of Abby Kelley and Stephen Foster, the relationship between Lucy Stone and Henry Blackwell was characterized by a mutual commitment to the rights of both to pursue their own interests. Like Kelley, Stone entered marriage cautiously. After marriage, both women discovered that the responsibilities of parenting were both rewarding and restricting. And again like Kelley, Stone refused to be constrained within the domestic sphere, although she took considerably longer to reenter public life. Fearing that marriage would lead to a loss of independence, Stone only agreed to marry Blackwell on the explicit understanding that it would not jeopardize her well-developed sense of individualism. Referring to the case of Angelina Grimké, Blackwell went to great lengths to convince Stone that marriage did not have to lead inevitably to an end to her reform career. Although he did admit that Grimké had at one point found herself in "difficult circumstances," Blackwell's positive assessment of the Weld-Grimké marriage was more than just a self-serving attempt to woo Stone. Following a discussion with Weld, Blackwell wrote to Stone in June 1853, offering his assessment of the changes in Weld and the Grimkés' reformism. Besides the problems he suffered with his voice, Weld had also cited his narrow escape from drowning as a factor behind the changes in his life. Blackwell accepted that Weld's "fighting era" was over, but counseled Stone not to be judgmental about Weld and Grimké: "I see plainly that in *their case* they have acted rightly."[71]

Writing to Stone the following month, Blackwell articulated many of his ideas regarding marriage. "I would not have my wife drudge, as Mrs Weld has had to do in the house," he assured Stone, "I would not even consent that my wife should stay at home to rock the baby when she ought to be off addressing a meeting, or organizing a Society." Seeking to convince Stone that her reform activities would not be impaired if they wed, Blackwell suggested that marriage was not responsible for the Grimkés' withdrawal from public life. Rather, it resulted from "a combination of physical, intellectual & moral causes." Indeed, even as Blackwell sought to convince Stone that any union between them would be different from the Weld-Grimké relationship, he praised their marriage: "If ever there was a true marriage it is theirs." And, referring to a maxim of abolitionism, Blackwell praised Weld and Grimké for their ability to "perceive their separate individuality *perfectly.*"[72]

Blackwell's entreaties failed to have any immediate impression on Stone. But her responses to his overtures reflected the ambiguities of the relationship between abolitionism and domestic values. Remarking that the "world may be more benefitted by the good brave children they [Weld and the Grimkés] stopped to rear, than it could have been if they continued in the field," Stone acknowledged the role of education and the domestic environment in reformism. She also noted that she did not think ill of the Welds, and admitted that "from their own standpoint they acted in harmony with their highest convictions." Yet she could not "understand" how Weld and Grimké could withdraw from the abolitionist movement before the slaves had been emancipated. Stone was not prepared to cease her efforts on behalf of the slaves, but she conceded that individuals must decide their own path. Although she ultimately agreed to marry Blackwell, there were two years of what their daughter subsequently described as "arduous courtship" before they married in 1855. Stone and Blackwell excluded the traditional vow from the wife to obey her husband, and by signing their protest against the legal, social, and economic inequalities of the marriage relationship, they publicly infused their wedding ceremony with an even clearer political purpose.[73]

Clearly, Lucy Stone did not rush into marriage, and was determined to retain her individualism within the relationship. Nonetheless, she did embrace many of the sentiments of other abolitionist women who had been less reticent about marriage. Like the Grimké sisters and Theodore Weld, there was a glorification of the home that paralleled domestic ideology. Stone and Blackwell regarded the home as an important location for the improvement of self, and, by extension, the world. "We must hallow that little place that *is* to be *our home,*" wrote Stone in April 1856, "with earnest effort at self-improvement, with noble aims, *and* good resolution coined into deeds. . . . It seems to me that in the little spot (God guard it!) unknown to us, yet existing *somewhere* in actual fact, we shall be able to live nearer our ideals, to make more of our time, and achieve what is more worthy to us."[74] Despite their assertions of women's right to participate in the public sphere, many of the roles of husband and wife embraced by Stone and Blackwell were consistent with domestic ideology. Consequently, while Alice Stone Blackwell's idealized account of her parents' marriage and their domestic arrangements must be viewed cautiously, her claim that Stone "rejoiced in having a home of her own" was accurate.[75]

Yet Lucy Stone's pleasure at having her own home was tempered by the difficulties of the early years of her marriage. Henry's frequent absences, along with Stone's continued lecturing activities, indicated that both sought to further their public reform goals within their marriage. Blackwell's later admission that housework was "a new and hard experience for a woman already 38," particularly one "accustomed for years to literary and intellectual pursuits," suggested the hardships faced by his wife. Any lingering romanticized vision of the joys of domesticity faded in the face of the reality of the situation. Lucy, pregnant for the first time at thirty-nine years of age, faced very real dangers from childbirth, and although Henry was at home for the birth of Alice in September 1857, his inability to find employment in the East soon compelled him to travel west again, leaving his wife and baby daughter.[76]

Alice Stone Blackwell subsequently claimed that her mother derived great pleasure and satisfaction from motherhood. But in the spring of 1858, with her husband away, a young baby to care for, and suffering from pleurisy, Lucy Stone discovered firsthand the difficulties faced by many women. Compounding these domestic tribulations were calls to reenter the public fight for abolition and women's rights. After having acceded to Susan B. Anthony's request to resume lecturing, Stone returned home to find that "a mishap or two" had befallen Alice while in the care of the nursemaid. This series of events, in conjunction with the loss of a baby boy through a miscarriage, prompted Stone to declare in early 1859 that she would refrain from lecturing until Alice had grown to the point where she could be confidently left in the hands of others. Stone's maternal feelings were revealed in a letter to Antoinette Brown Blackwell: "when I came home & looked in Alice's sleeping face, & thought of the possible evil that might befall her if my guardian eye was turned away, I shrank like a snail into its shell, & saw that for these years I can only be a mother—no trivial thing either."[77] Stone's letter captured many of the contradictions of the abolitionists' relationship to the domestic sphere, and the demarcation of gender roles. The fact that she had allowed herself to be drawn back onto the lecturing circuit evinced the strength of the call of public duty. Yet her sense of responsibility for Alice was obvious, and there was no inference that motherhood was an insignificant task.

While aspects of Stone's marriage resembled that of Abby Kelley, Stone's maternal obligations demanded a more lengthy commitment to domestic life. Nevertheless, domestic life was ultimately too confining for Lucy Stone. By 1863, with Alice no longer requiring her undivided attention, Stone was taking her first steps toward reentering the public fray. Even as she lamented the burden of domestic obligations, however, she remarked on the necessity of having a "quiet corner," where she was "free from criticism, or scrutiny." She was aided in these domestic aspirations by Henry Blackwell, who sought to provide support in the domestic sphere. Stone appreciated this support, noting in 1864 that she "felt like sitting down at once to write a treatise on 'Housekeeping Made Easy,' " wherein the "beginning and the end should be this: 'Choose a provident and thoughtful husband, who voluntarily will take all the burden on himself.' "[78] Yet even with Henry's support, a comment Stone made in 1877 attested to a timeless problem facing female reformers, or, indeed, any woman seeking to combine public activity with domestic obligations: "When I came home at night to find the house cold, the fire nearly out in the furnace, and none on the hearth, &c &c. it seemed as though the tired of a whole life came into my essence. I dont often complain, or feel like complaining. But I do wish there was some way of carrying on the Woman's Journal without such a hard constant tug—and if only the housekeeping would go on without so much looking after!"[79] Stone's remark revealed much about the experiences of female reformers: the ongoing tension between public reform and a desire for domestic organization; the interminable nature of domestic labor; and the reluctance to complain about one's personal situation. Although they received support from their husbands, and from domestic helpers, abolitionist women demonstrated remarkable ability and perseverance. Equally, while they did not accomplish all of their objectives, it is a testimony to the individual character and abilities of women reformers that they achieved as much as they did.

Wendell Phillips was reputedly the most eloquent public speaker of the abolitionist movement. His marriage with Ann Terry Greene—an "early and munificent friend of the slave"—involved a distinct rearrangement of gender roles, largely on account of the debilitating illness that struck Ann soon after their marriage.[80] Despite her best efforts, Ann's illness restricted Wendell's public life, compelling him to adapt his abolitionism around the responsibilities of caring for his wife. This raises important questions concerning their marriage: In what ways did Ann influence her husband's abolitionism; and how did her illness affect their marriage?

Was Ann Phillips, as one student of abolitionism put it, Wendell's "*silent* partner in the great business he was carrying on for freedom and humanity"? It is unlikely that Wendell Phillips would have accepted such a description. In an apparent affirmation of the moralizing influence of women as prescribed by domestic ideology, he credited Ann with being the individual who converted him to abolitionism. Here it is also helpful to consider other abolitionists' depictions of Ann's role. Elizabeth Cady Stanton emphasized to Wendell, "Never dream that I regard Mrs Phillips a mere echo," and Thomas Wentworth Higginson noted after Wendell's death that it was "impossible for those who knew them to think of him without her."[81] Besides suggesting that Ann was actively involved in abolitionist issues, these statements indicate that she and Wendell enjoyed a caring and close companionship that reflected their shared commitment to reform.

There is further evidence that Ann Phillips was not the passive and submissive wife prescribed by domestic ideology. Her influence over Wendell was revealed by her exhortation to him at the 1840 World's Anti-Slavery Convention in London to speak out vigorously on behalf of women's right to participate in the proceedings. "Don't shilly shally," she reputedly demanded, in an effort that won her praise from other female abolitionists.

Ann's illness did not prevent her from continuing to consider herself a part of the reform community. Having assured Maria Weston Chapman in 1839 that she had "*fought manfully,*" Ann later urged Deborah and Anne Weston to do all they could to "stir up" support for a fugitive slave who had been arrested. Equally revealing of Ann's sense of self-involvement in the movement was her assertion that: "We may as well disband at once if our meetings & papers are all talk & we never do anything *but talk.*"[82] Alongside her implicit suggestion that moral suasion had run its course—a theme explored in chapter 5—Ann's use of the word "we" affirmed that she continued to regard herself as an active member of the movement.

This continuing sense of involvement in abolitionism was remarkable given the ill-health that Ann endured over nearly five decades. A year after her marriage in 1837, Ann's precarious health, which had shown a dramatic improvement when she became engaged to Phillips, deteriorated. Ann was thus rendered housebound, and confined to bed for much of the rest of her life. Yet in much the same way that Stephen Foster and Henry Blackwell were determined their marriages would not limit their wives' reform activities, Ann Phillips struggled to ensure that her ill-health did not curtail Wendell's public role. Writing to Maria Weston Chapman in 1839, Ann stressed that she was "trying hard to get health," so that she would not be such a "stumbling block" in her husband's path. She sometimes sought to reassure Wendell that she was coping without him, and endeavored to place the abolition cause above her own illness. On one occasion, for example, she urged him not to hurry home, if he could serve the cause by remaining in Pennsylvania. In telling Wendell not to "*think* of coming home at least until Monday if you are enjoying yourself" Ann acknowledged that reformism was an enjoyable activity for her husband, an escape from domestic demands. Yet there were also many times when she implored Wendell to return home. Sometimes, Ann's urgings to Wendell to return home were implicit. "You do not know how long it seems to me," she lamented in December 1856, "since you went away—it seems ages." On other occasions, however, these requests were unambiguous. "No better," she told Wendell in an 1858 telegram, "Come home as soon as you can."[83]

Wendell's devotion to Ann was also apparent, both in deeds and words. His oratorical skills were in great demand, but in order to care for Ann, he limited his public commitments. This signified a reversal of the prevailing pattern of domestic organization; indeed, many of the conventional roles of husband and wife were inverted in the Phillipses' relationship. Responding to an 1846 request to attend an antislavery meeting, Wendell told Samuel Joseph May that because Ann had been "very ill a great while," he left her "very little." Wendell was conscious of Ann's sacrifices, noting that she would willingly let him "fly afar." In hoping that one day he would be "infinitely more free to stretch away to moderate distances" for the cause of the slave, Wendell explicated his frustrations in 1852. For many years, he and Ann sought a cure for her ailment, but these efforts failed, and in the mid-1850s they resigned themselves to coping with, rather than curing, her condition.[84] Despite the demands placed on him, Wendell generally responded with sympathy and patience to Ann's illness. The Phillipses' marriage was an unusual mix. Whilst Wendell fulfilled the masculine role of participation in the public sphere, he also performed a nurturing function commonly ascribed to women. And even though Ann was housebound, she continued to involve herself in reformism, albeit vicariously through her influence on Wendell.

Partly because William Lloyd Garrison was long regarded as the most significant abolitionist, and partly because his public defenses of women's right to participate in the public sphere were so controversial, it is important to assess whether his own marriage involved radical changes in gender roles. Paradoxically, the domestic arrangements of the man who lent his name to the most radical wing of the abolitionist movement conformed more closely to the prevailing pattern than some of his less well known colleagues' marriages. Indeed, in many ways his marriage corresponded to the model espoused by advocates of domestic ideology: while he was a public man, his wife was largely a private woman. Typically depicted as a dutiful and loyal wife, who was content to avoid a public role in abolitionism, Helen Garrison has received only cursory attention from historians. Aside from her involvement in local antislavery societies, she played a limited public role in abolitionism. Instead, Helen not only filled a position in relation to her husband that accorded with much of what domestic writers advocated in their tracts, but was also prepared to concede that men should make the decisions. Yet while her reformist role was largely indirect, Helen's contemporaries were not reticent about describing her contribution to abolitionism, and some of the domestic difficulties she faced—including the expectation that her home would serve as a social center for the abolitionist community—paralleled those of women more actively engaged in the public sphere.[85]

Perceiving her role as a supportive one, Helen Garrison shunned public controversy, and her comments prior to her marriage differed markedly from the sentiments expressed by some of the other women assessed in this study. Shortly before she wed, fearing that she would be unable "to serve" Garrison as she "ought," Helen described how quickly the time was approaching when she would "surrender" herself to him, "with a holy pledge to endeavor to live always" so as to secure his "approbation and love." Alongside the sexual connotations of her statement, her language betrayed a belief (common to most abolitionists as well as domestic reformers) that marriage was endowed with a religious significance. In marriage, she hoped her efforts would "approximate nearer His throne, who is infinitely lovely & worthy our highest adoration and praise." On one level, at least, the Garrisons' marriage lived up to Helen's expectations. Describing her good fortune in having William L. Garrison as a husband, Helen noted after a quarter-century of marriage that her "only regret" was "that in the performance" of her "duty as a wife" she had fallen "far short" of what she had "ardently desired." Garrison affirmed his love for Helen and referred to the "unalloyed bliss" they had enjoyed "in wedded life." But, praising her efforts to "smooth the rugged pathway" of his "public career," he also made it clear that he appreciated her work in the domestic sphere. Noting in 1861 that he had rarely thanked Helen for her domestic labors, he explained that the "highest praise is conveyed where no fault is ever found with the manner in which you discharge the daily household responsibilities resting upon you, but, on the contrary, every thing is satisfactorily recognized as complete and perfect."[86]

Helen Garrison provided further evidence of the wide-ranging influence of domestic and separate spheres ideologies. An 1837 episode was particularly revealing of her attitude toward motherhood. Following an incident in which the Garrison's second child, William Lloyd Jr., fell out of his carriage, Garrison wrote to Helen's mother, detailing the injuries the young child had sustained. Assuring his mother-in-law that the child was not seriously hurt—and pointing out that responsibility for the accident lay with their domestic helper—Garrison also remarked: "Helen did not wish me to inform you of the accident, lest you think she was to blame on the score of carelessness." Helen was clearly troubled by the prospect that the accident would be interpreted as evidence that she was failing in her maternal responsibilities. For his part, while Garrison spoke eloquently about women's rights, and enjoyed spending time with the children, he considered his wife's domestic responsibilities in terms akin to those prescribed by domestic writers. His 1846 statement that by coping in his absence, Helen was "signally manifesting the spirit of self-sacrifice in being willing to have me undertake my present mission, in accordance with my own convictions of duty" must not only be seen as an expression of the sense of obligation she felt to "the friends of emancipation." It must also be viewed in terms of the spirit of self-sacrifice ascribed to women by the advocates of domestic ideology.[87]

Yet while Helen Garrison assumed her domestic obligations with a stoicism that would have made any advocate of domestic ideology proud, her expressions of contentment with her role must be considered alongside subtle hints betraying the frustrations of an existence restricted to the domestic sphere. With a large family to care for, Helen's domestic workload was for three decades compounded by the seemingly endless procession of visitors in her "hospitable mansion." Indeed, when she told Sallie Holley in 1862 that her "hands are full," it was evident that the presence of these guests—black as well as white—intensified her workload immeasurably. Helen occasionally betrayed a longing for a respite from those responsibilities, which were exacerbated by Lloyd's frequent and sometimes lengthy trips away from home. Unlike most of the other women in this study, Helen rarely traveled from home. It was not surprising then that she looked forward to the opportunities she had to escape the domestic circle. And all the while, although William Lloyd Garrison publicly endorsed women's claims for equality, he provided little support to Helen in the domestic sphere. It is in this sense that their marriage is most revealing. Yet as was the case in other abolitionist marriages, gender roles were not static. In the Garrisons' case, the divergence between ideological pronouncements and private behavior declined somewhat after Helen suffered a debilitating stroke in December 1863. This compelled Garrison to assume greater responsibilities within the domestic sphere.[88] Nevertheless, the Garrisons' marriage illustrates that even amongst those abolitionist men who were devoted public supporters of the principle of women's rights, their behavior reflected the deep hold of the gender spheres ideology.

David and L. Maria Child's marriage reveals much about the conflicting imperatives that affected the public and private practices of abolitionism. In part these imperatives reflected the unique reversal of gender roles that occurred in the Childs' marriage. Maria remained committed to the ideal of domestic life, but her own marriage contradicted the ideal as it was commonly espoused. Both David and Maria were "intensely ambitious," but it was Maria who became the celebrated author, domestic writer, and abolitionist.[89] Much of Maria's importance derives from the way in which she functioned as a bridge between radical abolitionism, and the more conservative domestic ideology. Moreover, she found many aspects of her own marriage deeply dissatisfying. Yet the tensions within the Childs' relationship did not detract from their shared commitment to each other, and Maria's endorsement of many of the principles of domestic ideology reflected her "extreme aversion to mixing with the world." But her desire for domestic serenity, where she could "hide in peace and quietness from the world and its ways," was complicated by her sense of public duty, and by her devotion to David, which frequently compelled her to leave the domestic sphere. Although Maria's public activities were less self-consciously radical than those of some other female abolitionists, she did transgress the boundaries of women's sphere, and helped pave the way for the subsequent entrance of women reformers into public life.[90]

David Lee Child spent considerable time away from his wife. At different times Child worked as an agent of the AASS in Washington D.C., and as editor of the *National Anti-Slavery Standard* in New York City. But it was his infatuation with an array of mechanical and agricultural pursuits that most exasperated his wife. Child's schemes were intended to assist in the emancipation of the slaves and the elevation of African-Americans. His most persistent plan, a component of the free produce movement, was a proposal to grow beet sugar, to undercut Southern-grown sugar on the world market. These projects led him to travel widely throughout the United States, and in 1837 he journeyed to Europe to study beet culture.[91] With that abolitionist objective in mind, Maria's patience with her husband's fascination with what might be construed as impractical schemes becomes more plausible. But it is necessary to return to the early stages of their marriage to appreciate her frustrations.

L. Maria Child became aware of David's foibles soon after they wed in October 1828, and the early years of their marriage were marked by privation and transitoriness. While Maria was hopeful that their situation would eventually improve, she resigned herself to financial insecurity for the time being. These financial woes thwarted Maria's quest for domestic tranquility.

By 1831 she was regretting that they were again moving house. "The prime of our life," she lamented, "must be spent in one perpetual struggle with poverty." For a woman who dearly wanted "to go housekeeping," the financial insecurity and lack of a permanent home were persistent disappointments. Yet there was an underlying duality to Maria's perception of the early years of marriage, as evidenced by an 1835 comment: "How much we have suffered and enjoyed since you first called me wife!"[92] Maria's public interest in helping women to run their households efficiently was one response to her own personal situation, and it was no coincidence that it was during that period that she penned her domestic tracts.

In the longer term, many of the difficulties in the Childs' marriage resulted from financial problems. Notwithstanding the egalitarian rhetoric of Jacksonian America, David Lee Child's pecuniary anguish was shared by many of his contemporaries, including a number of his abolitionist colleagues. Of the abolitionists assessed here, only Wendell Phillips came from what could be described as a wealthy background. Others, such as Elizabeth Cady Stanton, came from privileged families, but most were toward the lower end of the middle-class continuum. All experienced a degree of economic indigence, and even Phillips's economic status declined during the course of his life. Stephen Foster, referring to his financial woes, told Abby Kelley in 1851 that he hoped "we shall never be so much troubled again as in the four years that are past." Typically, however, Foster saw a positive aspect to financial privation, arguing that it enhanced their reformism. "But this experience may not be wholly useless to us," he wrote, "as it will help us to sympathize with those who are in straightened [*sic*] circumstances."[93]

In the Childs' case, David's financial difficulties were eased by the income Maria derived from writing, and by the support provided by her father. Following his trip to Europe, David purchased a one-hundred-acre farm near Northampton, Massachusetts, with funds provided by his father-in-law. Like Henry and Elizabeth Cady Stanton's move to Seneca Falls, the Childs' departure from Boston reflected the husband's ambitions and desires. Maria had missed David when they lived in Boston, but at least there she had been able to enjoy the "good, warm, abolition sympathy" of her friends and colleagues. The situation in Northampton, however, was very different.[94] Maria's dissatisfactions with her life there paralleled those of Stanton in Seneca Falls, and, as laudable as David's plans were, she became increasingly frustrated.

Adding to Child's gloom was the fear that her writing career appeared to be at an end. A number of women became writers in the nineteenth century, but the first women who did so encountered criticism for stepping beyond the limits of their designated sphere. Child initially sought to circumvent such opprobrium by keeping her authorship secret, but the publicity that followed the publication of her novels quickly worked to her favor, as she achieved popular acclaim as a writer. Living in Northampton in the period after her marriage, however, made writing difficult, and Maria's frustration at not being able to write contributed to her disappointment. Kirk Jeffrey was correct to point out that Child's marriage was "never so unsatisfying" that she regarded it "as an entirely restrictive and repressive factor in her life." Nevertheless, sensing the disjunction between the idealized picture she had presented in her domestic tracts, and the reality of her own life, Child's enthusiasm for domestic life was undermined by the duties of wife and housekeeper.[95] Maria's experiences in Northampton steered her toward an affirmation of her independence as an individual with the capacity—and the right—to determine her own life course.

It was L. Maria Child's dual reputation as an abolitionist and a writer that combined to present her with the opportunity to take a step toward independence. David Lee Child was responsible for much of his wife's conversion to abolitionism, but once alerted to the slaves' plight there was no questioning her antislavery commitment. Maria's abolitionist credentials, firmly established by her 1833 *Appeal in Favor of that Class of Americans Called Africans,* coupled with her renowned writing skills, ably qualified her to accept the offer to serve as editor of the *National Anti-Slavery Standard,* a weekly New York abolitionist newspaper. The impact of Child's editorship of the paper during the early 1840s should not be underestimated. Although her tenure was characterized by a determination to avoid fomenting controversy within the antislavery movement, the appointment of Child symbolized the ways in which women's involvement in abolitionism undermined the gendered distinctions between public and private life. Lucretia Mott, stressing the radical nature of having Child as editor of the national organ of the AASS, and connecting abolitionism to women's rights, commented in 1841 that "by acquitting herself so nobly in the Editorial Chair," Child was not only doing much for the antislavery cause, but was also achieving much "for woman." Postbellum advocates of women's rights, too, acknowledged the importance of Child's editorship of the *National Anti-Slavery Standard.* Besides demonstrating her "very great ability" as a manager, the delegates at the 1870 women's rights convention believed that Child's editorship of the paper "marked an era for woman and introduced her to that field of labor which is now occupied by so many." Child's "steady, brave, persistent demand for freedom for the slave," they argued, had "done much for woman."[96]

Child's editorship of the *National Anti-Slavery Standard* was also significant on a personal level. The tensions associated with accepting the position were evident in her ambivalence about moving to New York City. In leaving Northampton she was rejecting aspects of her life there, and asserting her right to determine the course of her own life. But the reasons she outlined for her move to New York reveal that an alternative set of priorities underpinned this difficult decision. Not only was David listed as "assistant editor" of the paper, but Maria explained to readers of the paper that if "Mr. Child's business" had "made it possible for him to remove to New York, his experience in editing, his close observation of public affairs, and the general character of his mind, would have made it far better for the cause to have him for a resident [editor], and myself for an assistant editor." Despite the disappointments of her life in Northampton, Maria maintained a keen affection for David, and longed for the time when she could be with him "and find sufficient happiness in making him happy."[97]

These sentiments evince an underlying tension in L. Maria Child's life. By making her happiness dependent upon her ability to please David (whom she described as the "kindest and worthiest of husbands") she echoed the ideology of Catharine Beecher and other domestic reformers. But the form of Maria's efforts to make her husband happy cast her outside the domestic sphere prescribed both by Beecher, and, judging by what she had suggested in *The Frugal Housewife* and other domestic tracts, the roles she herself implied women could best fulfill. Child's dilemma was apparent in an 1841 letter to Gerrit Smith. As well as asserting that she was "willing to make any exertions, or any sacrifices" to help her husband, she noted: "My domestic attachments are so strong, and my love of seclusion so great, that nothing but my husband's pecuniary embarrassment would have driven me here [to New York]." Explaining why David was experiencing financial difficulties, she claimed he had been compromised by unscrupulous business associates.[98] Maria was defensive about David's financial problems; while she held him primarily responsible for his predicament, there was also an implicit suggestion that the turbulent nature of nineteenth-century

American capitalism provided the context for his difficulties. That perception was one of the principles underlying her works on domesticity: she believed that by projecting domestic values beyond the home, the exploitative and manipulative excesses of capitalism could be contained. Nonetheless, Child maintained her faith in the virtues of a free market, albeit one tempered by the influence of domestic values.

L. Maria Child continued to feel torn between a desire for independence, and an attachment to David. Kirk Jeffrey has implied that since there was little to be gained financially by accepting the editorship of the *National Anti-Slavery Standard,* the major factor behind Child's move to New York was her desire to escape from the unhappiness she felt in Northampton. Support for this argument came from Maria's decision to remain in New York after she resigned as editor of the paper in 1843. There is further evidence of her search for individual autonomy. Beside choosing to remain in New York, she also separated her financial affairs from those of her husband for several years—a radical step for a woman in the mid-nineteenth century. The separation of their lives might appear to have been almost total, given that apart from a brief period in 1843, when David edited the *National Anti-Slavery Standard,* they spent little time together until 1850.[99] Nevertheless, Maria's correspondence from that period reveals an ongoing tension. Although she had resolved to cease following her husband's movements, the explanation she offered for her decision indicated the strength of her attachment to David. By remaining in New York, she hoped to "earn as much" as she could, "to prepare a home always for him."[100] That explanation also casts a different light upon her decision to separate her financial affairs from David's. Maria's continued love for her husband, and reverence for a proper domestic life, might suggest she was more conservative than some other abolitionist women. Yet while the contradictions in Child's life led to considerable anguish, she stressed that the best way for women to gain their rights was by acting, rather than by philosophizing.

Not only did Maria's love for David remain constant during the 1840s; she continued to accept partial responsibility for his financial woes. Returning to a tenet of domestic ideology, Maria attributed David's financial problems to "his organization." She made it clear, however, that she could not let him down, and admitted that she would "probably have to meet his personal expenses." Feeling responsible for his "personal" expenses was a different proposition to injecting funds into his business ventures, but it did represent her abiding loyalty and commitment to David. Maria hoped that they would be able to spend all of the summer of 1847 together in New Rochelle. Knowing that he was ill brought to the surface all the affection she felt for him. In a statement congruent with the doctrine she had enunciated in her domestic tracts, she planned to devote the coming months to the "business of recruiting his health and cheering him up."[101] So, while David and L. Maria Child lived apart from each other for much of the 1840s, their separation was never complete, and Maria's domestic hopes remained consistent. Although she was destined to remain frustrated in many of these aspirations, Child retained an abiding commitment to the domestic sphere, and her disappointments did not dissuade her from continuing to proclaim the virtues and value of a satisfying home life.

For radical abolitionists, as for their contemporaries, the home was glorified and elevated as a sacred place, where refuge could be found from the tumult of the outside world. Like their public statements concerning domestic ideology, their domestic arrangements reflected trends that were apparent in the wider, nonabolitionist community. Yet in confronting the contradictions of domestic ideology, and the confinement of women to the private sphere, radical abolitionists challenged many of the prevailing conventions regarding gender roles and familial relations. In the process of seeking to reallocate domestic roles, they went a long way toward constructing household arrangements that took into account individual rights and desires. Radical abolitionists' distinctiveness arose from the practical and ideological role reversals that took place in their relationships. It was that reordering of gender roles (which was also a practical demonstration of the depth of the abolitionist challenge to the patriarchy of slave society) that enabled some women to continue their public abolitionism. Domestic values and experiences were not only important elements of the abolitionists' reformism; as the next chapter reveals, they also helped shape the construction of abolitionist sorority.

FOUR

Antislavery Sisters:

Sorority, Family, and Individualism

FRIENDSHIPS BETWEEN NINETEENTH-century women, and the political and social implications deriving from women's networks, have attracted considerable historiographical attention.[1] Marginalized from traditional avenues of power, women established relationships with each other that differed from those between men and women. Examining abolitionist sorority helps to delineate the boundaries of the antislavery family as a social group, and of abolitionism as a reform movement. Sororal feelings not only provided a foundation for female abolitionists' empathy with the enslaved women of the South; as their self-conscious use of the term "sisters" suggested, there were important social networks among abolitionist and other reforming women.[2] The associations forged between women's antislavery organizations mirrored the links between women's moral reform societies, as well as those between groups that were less obviously political or controversial. Yet while abolitionist sorority located abolitionists within the wider culture of nineteenth-century gender relations, equally apparent was the isolation that antislavery women felt from many of their contemporaries: exclusion from the majority bred unity among the minority. Abolitionist sorority was also a response to women's disappointments within those public institutions, including many antislavery societies, which refused to admit them as equals.

Preceding chapters have established that even as radical abolitionists challenged the division of men and women into distinct spheres, they appropriated many of the precepts of domestic and separate spheres ideologies. This ambivalence held implications for relations between abolitionist women. At the same time as they tested—and sometimes transcended—the boundaries between public and private life, abolitionist women were certain that the gender spheres of the nineteenth century were not simply oppressive. Besides leaving room for female bonding, the development of a distinct "social space" for women fostered the evolution of a female culture that was an important expression of women's subordinate status.[3] Complicating abolitionist sorority was the vexed notion of individualism, which stood in tension with a sense of responsibility to much-valued collective social units—of which the family was the most significant. A faith in individualism also shaped the abolitionists' perceptions of class relations, and blinded them to many of the inequalities of nineteenth-century America. Nineteenth-century sorority often rested on assumptions concerning women's common position, and on the amorphous concept commonly described as "woman's nature." Abolitionists were influenced by all of these aspects of American culture. While abolitionist women considered themselves different from other women, and valued individualism as a goal, the mobilization of women as a group was often predicated on the alleged universality of certain female experiences and traits. Hence the practice of abolitionism frequently tended to conceive women as an abstract singular: woman.[4]

Abolitionist sorority was much more than a defense mechanism against the practices of a patriarchal society. Female abolitionists' conception of sorority as an agent of positive change was wide-ranging, and—on the surface at least—not constrained by perceptions of social hierarchy. The Grimké sisters' optimistic perception of women's power, and their sense of women's shared responsibilities, were revealed in an 1839 letter to Queen Victoria.

The Grimkés believed that gender involved particular perceptions and obligations, but they were also conscious of social hierarchies and utilized those perceptions to further the cause of the slave. Their faith in the American democratic and republican ideal, and Sarah's subsequent praise for aspects of the French Revolution, did not preclude an appeal to the British monarch to help emancipate the slaves. Accordingly, as "moral and immortal beings," and standing "on the same platform of *Human Rights,*" they argued that all women had "the same duties and the same responsibilities." Invoking the duties of all women who were "in common with thyself invested with privileges & bound by obligations," the Grimkés referred to the "peculiar duties and great responsibilities," that devolved upon her as "Queen of a mighty people."[5]

This suggests that sorority was a powerful impulse among abolitionist women. Equally telling, however, were the limits to abolitionist sorority. Through their reform activities, female abolitionists maintained friendships and working relationships with men that belied prevailing stereotypes concerning the division of the sexes into separate spheres. Here, male abolitionists' use of the term "sisters" is revealing. Theodore Weld's description of Anne Warren Weston as "My Dear sister" not only revealed that abolitionist men employed the language of sisterly sentiments, but—given the religious imperative behind radical abolitionism—also implied a sense of shared religiosity between male and female reformers. Hinting that radical abolitionists' networks of reformist friends were not divided along gender lines, Weld's statement also suggested that radical abolitionist men perceived their movement as a family in which "brothers" could turn to their "sisters" for support. This raises a broader issue, concerning the relationship between abolitionist women's sororal friendships, and their marriages. Unlike the members of the postbellum Woman's Christian Temperance Union, abolitionists' sororal sentiments did not amount to a conscious effort to construct a formal sisterhood that emphasized the virtues of women's lives separate from men's.[6] Indeed, there is compelling evidence that female abolitionists' sororal friendships were subordinate to their marital relationships. Of the fifty-one women assessed in Blanche Hersh's study, thirty-seven were married. Postbellum women reformers, by contrast, were less likely to be married, which partly accounts for their greater emphasis on sisterhood and the plight of unmarried women.[7] With the exception of Sarah Grimké, the women studied herein were married, but even among those who did not marry, there was a recognition of the value of marriage. Lucy Stone insisted that it was only within marriage that individuals could find complete self-fulfillment. An "unmarried life, made the best yet," she told Henry Blackwell in 1854, "is yet only a half-life." That emphasis reflected the abolitionists' conviction that in marriage, as Sarah Grimké put it, "the highest affections of our nature can find a sufficient field for growth." Grimké's comment, all the more revealing because she never married, suggested that abolitionist women's sororal relationships were complementary to, rather than substitutes for, their marriages.[8]

Abolitionist sorority was further bounded by considerations of social hierarchy, ethnicity, and race. These considerations were evident both socially and institutionally. Female abolitionists expressed sympathy for the plight of oppressed women, but their hierarchical perspective transcended their loyalty to other women. Equally, as their black coadjutors recognized, white abolitionists' dichotomic perception of slavery and freedom as polar absolutes blinded them to many of the realities of individual and institutional racism in the United States.[9] Garrisonians denied the immutability of racial differences and white abolitionist women sought to treat African American women as equals. Nevertheless, their patronizing statements, and their public and private behavior, frequently betrayed a deep-seated belief in racial differences. This ambivalent attitude toward black women was expressed succinctly by L. Maria Child. She referred to her "sisters in bondage," and drew attention to those who were "suffering wrongs so foul, that our ears are too delicate to listen to them." Yet Child's condescension toward African Americans was demonstrated by her willingness to adopt the role of editor of Harriet Jacobs's *Incidents in the Life of a Slave Girl.* In her introduction to Jacobs's book, Child emphasized that the changes she had made were minor, and noted that with "trifling exceptions, both the ideas and the language are her [Jacobs's] own." Nonetheless, Child considered her role to be the senior one. Moreover, while her sense of bonding with African Americans was evident, her claim that literature written for white readers was unsuitable for blacks betrayed her belief that there were distinctions between people of different complexions. Child's racial values were sometimes explicit. Referring to "the colored Refugees," she asserted in 1864, "*Our* literature is not, in *any* of its departments, adapted to *their* state and condition. I think I can plan some books that will help to encourage, enlighten, and entertain them, at the same time. I have a faculty at writing with *simplicity,* and my sympathies are so entirely with them that I think I can put myself in their stead, and imagine what *I* should like in *their* place."[10] As Margot Melia has noted, it "was not easy" for black and white women "to become friends" in the racist environment of antebellum America, but white abolitionist women's references to African American women as their "sisters," were signals of intent rather than expressions of reality. Despite their avowed determination to treat black women as equals, white abolitionists' friendships with African American colleagues lacked much of the intimacy evident in relationships between white female abolitionists.[11]

Institutionally, too, black women encountered discrimination. Efforts were made to accommodate African American women in the female antislavery societies, and Julie Winch has argued that blacks "played a much more active role in the female antislavery movement than they did in the American Anti-Slavery Society." Similarly, Debra Gold Hansen has averred that the Boston Female Anti-Slavery Society (BFASS) "was integrated from its inception." Nevertheless, the racial attitudes of the nineteenth century worked against the admission of black women as equals, and Hansen's remark that "most black members were not particularly active in the organization and very few took a leading or policy-making role" is a revealing hint of the attitudes of Boston's white women abolitionists to their black coworkers.[12] There is evidence, moreover, that black women's involvement in the BFASS was not a spontaneous expression of racial equality on the part of the Boston women. Writing to the BFASS in April 1834, William L. Garrison—himself imbued with many of the racial values of the nineteenth century—described his shock at discovering that African American women were not being admitted to the Society. Declining an invitation to attend their meeting, Garrison's letter must have had some effect, since Mary Grew, the Society's corresponding secretary, promptly replied that a decision had been made to welcome black women into the organization.[13] This change of heart showed both sides of white abolitionist women's sororal feelings for black women. On the one hand, there was a desire to improve relations between white and black Americans. This, of course, was a challenge to the social mores of the nineteenth century. But at the same time, there was undeniable evidence that even radical abolitionists were affected by the racial beliefs that pervaded nineteenth-century America. The influence of these beliefs varied in intensity. Whilst the experiences of black women in the BFASS contrasted with the relatively tolerant attitude of the Philadelphia Female Anti-Slavery Society (PFASS), even in the case of the Philadelphia Society, African American women faced prejudice. Although Jean R. Soderlund has remarked that the black "women who helped establish" the PFASS "remained among the core of its leaders," Melia has demonstrated that the "participation of black women as the upper level" of the PFASS "was minor and brief."[14] On this issue, as elsewhere, white abolitionism reflected deeply felt ideas regarding social hierarchy as well as race. The African American women who were involved in the BFASS, "enjoyed prominence and economic standing in their own community," and the black members of the PFASS were drawn from that city's black "elite."[15] The inference from all of this is clear: although they proclaimed the virtues of a wide-ranging reforming sisterhood, the white women of the Boston and Philadelphia female antislavery societies had little social or institutional contact with the black populace.

Relations between white abolitionist women were less inhibited than those between black and white women. This intimacy reflected a wider pattern. Friendships between individuals of the same sex in the nineteenth century were frequently close, both emotionally and physically. Historians have remarked on the friendships between antislavery women, and Lawrence Friedman has contrasted abolitionist fraternity and sorority. Noting that the sorority "forged" by abolitionist women "differed in important respects from the fraternity of their male counterparts," and specifically contrasting the relationship between Sallie Holley and Caroline Putnam with that between Theodore Weld and Charles Stuart, Friedman has concluded that whereas fraternity "centered upon a quest for free-flowing mutually spontaneous if sometimes guilt-inducing bonds of the heart," abolitionist sorority "was less private and more formalized." Abolitionist sorority, he argued, "was more directly oriented toward the strategic and theoretical ramifications of woman's assumption of public roles in behalf of the dispossessed." Friedman was right to point out that female abolitionists spent considerable time "adjusting" to the circumstances and implications of their reformism, and his argument that "whereas abolitionist fraternity has left us with many deeply emotional but highly idiosyncratic documents, abolitionist sorority has provided a much more substantial intellectual legacy" has merit. But it is also important to pay due attention to the profound sense of intimacy that underpinned abolitionist sorority.[16]

An obvious sign of that intimacy was the undisguised adoration expressed in correspondence between abolitionist women. Like their non-abolitionist peers, female abolitionists effusively affirmed their love for each other, and unhesitatingly used affectionate terms of endearment. Convinced that honesty was essential if individuals were to maintain meaningful relationships, they were determined to express their feelings for each other.[17] The respect they felt for Lucretia Mott has been noted, but other women reformers also earned the acclaim of their peers. These expressions of affection were often marked by admiration for an individual's concurrent devotion to reformism and family. Sallie Holley made her feelings clear in an 1853 letter to Abby Kelley: "I love and admire you dear Abby, & wish I was as much as half as true and heroic as you." Holley's enthusiasm for Kelley stemmed partly from her relative youthfulness and inexperience in reformism, but her sentiments were echoed by other abolitionist women, in the postbellum as well as antebellum period. Sending her love, and a "scrap of poetry" to Helen Garrison, Sarah Grimké typically closed an 1872 letter "Good bye dear, Your loving S.M.G." Writing to Elizabeth Daniels, Grimké also hinted at the physical nature of nineteenth-century sorority: "How I wish I could clasp you to my bosom," she wrote, and "feel the throbbings of your warm heart."[18]

There were institutional parallels to these expressions of individual intimacy. In a form of institutional sorority, female antislavery societies communicated freely. Mary Grew's exhortation regarding the necessity for cooperation between "sister associations" was representative of the sentiments expressed by members of the female antislavery societies. Although these relationships often arose from such apparently innocuous social activities as women's sewing circles, female abolitionists understood the far-reaching consequences of women's associations. "Sarah S[outhwick] hopes the sewing circle or something to bring people together frequently in a social way," Abby Kelley told Maria Weston Chapman, "will be continued, as the diffusion of our principles by this means is constantly going forward."[19] Female friendships were thus linked to the extension of proper values in society.

Besides providing a forum for women to discuss their responsibilities, female antislavery societies furnished a supportive network for those women who had transcended the boundaries of women's designated sphere. Following the appointment of Angelina Grimké as a lecturing agent of the American Anti-Slavery Society (AASS), the women of the PFASS debated the propriety of women addressing audiences that included men. They had no qualms regarding women's right to speak before gatherings of women, but the question of whether they should address mixed audiences proved divisive. Yet while the Philadelphia women declared they "would never overstep the bounds of propriety," they concluded that the evils of slavery necessitated vigorous action. Depicting their bonding with the slaves in familial terms, they referred to the suffering of their "brethren and sisters" who lay "crushed and bleeding under the arm of tyranny." Distinguishing between what was morally required of women, and the standards set by society, their obligation to the slaves was unambiguous: "we must do with our might what our hands find to do for their deliverance, pausing only to inquire 'What is right?' and not 'What will be universally approved.' " Given that determination, it is not surprising that the Pennsylvanian women supported Sarah and Angelina Grimké in their public abolitionism. Moreover, the reference in the 1837 Annual Report of the PFASS to the Grimkés as "our beloved sisters" typified the affection female abolitionists felt for each other.[20]

On an individual basis, too, the Grimkés drew support from their female friends. Angelina's friendship with Jane Smith was particularly important, and Sarah also maintained friendships outside her immediate family. Although Sarah regarded herself as a member of Theodore and Angelina's family, and respected the marital relationship, the fact that she was unmarried led her to place a high value on her own friendships with other women. Perhaps most significant, the Grimkés supported each other. They had their share of disagreements but Sarah and Angelina helped each other in many ways, and their relationship was of continuing significance. Angelina's expressions of love to Sarah revealed both affection and guilt: "There are times dear Sister when I feel humbled in the dust, because I never have been willing to share my blessings with you *equally.*" Contrasting "all that" Sarah had done for her, with her own "ingratitude & selfishness," Angelina wished that God would give her "a *good heart.*" And despite Angelina's references to differences between herself and Sarah, she was certain that Sarah should remain in their domestic circle: "we all feel this to be your right place, the home of your heart—we all want you with us, & w*ld* feel a great blank if you were not with us."[21]

Having experienced firsthand the vilification associated with public lecturing, the Grimkés were sensitive to the demands placed on other women who entered the public sphere. Several abolitionist women commented on the trauma involved in their original decision to enter the antislavery field. Again, the support of female friends was vital. Angelina Grimké, encouraging Abby Kelley to devote herself to abolitionism, described her own reaction to an offer from the AASS to promote the cause. Grimké attested to her perception of abolitionist women's special ability to empathize with each other's difficulties. "I know by sorrowful experience," she assured Kelley in 1838, "what it is to feel just as thou describest, having a work to do & yet not knowing *how* to do it." Discussing how she had spent two agonizing years contemplating her future, Grimké recalled the loneliness of that experience: "If I had only had a companion to go out with me—how easy comparatively—but there was no one." This indicated the importance abolitionists attached to a supportive social circle. For those women whose reformism drew them away from home for extended periods, the absence of a coterie of antislavery companions—particularly female friends—was a source of great discomfort. Anne Warren Weston, praising Kelley for her courage, and inferring that the hardships associated with "travelling up & down by night & by day" were exacerbated by the fact that Kelley was "always with men & never with women," suggested the value that women abolitionists attached to their specifically female networks.[22]

The lack of female traveling companions was compounded by the specific criticisms directed at women abolitionist lecturers. Characteristically, however, in describing the discomforts of public lecturing, Abby Kelley affirmed the significance of the marital relationship. Kelley, who maintained a frank correspondence with Maria Weston Chapman, defended Foster in a letter of November 1843. Asserting that Chapman was undervaluing Foster, Kelley considered her friend to be "greatly prejudiced against him." Exhibiting pride in her future husband, and perceiving her role as a mediator between Chapman and Foster, Kelley's depiction of Stephen as "one of the best and most devoted life offerings," was suggestive of her belief in the significance of relationships between men and women. Kelley's conciliatory statements (including her defenses of Chapman in her correspondence with Foster) amounted to an effort to maintain harmony within the antislavery family. This paralleled another pattern of familial relationships in the nineteenth century. Historians have noted the significant role played by females in maintaining family ties during that period. Kelley's statement implied that abolitionist women conformed to that pattern.[23]

As the 1840 split in abolitionist ranks revealed, such efforts to maintain harmony within antislavery circles were often unsuccessful. The rejection women abolitionists suffered from some male-dominated antislavery societies strengthened their burgeoning institutional sorority. Institutionally and personally, the schism in the AASS, and the subsequent exclusion of women from the 1840 World's Anti-Slavery Convention, contributed to female abolitionists' sense of sorority. Aside from the obvious anger felt by many abolitionist women at their exclusion from the London Convention (which led Elizabeth Cady Stanton to proclaim subsequently that the women's rights movement could be dated from that particular example of male injustice) there were other, more subtle effects on women. Of the friendships established between abolitionist women at the 1840 meeting, perhaps the most significant was that between Elizabeth Cady Stanton and Lucretia Mott. Stanton recalled later that the relationship she forged with Mott "opened to me a new world of thought," but the twenty-four-year-old Stanton also influenced and inspired Mott.[24] That relationship, and others formed as a consequence of similar experiences, were important foundations on which the women's rights movement was based.

Less prominent women also established friendships at the London convention. The relationship Ann Phillips established in 1840 with the British abolitionist Elizabeth Pease survived many years. We have seen that Phillips's illness did not prevent her from continuing to regard herself as a member of the abolitionist community. One sign of that process was the network of friendships she maintained with other women. Phillips drew support from sympathetic abolitionist friends, even if she did not see them very often. Her relationship was Pease was especially valuable. Ann's gratitude, along with her sense of isolation from many of her former companions, was evident. "Since I have been ill," she told Pease in 1841, "the world has worn quite another aspect to me, for many that I had thought friends have fallen off, & many have misunderstood the nature of my state of health so much that there is no pleasure in communication with them." Praising Pease for understanding "the little numerous ills that sickness brings," Phillips thanked her English friend for having made her so happy.[25] This companionship supplanted the support Ann received from her family. While her relations were "kind as far as they understand," she noted they had "no sympathy" in subjects that interested her, nor did they have any idea of her "feeble state of health." This indicated that some abolitionists were isolated from their families of origin. Yet Ann's affection for Pease did not signify a lack of support or empathy from her husband. Ann's relationship with Pease was not a substitute for a dissatisfying marriage; Pease also maintained a friendship with Wendell Phillips that complemented her relationship with Ann. Wendell attested to the complementary nature of these friendships. Appending a note to one of Ann's affectionate letters to their English friend, he signaled just how deeply Ann cared for Pease, and revealed that he too valued Pease's role: "Ann's lines, affectionate as they are, dear Elizabeth, tell you no more of her heart than a drop of water can imagine the ocean. She moans for you. I was forbidden to mention your name, to keep away the tears. . . . I thought we were going home, but we leave full half of home behind us, where your kind heart is. I want Webb's Irish tongue [to] tell you how much we love you." Moreover, despite the depth of Ann's friendship with Pease, she related those feelings in terms that expressed the significance of her marriage. Comparing her feelings toward Wendell prior to their marriage with the sentiments she felt for Pease, Ann recalled that she had felt herself unworthy before her marriage, and stated that she felt the same toward her English friend.[26] In each of these ways, Ann Phillips's friendship with Pease was an adjunct to her marriage.

Ann Phillips's illness was particularly severe, but other abolitionist women also suffered various ailments. They carried their sympathies for each other's illnesses into their reformism. In a society where women's alleged vulnerability to ill-health was exaggerated and turned into a rationale for their subordinate status, female abolitionists' personal experiences merged with their public concerns: individual, private experiences were again shaping public reformism. Many women in the nineteenth century, affected by diseases frequently misdiagnosed by the predominantly male medical profession as psychologically based, valued the support of female friends.[27] Female abolitionists' attitude to illness not only evinced the supportive nature of their sororal relationships; it also revealed much about their perceptions of women's particular physiological and emotional vulnerabilities. Although they believed that women's true capacities were not recognized by society, abolitionist women accepted and utilized aspects of the ideology that underpinned women's second-class status. Female abolitionists' attitude toward women's medical role reflected this unusual mix. By encouraging women to enter the medical profession, they defied prevailing stereotypes regarding women's intellectual abilities. At the same time, however, the arguments they used to justify that expanded professional role for women, emphasizing women's nurturing role, and women's fragility, rested on the notion that the sexes were fundamentally different.

Since many illnesses were believed to be the result of an improper domestic environment, women were generally held responsible for the health of their families. To varying degrees all abolitionist women felt these responsibilities. But some also sought to reform the practice of medicine, and a general abolitionist cynicism toward the medical profession was reinforced by individual experiences. The death of children occasioned passionate expressions of affection among abolitionist women. Like their contemporaries, several abolitionists lost children to illness, and a shared sense of loss and compassion was evident in their letters of condolence. Lucy Stone's 1852 comments indicate the sorrow and anger women reformers associated with the influence of the predominantly male medical profession: "My brother's little children are both dead—killed we think by the Drs. I do believe they kill more than they cure." Since the medical profession was largely a male domain, Stone's comments, like Elizabeth Cady Stanton's reference to the "ignorance of physicians," amounted to a thinly veiled criticism of men.[28]

Radical abolitionists were sure benefits could follow the entry of women into the medical profession. As abolitionist women saw their public and private reformism as proof that women could function in both the public and private spheres, female doctors were tangible evidence of women's capabilities and a refutation of the prevailing view that linked women's illnesses to their reproductive function. Elizabeth Blackwell, a sister of Henry Blackwell, achieved fame for becoming the first female to receive professional medical qualifications. Harriot Kezia Hunt—whose expulsion from Harvard Medical School in 1850, along with the black nationalist Martin Delany and two other African Americans, revealed how the forces of patriarchy perceived blacks' and women's acquisition of medical skills as a threat to its dominance—was another well-known female doctor. Angelina Grimké advised Hunt to confine herself to the "Nervous Diseases," which she noted were difficult to treat. In this way Grimké demonstrated clearly her faith in women's intellectual abilities, and inferred that women were capable of working in the public sphere. Yet she also affirmed the strength of the assumptions concerning women's particular vulnerabilities: by admitting that "women are the principal victims of nervousness," she endorsed the stereotypes presented by male medical practitioners.[29]

Sarah Grimké exhibited a similar duality. Encouraging Harriot Kezia Hunt to pursue her medical studies, she accepted that it was "particularly" women's "sphere to minister to the sick." By suggesting that the "medical profession opens more than all other things a highway of improvement to woman," Grimké revealed her high expectations concerning the benefits that women could derive from acquiring a more significant role in medicine: "it affords such an extensive field to physiological research to an investigation of all that pertains to the structure & uses of our organs—to the injury sustained by those organs from the abuses to which they are subjected." Characteristically optimistic about the virtues of a scientific understanding of the world, and referring again to the abuse of women, Grimké thus infused women's medical role with an explicit reformist purpose. But her attitude was based on more than the self-interest of the female sex. Typically, women's role as defenders of the domestic realm was emphasized, and she asserted that "no women" could "justly fulfil her mission as a physician without a love spirit." It was only with that spirit (which she believed distinguished women from men) that women could achieve "unity & internal correspondence with those whom we are in outward communication." Indeed, Grimké later attributed great importance to the "love element," which she lauded as woman's "crowning blessing."[30] Grimké's comments were an implicit affirmation of the ideology that assigned a higher spirituality to women than to men. Unlike domestic writers, however, she refused to accept that the preservation of those attributes was dependent upon women remaining within the domestic sphere. Instead, convinced that women's special qualities could be projected beyond the home, she reasoned that it was incumbent upon those women who were capable to utilize those qualities to reform the world.

We have seen that abolitionists and other reformers regarded education as an essential means of promoting reformist values. But there were other implications of this concern for education. Carroll Smith-Rosenberg's emphasis on the significance of women's education as a bonding process applied also to abolitionists, and her argument concerning girls' experiences of boarding school as important stages in the development of sororal relationships was particularly true of two prominent nineteenth-century reformers, Lucy Stone and Antoinette Brown. Suffering the injustices of the sexist practices at Oberlin College, Stone and Brown established a lifelong friendship.[31] Equally important, it was at Oberlin that Stone and Brown—

who subsequently achieved fame as the first woman to be ordained a Protestant minister—became interested in reform issues. Complementing their friendship, the ideas to which they were exposed while at Oberlin played a part in opening their minds to the connections between their individual frustrations and broader patterns of oppression. An important influence on Stone was Abby Kelley, who along with Stephen Foster delivered antislavery lectures at Oberlin in 1846.[32]

Aside from the common experience of boarding school, there were other ways in which abolitionist sorority was linked to the wider pattern of nineteenth-century women's friendships. Domestic ideology defined women largely in terms of their maternal role, and the shared experience of motherhood was an integral element of nineteenth-century sorority. This was equally true for abolitionist women, who not only supported each other during pregnancies, childbirth, and the raising of children, but who linked maternalism to public reform. Indeed, much of that praise female abolitionists expressed for each other recognized motherhood as being of equal importance to the role of public reformer. This celebration of motherhood was of long-term significance in American reformism. As the resolution of the 1870 women's rights meeting praising Elizabeth Cady Stanton's "benignity and motherliness" suggested, maternal values were important in the women's rights movement. These affirmations of the value of motherhood were firmly grounded in reformers' own domestic experiences. Lucretia Mott served as symbol of motherhood for many abolitionists. As well as affecting Elizabeth Cady Stanton, Mott influenced other female abolitionists, including Sarah and Angelina Grimké. The Grimkés' conversion to abolitionism alienated them from their own mother, who refused to emancipate her slaves. Spending time in Philadelphia, in the company of a circle of busy abolitionist women, the Grimké sisters turned to Mott to supplant the nurturing role formerly provided by their own mother.[33]

The celebrated relationship between Elizabeth Cady Stanton and Susan B. Anthony illustrates the complexity of nineteenth-century sorority. Initially drawn together by a shared sense of women's oppression, their longstanding friendship was both a forum for an ideological discourse, and a concrete example of the support women could provide to each other. Elizabeth Cady Stanton's criticism of Henry Stanton revealed her need for support and encouragement, and her relationship with Susan B. Anthony provided an avenue to vent her marital frustrations. Stanton's dissatisfactions were evident in an 1855 letter to Anthony. "Henry sides with my friends," she explained, "who oppose me in all that is dearest to my heart. They are not willing that I should write even on the woman question." Stanton relied heavily on Anthony for support, and their relationship revealed much about domestic politics in nineteenth-century reformers' households. Anthony encouraged Stanton's burgeoning sense of independence. By assuming some of Stanton's domestic responsibilities, Anthony made it easier for her friend to contribute to the women's rights movement. Moreover, Anthony's indignation at Stanton's confinement to the domestic sphere helped both women articulate their frustrations with the demands of domestic life.[34]

As close as her friendship with Anthony was, however, Stanton continued to attach great importance to her own family. As Kathleen Barry has noted, Stanton "kept her marriage as an ever-present emotional wedge between" herself and Anthony. And notwithstanding the abolitionists' public eulogization of their relationships, and the romanticized descriptions of those relationships by some historians, sororal friendships, like all human relationships, revealed differences of opinion. Despite Stanton's later claim that "not one feeling of envy or jealousy has ever shadowed our lives," her friendship with Anthony was not free of stresses. Many of the tensions that emerged between husbands and wives were replicated in relationships between female friends. Anthony, and other female abolitionists, endeavored to alleviate Stanton's home duties, but they were frustrated by her inability to escape the burdens of domesticity. Urging Stanton to attend a planned women's rights convention in Philadelphia, Lucretia Mott sternly asserted: "*You are so wedded to this cause, you must expect to work as pioneers in the work.*"[35] Mott's language, however, suggested more than just her wish that Stanton could attend the convention. By presenting Stanton's responsibilities in terms of a marriage to the cause, Mott inferred that an appeal that emphasized public obligations as an analogue of marital responsibilities would be the most difficult to resist.

Elizabeth Cady Stanton's comments regarding her differences of opinion with Anthony are noteworthy not only for what they reveal about their friendship, but also for her ideas concerning marriage, and the distinction between the public and private spheres. When she and Anthony were alone, observed Stanton, they "indulged freely in criticism of each other," and "hotly contended whenever" they "differed." "To the world," however, "we always seem to agree and uniformly reflect each other." Distinguishing between the public and private realms, Stanton drew an overt parallel between her relationship with Anthony, and her prescription for a proper marital relationship: "Like husband and wife, each has the feeling that we must have no differences in public."[36]

At first glance, and undoubtedly influenced by Elizabeth Cady Stanton's experiences, Susan B. Anthony considered that marriage was for women a step into inevitable drudgery. Commenting on the marriage of Antoinette Brown Blackwell, Anthony reiterated the role of individualism in nineteenth-century reformism. Regretting that Blackwell (who had earlier vowed to remain single) was unable to engage in public reformism after her marriage, Anthony lamented: "Thus does every married woman sink her individuality." Anthony's view of marriage, judged by her reaction to Stanton's and Blackwell's marriages, was largely negative. Yet despite her denunciations of the effect of marriage on women, Anthony continued to believe in the *ideal* of marriage. In the postbellum period, even as she demanded the right of single women to have homes of their own, she made it clear that she did not wish to question "the *superiority* of the time-honored plan of making a home by the union of one man and woman—in marriage."[37] Other abolitionist women recognized the difficulties associated with establishing equitable marriages, but they did not let Anthony's criticisms go unanswered. After Anthony expressed disappointment at Lucy Stone's decision to marry, Stone responded by asserting: "I wish you had a good husband; it is a great blessing." Similarly, Lydia Mott's response to Anthony's negative assessment of Antoinette Brown Blackwell's marriage affirmed radical abolitionists' conviction that marriage did not necessarily entail the forfeiture of individuality. Presenting human relationships in terms of mutual interests, Mott inferred that to abstain from familial—and marital—relations was unnatural: "when you speak of the individuality of one who is truly married being inevitably lost, I think you mistake. If there ever was any individuality it will remain. . . . I like the expression 'we' rather than 'I.' I never feel that my interests & actions can be independent of the dear ones with whom I am surrounded. . . . This standing alone is not natural and therefore cannot be right."[38]

Just as radical abolitionists did not regard their idealized version of true marriage as a threat to their individuality, their construction of sorority did not preclude an abiding faith in individualism. Indeed, they sought to draw strength from the difficulties faced by abolitionist women. Angelina Grimké's comments on Abby Kelley's decision to lecture on behalf of the AASS have been mentioned. But even as Grimké recognized Kelley's difficulties, she expressed confidence in women's abilities. Suggesting that "perhaps it was all for the best that Abby had to stand alone," and emphasizing "how strengthening it is to feel that we have no arm of flesh to lean on," Grimké referred to her own experience. This belief that individual suffering could be a strengthening experience was balanced with a determination to assist other women through periods of loneliness. Abolitionist women supported each other during their husbands' absences. Helen Garrison found support from her female friends. Describing William L. Garrison's absence from his family as a "temporary bereavement," Mary Grew noted that Helen's loneliness and sorrow would have been mitigated, at least in part, by the knowledge that her husband was "on a noble mission for humanity." Specifically, she predicted that "the remembrance of the bereaved slave wife and mother" would "do much to reconcile" Helen to her husband's "temporary absence."[39] Besides suggesting sororal bonds, Grew's comments are significant because they also included Helen Garrison in the abolitionist community.

The empathy among abolitionist women was evident too in their common awareness of the difficulties of managing the domestic sphere. Women's common experiences within the private sphere were not only a foundation of their sororal relationships; they were central to abolitionist women's perception of domestic politics, and the ideology of women's rights. Chapter 3 revealed that despite the romanticized descriptions of her domestic skills, Lucretia Mott was conscious of the demands of family and household. Mott's domestic experiences helped her to empathize with Elizabeth Cady Stanton's plight. Historians have identified the dissimilarities between Mott and Stanton's domestic lives, but notwithstanding their different ages and geographical locations, and varying levels of support from their husbands, there were parallels between the two women's domestic experience. These domestic experiences were raised in abolitionist women's correspondence. Abby Kelley's comments are instructive. Writing to Sydney Howard Gay, she hoped that if she could "see Lizzie [Gay's wife] I should have a long yarn to reel off to her in relation to domestic matters." Given that such a conversation was not possible, however, there is evidence of the abolitionists' emphasis on relationships between men and women. As Kelley's plea to Gay to "tell me what you can about *domestically*" inferred, she considered the domestic sphere as more than women's place.[40] Kelley's comment reflected the nature of her individual friendship with Gay, but the fact that she directed her inquiry to him implied that she expected him to be thoroughly acquainted with domestic details.

While abolitionist women discussed the difficulties of managing the domestic sphere, much of the actual labor in their homes was performed by paid servants. Reforming women appreciated the domestic problems faced by members of their own coterie, but they were less sensitive to the difficulties facing the women who frequently labored in the homes of middle-class families. This raises the important question of whether abolitionist women's primary loyalty was to other women, or to their class. The relationship between gender and class is a contentious one, fraught with contradictions. Abolitionist women, like their feminist successors, were unable to resolve the tensions inherent in this question. Not only did abolitionists prize individualism as a goal, but their belief that many of America's social ills derived from the breakdown of individual social relations led them to emphasize the value of individual reform. On this issue, as on others, exceptionalist assumptions shaped the practice of abolitionism. Although abolitionists depicted Jacksonian America as "this wicked land," the common conviction that there was a greater degree of social mobility in the United States than elsewhere shielded many from a deeper analysis of the inequalities of their society. Convinced that all whites were essentially free, abolitionists often failed to recognize, or refused to accept, that nineteenth-century America did not offer equality of opportunity to all. Aside from slavery and marriage, they paid scant attention to the institutional foundations of inequality in the United States. Instead, they often regarded an individual's failure as a reflection of personal shortcomings or circumstances. Even in the postbellum period, most of the hierarchical assumptions that were evident in abolitionism remained in place. This goes part of the way toward explaining the general abolitionist reluctance to address questions such as labor reform, which demanded a more thorough critique of the nation's social and economic structures. Much has been written about the abolitionists' relative neglect of what proslavery writers, Northern labor spokespersons, and utopian communitarians alike denounced as the "slavery" of wage laborers. Despite Herbert Aptheker's claim that abolitionism was "afire with egalitarianism," the movement was bounded by notions of ethnic difference and social hierarchy.[41] An examination of abolitionists' domestic organization enhances our understanding of this issue: their hierarchical perspective was firmly grounded in their day-to-day practice of employing domestic helpers.

In the broadest sense, radical abolitionists and advocates of women's rights were well aware of the problems facing women in the domestic sphere. Conscious of the inequalities arising from the commodification of women, they believed that women's problems as unpaid laborers began with the assumptions underlying marriage. Proponents of women's rights, expanding on Angelina Grimké's assertion that "woman never was given to man," rejected the notion that woman's mission was to cater to men's desires. Challenging the prevailing view that women's primary role should be to serve others, and stressing the importance of individuality, they sought to overturn prevailing assumptions concerning women's function. Proclaiming a "new doctrine," Elizabeth Cady Stanton and Susan B. Anthony declared in 1856 that "woman, equally with man, was made for her own individual happiness." Objecting to the multifarious ways in which women's lives were shaped around caring for men, and referring to the objectification of women, they asserted that woman "is given in marriage like an article of merchandize." In an indication that abolitionist sensibilities extended beyond the movement to free the slaves, it was common for advocates of women's rights to compare the position of women and slaves. The Polish-born abolitionist and women's rights advocate Ernestine L. Rose used the slavery-marriage analogy to describe how men reduced women to property: "Woman is a slave, from the cradle to the grave. Father, guardian, husband—master still. One conveys her, like a piece of property, over to the other." Linking the plight of women with slaves was common among proponents of women's rights, and the commodification of women was apparent in the exploitation of their labor. Believing that woman "has been the great unpaid laborer of the world," women's rights advocates presented women's largely unacknowledged economic contribution in terms of the well-being of the American family. It was on this basis that some reformers sought to ameliorate domestic financial arrangements. Elizabeth Cady Stanton argued in 1851 that since "the economy of household" was "generally as much the source of family wealth as the labor and enterprise of man," wives should "have the same control over the joint earnings" as their husbands.[42]

Yet while radical abolitionists and advocates of women's rights incisively critiqued the exploitation of women by men, the exploitation of women by other women was less well understood. It is necessary to distinguish the abolitionists' high-sounding rhetoric—such as Lucy Stone's 1857 statement that her experiences gave her "a deeper detestation of" America's "social systems"—from their reformist priorities and practices. Abolitionist women's equivocal response to the exploitation of working-class women was one aspect of the broader abolitionist faith in the ability of individuals to defend their own interests. Long after the abolition of slavery, this issue remained important for those reformers interested in women's rights. Although L. Maria Child claimed in 1869 that she did not believe in "*classes,*" only in "*individuals,*" her earlier reference to "all classes of people" was a more accurate representation of abolitionists' views regarding social relations. Writing in 1877, Child lamented "an increasing tendency toward a strong *demarcation of classes*" in the United States, but she knew that tendency could not be wished away, and she was aware of social hierarchies. Indeed, in response to the bloody clashes between workers and troops that accompanied the Great Railway Strike of 1877, Child unambiguously expressed her fears—and her prejudices. Telling Sarah Shaw that she had long regarded the "vexed question of Labor and Capital" as a "volcano seething and rumbling beneath our feet," Child's "frightful sense of insecurity" was exacerbated by the presence of "an ignorant desperate rabble, ready for any work of destruction, whenever opportunity offers." Insisting there was "no excuse" for such behavior in the United States, because "every man who is unjustly" treated "has ample legal means of redress," her distaste for the cause of labor rested on the same exceptionalist principles that underpinned other aspects of nineteenth-century reformism. In a statement that echoed the slaveholders' earlier denunciations of the mischievous work of foreign abolitionist provocateurs, Child pointed out that "most of these reckless rioters have had their training under European governments." Characteristically, she saw the problem, and the solution, in terms of reforming individual social relationships—particularly marriage. Not only did people from different classes not "intermix socially," but they also did not marry outside their social class. Although she would tell Shaw three months later that "neither your daughter, nor mine, if I had one, could marry a day-laborer," Child bemoaned the fact that the "genteel classes do not intermarry with the middle classes," and "the middle classes do not intermarry with the laboring class."[43]

Investigating abolitionist women's attitude toward the women who labored in their homes reveals much about nineteenth-century reformism. While middle-class reforming women valued domestic organization, their ability to merge public and private duties was usually dependent upon the labor of working-class women. The abolitionists' use of domestic helpers conformed to a wider pattern of the nineteenth century, when many middle-class women employed household helpers. Indeed, domestic service was an important source of employment for working-class women, particularly migrant women, in the nineteenth century. So common was this practice that domestic advisers such as Catharine Beecher counseled their readers on the efficient management of servants, cooks, and other domestic helpers. Relations between female abolitionists and their domestic helpers did not always correspond to the pattern advocated by Beecher, but abolitionist women shared Beecher's utilitarian outlook.[44]

Not all abolitionists employed domestic helpers, and some occasionally expressed satisfaction in their ability to cope without such assistance.[45] Yet as their correspondence revealed, middle-class reformers generally used domestic helpers. Writing to Sallie Holley, Helen Garrison signified that she was accustomed to having household assistance, even if, as she emphasized, it was "only one domestic." Similarly, despite Angelina Grimké's 1838 claim that "we all like doing without a girl very much," she subsequently employed domestic helpers. Listing her domestic obligations, she noted in 1857 that she had "a young woman" who relieved her from "a great deal of care."[46] Sarah Grimké's 1868 remark that "the family goes smoothly under the supervision of a housekeeper & two good servants," indicated the level of domestic assistance in the household at that time. Elizabeth Cady Stanton also employed domestic helpers. Following the birth of her fifth child in 1852, she wrote to Elizabeth Smith Miller, providing an account of the experience. Stanton's long-serving domestic helper, Amelia Willard was absent, but since her "nurse" was a "good cook," and because her "new girl" was "tolerable," Stanton had "not had to go into the kitchen yet." Evidently, while Susan B. Anthony provided assistance, it was the ongoing labor of Willard and other domestic laborers that really ensured the proper functioning of Stanton's home. Willard's significance can be measured by the fact that she stayed in the Stanton household for thirty years, and was regarded as an important member of the Stanton family. But other abolitionists, like many of their nonreformist contemporaries, found it difficult to secure satisfactory domestic help.[47]

Abolitionists' statements concerning the wages paid to domestic helpers cast light upon the nature of the relationship between middle-class women and the women who labored in their homes. While specific details regarding the wages paid by women reformers to their domestic servants are predictably elusive, certain patterns can be deduced. Given that there was a shortage of domestic helpers in nineteenth-century America, the length of service of some domestic helpers to women reformers suggests that a reasonable wage was being paid. Conversely, as the proceedings of the second women's rights convention signified, reformers were concerned that the women who labored in their homes were poorly paid. At that convention, held in Rochester in 1848, Elizabeth Cady Stanton "offered a resolution respecting the wages of house servants." Arguing that the wages paid to house servants were "quite too low for the labor they performed," she "urged the necessity of reformers commencing at home." A resolution was passed calling on women "to do all in their power to raise" the wages of working-class women, "beginning with their own household servants." This suggests that there was a genuine desire to help domestic laborers gain better remuneration for their labors. Yet L. Maria Child's subsequent claim that the women of New England paid their domestic helpers "generous wages" must be placed in its proper context. In making that statement, Child's concern was not to enumerate the conditions or wages of working-class women. Rather, she was seeking to contrast the virtues of New England with the evils of the Southern states. Furthermore, women reformers' complaints concerning the difficulty of securing and maintaining suitable domestic helpers implies they made no special allowances for the labor performed by their household helpers.[48]

William L. Garrison's comments concerning domestic assistance within his and Helen's household reveal much about the hierarchical assumptions underlying his reformism. Besides indicating that he took an active interest in domestic affairs, and affirming the value abolitionists attributed to notions of efficiency, Garrison's statement regarding the likely impact of the impending departure of their "German girl" conveyed the level of domestic assistance within the household. Explaining that the girl had "no efficiency," and that she would not be missed, Garrison added that their "cook would rather have her go than stay." Garrison did not actively practice a radical reversal of gender roles in his own marriage, but his statement did suggest that male abolitionists played a part in making decisions within the domestic sphere. Helen Garrison also discussed domestic helpers. Reflecting upon the capabilities of her domestic helper, she revealed the combination of condescension and praise typical of abolitionist women: "I think for a girl so young she has excellent judgment and possesses many good qualities." Garrison thus indicated the qualities she deemed desirable in women, and by remarking that she hoped her domestic helper would "make a useful woman," she signified a utilitarian outlook toward the values of womanhood. Endorsing the principles of female influence within the home that were being popularized by domestic writers, Garrison subsequently criticized another domestic's disagreeable attitude, and expressed "dislike" for the "influence" that such a person would exercise within the home.[49]

Equally indicative of radical abolitionists' self-perception as a privileged group was Lucy Stone's statement concerning the apathy of many women to their plight. "One who is in total darkness," Stone told Elizabeth Cady Stanton in 1853, "finds his eyes pained by the sudden admission of bright light—and closes them. So too with many who are thinking of this woman question." Besides betraying the hierarchical assumptions characteristic of many nineteenth-century reformers, Stone's reference to women being in "blindness" was reminiscent of the way in which those who believed they were gifted with religious revelations looked down upon those who had not been so touched. Like Lucretia Mott's appeal to "those women whose 'eyes are blessed that they see,'" Stone's remark reaffirmed how female reformers perceived their mission in religious terms. The religious theme was also evident in the postbellum period, as evidenced by the emphasis L. Maria Child placed upon "educating 'the masses' to a higher stand point." Believing that certain cultures had grafted "superstition" onto Christianity, she reasoned that the "Italian peasant woman is doubtless comforted by praying to a doll dressed up in tinsel, which she worships as the 'Mother of God.'" Child's sense of superiority was obvious: "It is the business of *grown* people to lead children away from the necessity of toys." Evidently, Child's assumption that all women were endowed with a common feminine nature did not preclude her from speaking in hierarchical terms about women's abilities and conditions. Her statements concerning Asian women were similarly revealing. After comparing the "ignorant, stupid, listless women of the [Asian] harems," with the "intelligent and capable wives and mothers of New England and the West," Child noted in 1877 that the "women of Asia have the same human nature, and the same natural capabilities, that we have; but in those countries they spend their time playing with dolls and chattering with parrots." Yet while Child's comments were an apparent endorsement of those whose campaign to exclude Chinese immigrants from the United States bore fruit with the passage of the Chinese Exclusion Act in 1882, her belief in ethnic difference rested on the assumption that within all people there was the potential to become Americanized. Child argued that given the proper educational and domestic environment, all women were capable of achieving the levels that she and her coadjutors believed American women, especially those from New England, had reached. "If they had been brought to New England as soon as they were born," she wrote, "they would become clerks, authors, doctors, painters, and sculptors, and enlightened domestic companions for intelligent men, and sensible, judicious mothers of coming generations."[50] Child, and other female abolitionists, thus believed women could be elevated; their second-class status was the result of environmental, not biological factors.

Distinguishing between the institutional evil of slavery and the individual problems arising from middle- and upper-class women's relations with their working-class domestic helpers, the abolitionists' faith in the social mobility of the United States led them to argue that those women who worked as domestics could eventually reach a higher station in life. But at no stage did they envisage a social system in which all women performed the same tasks. L. Maria Child explained in 1835 that domestic helpers "only" differed from their employers "in having, for the time being, a different use to perform in society." Child employed the language of a sisterhood, but hierarchical assumptions shaped her reformism, as her 1840 statement that "her girl" needed "constant guidance" implied. Her earlier call to American women to "consider their domestics as sisters of the great human family" suggested that she was seriously concerned about the plight of domestic helpers, and indicated that sorority was a powerful connection between women of different social classes. Condemning the widespread habit of regarding domestics "as pieces of property," and advising women not to treat them as "pieces of machinery," she argued that if middle-class women treated their domestic helpers more equitably, there would be fewer problems between servants and mistresses.[51] Yet while Child was interested in the plight of domestic helpers, and although she denounced the commodification of women, there was no suggestion that middle-class women should manage without domestic helpers. The underlying system was not challenged.

Other abolitionist women held similar views. Abby Kelley, pitying a young Irish girl employed as a domestic, noted in 1845 with considerable condescension: "When I talked with her and tried to console her, and told her that we were trying to bring about a better state of things, a state in which she would be regarded as an equal, she wept like a child and seemed full of gratitude." Kelley was critical of the "slavish manner" in which many women treated their domestic helpers. But beyond glibly urging Stephen Foster to "be faithful in the families" with whom they stayed, "and bear testimony against this great wickedness" she offered no coherent prescription for the alleviation of their plight. Like some of her colleagues, Kelley found it difficult to secure satisfactory domestic help. Sallie Holley "truly" regretted Kelley's "disappointment about housekeepers," and noted in 1852 that she could "well imagine the trial" her friend was enduring "under the circumstances." Holley's statement pointed to both the strengths and weaknesses of abolitionist sorority: while there was a deep empathy for Kelley's plight, there was also an underlying assumption that Kelley should be able to find a suitable domestic helper. Moreover, even the fact that Kelley's colleagues felt it necessary to praise her specifically for her treatment of Irish girls staying in her home implied the gulf between women of different classes.[52]

Similarly revealing were Elizabeth Cady Stanton's postbellum comments regarding the treatment of domestic helpers. Emphasizing that the "freer the relations between human beings, the happier," Stanton asked her audience to consider "the servants in our households; with how much more care and consideration, we treat them, knowing that they can leave us when they choose, than we should if they were our slaves absolutely in our power, that if they left us, gospel and public sentiment would drive them back. The necessity on our part of greater kindness and generosity to *hold* them, while it ensures greater happiness to them, is the most desirable discipline for ourselves."[53] By assuming that her audience would have domestic helpers, Stanton betrayed much about the class composition of nineteenth-century reformism. But she also suggested that these women were conscious of the need to exercise their power judiciously. While reforming women perceived their power as differing from that of the slaveholders, the problem of retaining their domestic helpers, like the difficulties faced by the slaveholders in maintaining their slave laborers, required sound judgment. Abolitionist women had neither the desire nor the means to control their domestic helpers in the way that slave owners sought to control the slaves. Yet the awareness that power had to be exercised judiciously was a common theme.

Stanton had unwittingly suggested a parallel between slaveholders' relationships with their slaves, and female reformers' relationship to their domestic helpers. A further parallel can be drawn when we consider the question of race. White women reformers of the North certainly did not go so far as Southern slaveholders, who premised their racial ideology on the alleged differences between themselves and their black slaves. But abolitionists did distinguish themselves from their domestic helpers, in ethnic as well as class terms. Reformers who proudly traced their genealogical roots to the pre-Revolutionary period considered themselves superior to migrant women. This was sometimes evidenced by such innocuous statements as Wendell Phillips's 1852 comment to Helen Garrison: "we are succeeding in getting a *native* American at last." These views on ethnicity had echoes in other reformist movements. Despite protestations to the contrary, an almost nativist set of assumptions regarding the alleged superiority of American institutions remained evident in the postbellum women's rights movement. Demands for the vote for women were sometimes couched in terms of the need to use women's vote to protect the United States from the influence of what Henry Blackwell derided as "the ignorant minority one-half." This attitude put the abolitionists closer to the views expressed by the antiforeign and anti-Catholic Know Nothing Party than would be expected from reformers who proclaimed their determination to overcome racial prejudice. Even as he rejected the principles and tactics of the Know Nothing Party, Blackwell exhibited many of the essentially racist tenets of their platform. Depicting the Know Nothings as despotic and secretive, he nonetheless accepted the need to "remedy" the "ignorance, credulity, the superstition of the foreign elements."[54]

L. Maria Child's hierarchical assumptions were complicated and obscured by her financial situation. One consequence of David Lee Child's financial ineptitude was that his wife was compelled to borrow money from her better-off friends, especially Ellis Gray Loring. But even as she reluctantly accepted financial support, Maria noted the differences between herself and Loring's wife, Louisa, with whom she was also a close friend. Child sought to place her pecuniary difficulties in a positive light, and in affirming the values she had emphasized in her domestic tracts, rebuked the excesses of the wealthier elements of society. "I dare say I took more satisfaction in stitching away at midnight," she remarked in 1856, "than Louisa Loring does in saying 'Ellis, dear, I want $100 to pay a seamstress for sewing for Kansas.' "[55] This implied middle-class abolitionists' perception of the differences between themselves and the wealthier elements of society. Abolitionists perceived an even more distinct gulf between themselves and those of the lower classes.

The abolitionists' perception of class and social hierarchy was a complex mix; economic standing played a part, but notions of respectability and cultural awareness were also important. Indeed, abolitionists' attitudes reflected their sense of cultural superiority over those whom L. Maria Child denigrated as "the rude and illiterate." Child's views on marriages between individuals from different social classes have been noted, but underlying her concerns was a belief that marriages that lacked "congeniality of manners, habits, and tastes" were doomed to failure. This consciousness of social hierarchy frequently reflected differences in social behavior and circumstances. Ann Phillips's counsel to Wendell—"I think if you could get to some *new* Hotel you would not have so many beggars"—symbolized the widespread abolitionist distaste for, and disinterest in, many of the problems facing the lower classes. Angelina Grimké's 1853 statement regarding a married couple with whom she stayed also represented a common abolitionist perspective. Grimké considered her hosts to be "very kind pleasant people," but she also condescendingly asserted that they were "uncultivated." Writing in the postbellum period, Sarah Grimké was even more explicit. Referring to the child of one of their housekeepers, Grimké remarked that "children of that class are brought up in such uncleanly habits." More obliquely, Abby Kelley revealed her self-perception when she wrote to Stephen Foster in 1845: "I will tell you all confidentially that I am situated very uncomfortably . . . and so are all the others of *our class.*" Kelley's imprecision regarding the meaning of that phrase does not diminish the fundamental point that while abolitionists presented themselves as representatives of true American values, they *felt* different from many of their contemporaries.[56]

This cultural antagonism reflected racial, as well as hierarchical preconceptions. These preconceptions were shown in one of L. Maria Child's "Letters from New York," written while she was editing the *National Anti-Slavery Standard.* Child's interest in spirituality reflected her consciousness of social hierarchies, as her comments following an 1841 lecture by Julia Pell, an African American, suggest. Believing that her understanding and awareness of spiritual matters exceeded that of most Americans, her sense of social solidarity was bounded by her condescension toward those she considered more vulnerable to material, or "outward" attractions. After hearing Pell preach in New York, Child remarked on the power of her oratory. Yet Child's condescension was also evident: "if she [Pell] gained such power over my spirit, there is no cause to marvel at the tremendous excitement throughout an audience so ignorant, and so keenly susceptible to outward impressions."[57]

While there was no simple resolution to the tensions in Child's mind, other abolitionists shared her interest in the relationship between marriage and social hierarchy. Lucy Stone's views emerged in her correspondence with Henry Blackwell. Responding to Blackwell's plea not to judge other people's marriages by her own standards, but rather by the standards of the individuals directly involved, Stone revealed her sense of superiority over the mass of people around her. "Being what they are," she asserted in 1853, they "do not suffer" as "I should in their place." Furthermore, she reasoned, the "character of the parties, no doubt, has much to do with that of the rest of the relation, but the idea of marriage as held by the mass of people is a false one." Consequently, she contended, "they do not rise higher than their own idea." Blackwell's self-perception resembled that of his future wife. Discussing the possibility of having children, Blackwell outlined the criteria he would set for his children, and suggested something of his own self perception. "I am too proud & too *aristocratic,*" he told Stone, "to be willing to have any but fine, noble children." On the surface, the language of that self-perception sat uncomfortably alongside the more general abolitionist critique of Old World class structures. But while Blackwell was born in England, his use of the term "aristocratic" was more than a reflection of the class ideology of the society that had borne him. Instead, his hierarchical perspective signified that even the most determined critics of inherited aristocracies presupposed the existence of a "natural" aristocracy, based on merit and achievement. The hierarchical values underpinning Blackwell's statement were of continuing significance in American reformism. Describing the events at an 1869 Woman's Suffrage Convention in Newburyport,

William L. Garrison remarked that many of the women present represented "some of the most respectable families of the town." Garrison's statement may have been euphemistic, but the underlying premise was again clear: public reformism was a respectable activity.[58]

This question of social refinement particularly interested L. Maria Child. She inferred that, at least in part, gender accounted for the different levels of refinement and civilization in society. Explaining in 1846 why she was living apart from her husband, Child noted that whereas David was "living in the woods, with animals and coarse men," she was "growing more refined and poetic every day, under the influences of music, pictures, and mystical contemplation." Yet Child did not consider all men unrefined; part of the attraction she felt for the visiting Norwegian violinist, Ole Bull, was his ability to open "unknown depths" in her soul. This implied that radical abolitionists' hierarchical perspective was evident in their understanding of gender differences. Child's sense of intellectual superiority shaped her opinion of men, and transcended hierarchies of political achievement. Although she praised Abraham Lincoln as "an honest man," who "conscientiously" hated slavery, she also regarded him as "a man of slow mind, apparently incapable of large comprehensive views." Commenting on the nature of women's friendships, and attesting to the important role played by her female friends, Child noted that while "as a general rule" friendships between men were more enduring than those between women, her own female friends "had been more stead-fast" than her "gentlemen friends." Child's belief that her social circle was comprised of intelligent and well-informed women was evident when she explained that she and her close female friends "have always talked about books we have read, the scientific discoveries we have heard of, and the state of public affairs." But in clarifying why she considered it easier for men to establish longer-standing friendships, Child denounced the ways by which society limited the range of options available to women. Arguing that "frivolous people will form frivolous friendships," and that there "are *more* frivolous women than there are frivolous men," she reasoned that such a state of affairs was neither natural nor inevitable. Rather, since society excluded women from "business, politics, art and literature," they were unable to "talk on sensible subjects." Men, however, given "more solid and enduring subjects of interest in common," were able to maintain different relationships than those of women. Other abolitionists concurred with Child. Henry Blackwell, keenly interested in the issue of women's rights, pointed out that women were "so fettered & dwarfed intellectually" that they were "compelled to live too exclusively in the region of sentiment & of affection at present."[59] These statements suggest that women had not yet formed a separate public sphere. But radical abolitionists believed that their efforts to encourage women to operate beyond the domestic circle—complementing their efforts to promote women's position within the home—would also benefit men. In addition to improving the world, the elevation of women would lead to more satisfying marriages, and would also enable them to construct sororal relationships around subjects considered more edifying.

L. Maria Child was deeply concerned with this issue. Having distinguished between the relationships she established with men, and those she forged with women, Child attested to the strength of her friendships with men. In so doing, she offered an apparently contradictory version of the relative importance of male and female friendships in her own life. Although she acknowledged that she owed "much to the elevating influence of several women," she claimed that her "best friendships have generally been with men." During a period of particular personal dissatisfaction, Child commented that in addition to the "star of domestic affection," she had been immensely strengthened by "the star of friendship, with healing in its rays." Specifically, she expressed gratitude to Francis George Shaw, as well as Louisa and Ellis Gray Loring, for their "continued sympathy." In understanding why Child placed such a high value on her relationships with male friends, it is helpful to recall the hierarchical assumptions evident in her pronouncements on women's relationships, wherein she revealed that she considered herself superior to most women. Accordingly, since she believed she was able to understand and discuss subjects that were generally considered to be "masculine" rather than "feminine," it was perhaps inevitable that she would establish meaningful relationships with men. As always, however, there were tensions in Child's mind; she not only noted, apparently with some regret, that "the woman greatly predominates in me," but further asserted, "I cannot live without being loved."[60]

Abolitionist sorority revealed much about nineteenth-century reformism. Besides indicating the distinctiveness of women's experiences, abolitionist sorority attested to the pressures inherent in trying to resolve the frequently competing demands of domestic and public reform. Abolitionist sorority thus signified the tensions between public and private life, and between individualism and responsibility to collective social units such as the family. Similarly, although the separate spheres of the antebellum period were oppressive, they did leave room for women to form friendships, and to develop a women's culture that was both an expression of, and a means of countering, their subordinate status. Consequently, while abolitionist sorority was a manifestation of women's public as well as private grievances, some women were empowered by sororal practices and sentiments. Ultimately, however, abolitionist sorority was notable not just for its strengths, but also for its limitations, which were suggestive of the wider limitations of nineteenth-century reform, especially in terms of race, ethnicity, and class. There were other boundaries to abolitionist sorority, and the friendships and working relationships between antislavery men and women suggest the limits of the separate spheres ideology. Abolitionist sorority was considered an adjunct of marriage. Indeed, the loneliness felt by abolitionist women, typified by Lucretia Mott's reference to "the void occasioned by the departure of our husbands," attested to the significance they attached to their marriages. A letter from Helen Garrison to Ann Phillips, written during one of William L. Garrison's absences, captured the depth as well as the limits of abolitionist sorority. Connected by their husbands' prominence in the abolitionist movement, and accustomed to being left at home, there was undoubtedly a bonding between the two women. Yet while Helen emphasized that Ann was "kind and sympathetic," her loneliness was evident: "I feel lonely and forlorn without my darling. For who else is there that can supply his place[?] Not one."[61] Chapter 6 examines intimacy between abolitionist couples, and the strength of their marital bonds. But before exploring specific aspects of those marriages, it is necessary to turn to the male abolitionists, and analyze their construction of masculinity, and its role in both the private and public spheres.

FIVE

"A True Manly" Life:

Abolitionist Men at Home and Beyond

WHILE STUDIES OF ABOLITIONISM have traditionally focused on the activities of its male participants, there have been few attempts to assess the specific meanings that abolitionists ascribed to masculinity.[1] This omission is one aspect of the larger historiographical neglect of what E. Anthony Rotundo has labeled "the cultural invention called *manhood.*" Radical abolitionists shared antebellum moral reformers' conviction that "men stood in the way of virtue," but they did not believe men were beyond redemption. Among the competing versions of masculinity evolving in Jacksonian America, Garrisonian abolitionists renounced power and domination, favoring instead intimacy and cooperation. Accordingly, although radical abolitionist men were concerned with traditional codes of masculine behavior such as bravery and cowardice, as Angelina Grimké's lament that "some of the noblest virtues are too generally deemed *unmanly*" implied, there was a more significant side to abolitionist masculinity, one that defined men's role in terms of their domestic and affectionate qualities, and that attributed an important role for men in the private sphere.[2] Representing and shaping a gender ideal that historians have labeled the "Christian Gentlemen," and anticipating the pattern of "masculine domesticity" recently identified by Margaret Marsh, radical reformers believed there were positive traits to masculinity.[3] The delegates at the 1870 women's rights convention detailed these qualities. Praising James Mott's role at the first women's rights convention, they declared he was "a man in whose pure soul there was no guile, no shadow of fear, no faltering or failure of principle; truthful, just, generous and loving."[4]

Radical abolitionists' belief that a "true manly life" was compatible with reformism held implications for reform in both public and private life; just as women's abolitionism casts light upon the nineteenth-century meanings of "private" and "public," abolitionists' versions of masculinity signify the intersections between women's and men's worlds.[5] As the next chapter explains, radical abolitionist men devoted considerable attention to establishing and maintaining intimacy with their wives. But as this chapter reveals, by maintaining social and working relationships with female as well as male coadjutors, they also challenged the division of the sexes that was prescribed by gender spheres ideology. By explicitly supporting the women's rights movement, some abolitionist men carried these principles into their public reformism, further exasperating their opponents. Not all abolitionist men embraced the "feminine" strategy of Garrisonian moral suasionism, and many antislavery activists did not abjure the masculine world of antebellum party politics. During the 1850s, moreover, radical abolitionists' commitment to nonviolence was tested by the increasingly violent struggle over slavery. The shifts in antislavery tactics that occurred during the period preceding the Civil War, and abolitionist men's personal confrontations with the forces of slavery, constituted a tentative "masculinization" of abolitionism. Because they belonged to the more radical strand of abolitionism, the abolitionist men analyzed herein represent the possibilities—and boundaries—within antislavery.[6] And all the while, male abolitionists' construction of masculinity was underscored by a thorough revulsion at the perversion of masculine powers and values in the South: if, as radical abolitionists believed, existing marital practices had parallels with slavery, abolitionist men were determined not to be viewed as analogues of slaveholders.

Abolitionist men confronted the tensions of resolving their emphasis on individualism—so important to abolitionism, and to the notion of individualistic masculinity—with their determination to be considerate and loving companions. Male abolitionists also faced the popular perception, implicit in many nineteenth-century stereotypes of masculinity, that marriage was a form of captivity and restraint. The most famous abolitionist voiced these concerns during the 1840s. Confiding to fellow reformer Samuel J. May that he found his "family to be a considerable drawback" on his "public usefulness," William L. Garrison betrayed a tension between public and private obligations. Yet Garrison's commitment to his family was deeply felt. Besides reassuring Helen that he took very seriously "the sacred claims which are binding upon me as a husband and a father," he signaled the extent to which abolitionist men were judged in the context of their affectionate qualities. With reference to Wendell Phillips, Garrison told Ann Phillips in 1848 that "If any one thing has served to exalt him in my eyes more than any other, it is the rare consecration of himself to you, through the years of your great debility and sad affliction." Garrison thus foreshadowed L. Maria Child's 1877 assertion that "the most perfect man" was one who was "affectionate as well as intellectual." Insisting that "God intended a participation of the masculine and feminine element in every relation and every duty of life," and indicating that the antebellum concerns of radical abolitionists continued to influence postbellum reform, Child remarked on the importance of establishing the correct balance between the sexes. "I think every individual, and every society," she wrote, "is perfect just in proportion to the combination, and cooperation, of masculine and feminine elements in character."[7] Child's remarks hinted at an underlying tension within radical abolitionists' conception of gender relations. Abolitionists such as Child knew that the belief that women were different from men led in practice to the subordination of women. But, demonstrating that abolitionists could not entirely escape the nineteenth-century habit of conceiving gender relations in terms of differences and opposites, Child also spoke in terms of underlying differences between men and women.

Many of the issues faced by male abolitionists paralleled those encountered by other middle-class men. Stephanie Coontz's contention that it is possible to see "the revival movement of the 1830s and the emergence of new associations aimed at individual transformations" as answering the concerns of middle-class men helps to explain abolitionist interpretations of masculinity. These associations and movements, including antislavery, provided a context for the discussion of questions pertaining to the redefinition of masculine roles and tasks—questions especially significant for abolitionists due to the relationship between slavery and the geographical expansion of the United States. Indeed, the frontier was not only gendered in such a way that emphasized masculine values and power; it was also highly politicized, since the geographical expansion of antebellum America was linked closely to the survival of the very institution abolitionists sought to destroy.[8]

The frontier, as both a concept and as a reality, played a part in shaping abolitionists' constructions of masculinity. One nineteenth-century version of masculinity emphasized the image of the independent man, who, unrestrained by the confines of "civilized" society, set out alone to forge a path that would ultimately benefit other members of society. In an oblique way radical abolitionism amounted to a quest for similar ideals. Wendell Phillips remarked that in alerting others to their abolitionist duty, William L. Garrison had allowed them to be "redeemed into full manhood." As Robert Abzug has noted of Theodore Weld, "he pursued manhood and a sense of self through the rebellious calling of abolitionism." This aspect of abolitionism mirrored transcendentalism. Just as Ralph Waldo Emerson urged resistance to the pressures evident in "communities of opinion," abolitionist men knew their reformism entailed a certain isolation from society.[9] The antislavery community provided a supportive network for abolitionists, but abolitionism remained an isolating and individualistic activity. Moreover, abolitionists' belief that they were traveling along paths hitherto unexplored was analogous to those explorers who placed their determination to fulfill what they considered their individual destiny above their social connections. Where explorers journeyed along uncharted physical paths, radical abolitionists were investigating unexplored social possibilities.

Some abolitionist men experienced a tension between a determination to present masculinity as a positive, civilizing force, and a desire to abstain from many of the duties associated with "civilized" life. Underpinning this tension was a conviction that Southern men, especially slaveholders, represented the antithesis of refined culture and civilization. Mortimer Thomson, the author of an 1859 antislavery tract, described the men present at a slave auction in typically hierarchical terms: "The buyers were generally of a rough breed, slangy, profane and bearish, being for the most part from the black river and swamp plantations, where the elegancies of polite life are not, perhaps, developed to their fullest extent." Yet certain abolitionist men apparently spurned aspects of civilized society. Theodore Weld's romanticized description of himself as a "*Backwoodsman untamed,*" whose "bearish proportions" had "never been licked into *City shape,*" was in part nothing more than an excuse to avoid many of the polite obligations associated with abolitionism. But his use of the word "bearish" is interesting given Thomson's later use of the same term to describe slave buyers. Always uncomfortable at antislavery conventions, Weld's depiction of himself as "too uncultivated and shaggy for 'Boston notions'" also reflected his self-image as a rural, independent individual, conforming to a common nineteenth-century masculine tradition. Weld's statement is open to a range of interpretations. Given the perceived relationship between the "masculine" experience in the wilderness or on the frontier, and "feminine" civilization, his language suggested a rejection of what was widely portrayed as the civilizing influence of women. This attitude resembled the values presented by the authors of the Davy Crockett almanacs, published widely after the mid-1830s. It was on the frontier that the alleged contrast between the masculine characteristics of violence and independence, and the feminine traits of "civilization" and peaceful persuasion was most clearly defined. Indeed, the popular imagery of what L. Maria Child described as "the untrammelled West" contributed significantly to the demarcation of gender roles.[10] Yet taking into account that the frontier ideology included the idea of carrying Christian "civilization" to an untamed wilderness, Weld was also implying an extension of the reformers' mission.

Weld's self-image did not preclude him from forming a passionate and enduring relationship with Angelina Grimké, nor from embracing what was for the time an egalitarian attitude toward women. Rather than perceiving his love for Angelina as an impediment to his individualistic masculinity, Weld presented his feelings for Grimké as the pinnacle of his own self-development. Referring to traits widely regarded as "masculine," he linked his love for Grimké to his commitment to reformism: "Dearest, at one thing I marvel. It is that when this yearning love and pining of spirit for you pervades me *most*—even when the *deepest* tide of tenderness swells over me—instead of its having a tendency to *weaken* and *effeminate* my character, it seems to wake up within me new strength and to summon me to higher daring and more immoveable endurance. Strange as it may seem, I have never so panted for the thickest of the conflict as within the last few weeks. I feel that my love for you Angelina girds me to *do* more, to *suffer* more, and to *dare* more than I was ever girded for before."[11]

Henry Blackwell and Lucy Stone confronted the issue of a masculine environment in specific geographical terms. Prior to their marriage they discussed where they would reside after their wedding. With business interests in the West, Blackwell naturally saw advantages there. Stone, at home among the reforming communities of the Eastern cities, preferred to live in the East. On this issue, Blackwell and Stone contradicted a pattern described by E. Anthony Rotundo, who has noted that nineteenth-century men generally made the decisions regarding their families' place of residence. Blackwell, keen to accede to Stone's wishes, conceded ground during the course of their courtship. Initially agreeing to let Stone select their place of residence, he revealed a dislike of "Western men." Determined not to resemble such men, Blackwell thought that while the West was "grand in possibility & in the future," it was "mean in its actuality & in its Present." Following their wedding, however, Blackwell spoke with considerably more affection of Western men, whom he implied were more liberal and broad-minded than their Eastern counterparts. Embracing a more assertive stance regarding their place of residence, he also implicitly disparaged what he considered the acquisitive values of Easterners. "I tell you, dear Lucy," he wrote in January 1856, "we must make our home in some community of simple, earnest, alive people, who are not absorbed in money-making." Yet Blackwell's determination to live in the West was short-lived. Four months later, he agreed that as "a *permanent* residence," the East was "far preferable," and their movements reflected that conclusion. Stone and Blackwell initially resided in Cincinnati, but after spending three months surveying and certifying the six thousand acres of land they owned in Wisconsin, they moved East. The geographical issues raised by Blackwell and Stone were also evident in the practice of Garrisonian abolitionism; while Blackwell did not specify whether his comments concerning Western men were made in specific reference to Western antislavery men, or Western men in general, Abby Kelley noted in 1853 that the "greatest fear" she held "for the West" was "its dreadful tendency to politics." It was partly for that reason that Kelley spent time in the West, spreading the Garrisonian message.[12]

Considerable historiographical attention has been directed toward relationships between abolitionist women. Less attention has been paid to relationships between abolitionist men, which reveal much about the significance they attached to ideals of intimacy and love. Lawrence Friedman has suggested that many male abolitionists were cautious about forming relationships with women, and that some actually feared the prospect of marriage. Friedman's points were well made, but other aspects of abolitionist men's perceptions and construction of gender relations warrant investigation. While friendships between abolitionist men denote the limitations of fraternity, as they placed great emphasis on their relationships with women, abolitionist men did establish important friendships with their male coworkers. On the most fundamental level, the oft-repeated phrase "Am I Not a Man and a Brother?" like the abolitionists' frequent references to each other as "brother," evinced their efforts to infuse their public reformism with fraternal sentiments.[13] Not only was there intimacy and bonding between particular abolitionist men; there is also evidence of "romantic friendship," which mirrored a wider pattern amongst middle-class males.[14] An obvious example was the relationship between Theodore Weld and the iconoclastic British abolitionist, Charles Stuart.

The correspondence between Weld and Stuart illustrates the depth of their friendship. Affectionately describing Weld as "my Theodore," Stuart's references to his American friend as the "dearly beloved of my soul," and "long the most intimate brother of my heart" resembled the language used in correspondence between nineteenth-century women. Stuart, believing his friendship with Weld was inspired by and infused with heavenly sanction, described their relationship similarly to the way many abolitionists viewed their marriages. "I am persuaded that our love," wrote Stuart in 1846, "apart from all other agreement and disagreement, is holy & eternal, in its measure, like Him, from whom it flows."[15] A lack of surviving correspondence from Weld to Stuart renders the task of ascertaining the American abolitionist's feelings toward his eccentric friend more difficult. Fortunately, Stuart's impact on Weld emerged in the latter's correspondence with other abolitionists, particularly Angelina Grimké. As he revealed to Grimké in 1837, Weld's undisguised adoration of Stuart, couched in unambiguously religious tones, merged with an acknowledgment of the British reformer's influence:

> How I mourn that you could not have known CHARLES STUART. I can hardly trust myself to speak or write of him: so is my whole being seized

> with love and admiration of his most unearthly character that whatever I say of him seems to others like the extravagance of *enthusiasm.* I feel humbled and shrink with a sense of conscious and sometimes almost overpowering unworthiness when I look upward to the pure heights of his heavenly character. *I have never known such a character!* Like the eagle he flies alone! His absence almost seems like the subtraction of a portion of my being; and I daily render thanks to my Lord and master and "elder brother" that he has stooped so low as to take a man of earth and cloathe him so richly with the beauty and purity and majesty of his own spirit, making such a reflection of the light of His own blessed countenance as to lure upward to the source of all overcoming loveliness and glory the low and earthly *fellow* worms that crawl and grovel so far below him.[16]

Such effusive assertions of intimacy between men could be construed as evidence of a homosexual content to the Weld-Stuart relationship. But despite the numerous expressions of love between the two men there is little to infer that the feelings between them were homosexual. Moreover, Donald Yacovone's point that "preoccupation with elemental sex says more about the twentieth century than about the nineteenth," reinforces Anthony Barker's suggestion that Stuart's "emotion-charged relationship with Weld was the outlet for a repressed heterosexuality." Alongside the paternalistic nature of their relationship (typified by Weld's comment that "Charles has for me more than a fathers [*sic*] affection for his first born") Weld's gratitude to Stuart paralleled that of some younger female abolitionists to their elder colleagues. "While yet a boy," he told Angelina Grimké in 1837, "I became acquainted with him, and from that time till now our intimacy has been that of an *indivisible existence.*" For her part, Grimké drew a specific comparison between her friendship with Jane Smith, and Weld's relationship with Stuart. Grateful to her "Father in Heaven" for giving her "*such* a FRIEND," Grimké praised Smith as "*my* Charles Stuart."[17]

Historians have recognized the depth of the friendship betwen Weld and Stuart.[18] Yet there was another aspect to the friendship, one that not only attested to the importance of their relationships with women, but that also revealed that the characteristics valued in marriage were also relevant to their fraternal friendships. Besides emphasizing that the strength and ardor of their respective relationships with Stuart and Smith were not impeded by differences of opinion, Weld and Grimké urged each other to meet and converse with Stuart and Smith. This willingness to discuss the depth of their respective friendships with Stuart and Smith was suggestive of the intimacy between Grimké and her future husband. Keeping in mind their determination to preserve their individuality within marriage, Weld and Grimké's enthusiastic statements about Stuart and Smith might have reflected attempts to prove to each other that they would maintain such friendships, and that they would not become solely reliant on the marriage relationship. Weld perceived his concurrent love for Stuart and Grimké as complementary associations, equally necessary and important. Supporting this interpretation was his invitation to Stuart, presumably made in conjunction with the Grimké sisters, to live with them.[19] As Angelina's sister made her home in the Weld-Grimké household, so Theodore hoped his "brother" could also be a member of their reforming family.

As important as the Weld-Stuart relationship was, however, differences between the two men eventually disrupted their friendship. That discord conformed to a pattern described by E. Anthony Rotundo, who has noted that "young men" often "believed that intimate male attachment was a passing fancy." Equally significantly, while Weld was emphatic in his expressions of love for Stuart, he explicitly differentiated between the emotions aroused by his relationship with Angelina Grimké, and those provided by Stuart. "Many a time," he told Grimké in 1838, "I have wept on his neck from *very love to him* and yet at those very times I have felt in my inmost soul that there remained other intense necessities of my compound *human* nature untouched by the ministrations of his love and communion and panting for *congenial* affiliation. Those necessities *you alone* have reached and filled."[20]

Stuart and Weld were not the only abolitionist men to forge an intimate friendship. Again, however, the complementary nature of male and female friendships within the abolitionist movement was apparent. These friendships must always be seen in the context of the separate spheres ideology. Writing the year after William L. Garrison began publishing the *Liberator,* the British writer Fanny Trollope opined that "with the exception of dancing," the "enjoyments of the men are found in the absence of women." Radical abolitionism, as a social as well as a reform movement, represented a challenge to that division of the sexes. This challenge was evident within and outside marriage. Writing to his future wife in April 1834, Garrison signaled the priority he placed upon his marriage: "Your solitary love for me is dearer than the multitudinous friendships of all my admirers. Not that I undervalue those friendships, for they are very precious; but your love is a part of my being, and deprived of it I should droop and sicken." Garrison spoke proudly of his love for his fellow abolitionist men, and there were close male friendships within other antislavery circles.[21] But abolitionist men also sought to achieve intimacy, in a nonsexual sense, with their female coadjutors. At the same time as Garrison was describing the New Hampshire abolitionist Nathaniel Peabody Rogers as his "increasingly beloved friend," he enjoyed an intimate friendship with Maria Weston Chapman and other female members of the social network described by Lawrence Friedman as the "Boston Clique." Writing to Chapman in 1848, Garrison suggested the depth of his feelings for his coadjutor. "How immensely indebted am I to you," he wrote, "for counsel, encouragement, commendation, and support!" In fighting for the abolitionist cause, he noted, "we have seen eye to eye, and stood side by side. May we continue to do so while we both have breath." Maria Weston Chapman was a vigorous participant in the public fight against slavery, but Garrison also felt intimacy for women who were unable to violate gender prescriptions. Expressing particular sympathy for Ann Phillips, Garrison not only remarked that "the first wish of his heart" would be to see her restored to health, but also sent several New Year's messages to that effect.[22]

This pattern of intimacy was evident in official abolitionist matters. Institutional fraternity within antislavery societies did not replicate that which evolved in many other nineteenth-century men's organizations. Encompassing both social and business activities, this male world emphasized the exclusion of women, and the construction of a specifically male space.[23] Garrisonian abolitionism, as an institutional activity, reflected individual abolitionists' efforts to forge closer relationships between the sexes. David Lee Child demonstrated this process. Writing in his capacity as an employee of the AASS, Child's tactical differences with Maria Weston Chapman did not prevent him from addressing her as "my dear friend." Nor did he suggest that he found it demeaning to report to a woman. As the Washington, D.C., agent of the AASS, Child was accountable to Chapman, and while they had their share of disagreements over antislavery tactics, there is nothing to indicate that these stemmed from Child's being accountable to a woman.[24]

There were always differences of opinion among radical abolitionists, and true to their pronouncements in favor of individual freedom, an admirable degree of tolerance was shown to divergent points of view. Some differences, however, were apparently irreconcilable. These differences paralleled the declining significance of the Weld-Stuart friendship. Nathaniel Rogers was a widely respected member of the New England abolitionist community. But his radical views on the issue of free speech eventually alienated even his closest friends, and by 1844 he was effectively expelled from the circle of Boston abolitionists. Members of the Boston Clique may have hoped that their friendships with Rogers could continue undisturbed. Yet the necessity of sacrificing their individual desires for the good of the antislavery organization meant that their relationships with Rogers broke down. The Rogers episode was significant not just for the breakdown of those friendships, but also for affirming that intimate relationships between male abolitionists were considered less important than the demands of the wider abolitionist "family."[25]

By striving to strengthen the bonds of intimacy between women and men, radical abolitionist men were moving in largely uncharted waters. Unlike women, for whom countless books and articles provided advice concerning the roles of wife and mother, expectations of masculine behavior within the family were often unstated. Consequently, while there were guidelines prescribing men's behavior in the nineteenth century, and although particular masculine traits were deemed essential if a marriage was to succeed, there was much less public discussion regarding the correct means of fulfilling masculine functions. Radical abolitionists valued such widely lauded virtues as sobriety, and they sought a true understanding of their prospective wives. But their interest in women's condition rendered them atypical.[26]

Some abolitionist men believed they were playing a part in liberating their fiancées and wives from the restrictions of their families of origin. Ironically, while Henry Stanton's attitudes and behavior played a role in alerting his wife to the question of women's rights, before his marriage he implicitly portrayed himself as a factor in her emancipation from her family of origin. Prior to his departure for London in 1840, Stanton wrote to Amos Phelps: "We thought of putting off the whole affair till my return—but, as the time draws near for my departure, she will not consent to be left behind in the hands of her opposing friends." Yet Stanton's language betrayed another perception of the nature of the marital relationship. His April 1840 comment to Gerrit Smith that Elizabeth Cady might be "*in chains*" by the time of their next visit was undoubtedly ironical, but it portended Elizabeth's eventual perception of herself, and other women, within marriage. Although Stanton was pleased that he and Elizabeth were sailing together to England, he also betrayed the contradictions in his perception of the marital relationship. His depiction of Elizabeth as "my newly acquired treasure" (notwithstanding his disclaimer that he used such terms "not because Elizabeth is *mine*") was more than a hint of his excitement upon marriage. Even though he was ten years her senior, his subsequent reference to his wife as "my dearest daughter" was an inadvertent admission of the extent to which he considered himself to be the senior member of the family.[27] Henry Stanton was sincerely devoted to his family, yet his behavior and attitude contributed significantly to the evolution of his wife's feminist consciousness.

Peter Stearns has identified among some modern men "an almost masochistic sense of guilt about the real or imagined woes of women, a desire to be in the forefront of the fray against 'maleness.'"[28] Certain abolitionist men, perhaps, were representative of that phenomenon, although their motivations and their experiences were more complex than Stearns suggested. Stephen Foster was one of these men. At first glance, Foster's language resembled that used by William L. Garrison and Henry Stanton. But a closer analysis reveals that from the outset of his friendship with Abby Kelley, Foster was sensitive to her determination to retain her independence. Kelley and Foster were wrong to assume that Angelina Grimké's withdrawal from public reformism resulted solely from her marriage to Theodore Weld. But their reading of the Weld-Grimké relationship, and their understanding of freedom and slavery, shaped their own marriage. Above all, beyond their determination to preserve their individuality, Kelley and Foster were conscious that marriage frequently resulted in women being reduced to a form of domestic bondage. Accordingly, Foster's self-mocking assertion to Kelley that "I now feel that you are indeed my *own,*" was not an indication that he regarded her as a chattel. The lengths he went to discuss the issue signified his concern for Kelley's individuality. Ironically appropriating the language of public abolitionism, Foster revealed his preoccupation with the marriage relationship, and affirmed his anxieties concerning husbands' rights over their wives: "now you are my *own.* Perhaps you do not like this idea of being so thoroughly possessed by another, even though he be your own S.S. [Foster], but I cannot help it. I have made good my title to you & now I shall hold you *fast.* I have come honestly & honorably by you, & now, depend upon it, I shall keep you in my strong arms; so you may resign all hope of ever effecting an escape. . . . I shall henceforth claim & hold you as my *own property*. . . . I shall now *tyrannize* over you to my heart's content, so you may prepare for it, & make a virtue of submission, if you please. 'Wives submit yourselves unto your own husbands,' you will bear in mind is the command."[29]

Eleven years later, Henry Blackwell demonstrated similar concerns. Believing that marriage should allow Lucy Stone to retain her individuality, and maintain her public activism, his language reaffirmed how abolitionist men's concerns over slavery affected their personal lives. Having reassured Stone in May 1854 of his "determination that my love shall *never fetter you* one iota," Blackwell counseled Stone that a refusal to consider marriage, on account of the existing marriage laws, would be to "subject oneself to a more abject slavery than ever actually existed." Blackwell's wooing of Stone was a determined effort to win her heart. Yet just as Stephen Foster had criticized the "wily arts of courtship" as "another name for deception and fraud," Blackwell was emphatic in his resolution not to mislead Stone. Declaring that he would "consider it a *crime*" on his part if he succeeded "in *mesmerizing*" Stone, Blackwell's self-conscious correspondence during the period prior to their marriage revealed his concern that she retain her individuality.[30] Wendell Phillips, too, was determined to respect his wife's wishes. Following his ironic declaration that he was "the HEAD of the family," his 1873 remark that "nothing pains me so much" as Ann's disapproval (made after three and a half decades of marriage) was revealing of his broader attitude toward women.[31]

Abolitionist men such as Phillips, Blackwell, and Foster were deeply concerned with domestic life. Suggestive of the importance they attached to the domestic sphere was their praise of women who effectively managed their homes and families. Equally telling was their abiding interest in home life. These sentiments, typified by William L. Garrison's postbellum comment that "every home incident is of interest to me," were keenly felt during absences from home. Garrison was not the only man whose abolitionism took him away from home and family. Theodore Weld emerged from "retirement" in 1841 to work for the AASS, but despite the tensions between his commitment to public abolitionism, and his inability to fulfill the obligations of home life, his marriage to Angelina Grimké "remained his foremost commitment in life."[32]

This commitment was evident in abolitionist men's consciousness of their paternal responsibilities. In some cases, such as William L. Garrison, whose drunkard father had abandoned his family when Garrison was three years old, abolitionist men's awareness of paternal responsibilities reflected a determination not to replicate the errors of their own fathers.[33] All antislavery men expressed love and attachment to their children, and some provided more than rhetorical and emotional support to the parenting process. One of the most dramatic examples of an abolitionist man assuming an important role in parenting was in the marriage of Abby Kelley and Stephen Foster. Foster remained at home and assumed much of the responsibility for raising Paulina (Alla), thereby enabling Kelley to resume her public abolitionism. Foster provided clues to his perception of his parental obligations, and to the effect of those responsibilities on his abolitionism. Responding to Abby's request that he join her at a forthcoming antislavery convention, Stephen insisted in 1851 that he was "very unwilling" to leave Alla "for so long a period." "She is now at an age," he sternly reminded Abby, when "she needs a parent's care." These concerns were thrown into sharp relief when children fell victim to illness. Like their female companions, abolitionist men empathized with the difficulties caused by sickly children. When Alla was ill, Foster was frequently the one who assumed the role of carer. There were occasions when Foster's commitment to Alla compelled him to abstain from public reform. Apologizing that he was unable to help raise money for the antislavery cause, Foster explained to his abolitionist colleague Lysander Spooner in 1859 that he was "closely confined at home by" Alla's "illness." Alla was so dependent on him, he noted, that he was unwilling to leave her "even for a single day," unless it was absolutely necessary.[34] Foster and Kelley concurred with domestic writers that parenting was an important responsibility. But by modifying the prescribed gender role of feminine nurturance and masculine engagement in the public sphere, they were disproving a central assumption of domestic ideology. Male abolitionists' affirmations of love for their children contrasted with their belief that slaveholders abused their paternal responsibilities. Again, private life merged with the imperatives of public reform. Radical abolitionists believed that the ideology and practice of Southern fatherhood was not only a pillar of the racism underpinning slavery, but also a rationale for the continuing oppression of women.

The willingness of some abolitionist men to adopt roles widely designated as women's responsibility did not mean they regarded their masculinity as unimportant. On this question, there were differences, as well as similarities between African American abolitionists and their white counterparts. Lucretia Mott's postbellum reference to the importance of securing "manhood" for the "long bound and enslaved" revealed that white abolitionists acknowledged the damage inflicted on the self-image of male slaves. It was, however, African American men who most clearly understood the diminution of their masculinity, and who most explicitly linked their masculine identity to their quest for freedom. The most notorious example of a black abolitionist linking the quest for freedom to masculine traits was David Walker's 1829 *Appeal,* wherein he called African Americans to action by referring specifically to their masculine traits. Answering his own question "Are we Men!!" in the negative, he declared that "if we ever become men we must assert ourselves to the full." Walker's pamphlet earned him a reputation for extremism, but other black abolitionists also expressed concern with masculine traits. Tracing the textual changes in different editions of Frederick Douglass's autobiography, David Leverenz has demonstrated the significance Douglass attached to his physical efforts to achieve his freedom. Similarly, as James Oliver Horton and Lois E. Horton have argued, notions of manhood played a part in black Garrisonians' more militant stance on the slavery issue.[35]

Inferring that the destruction of the slaves' masculinity was one of the most ruinous effects of slavery, African American men's concern for their masculine self-image owed much to the sexual and domestic abuses that occurred under slavery. Besides being unable to protect their wives from the wanton desires of white slave owners, African American men could not properly fulfill their role as fathers, since their children, as well as their wives, were the property of white men. This inability to render assistance to their children was a source of anguish, and a tormenting challenge to male slaves' masculine identity. Henry Bibb expressed his frustration at being the "father of slaves" who were "still left to linger out their days in hopeless bondage." After one failed attempt to rescue his family from slavery, Bibb noted: "I felt it to be my duty, as a husband and father, to make one more effort." Ex-slaves also lamented their inability to assist their mothers. The Reverend J. W. Loguen, describing a scene where he felt helpless to assist his mother who had been flogged, and referring explicitly to the erosion of the masculine self-image, noted in 1859 that to "be a slave, he must cease to feel that he is a man." Ex-slaves realized that fleeing the South was only a partial solution to their predicament: those who left wives, children, and other loved ones in slavery were never really free. White abolitionists proclaimed their empathy with those in bondage, but for former slaves, the phrase "bound with them in chains" was more than a rhetorical device.[36]

At the heart of black abolitionists' construction of masculinity was repulsion toward slaveholders' abuse of masculine power. In articulating that sense of repulsion, African Americans endorsed the principles underpinning other antebellum moral reform movements, including the temperance movement. Black and white abolitionists believed that Southern intemperance was symptomatic of the overall failure of domestic values in the slave states. Abolitionists regularly depicted white masters as being drunk when they forced themselves upon slave women, or when they flogged their slaves. They also suggested that slave owners deliberately used alcohol as a means of placating their slaves, and rendering them insensible to their plight. Ex-slaves attested to the significance of such behavior. The description by one slave of an alcoholic binge, exacerbated by the fact that it occurred on a "holy day," encapsulated many of the abolitionists' concerns: "I had resolved to go to carouse, with my fellow slaves, and master was even more complacent than usual, and gave me a generous allowance of money. He warmly encouraged my going, as masters always do, because whatever sinks the man secures the slave."[37] Maria Stewart, a pioneer African American abolitionist and public speaker, was also concerned with these issues. In 1833, she urged a group of black Bostonians to "throw off" their "fearfulness." "If you are men," she declared, "convince [whites] that you possess the spirit of men." Enjoining black men to serve their communities, and arguing that if he was given "equal opportunity," the black man could become a "dignified statesman, the man of science, and the philosopher," Stewart's was not a call to violence. Indeed, when she implored "our men, and especially our rising youth, to flee from the gambling board and the dance hall; for we are poor and have no money to throw away," Stewart's image of masculine virtue had much in common with the bourgeois values associated with the Northern middle class.[38]

Like their African American coadjutors, white abolitionists vehemently condemned the violence associated with slavery. Yet while they experienced real terror when they confronted hostile mobs, they did not directly encounter the institutionalized violence of slavery that had shaped the attitudes of many black abolitionists. This difference was reflected in white abolitionists' responses to violence. Although the AASS assured its lecturers that the "only way to put down mobs" was "not to fear them," white abolitionists did not seek to prove their manhood by mimicking those whose behavior they detested.[39] Having defined civilization in terms of the advancement of feminine values (which implied the use of "feminine" strategies of social reform, such as peaceful persuasion) radical abolitionists were reluctant to embrace violent means. Generally, white abolitionist men shunned physical violence, which their religious and reforming ideologies denounced as barbaric and uncivilized. These convictions were increasingly put to the test during the antebellum period. As will be described below, the Garrisonians' attitude toward violence shifted slowly and reluctantly; by the time of the Civil War, when the question became less abstract, many were too old to participate directly in that struggle.

There were, however, alternative arenas of masculine conflict during the nineteenth century. Business, for instance, has been described by some historians as the successor, or substitute, for military activity. Even in the preindustrial era, as Nancy Cott has noted, to "act like a man" meant supporting a wife. Industrialization, and the consequent division between home and paid work, strengthened that assumption: as Samuel K. Jennings assured American wives in 1808, their husbands were "bound to provide for you and your children." Many tasks in the industrializing world of the nineteenth century were couched in terms of satisfying inherently masculine instincts or talents. Indeed, the gender ideal of the "Masculine Achiever" was often tied to the evolving system of commercial capitalism. Abolitionist men eschewed many of the values associated with the Masculine Achiever, but in their domestic lives and in their public reformism they were influenced by the imperatives of the market.[40] The reevaluation of gender roles did not preclude some abolitionist men from considering themselves providers for their families. In the economically volatile antebellum era, many men expressed anxiety over their ability to fulfill the provider role. For abolitionists these anxieties were compounded because the economic activities they sought to incorporate into their reformism, such as petty proprietorship and small-scale agriculture, were rapidly being eclipsed in the antebellum market economy.

For male abolitionists, the need to accomplish "masculine" tasks in the public sphere had to be balanced with private responsibilities. These conflicting demands were evident in the case of Henry Blackwell. Blackwell spent considerable time away from home in the period following the birth of Alice Stone Blackwell in 1857, but his love for his daughter was not diminished by his absences. Like abolitionist women, Blackwell regretted that he was away from home, and justified his absence on the grounds of the necessity of performing a duty for a greater cause: "Lucy dear—please God! I will *never* leave you & baby again for so long an absence. Forgive me this once. It was *not for myself that I did it.*" Blackwell's guilt at leaving Stone to care for Alice was also apparent: "It is a great shame & pity that I have had to leave you all the burden & weariness of it." Blackwell's reference to a "father's love"—based on his absence from his own child—provided a foundation on which to empathize with slave fathers, who were forcefully separated from their children. As his 1853 statement that while women were fettered with "household cares & ties," the "whole burden of acquiring subsistence" fell upon men suggested, Blackwell keenly felt an obligation to assume the provider role. The financial arrangements of the Stone-Blackwell relationship are assessed below, but given that Stone's lecturing skills had enabled her to achieve considerable financial independence, Blackwell's anxieties possibly reflected a desire to *establish* a role for himself.[41]

Demonstrating the extent to which business shaped nineteenth-century constructions of masculinity, the responsibilities to which Blackwell alluded illustrated how the influence of the market was felt in such material concerns as employment. Aside from their public reformism, abolitionist men were involved in a range of activities characteristic of the emergent middle class in the nineteenth century. Although they repudiated many of the acquisitive values of their society, Garrisonian men supported efforts to utilize market forces on behalf of the free produce movement, and they were unavoidably entangled in the wider material world of the market, with all of its implications and contradictions for women's status. To support themselves, and to fund their reform activities, abolitionists relied upon a range of occupations that adhered closely to the mainstream of their era. Their abolitionism did render them distinct, but their ability to maintain that distinctiveness was often dependent on activities that were far from unusual. James Mott's employment history was representative of the evolving middle class. After having worked as a bank clerk and a bookkeeper, he eventually found success as a shopkeeper. As other Americans suffered during economic downturns, the abolitionists' woes were compounded by the recessions that regularly affected the United States in the nineteenth century.[42]

Few abolitionists relied solely on the income they derived from their antislavery endeavors. Not only was the rate of remuneration low, but there was little reliability attached to the income provided by the antislavery societies, which were themselves usually in a state of near poverty. Accordingly, agents of the antislavery societies were frequently paid late, or underpaid, meaning all but a few had to supplement their income by other activities. Regardless of the definition of what constitutes "business," abolitionist men were involved in the marketplace. Nonetheless, their involvement was generally either on a small scale, or was typified by the frugality associated with domestic ideology.

Those frugal values were evident in abolitionist men's public pronouncements on domestic matters. James Mott's 1824 tract *Brief Hints to Parents, on the Subject of Education,* was a characteristically didactic document, exalting values similar to those championed by domestic writers. Lauding frugality, hard work, and the family unit, he urged parents to assist their children in acquiring a proper education. These values were well regarded in other abolitionist households. Praising the Weld-Grimké family circle, Elizabeth Cady Stanton told Lucretia Mott in 1848 that "Theodore teaches" their "charming" children "himself." "It would do you good," wrote Stanton, "to see Theodore wrestle & play with his children." Stanton's positive presentation of Weld's fatherly role must be viewed against the subsequent psychological problems faced by Weld's second son, Theodore ("Thoda" or "Sody"). Thoda's difficulties, first manifested during the 1850s by stuttering and "inexplicable dreamy states," raised concerns that he was edging toward insanity. Confronted with conflicting explanations for Thoda's condition, Theodore and Angelina tried a variety of treatments, none of which proved effective in the long term. Robert Abzug's conclusion that Weld, "who so sensitively shaped the characters of other men's children, helped devastate the character of his own son," rests in part on the implication that Thoda's problems could have been avoided if Theodore and Angelina had fulfilled their parental responsibilities more adequately.[43] Abzug's interpretation, based on the assumption that Weld's troubled relationship with his father shaped his relationship with his own offspring, must be seen, however, in conjunction with the persuasive evidence of Weld's affection for his children. Weld's active participation in the rearing and education of his children modified prevailing gender roles, and suggested options for other reformers as well as for those Americans not dedicated to the improvement of society. Besides implicitly presenting fatherly duties in terms of God's love, a letter from Weld to his sons revealed that the bonding process between abolitionist fathers and their children paralleled that which domestic literature promoted between mothers and their children: "My precious boys! Father's heart yearns for you every day and is full of prayer, that Heavenly Father's sweet breath of love and truth may so warm and quicken your hearts, that all good, true, noble unselfish loving God-like thoughts and feelings may nestle there so closely, and cluster so thick and strong that nothing evil can find room there."[44] Weld's affection for his children, and his efforts to inculcate values prized by reformers, were indicative of radical abolitionists' wider faith in education. By seeking to shape children's minds in appropriate educational institutions, Weld and the Grimkés effectively fused private and public labors.

Alongside that reform imperative, Weld's involvement in the Raritan Bay Union school reflected his quest for financial security.[45] Similarly, his farming activities were suggestive of his desire to provide for his family. Moreover, not only did Weld and Stephen Foster seek to support their families by farming, other abolitionists endorsed agriculture as a means of reform. Henry Blackwell's conviction that "the *hope of the World* lies in Agriculture," had direct relevance for abolitionism. Blackwell's belief that a "man who does not live on his own land is a factious and artificial being" echoed and informed the abolitionist understanding of the plight of the slaves, who could never achieve individuality while they were unable to own land on which they worked. The ideal of the yeoman farmer, enshrined in Jefferson's vision of the democratic republic, was hardly unusual in antebellum America. In Blackwell's case, his belief that landowners would be responsible and virtuous citizens was undermined somewhat by the fact that he was also willing to rent land out to those unable to own property. While Blackwell declared his "contempt for the whole sphere of business," and remained a small-scale entrepreneur rather than a large-scale capitalist, he noted that "a little income from rents, or interest" would be a useful supplement to his and Lucy's income.[46]

Few abolitionists, with the notable exception of Gerrit Smith, owned significant amounts of land. This suggests another disjunction between the abolitionist and Southern versions of masculinity. Claiming that slavery was based on moral, not material relationships, proslavery writers criticized what they regarded as the acquisitive nature of Northern society, and argued that capitalism exacerbated social differences. Yet status in the South was largely determined by the size of one's landholdings, and the number of slaves one owned. That process of social organization contrasted sharply with James Mott's explanation as to why he valued financial security. After working (presumably on a voluntary basis) at a local soup house, Mott philanthropically declared that he would "like to be rich," so as to be able to "relieve the necessities" of his "fellow suffering creatures." The experience of working with such people, he continued, had made him "grateful for his good fortune" and thankful that he had "food and raiment."[47] On the surface, Mott's statement resembled the rhetoric of Southern paternalism. But in addition to revealing that some male abolitionists were willing to work in areas that allegedly fell into women's sphere, Mott implied the differences between the abolitionists' construction of social responsibility, and the determinants of social station in the slave states. Abolitionist men did not achieve all their reform objectives, but they sought to turn their words into deeds. Indeed, they regarded reformism, rather than material gain or an acquisitive spirit, as the means to individual self-fulfillment. In this way they located themselves within a middle-class reform tradition that—as Lori Ginzberg has noted—regarded "virtue" rather than "wealth" as the determinant of both individual and national "success."[48]

David Lee Child sought individual self-satisfaction through the application of agricultural advances to reformism. Alongside his quest for personal financial security, his business activities (including his unsuccessful efforts to promote the production of beet sugar) reflected a desire to help free the slaves. In this way, he sought to recover his masculine identity. Yet despite Child's humanitarian motives, which distinguished him from the prevailing model of individualistic masculinity, his faith in scientific and technological advancements placed him in the mainstream of antebellum middle-class American culture. Similarly, James Mott's business ventures, like Child's, were typified by altruism, and were always on a small scale.[49] Other abolitionist men also could not escape taking at least a grudging interest in business affairs. The *Liberator* was the best-known abolitionist newspaper, but its notoriety did not provide a sizable or steady income for William L. Garrison. The perennial impecuniosity of the *Liberator* compelled Garrison to borrow money regularly. In 1847 he linked his financial predicament to masculine honor. Asking one of his brothers-in-law to help procure a loan for three hundred dollars, Garrison not only offered as security "whatever belongs to me in the shape of personal property," but also his "personal integrity as a man." Garrison's financial concerns did not abate over the years, and an indication of his postbellum economic situation was his response to an 1868 invitation to lecture. "I would not think of going," he admitted to one of his sons, "were it not that I needed the money to defray household expenses, and that I am doing nothing to insure a lively income."[50] On this occasion, as on others, Garrison's reluctance to leave home was outweighed by the obligation he felt to provide for his family.

The anxieties arising from the belief that men should provide financial security for their families were well shown by Henry Stanton in the months preceding his marriage. Stanton's confidential correspondence with Amos Phelps betrayed both his excitement and his fears regarding his financial position. Referring to his plans to marry, Stanton implored Phelps to confide in no one, not even his wife. Conscious of Elizabeth Cady's privileged background, and of the pressure being applied by Judge Cady on his daughter not to marry, Stanton possibly feared that a wider awareness of his precarious financial situation would jeopardize his chances.[51] His pleas to Phelps not to confide in his wife perhaps reflected a fear that if Phelps's wife learned of Stanton's plans, and his financial woes, other female abolitionists might also soon know. It is unlikely that Stanton feared other abolitionist women would seek to dissuade Elizabeth Cady from marriage, since most believed that women should make up their own minds over their choice of marriage partners. A more likely interpretation is that Stanton feared Judge Cady would become even more entrenched in his opposition to his daughter's marriage plans. Stanton's comments also suggest that his fraternal feelings for Phelps were being utilized for the purpose of aiding his chances to fulfill another, more important relationship: marriage.

There were parallels between Stanton and David Lee Child. Both worked for a time as lawyers, both married women who eventually became more well known than themselves, and both received support from their fathers-in-law. We have seen that L. Maria Child's father provided the funds to purchase the farm in Northampton, and Daniel Cady provided direct support to Henry Stanton.[52] Despite that assistance, Henry Stanton's financial worries continued after his marriage. Having left his wife at home soon after the birth of their first child, Stanton remained away for long periods. Like other men, he was expected to provide for his family, and if he could most effectively do so away from home, there was no choice but to move to where employment opportunities were forthcoming. His determination to "get an honorable and competent practice," for the sake of Elizabeth and "the kid," was typical of many men. The tensions in Stanton's mind were evident in 1851. Remorseful at his "inability to be at home," he implored Elizabeth to provide him with details on the health of the family. While Stanton's public commitments, especially his involvement in the political machinations in Albany, had priority over his interest in the domestic sphere, he keenly felt the responsibility of fatherhood.[53]

Abolitionist men's sense of intimacy and bonding to their children affected their perceptions of slave society. While many slaves could never be certain about their father's identity, abolitionists acknowledged the bonding between slave parents and children. Besides suggesting that maternal and paternal sentiments were natural, rather than the result of social conditioning, Isaac Hopper's claim that parental "feelings" were "not acquired," but "natural" and therefore "as poignant in the breast of a black, as a white mother," revealed that antislavery men were attuned to the strength of maternal attachments. Abolitionist women also appealed to paternal sentiments. Sarah Grimké, describing a scene of domestic bliss, where children were happily embracing their parents, beseeched her readers to "look in upon" their "slave." "He too is a father," Grimké asserted, "and *we know* that he is susceptible of all the tender sensibilities of a father's love. He folds his cherished infant in his arms, he feels its life-pulse against his own, and he rejoices that he is a parent; but soon the withering thought rushes to his mind—I am a slave, and tomorrow my master may tear my darling from my arms."[54]

The paternal theme also influenced the institutional practices of abolitionism. Lawrence Friedman's depiction of William L. Garrison's "fatherly management" of the Boston abolitionists demonstrates that the characteristics radical abolitionist men valued in their individual domestic relationships were significant in their public lives. Garrison's fatherly leadership of the Boston coterie, as described by Friedman, reflected what many regarded as Garrison's extremism and his eccentricities. Yet Garrison sought to foster unity and tolerance.[55] At first glance, Garrison's fatherly leadership of the Boston group resembled the Southern model of a benevolent patriarch. The resemblance, however, was superficial, and radical abolitionists' version of fatherly love constituted a challenge to the authority of Southern slaveholders.

Since the values associated with Southern men were also evident in the North, the abolitionists' denunciations of Southern patriarchy transcended the struggle to emancipate the slaves. Patriarchy fused masculine authority with the paternalistic idea that men should protect women. Radical abolitionists were not entirely dismissive of this notion. Invoking the "fashions of chivalry," Abby Kelley jokingly demanded that Stephen Foster bring forth "trophies of victory, shackles broken, whips dust-trodden, sword in the left hand and a proclamation of emancipation in the right, before your lady love shall yield to her good knight." Kelley's comments were made in jest, but she was nonetheless using explicitly masculinist terms to connect abolitionism with Foster's romantic prospects. There were, moreover, occasions when female abolitionists allowed their husbands to adopt a protective role. The persistent charges that lecturing had rendered Kelley unfit for marriage, and that she not only had relationships with abolitionist men, but, most significantly, with African Americans, continued after her marriage. After one heckler at an antislavery meeting made such an accusation, Kelley proudly noted that Foster "called out the scamp and made him tremble before the meeting."[56]

Radical abolitionists knew, however, that men's assumption of a protective role, often expressed in terms of gallantry and chivalry, perpetuated the subordination of women. Prior to her marriage, L. Maria Child had been impressed by David Lee Child's valor and chivalry.[57] With the passage of time, however, her attitude toward these masculine characteristics shifted. By 1843, convinced that the "physical-force principle" was antithetical to the interests of women and civilized society, Child was depicting gallantry as "an odious word to every sensible woman, because she sees that it is merely the flimsy veil which foppery throws over sensuality." Rather than "indicating sincere esteem and affection for women," she thought "the profligacy of a nation may, in general, be fairly measured by its gallantry." Along with gallantry, chivalry was an essential component of the Southern masculine ideal. Child's 1839 statement that chivalry should "pass away with barbarism," like William L. Garrison's later remark that chivalry "practically crushes and degrades woman," revealed the abolitionists' understanding that chivalry was symptomatic of the Southern oppression of women. The implicit connections between chivalry as representative of an outmoded pattern of gender relations, and slavery as also belonging to the past, were evident. Abolitionists realized that Southern men were not the only ones to abuse the notion of chivalry. L. Maria Child condemned "those dissipated despots" who boasted "of their *chivalry,*" but she was not content just to denounce Southern hypocrisy. As she revealed in an 1860 letter to Charles Sumner (perhaps the most celebrated victim of the Southern code of honor) Child was also aware of the North's complicity in the perpetuation of slavery; she noted that she was even "more indignant" that Northerners "are so generally willing to *allow* the impudent claim."[58] Yet while radical abolitionists knew that reform was required throughout the nation, they believed that their version of mutual respect between men and women contrasted with what they considered the self-serving rhetoric of Southern paternalism. This difference echoed the perceived differences between Southern claims that their slaves were well treated and contented, and the abuses that actually occurred under slavery. As Garrisonians saw it, the contrast between the North and the South was one between truth and dishonesty. Their vision of true marriage, and their desire for racial harmony, contrasted with the disingenuous ideology of Southern racism and paternalism.

This question of paternalism raised the question of women's financial independence, and women's contribution to their family's income. E. Anthony Rotundo has noted that during the nineteenth century the responsibility for familial finances was an area "in which man's right to decide was undoubted." Some abolitionist women were apparently content with such a situation, but in other cases, the issue proved more contentious. We have seen that L. Maria Child's decision to separate her financial affairs from those of her husband was a difficult one, and that their "separation" was always ambivalent. The experiences of other female abolitionists were similarly complex. Lucy Stone, as well as making a number of sizable loans to Henry Blackwell, placed the money she had earned from her lectures, amounting to the not-insignificant sum of five thousand dollars, in the hands of her future husband and his brother Samuel. Andrea Moore Kerr has argued that from the beginning of Blackwell's marriage with Stone, he showed "himself unwilling to relinquish the traditional 'masculine' role." To be sure, Blackwell believed—erroneously—that his business acumen was superior to Stone's. As noted above, it is also possible that he was concerned with establishing a role for himself within marriage. Yet the early stages of the Stone-Blackwell marriage also revealed that some abolitionist relationships could accommodate changing views about women's abilities to manage their finances. Indeed, Blackwell's attitude toward women's economic status was evidenced by his willingness to discuss financial issues with Stone before they were married. While Blackwell was prepared to assume responsibility for Stone's pecuniary affairs, he did not consider himself naturally entitled to control her finances. Careful to couch his comments in terms that took cognizance of Stone's determination to maintain her independence, Blackwell asked her not to worry about monetary matters. Asserting that "feelings of [financial] *gain*" should not affect the "spontaneity of her labors," and assuring her that "Lucy Stone Blackwell" was "more independent in her pecuniary position than was Lucy Stone," he took pride in his ability to provide financial security for his bride. Blackwell implored Stone not to "feel humbled, or subservient" in "accepting his earnings," since they would be of no value to him unless they were shared with her.[59]

Despite Blackwell's promises that marriage would not constrain Stone, he underestimated her determination to retain her individuality. In a period when most women took their husband's surnames, his apparent assumption that Stone would choose to be called "Lucy Stone Blackwell" was a sign of his liberal attitude toward women's position within marriage. Yet Stone elected not to add her husband's name, preferring instead to continue to be known as "Lucy Stone." Equally significant, Stone was determined to preserve her hard-won financial independence. Echoing the abolitionists' condemnation of the slaveholders' paternalistic protestations that they were best able to care for the slaves, and foreshadowing the women's rights movement's efforts to encourage women to achieve financial independence, Stone was skeptical of Blackwell's protestations that "the *presence* of love" rendered "dependence *mutual* & financial details simply *trivial.*" Accordingly, she sought to ensure that the home they bought in Orange, New Jersey, in April 1857 was purchased in her name. Attesting to the importance of financial independence, Stone told Blackwell: "It is more important to me than you have ever known, that I should have the income of my property. Now that there is no reason why I should not, I greatly prefer to arrange so that our properties may be separate."[60] Blackwell's concession to Stone's determination for fiscal independence contrasted sharply with Southern practices, which—until the turmoil of the Civil War expanded many Southern women's role in the public world of business and finance—emphasized masculine responsibility for financial management.

Abby Kelley shared Lucy Stone's determination to retain her individuality. But in the Kelley-Foster household, alongside Stephen Foster's continuing concern for financial matters, there were ambiguities regarding the reversal of gender roles. Prior to her marriage, Kelley sarcastically derided Foster's lack of financial acumen. Later, however, in urging the AASS to pay the salaries of other agents, rather than to herself, she remarked that she did not "look out for rainy days." "My husband does that," she explained to Maria Weston Chapman in 1846, "because he feels it is his duty." Noting that while she would be happy to "work for nothing and trust the consequences," Kelley claimed that her husband felt a responsibility to manage their financial affairs. Significantly, she opted not to dissent on the matter, since she liked "every one to be at liberty." Moreover, concerning herself and Stephen's decision to continue working in the western states, Kelley told Sydney Howard Gay in 1845 that she "left it with Stephen to decide."[61]

An 1851 letter from Foster to Kelley, wherein he replied to legal queries she had directed toward him, revealed the dual nature of male abolitionists' self-image. Advising Kelley that he had "looked at the statutes" and was "satisfied" of her "right to damages," Foster adopted a characteristically masculine attitude toward the role of the husband as the arbiter of certain decisions within the domestic sphere. The nature of Kelley's legal query, however, illustrated that other imperatives were at work, since Foster also assured her that she was entitled to financial compensation, separate from him. Discussing the differences between himself and his wife, and regretting that she attached "undue importance" to his "cooperation," Foster expressed frustration when Kelley did not exercise the independence for which she was publicly renowned. Foster's declining status and importance within the abolitionist movement, coupled with his wife's continuing prominence in public reformism, constituted an indirect challenge to his self-image. One consequence, as Joel Bernard has noted, was that Foster suffered from depression. Yet Foster did not allow his relative lack of public success to detract from his marriage. Instead of responding to Kelley's success with bitterness or jealousy, he remained a loving husband and devoted father, who expended time and energy into their Worcester farm. Foster told Wendell Phillips in 1857 that above all else he sought "the privilege of retiring altogether from the lecturing field to the quiet of private life." Hoping to be able to devote himself to "some occupation" that was "less laborious, & more congenial" to his tastes, Foster described his "craving for retirement." Moreover, in claiming that he had "no desire for an [antislavery] agency," and pointing out that the AASS was not organized for the purpose of providing employment for abolitionists, he refuted criticisms of the motives of reform movements.[62] Foster's desire for domestic tranquility complemented his wife's determination to participate in public abolitionism. Kelley's antislavery activities, along with those of other female abolitionists, were a prelude to the emergent women's rights movement.

Partly on account of the activities of female abolitionists such as Abby Kelley, the issues of slavery and women's rights were commonly considered together. While women abolitionists' determination to engage in reform beyond the domestic sphere elicited a range of responses from their male colleagues, endorsements of women's public role in abolitionism did not necessarily amount to tangible support for women's rights. As the acrimonious divisions within antislavery organizations indicate, women's demands for their rights did not attract universal support among male abolitionists. From women's first tentative steps toward public activism, abolitionist men's response varied, both over time and between individuals, from outright rejection, to cautious opposition, to unreserved endorsement. The abolitionist men reviewed herein were self-conscious about the demarcation of men's and women's spheres, and some sought to redress imbalances in gender roles. Few went as far as Henry Blackwell, whose long courtship of Lucy Stone led him to state, "I *wish* I could take the position of the wife under the law & give you that of a husband." But there was an appreciation among radical abolitionist men that women's domestic role did not preclude them from playing a role in the world beyond the home. Some explicitly portrayed the home as merely the starting point for women's broader area of responsibility. Theodore Parker was convinced that "the domestic function of woman, as a housekeeper, wife, and mother," did not "exhaust her powers." Like charity, he argued in 1853, women's function began at home, and then, again like charity, went "everywhere." Determined to utilize women's abilities fully, Parker thought that to "make one half of the human race consume all of their energies in the functions of housekeeper, wife and mother," was a "monstrous waste of the most precious material that God ever made." The notion of civilization also influenced male abolitionists' attitude toward women's rights, and Samuel J. May's 1845 admission that men "have more brute strength" than women augmented the case for women's rights. Arguing that "moral power," "influence," and "will" were more valuable attributes than physical strength, May contended that "civilization implies the subordination of the physical in man to the mental and moral."

He was certain that the "progress of the melioration of the condition of our race" was "everywhere marked by the elevation of the female sex."[63] Since men were commonly defined by their physical prowess, and women by their influence and moral virtues, May's contention that the progress of humanity was not defined or measured by physical strength, but rather by moral and intellectual advancements, amounted to an implicit demand for the elevation not just of female virtues, but of women's rights.

The reactions of those male abolitionists whose wives sought independence hold clues to men's contribution to the struggle for women's rights. The case of Theodore Weld provides an interesting example of the various factors influencing abolitionist men. Weld initially sought to dissuade Angelina Grimké from bringing the "woman question" into her antislavery activities, but his position was complicated because it soon became apparent that not all men opposed the Grimkés' public association of women's rights and abolitionism. The radical reformer Henry Clarke Wright was a consistent supporter of the Grimké sisters. Wright, who also urged Abby Kelley to lecture in public, encouraged the Grimkés to broach publicly any topic they considered important. Wright's attitude toward women's rights, and his support for the Grimkés, contributed to his differences of opinion with Weld. But there were other, more personal, sources of disagreement between the two men. Peter Stearns has noted that while "it was still widely assumed" in the nineteenth century "that love legitimately brought the possibility of jealousy," it was also thought that "well-arranged love would limit its sway." Weld disliked Wright and while their differences stemmed partly from conflicting views of the nature and direction of reform, tensions were exacerbated because Weld envied Wright's "easy manner with women." Given the restraint Weld exercised in his early dealings with Grimké, the potential for personal rivalry was obvious. Moreover, the close friendship between Wright and the Grimké sisters may have prompted Weld to view him as a potential rival for Angelina's affections. Possibly influenced by Wright's liberal contribution to the women's rights movement, and certainly affected by his relationship with Grimké, Weld became a supporter of women abolitionists' right to work in the public sphere.[64]

The most prominent abolitionists, black and white, publicly advocated women's rights. But Frederick Douglass's and William L. Garrison's pronouncements on women's behalf sat somewhat uneasily alongside the division of labor within their own homes. Douglass, praised by Elizabeth

Cady Stanton for his efforts at the 1848 Seneca Falls women's rights convention, declared in 1850 that "the truths on which" the women's rights movement were "founded are invulnerable."[65] Yet Douglass's marriage did not entail dramatic challenges to gender roles as they were codified in separate spheres ideology. Anna Murray Douglass was not quite the "totally domestic woman" she has been labeled. According to the testimony of Rosetta Douglass, Frederick and Anna's eldest child, Anna was a "recognized co-worker" in the Lynn and Boston antislavery societies. She was, nonetheless, responsible for household affairs, including raising five children. Frederick Douglass, whose autobiographies include scant mention of his domestic life, was apparently content with such an arrangement.[66]

William L. Garrison was widely regarded as an early and emphatic supporter of the women's movement; after having declared his support for women's rights in 1837, he encouraged women to seek political equality. In 1846 Garrison enunciated his vision of women's rights: "What are the Rights of Woman? Define what are the Rights of Man, and thou hast answered the question. Rights are of no sex, and may never be innocently usurped or [condemned?]."[67] Garrison asserted that women's rights, rather than deriving from women's particular qualities, were based on the principles of human rights. The implication deriving from that assumption—that the sexes were by nature equal—placed Garrison at the radical end of antebellum reformers. While his support for women's rights wavered briefly in the immediate postbellum period, Garrison subsequently argued that women were entitled to political as well as social and economic equality, noting in 1870 that the "claim of women to the ballot is so reasonable, in such conformity to the theory of popular government, and so important in its bearings upon whatever concerns the interests of the people, that I marvel that any man with ordinary intelligence and sense of justice, on giving any consideration to the subject, can resist or deny it." This demonstrated (albeit in characteristically hierarchical terms) his support for women's claim to political equality. For this, Garrison earned the praise of at least some of the leading proponents of women's rights. Lucy Stone implored Francis Jackson Garrison to ensure his memoirs spelled out his father's "support for the American Woman Suffrage Association."[68]

William Lloyd Garrison's support for women's rights reflected his long-standing belief that women made a telling contribution to the antislavery movement. Indeed, Garrison was effusive in his praise of female abolitionists, commenting to Elizabeth Pease in 1837 that women had done "more for the extirpation of slavery than the other sex." Yet Garrison's reaction to the Grimkés' entrance into the public realm suggested that his enlightened views stood alongside rather traditional assumptions concerning gender differences. Certainly his prescriptive statements regarding gender roles did not accurately describe his own marriage. While Garrison supported the Grimkés' right to participate in public reform, he continued to see their role in terms of women's traditional virtue, as his private comment to Pease that the South Carolinian sisters were "exerting an almost angelic influence" implied. Garrison's use of the word "influence" inferred that there was another side to his attitude toward women, and hinted at his perception of his own marriage. Soon after he wed, Garrison raised these matters with Samuel J. May. Besides suggesting that he did not regard marriage as an impediment to his public reformism, Garrison unintentionally portended the evolution of widely different perceptions among some abolitionists and advocates of women's rights concerning the nature of marriage. Metaphorically relating slavery to marriage, Garrison jokingly castigated May: "You! Who took away my liberty and put me in bondage with another? You! Who put such a noose around my neck and tied such a knot, as to defy my industry and skill in emancipating myself." Garrison's irony may have masked a genuine anxiety concerning his masculine identity within marriage. But despite the accolades he received from women's rights activists, his marriage conformed to the pattern prescribed by gender spheres ideology. In an 1835 letter to his brother-in-law, Garrison explicitly, and with no suggestion of embarrassment, explained his motives for marrying Helen. "I did not marry her," he remarked, "expecting that she would assume a prominent station in the anti-slavery cause, but for domestic quietude and happiness. So completely absorbed am I in that cause, that it was undoubtedly wise in me to select as a partner one who, while her benevolent feelings were in unison with mine, was less immediately and entirely connected with it."[69] Garrison's egotism was apparent; but his letter also revealed that he viewed marriage as a means of facilitating his work outside the home.

Garrison's view of women can be traced to the period preceding his marriage. His public comment in 1828 that nobody had "more respect" for the "character of woman," echoed views expressed by domestic writers. Garrison reasoned that the continuation of that respect was dependent on women devoting themselves to "exerting" their "proper influence" and doing their "proper duty." Again like domestic writers, Garrison expressed reverence for the idealized role attributed to mothers. "Above all," he stressed, "on the mother it depends (as far indeed as such a thing can depend on earthly power) whether her children shall be happy or miserable forever." Women were to suppress their own ambitions, and pass their "*whole*" lives in "softening the character, exciting the affections, and rewarding with a love beyond all price the toils of man." Women were also to act as educators, providing moral guidance and an understanding of the importance of religion. Garrison maintained his views on women's appropriate role, noting publicly in September 1834 (the same month that he married) that nature "provided opposite spheres for the two sexes." He reiterated such sentiments, albeit with more subtlety, in his private correspondence. Writing to Lucretia Mott in 1840, he demonstrated his adherence to the ideology that prescribed women's function in domestic terms. While he contradicted one element of the separate spheres ideology by lauding Mott's "intelligent vigor," he carefully praised her "moral worth and disinterested benevolence"—characteristics commonly attributed to women by domestic writers.[70]

Other abolitionist men, black as well as white, also betrayed attitudes toward women that were congruent with domestic ideology. Henry Blackwell, grateful for the positive effect Lucy Stone was having upon him, remarked in 1853 that he would "try to show" Stone "that a woman can serve as a mediator to point her friend to higher views of duty and of God." Noting that a "soft answer turns away wrath," and pleased that Stone was "not very combative in" her "spirit," Blackwell expressed faith in the efficacy of peaceful persuasion, a skill, or tactic, generally attributed to women.[71] Like their white colleagues, certain black abolitionist men declared their commitment to gender equality. On occasions, these declarations of support for women's rights were couched in terms of sexual equality. Arguing that women's "mental capacities are equal to their brethren," the editor of the *National Reformer*, a black Garrisonian newspaper published in Philadelphia, noted in 1838 that "our organs of sense, and reasoning powers, belong not to us peculiarly as males, or females, but as human beings." Nonetheless, as in the case of Frederick Douglass, these statements must be viewed alongside evidence that African American abolitionist men continued to view women's role and nature in terms congruent with domestic ideology. As Henry Bibb's 1850 remark that it was "truly marvellous to see how sudden a man's mind" could be changed "by the charms and influence of a female" suggested, African American men attributed considerable redemptive moral powers to women.[72]

Notwithstanding these measured affirmations of support for the gender spheres ideology, a number of abolitionist men followed Stephen Foster's example, and accepted some responsibility for domestic life. This was even true in the case of William Lloyd Garrison. Lawrence Friedman has portrayed Garrison's attitude toward women in terms of an evolution, and on one level, Garrison's ideology, and his treatment of women, did change over time. In the period following December 1863, when Helen Garrison suffered a stroke, he assumed a greater share of the domestic obligations. Consider, too, his 1866 comment to James Miller McKim, when he explained why he could not journey to Chicago. "The case of dear wife is attended with considerable anxiety," he wrote, "and I am obliged to act the part of nurse, and to watch over her by night." There were parallels between Garrison's post-1863 situation and that of Wendell Phillips over a much longer period. When considering Garrison's actions during that period, it is necessary to note that the demands of women were much better known, and more widely accepted, at least among reformers, than they had been in earlier decades. Yet while Garrison commended Helen's contribution to the antislavery struggle, his attitudes toward gender roles revealed the continuing influence of domestic and separate spheres ideologies. After remarking in 1869 that Helen "never thinks of herself," and "is always disinterested and self-denying," Garrison published *A Memorial* to Helen in 1876, wherein he praised and thanked her for her contributions. That document revealed that Garrison continued to regard women as auxiliaries or adjuncts, operating in the private domestic sphere, while their husbands engaged in public activities. Referring to his "large indebtedness" to Helen as "a helpmate," Garrison blessed "her memory for a cooperation that was so essential" to his "domestic tranquillity and public service." Although he mentioned the responsibilities and difficulties faced by his wife, Garrison judged such "burdens" as "too common in the conjugal relation for special consideration here."[73]

Abolitionist men's attitudes to women's right to participate in the public sphere came to the public eye in 1840. The annual meeting of the AASS, and the World's Anti-Slavery Convention in London, provided male abolitionists with the opportunity to demonstrate their support for women. For the American delegates to the convention, the issues arising there paralleled those of the preceding months, when the question of women's role in the abolitionist movement had contributed significantly to the schisms within the Massachusetts and American Anti-Slavery Societies. Those in favor of women's rights had achieved a dubious victory at the AASS meeting, but events in London did not work to their favor, since the delegates to the world convention decided against admitting women as participants. Of the male abolitionists under review in this study, four attended the assembly in London. Garrison traveled to England alone, but Wendell Phillips, Henry Stanton, and James Mott were accompanied by their wives. Garrison arrived late to the convention, after the decision had been reached to exclude women. But his subsequent refusal to involve himself in the proceedings of the convention earned him the accolades of many women reformers, and while he regretted that "the woman's question" was "launched with so little combination, so little preparation, [and] so little knowledge of the manner in which it had been entangled by the fears of some and the follies of others," he optimistically concluded that the "coming of those women" to the London convention would "form an era in the future history of philanthropic daring."[74]

The responses of other prominent male abolitionists to the debate in London were more ambiguous. Although there are uncertainties regarding Wendell Phillips's response to women's demands for participation at the London convention, he has been widely credited with being a supporter of the women, and Lucretia Mott specifically praised him for "manfully" pleading on their behalf.[75] Less has been said of Henry Stanton's role at the London meeting. Differing from Garrison and Phillips in many ways, Stanton was nonetheless conscious of the demands of women reformers. Since the proceedings of the convention in London do not record the way in which delegates voted on the question of admitting women delegates, it is not always easy to determine how particular individuals voted. In Stanton's case, the evidence is contradictory. Although Garrison stated that Stanton had voted to admit women, and Elizabeth Cady Stanton claimed later that her husband made an "eloquent speech" on the women's behalf, Henry Stanton denied that he had actually voted in favor of admitting women as delegates.[76] Caught between public and private commitments, he was in an increasingly difficult position. Publicly he was aligned with the political abolitionists, whose more conservative views on gender roles were expressed in their 1839 and 1840 efforts to exclude women from equal participation in the AASS. But his wife was becoming increasingly conscious of the inequalities arising from the exclusion of women from the public sphere. Elizabeth's close association with Lucretia Mott and other Garrisonians was undoubtedly a topic of discussion between herself and Henry. Her unwillingness to accept the criticism of Lucretia Mott by the British abolitionist John Scoble was a further source of disagreement. Annoyed at Elizabeth's response to Scoble's ill-mannered criticism of Mott, Henry chastised Elizabeth and hoped she would restrain herself in the future. Subsequently describing Scoble as "one of the most conceited men" she "ever met," Elizabeth condemned his "narrow ideas in regard to women," and expressed "intense satisfaction" at the seasickness Scoble suffered on the return voyage to the United States. Yet in an indication that she abided by her own prescription for married couples not to air their differences publicly, Elizabeth made no mention in her 1898 memoirs of Henry's request that she conduct herself more demurely. After that incident it appears that they decided not to allow their differences to interfere with their immediate plans. Recalling that Elizabeth had gone to London not as a delegate to the World's Anti-Slavery Convention, but as a newlywed, the other purpose of their trip, aside from attending the London meetings, was to enjoy their honeymoon. According to the available evidence, that is precisely what they did.[77]

To understand the Stantons' marriage, Henry's response to his differences with Elizabeth over abolitionist ideology must be distinguished from his response to her women's rights activism. Blanche Hersh has suggested that while the Stantons' marriage was "less harmonious than that of most feminist-abolitionists," the fact that Elizabeth was a Garrisonian, and Henry a New York abolitionist, was not a source of conflict. Hersh's conclusions regarding the Stantons' differences over antislavery ideology are sound. But, keeping in mind her tendency to view abolitionist marriages as generally successful and peaceful, her assessment of the Stantons' marriage requires clarification. Elizabeth Cady Stanton's abolitionist allegiances were more complicated than Hersh suggests. Given that Stanton became a devout advocate of women's political rights it was perhaps not surprising that she acknowledged the value of politics as an antislavery tactic. It is also helpful to recall that for a number of years Elizabeth was not an active participant in the public abolitionist movement, meaning that her differences with Henry were less divisive than they might otherwise have been.[78]

In the longer term, as Elizabeth became increasingly interested in the women's rights movement, she and Henry apparently reached an agreement whereby neither interfered publicly with the other's reform activities. There is evidence that Henry resented Elizabeth's increasingly public demands for women's rights. But they preferred to keep their differences relatively private. Moreover, Henry's attitude toward women's rights cannot be easily dismissed; despite indications that he opposed Elizabeth's efforts to improve women's position, and despite his refusal to attend the 1848 women's rights convention in Seneca Falls, he embraced a liberal attitude on several issues pertaining to women's role. In 1851, he presented petitions to the New York legislature on behalf of women's rights. When two of Stanton's fellow Senators "tried to throw ridicule upon" the petitions, he told Elizabeth that he "pounced upon them," whereupon "they backed out." Henry was not only pleased to report that he had presented the petitions. Clearly, he was also keen to tell Elizabeth of his success over his political adversaries, which he couched in terms of a victory for his masculine credentials. Henry also supported Elizabeth's reformism in other, more personal ways. When Elizabeth decided to wear the controversial Bloomer costume, he raised no objections, and was prepared to accompany Elizabeth in public when she was wearing the costume. For a politically inclined individual such as Stanton the potential damage from such actions was considerable, but he did support his wife. Other abolitionist men also supported their wives' determination to embrace the Bloomer costume. Henry Blackwell noted that he was "willing to *help*" Lucy Stone wear the costume, and Gerrit Smith, believing that women's dress imprisoned and belittled females, was an emphatic advocate of the Bloomer costume.[79]

Publicly and privately, James Mott demonstrated his sensitivity to radical women's demands. Mott's devotion to his family included the traditional assumption of responsibility as economic provider, and the reverence accorded Lucretia Mott's domestic skills suggests that James contributed little physical help within the home. He did, however, support his wife's public reformism. Mott's attitude was shaped by his experiences within the Society of Friends, where there had been disputes during the early nineteenth century regarding the respective powers of males' and females' meetings. Mott, concluding that such disputes were unnecessary, and confident that more enlightened ideas would ultimately triumph, hoped that women would "have an equal voice in the administration of the discipline." His support for women's rights was a natural extension of that egalitarian outlook. Evidence of the high esteem in which James Mott was held by female reformers was provided at the first women's rights convention, held at Seneca Falls in 1848. Tentative about the propriety of conducting the meeting themselves, and unsure of the correct procedures to adopt, the delegates elected Mott to be the presiding officer, a task he accomplished to the satisfaction of all present. By the time the women reconvened in Rochester two weeks later, their confidence had grown to the point where they did not hesitate to elect a woman to fill the chair. But the initial appointment of Mott to that role was an explicit affirmation of faith in his understanding of women's plight. Bearing in mind the role accorded to women as moral guardians within the domestic sphere, the choice of James Mott was an implicit endorsement of Lucretia's role in guiding him along the right path.[80]

Radical abolitionist men knew their support for women's rights distinguished them from their contemporaries. Just as female abolitionists were criticized for stepping beyond their designated sphere, their male supporters were vilified for their willingness to defend women's rights publicly, and for their apparently equal private treatment of women. Daniel R. Hundley's disparaging reference to "the Bloomer style of men" was representative of many men's responses to those male abolitionists who were interested in reforming marital practices. More generally, abolitionist men were assailed for their advocacy of sexual equality.[81] These criticisms were evident both institutionally and individually. Stephen Foster's condemnation of the churches for their failure to act against slavery earned him notoriety. But, revealing again how abolitionism aroused deep-seated fears concerning the sexual as well as the racial order, Foster's critics denounced his radical attitude toward women's rights. Even before his marriage the clergy chided him for his advocacy of gender reform. Calling upon Foster to correct his ways, the Church Committee of Dartmouth College noted in 1841 that Foster regarded the "gradations of society" as "a pretension & a contrivance for the elevation of the strong above the weak." The committee's claim that the "social distinctions of the sexes" were "taught by God equally in physical nature and the Bible" was no more convincing to Foster than arguments that slavery and racism were "natural" conditions, resulting from God's will. Not surprisingly, Foster was unmoved by the committee's decision to excommunicate him, and he continued to criticize what he considered the gross hypocrisy of the American churches.[82]

Foster, and other abolitionist men, were also sharply critical of the

Southern masculine ideal, which emphasized the importance of acknowledging the "natural impulse." That aspect of the Southern ideology, radical abolitionists believed, translated in practice to the oppression of all women. The contrast between the sexual mores of the South, including the tolerance of male infidelity, and the abolitionists' emphasis on purity and truth, could not have been greater. All abolitionists were appalled by the sexual violence endemic in slave society, and some repudiated the sexual abuse of wives by their husbands. But radical abolitionists' underlying distrust of masculine sexuality extended beyond the oppression of women in slave society and in marriage. Sexual excess of any kind was widely condemned in the nineteenth century, and immoderate sexual activity was perceived as a threat to "true manliness." For certain abolitionists, concern over what they judged as unnecessary sexual activity was an integral aspect of their reformism. Besides emphasizing the importance of physical health for women, abolitionists identified dangers to masculine self-development. In a period when good health was considered an essential prerequisite for the development of energetic and effective characters, great emphasis was placed on physical exercise and activity for both sexes. Like the proponents of "muscular Christianity," radical abolitionists were convinced that young men's intellectual and emotional improvement should be complemented by physical development.[83]

The abolitionists' interest in physical health, and their respect for manual labor—which foreshadowed the later nineteenth-century interest in sport as a symbol and agent of masculinity—merged with their determination not to allow the physical energy of American youth to be squandered by what Dr. Harvey Kellogg referred to as "self-pollution." Kellogg, John Todd, and other nineteenth-century writers railed against the perils of what William L. Garrison labeled the "dreadful vice of Masturbation." As Lewis Tappan's warning that "youthful lust" could cause "idiocy, insanity, disfigurement of body, and imbecility of mind" revealed, abolitionists believed masturbation threatened the intellectual and physical well-being of the nation's youth. Warning that the "vice of self-pollution" endangered the wider community, Garrison connected sexual impurity to the antislavery struggle. Critical of those who were "so fastidiously pure minded, (?) that they deem it indelicate (?) to be discussed," he argued that it was "as much the province of purity to hunt out and extirpate lewdness, as it is that of liberty to assail and destroy slavery." Abolitionists sought to ensure that their own children abided by these precepts. Having earlier advised their second son, Thoda, to engage in some "manly pursuit," Theodore Weld and Angelina Grimké connected what was diagnosed as a psychological disturbance with a fear that he was engaging in "willful sexual self-abuse." One of the commonly expressed fears of those who warned of the dangers of masturbation was that seminal loss detracted from a young man's physical strength, a particularly significant concern given that nineteenth-century masculinity was routinely couched in terms of men of action.[84]

For abolitionists—black as well as white—these issues assumed new urgency after the mid-1840s, when sectional differences made a civil war all the more likely, and when the women's rights movement achieved public prominence. We have seen that black abolitionists' long-standing concern with masculine values encompassed a range of attributes associated with different models of manhood. But in the decades preceding the Civil War, as they became increasingly exasperated at what they regarded as white abolitionists' proclivity toward abstraction and prevarication, African American abolitionists embraced a more activist approach to the twin problems of slavery and equality. This process was demonstrated by the changing responses to Henry Highland Garnet's "Address to the Slaves of America." Speaking to the 1843 "National Convention of Colored Citizens," Garnet argued it would be better for those in bondage to "die freemen than live like slaves." The issue was debated at length, but led by Frederick Douglass, a majority of delegates concluded Garnet's speech was too militant to be published. By the time the African American leadership reconvened in 1847, however, the mood had changed, and the delegates to the national convention voted in favor of publication. This shift is significant not only because it attests to changing black attitudes on the question of direct action. A close look at Garnet's speech indicates that even as he framed masculine values in terms of action and bravery, he had embraced many of the familial and domestic values that dominated antebellum America. Besides calling for black men to remember "the stripes your father bore," he spoke particularly of the injustices suffered by black women: "Think of the torture and disgrace of your noble mothers. Think of your wretched sisters, loving virtue and purity, as they are driven into concubinage, and are exposed to the unbridled lusts of incarnate devils." Black men, Garnet averred, were too passive. "In the name of God," he asked, "are you men?" The increasingly activist stance of black abolitionists in the pre–Civil War era included fresh calls to contemplate the question of emigration. On this issue, too, as

Garnet's 1849 assertion that he would "rather see a man free in Liberia, than a slave in the United States" suggested, African Americans' expressions of frustration with American society were gendered in a way that emphasized the emasculating effects of racism and slavery.[85]

The growing sectional crisis also prompted white abolitionists to reassess their attitude toward violence. While Garrisonians continued to praise the value of moral suasionism, they did exhibit a greater tolerance of violence. Stephen Foster, speaking soon after the passage of the notorious Fugitive Slave Act of 1850, summed up his feelings at the time and hinted at the changes in abolitionist sensibilities that would ensue during the next decade. Foster was reported as having been not personally "prepared to say we should kill any body in defence of the fugitive slave," but in the martyr tradition of which the abolitionists saw themselves, "he believed it was a cause to die ourselves." Moreover, while he declared that he "would not use the sword of physical violence, because there was a mightier sword, the sword of the spirit," Foster left the way open for others to use violent means. " 'But,' said he, 'if any of you are not acquainted with this sword [of the spirit], and know only the sword of steel, and believe in its use for your own defence, in God's name use it now.' "[86]

The conflict that erupted in "Bleeding Kansas" during the mid-1850s, when proslavery and antislavery settlers were warring over the future of slavery in the western territories, was a portent of the Civil War. Abolitionists Thomas Wentworth Higginson and Gerrit Smith described the struggle in Kansas in terms that stressed the masculine dimension to the free settlers' struggle there. The contest in Kansas also interested L. Maria Child, who argued that antislavery women were endowed with virtues characteristically attributed to men. Having remarked privately in 1855 that she admired "a *manly* woman, though I dislike a *masculine* one," Child noted later that she had never "been so proud of women," as when reading of the "patient endurance" and "undaunted heroism" of the women in Kansas. In 1856, Child alluded to the gendering of public abolitionism. "Would to God there were *men* enough on board of her [the North]," she declared, "to man a new Life-Boat, the Northern Republic."[87] Evidently, she believed that courageous action was required if the North was to achieve independence from the tyranny of the slave power.

Accusations that abolitionists lacked courage were coupled with criticisms of their advocacy of gender reform. One response to the challenge posed by radical abolitionism was to question the masculinity of abolitionist men. The editors of the *New York Herald* vigorously denigrated "henpecked" male abolitionists, by claiming they required the protection of women.[88] Besides insulting the abolitionists' audience, the editors of the Baltimore *Patriot* belittled abolitionists for their alleged lack of such masculine virtues as courage, chivalry, and honor—characteristics closely associated with the patriarchal ideal of Southern society. Wendell Phillips, declared the Baltimore editors in 1854, was "one of those ferocious champions of freedom, who denounce the dead or distant to assemblies composed of ladies, children and divines. He is one of those trumpeters who bray at the onset, but are never seen in the charge." The editors of the *Patriot* not only accused Phillips of cowardice but, implying that the women supporters of abolition were unable to find husbands, also disparaged women abolitionists' femininity. "Perhaps if a civil war should come," they sardonically suggested, "Mr. Phillips would be surrounded by a life-guard of elderly maiden ladies, and protected by a rampart of whalebone and cotton-padding."[89]

Some abolitionists systematically justified their willingness to advocate violent means to overthrow slavery. As Michael Fellman has explained, Theodore Parker's support for violent means rested upon the belief that abolitionists were heirs to the revolutionary heroes who had been compelled to take violent measures to expel the British.[90] It was John Brown who most effectively brought these matters to the public eye. Despite the Garrisonians' professed philosophical rejection of physical violence, Brown's failed attempt to promote a rebellion among the slaves elicited a range of responses from the antislavery community. Lucretia Mott, separating Brown's military endevors from his moral virtue, declared that "it is not John Brown the soldier that we praise; it is John Brown the moral hero." The pertinent point was that Brown's abhorrence of slavery, and his courageous and defiant attitude toward his impending execution, earned him the acclaim of abolitionists.[91] As with the death of the antislavery editor Elijah Lovejoy in 1837, abolitionists recognized the propaganda advantages to be derived from Virginia's decision to execute Brown. But there was a specifically masculine dimension to abolitionists' comments on Brown. Bertram Wyatt-Brown's suggestion that Brown, whose "demeanor and actions were unmistakably masculine," offered abolitionists "a champion, someone to represent Yankee honor," in tandem with the endorsement of Brown by Northern intellectuals, and the popular sympathy for his plight, points to his significance for the abolitionist self-perception. Wendell Phillips not only lauded Brown as a man of "action," but also specifically commended him for his valor. Similarly, Stephen Foster's praise for Brown's actions, his 1855 warning that the nation's only choice was "between slaveholding and revolution," and his 1859 call for "less profession, and more deed," signified his increasingly activist approach to the problem of slavery. By January 1859 Foster was speaking privately of beginning "the war."[92]

Stephen Foster had long enjoyed a reputation for extremism within the abolitionist movement, but his readiness to accept a more activist approach to the slavery issue was not unique. Even L. Maria Child, whose long-standing aversion to direct confrontation and violence was expressed in many ways—from her domestic tracts, through her determination not to allow the *National Anti-Slavery Standard* to become an organ promoting division within the antislavery movement, to her own search for domestic peace—reluctantly concluded during the 1850s that a war that led to emancipation might be preferable to allowing slavery to survive. "If the Slave Power is checked *now,*" she assured Sarah Shaw in 1856, "it will *never* regain its strength. If it is *not* checked, civil war is inevitable; and with all my horror of bloodshed, I could be better resigned to that great calamity, than to endure the Tyranny that has so long trampled on us." Four years later, although she continued to proclaim that it was her "business" to "use all my energies in creating the will" to emancipate the slaves, Child also betrayed an increasing tolerance of political action. By suggesting that "legislators" should decide "in what way it [emancipation] is to be accomplished," she accommodated at least part of the premise of political abolitionism and of the masculine political culture that had for so long defended slavery. In 1857, Abby Kelley told members of the Massachusetts Anti-Slavery Society that "every true friend of liberty here would rejoice to hear to-night that the slaves of Louisiana or of Tennessee had risen up against their masters." Referring to the ongoing institutionalized violence associated with slavery, Kelley disclaimed any abolitionist responsibility for bringing on sectional conflict that may lead to war. The real aggressors, she reported, were the slave owners. The "question is not whether we shall counsel the slave to forsake peace, and commence war;" she told her listeners, "*the war exists already,* and has been waged unremittingly ever since the slave has been in bondage."[93]

For Wendell Phillips, the rising tensions associated with the slavery issue prompted personal and ideological shifts. Frequently facing violent mobs, and willing to utilize the services of sympathetic bodyguards, Phillips carried a revolver during 1860 and 1861, when the dispute over slavery was approaching its zenith. Phillips's actions were in self-defense, but there is evidence of a deeper shift in his abolitionist outlook. Although he declared in 1857 that the "slave does not seek the help of your musket," his speeches of the 1850s reflected an increasing willingness to accept direct action against slavery. His lecture on the Haitian revolutionary leader Toussaint L'Ouverture implicitly endorsed a direct strike against the slave power. In his speech praising the actions of Crispus Attucks, an African American who had played a prominent part in the early stages of the American Revolution, Phillips couched his endorsement of direct action in terms particularly applicable to the American experience. Direct action on behalf of abolitionism, he inferred, was as justified as the actions of those eighteenth-century Americans who had taken up arms against the British. "It is an easy thing to fight when the blood is hot," Phillips said in his praise of Attucks, "but this man whose memory we commemorate tonight stepped out of common life, every-day quiet, and lifted his arm among the very first against the government. It is only pre-eminent courage that can do this." Similarly, Harriet Beecher Stowe, who at the beginning of the 1850s had placed domestic and feminine values at the center of *Uncle Tom's Cabin,* was by 1856 exhibiting greater tolerance towards a "masculine" solution to slavery. In the novel, *Dred: A Tale of the Great Dismal Swamp,* Stowe paid tribute to Denmark Vesey and Nat Turner, two slaves who had achieved notoriety for their efforts to end slavery by violent rebellion. Vesey and Turner failed to liberate the slaves, but their readiness to strike directly against the slave power signified their personal courage, and at one point Stowe specifically praised Vesey: "Denmark Vesey was a *man*!"[94]

On a more personal level, the actions of abolitionist men suggest the significance of their physical commitment to aiding the slaves during the 1850s. "The turn to violence and the tolerance or enthusiasm for armed resistance" among the abolitionists, may have remained, as Jane and William Pease have argued, "more symbolic than real." Yet there is evidence that abolitionist men welcomed the opportunity to involve themselves directly in the slavery issue. The plight of ex-slaves provided such opportunities. Many abolitionists' homes had long been used by former slaves as refuges on the "Underground Railroad," but the 1850 Fugitive Slave Act made it easier for ex-slaves to be returned to the South. Long convinced that the North was implicated in the perpetuation of slavery, radical abolitionists regarded the 1850 legislation as the fulfillment of their prophecy that slavery was poisoning social relations throughout the nation in ever more tangible ways. In seeking to subvert the Fugitive Slave Act, Garrisonian abolitionists were occasionally compelled to confront the forces of slavery head-on. Wendell Phillips suggested in 1854 that if necessary, opponents of slavery should resort to street fighting to thwart kidnappers intent on taking ex-slaves back to the South. Stephen Foster, even before his direct involvement in a slave rescue, had articulated his position on this issue. At the 1854 New England Anti-Slavery Convention, he spoke of the importance of helping protect ex-slaves. As the proceedings of the convention reveal, the masculine role was of undoubted importance to Foster. "Every man," he was quoted as saying, "should fight against slavery with his own weapons,—with those whose use he best understood, and in which he most trusted. If those were physical weapons, let him use them." Drawing a distinction between men in urban areas and those outside the cities, Foster "said that men in the country, (and he spoke especially of Worcester), were ready to combine and organize against kidnapping, if those in the city were not." Moreover, he argued, those in the country "were men who might be depended upon, in any extremity." Other delegates disputed Foster's implicit disparagement of city men, but the significant point was that manliness was considered important.[95] The conjunction of individual physical commitment to the slavery issue, and male abolitionists' self-image, were shown by Foster's and Henry Blackwell's personal participation in the liberation of slaves.

Blackwell's 1854 actions in assisting an African American secure her freedom helped him establish his abolitionist credentials with Lucy Stone, whom he was then courting. Appropriately, Blackwell was addressing an antislavery meeting in Salem, Ohio, when word arrived that a train would soon be passing through the town with "a colored girl with her master & mistress, on her way to Tennessee." Adjourning the convention, the delegates hurried to the train station, whereupon a tense confrontation ensued. Blackwell recounted to Stone his involvement in the events of that day:

> The child was asked if she wished to be free & replied yes whereupon I told the owners, the husband having meanwhile come in, that the child was now legally free under our laws & must go with us. I took the child's arm, & commenced lifting her from her seat, seeing that the passengers in the cars seemed to sympathize with the owners, & that there was no time to be lost. At that moment a young Cincinnatian of

> the name of Keyes collared me & remonstrated with me. I let go of the child, who was instantly caught up by the other members of the committee & passed out & carried swiftly off into the town in the arms of a colored man, and shook him off. . . . Altogether, it is a rather amusing affair, & I do not regret the part I took in it, notwithstanding the odium and misunderstanding which attaches to anything of the kind.[96]

Blackwell's enthusiastic description of his involvement in the events in the Salem rescue, rendered all the more powerful by the fact that he was helping a child secure freedom, signified his readiness to directly confront the slaveholders. That willingness to meet the forces of slavery head-on contrasted with the accusation that abolitionists were too cowardly to directly engage their protagonists.

Stephen Foster, too, was involved in a personal confrontation with the forced of slavery. Foster had no need to impress his wife, nor anybody else, of his commitment to the slaves, yet the events of late October 1854 reveal that he was pleased to be able to demonstrate his very direct involvement in abolitionism—as his subsequent letter to Abby confirmed. When a federal marshal arrived in Worcester looking for former slaves, a vigilance committee of abolitionists was organized to make his task more difficult. Following the marshal's attempt to detain an African American, a hostile crowd formed. But Foster and his abolitionist colleagues led the marshal safely through the gathering, eliciting a promise from him that he would leave town. Foster then made a brief speech, and the marshal was permitted to withdraw in safety. Foster's involvement in those events was doubly significant: besides preventing the return of an ex-slave to the South, he was able to combine that objective with the protection of the marshal.[97] His actions were symbolic of the abolitionism of the 1850s, when the waning commitment to moral suasionism continued to operate alongside a wider tolerance of direct action against slavery.

That ambivalence continued during the Civil War. Lacking military experience, and generally too old to contemplate direct involvement in war, few prominent abolitionist men took part in the fighting. Henry Blackwell established a Union League to oppose the antiwar societies that sprang up during the conflict, but his commitment to the war was not without limitations. Drafted to serve in the Union Army, Blackwell—like many other men who were able to do so—avoided military service by paying three hundred dollars for a substitute.[98] Nonetheless, despite the abolitionists' disagreements and uncertainties over whether force should be employed to emancipate the slaves, and the long-standing devotion of many to nonresistance and peace, once the Civil War began, abolitionists counseled Abraham Lincoln to engage the South as vigorously as possible. Abolitionists abhorred the war's bloodshed, but as Sarah Grimké's description of the Civil War as "the holiest ever raged" indicated, they believed its purpose was honorable—especially after Lincoln issued the Emancipation Proclamation.[99]

Lauding values such as peace and harmony, radical abolitionist men sought intimacy and equity in their relationships, both with each other and with the women they loved and worked alongside. Again, radical abolitionism said much about the demarcation between public and private life. Even while abolitionist men valued the domestic realm, they challenged the distinctions, both real and contrived, between the public and private spheres. Besides involving themselves in the private world of home and family, radical abolitionist men spurned the party politics of antebellum America, and advocated nonviolence—thereby abstaining from institutions and activities widely regarded as "masculine." Nonetheless, the politicization of antislavery during the 1850s drew some abolitionists nearer the political mainstream, and hence closer to the prevailing patterns of masculine involvement in the nation's political culture and system. As well as being unable, or unwilling, to discard completely all the elements of the prevailing view of masculinity, their eulogization of John Brown, and their ultimate endorsement of the Civil War, point to what might be labeled a hesitant "masculinization" of abolitionism in the 1850s and 1860s. These trends coexisted with an abiding commitment to family and marriage. Like their female coadjutors, male abolitionists sought to merge their desire for individual reform with the imperatives of public reformism. Abolitionists emphatically rejected the institutionalized violence they associated with the abuse of masculine powers in the slave states. While radical abolitionists' construction of masculinity did not signify complete equality between women and men, it did stand in stark contrast to the Southern view of gender relations, and foreshadowed the emergent emphasis on companionate marital relations throughout the nation. An essential aspect of companionate marriage was the increased emphasis on intimacy: having examined social and working relationships between abolitionist women and men, the final chapter further explores relations between abolitionist husbands and wives.

SIX

"My Heart's Dearest Idol": *Intimacy and Affection in Abolitionist Marriages*

THE SOCIAL AND REFORMING NETworks to which radical abolitionists belonged, and the oft-intimate friendships that underpinned these networks, challenged prevailing ideas regarding gender roles and transcended the division between the public and private realms. As significant as these relationships were, however, radical abolitionists continued to regard marriage as the key institution in civil society. Through their efforts to reform marriage, and to establish and maintain marital intimacy, they self-consciously pondered the emotional and physical aspects of the marriage relationship. These deliberations were linked to their reform priorities and to their role in testing the boundaries between public and private life. Radical abolitionists considered marriage and love as private matters, and they embraced a conversion model of reform that rested firmly on the perfection of the individual.[1] Nonetheless, during a period in which the notions of private and public were in flux, these abolitionists regarded their marital relationships as public statements, linking their antislavery commitment to gender and family reform. Convinced that public and private reform were interdependent, and certain that marriage was the most important of all human relationships, they carried matters of love, romance, and marriage into public discourse. Much of the significance of radical abolitionism derives from this reshaping of the public sphere.

Central to radical abolitionists' racial and gender ideologies, and to the response they generated, was the question of sexuality. Since sexuality is "socially constructed," analyzing abolitionists' sexual ideologies—and, where possible, aspects of their sexual relations—provides an opportunity to test popular and scholarly stereotypes concerning nineteenth-century sexuality.[2] Abolitionists' attitudes toward sexuality must be seen within the context of the evolution of romantic marriage. With its increased emphasis on an emotional attachment between women and men, the development of romantic marriage made it more likely that individuals would marry people of their own choosing, rather than respond to a situation imposed by their parents, or by economic and social circumstances. Within that process, however, new difficulties emerged; as expectations rose, so too did the potential for failure. Karen Lystra has referred to the contradiction arising from the evolution of companionate marriage. "Victorians conceived of marriage," she wrote "in terms of love and personal choice. Yet spousal roles were largely defined as compulsory social obligations. An act of self-determined choice, Victorian marriage nonetheless imposed a set of mandatory sex-role specific duties upon husband and wife." By questioning these gender-defined roles, radical abolitionists sought to resolve the contradiction to which Lystra referred. Underscoring their desire to establish equitable marriages was a conviction that intimacy (typified by Stephen Foster's description of Abby Kelley as "My heart's dearest idol") was essential to the marital relationship. This concern with intimacy, standing in contrast to the horrors inflicted upon slaves, held implications for gender reform, an issue that continued to interest radical reformers long after the emancipation of the slaves. As Elizabeth Cady Stanton remarked in 1870, when husbands and wives did "not own each other as property," but were instead "bound together only by affection," marriage would be "a life-long friendship, and not a heavy yoke from which both may sometimes long for deliverance." Yet while radical abolitionists ascribed great value to the elusive force described by Theodore Weld as a "love that baffles all expressions," they understood that affection did not necessarily equate with equality, and their marriages were neither static nor without tensions. L. Maria Child captured both sides of this process. "You and I are like two drops of quick-silver placed a few inches apart on a level surface," Child told her husband in 1836, "there is a continual restlessness and agitation, till at last they get together."[3]

The way radical abolitionists approached marriage revealed much about their perception of the relationship. Again, their experiences and attitudes were characterized by an underlying duality. The task was to balance conflicting urges and desires; abolitionists were not devoid of a desire to express their feelings, physically as well as emotionally. Confirming Karen Lystra's argument that love "was defined as one thing beyond individual control," some abolitionists admitted the depth of their initial attraction to their future spouses. Physical characteristics played a part of that initial attraction, but equally significant was a sense of personal union that could be a thrilling and liberating experience. Prior to her marriage Ann Terry Greene playfully recounted how she had crept into Wendell Phillips's room when he was away. Looking "in vain for a trace of" her "beloved," Ann's disappointment was alleviated by their impending reunion. "Tomorrow!" she exclaimed, "how much that little word bears on its bosom for me, for *us,* since, we trust it brings us together." Writing in March 1855, Henry Blackwell admitted to Lucy Stone "*I loved you at first sight.*" "It was not for nothing," he recalled, "that my heart leaped towards you & yearned for you when I first saw you in our store six years ago."[4]

Yet even in those cases of immediate attraction, abolitionists often held their feelings in check before they declared their love—as was common for the period. William L. Garrison attested to his initial attraction to Helen Benson, and to his caution. "From the very first moment" that he saw Helen, he noted in 1834, he was "most favorably impressed, in relation to her personal, mental, and moral worth." "Her image was with me constantly," he continued, "during my absence from the country—and it was with joy that I saw her on my return." But Garrison was unable to state his feelings: the need for restraint, a fear of rejection, or an inability to convey his feelings adequately served to inhibit a declaration of love. "At each successive interview," he wrote, "I felt a growing attachment, but I disclosed my feelings and predilections to no one." Garrison's caution appears repressive, but nineteenth-century courtships were more formal than those of subsequent eras. Alongside their circumspection, abolitionists carefully contemplated marriage. The principles of organization and efficiency, so important in both domesticity and abolitionism, also affected marriage. Reflecting a wider trend of the late eighteenth and early nineteenth centuries, abolitionists exercised increasing independence from their parents in choosing their spouses. These imperatives were evident in many ways: from Elizabeth Cady Stanton's defiance of her father's disapproval of Henry Stanton, to Wendell Phillips's refusal to be deterred by his mother's disapproval of his love for Ann Terry Greene, to Theodore Weld's reassurance to Angelina Grimké that his declaration of love was more than a mere "rhapsody of a lover." Indeed, Weld's assurance to Grimké that his love for her was "the combined dictate of my reason and judgement and conscience and self knowledge" revealed much about radical abolitionists' self-conscious efforts to approach marriage in a rational manner.[5]

Besides perceiving marriage as the fulfillment of the individual desires of husband and wife, radical abolitionists regarded true marriage as an expression of God's will. This belief was linked to their understanding of their reformist mission. Abby Kelley feared that romance and love would distract her from the task of liberating the slaves—a commitment, she believed, that required a special relationship with God. Apprehensive that love for a man would interfere with that relationship, and always anxious about her individuality, Kelley reacted warily to Stephen Foster's marriage proposals. Although she agreed to marry Foster, Kelley's concerns did not abate once she had made up her mind to marry. Abolitionist men betrayed similar concerns. Theodore Weld valued his relationship with God, but he ultimately concluded that a proper love, and marriage, would not threaten that relationship, and would actually facilitate his reformism. Angelina Grimké was also attuned to these imperatives. While Weld remained an advocate of individualism, Grimké feared that he was sublimating his own desires too much. Typically attentive to the special relationship between God and the individual, she urged Weld to take note of God's will, rather than "*what you think is mine.*" Henry Blackwell, too, was conscious of this issue. Writing to Lucy Stone in 1855, he summed up his feelings: "I am very glad dear Lucy that I can reveal, in spite of my imperfections, something of Divinity to your soul—I should like to stand in your heart & mind as a perpetual reminder of the nobler qualities of Man, as you must represent to me the highest elements of Womanhood." Beyond his feelings of gratitude that Stone was permitting him to express himself freely, and his inference that men and women were imbued with different qualities, Blackwell believed that a proper union of a man and a woman was an expression of God's will, infused with its own divine element.[6]

Determined to proceed along the path they deemed the right one, and conscious that their behavior was subject to intense public scrutiny, radical abolitionists realized the dangers of alienating or offending their nonabolitionist contemporaries. Some abolitionists recognized that marriage was a means of avoiding public opprobrium. Abby Kelley and Stephen Foster were particularly sensitive to these issues. Telling Foster in 1845 that there were many who wished her "married to get rid of me," Kelley pointed directly to the public perception of women's role: "they would say I was under *obligation to take care of your feeble constitution and nurse you.*" Kelley's determination not to be constrained by stereotypes concerning women's sphere did not mean she was prepared to attract criticism if it could be avoided. Nine months before their marriage, she cautioned Foster. "I do not know as it would be expedient for us to journey together," she wrote, "until we are one before the world." Following her wedding, Kelley was adamant that marriage was beneficial to both her personal happiness and her public reformism: "since our marriage our meetings have been much more successful than ever heretofore. We realize that even in the anti slavery cause a whole man and a whole woman are far better than a half man and a half woman."[7]

Kelley's statements hinted at the difficulties abolitionists faced in integrating public reformism with private feelings. All marriages involve differences between spouses, and abolitionists' close marital relationships did not preclude dissent over a range of issues. But these differences of opinion did not necessarily detract from what continued to be close marriages. Lucretia Mott noted in 1841 that while she and James differed on the subject of "Theology," such disagreements were not allowed to interfere with the peaceful domestic environment in their home. Stephen Foster, writing to Wendell Phillips, outlined differences between himself and Kelley regarding antislavery ideology and strategy. Yet Foster encouraged his wife's independence, and "to the extent" of his "ability," he sought to "aid her in the faithful discharge of her trust." The question of balancing reform priorities, particularly gender and race reform, sometimes proved difficult. Kelley and Foster disagreed over the relative importance of the women's rights issues vis-à-vis the struggle for African American equality. Following the Civil War, Kelley argued that the question of women's suffrage should be put to one side until voting rights had been secured for African Americans. Unlike his wife, who rejected linking the two issues, Foster publicly brought the women's suffrage question into antislavery meetings. His actions signified his commitment to the cause of women's rights, but he ultimately relinquished ground after Elizabeth Cady Stanton and Susan B. Anthony sought to place the women's suffrage issue above that of black suffrage.[8] There is no evidence, however, that Kelley and Foster permitted their public disagreements over that issue to interfere with their commitment to their own family. In other abolitionist marriages, differences and disappointments contributed directly to an emerging sense of female independence and consciousness. It is partly for that reason that caution should be exercised in labeling such relationships as "failures." And even in the marriage of Henry and Elizabeth Cady Stanton, with all its long-standing tensions, there were positive aspects of their relationship, not the least of which was the mutual satisfaction they derived from their children. Moreover, despite Elizabeth's dissatisfactions with her marriage, she and Henry continued to communicate on family matters.[9]

Abolitionists were committed to dealing honestly with differences of opinion. But they also hoped that some differences could be avoided if women and men were able to engage in an open dialogue before they married. Nineteenth-century ideas of propriety could inhibit such a dialogue during abolitionists' courtships. Elizabeth Cady Stanton referred to these conflicting imperatives. Stanton, whose memoirs include little mention of her husband, recalled in 1898 that there were advantages to be derived from having enjoyed an honest discourse with Henry before their marriage. She noted that when she first met Henry, he "had come over from Utica with" fellow abolitionist "Alvan Stewart's beautiful daughter, to whom report said he was engaged." That rumor proved false, but Elizabeth remembered that the fact that Henry was not viewed as a possible husband had its advantages. "Regarding him as not in the matrimonial market," she wrote, "we were all much more free and easy in our manners with him than we would otherwise have been." This inferred that the formality attached to courtship impeded a full exchange of views; but abolitionists sought to understand each other more fully before marriage. Convinced that the need for honesty transcended concerns about impropriety, they emphasized the need for absolute honesty before they wed. That determination conformed to a wider pattern among middle-class men and women, but for some abolitionists the "goal" of "learning as much as possible about the prospective mate," was all the more significant because of their determination to maintain their involvement in reformism after marriage. Hoping that an open exchange of views would assist in establishing the precise nature of their relationship, Lucy Stone and Henry Blackwell stressed the need for honesty: "we are going to be very frank," Stone told Blackwell in October 1854, "and very candid and very honest, with ourselves and with each other when we meet. And *then* we shall not misunderstand nor mistake."[10]

Angelina Grimké linked this sense of honesty to spouses' ability to understand each other more fully. Beyond confirming the primacy of the marriage relationship, and implying the boundaries of abolitionist sorority, Grimké viewed marriage as a means of individual self-fulfillment. Angelina enjoyed close friendships with her sister Sarah and with Jane Smith, and she noted that they were willing to tell her of her faults. But she assured Weld that he understood aspects of her character more fully: "you dear brother have, I must acknowledge, dived deeper into the *hidden* sins of my heart than any one ever did before, and you can therefore do me more good." Abolitionists' determination to maintain marital honesty did not mean secrets were not occasionally kept from spouses—as an 1859 exchange between Abby Kelley and William L. Garrison demonstrated. But Kelley's letter to Garrison was most revealing for its affirmation of the honesty and freedom of expression within abolitionist marriages. Believing that she had been slandered by Garrison, Kelley wrote to him, hoping to resolve their differences. Referring to a letter she had received from Garrison, she confided: "No one knows I have received it—not even my husband from whom I am not wont to withhold any thing." The implication, as Kelley made clear, was that such circumstances were unusual.[11]

Radical abolitionists' mutual desire for an honest exchange of views helped them express their romantic attachments. Lawrence Friedman has identified an "awful strain" felt during the initial years of the abolitionists' marriages, when the "marital bond" usually "appeared quite frail." But tensions and difficulties should not mask the happiness, and sense of personal liberation, that many abolitionists felt upon marriage. As well as overstating the fragility of the abolitionists' marriages, Friedman does not pay due cognizance to the role of the mutual love felt by abolitionists during the early stages of their marriages. The affection between abolitionists husbands and wives played an important role in helping them to overcome marital tensions. Friedman has suggested that William L. Garrison "experienced sharp strains early in his marriage." Yet Garrison left evidence that his marriage began happily enough, a pattern not uncommon for the period. After proudly describing himself in 1822 as "An Old Bachelor," he later explained his joy at marriage. Having "jumped, body and soul, into matrimony," Garrison pointed out that he had "sunk the character of bachelor in that of husband."[12]

Domestic values permeated the abolitionists' romantic lives, and shaped their perception of the value of home life. Their celebrations of domestic harmony were premised upon undisguised affirmations of intimacy and affection—emotions most fully achieved, they believed, within the home and true marriage. Given that William L. Garrison's public endorsements of women's rights were underpinned by a marriage that provided few opportunities for Helen to move beyond the private sphere, it was perhaps not surprising that his affirmations of love for her were premised upon an appreciation of domestic tranquility. Describing his joy at achieving what he had long "been yearning to find," he expressed his good fortune in having "a home, a wife, and a beautiful retreat from a turbulent city." Following his 1840 trip to London, Garrison attested to the importance of his home. " 'There is no place like it,' at least to me," he wrote, "Surrounded by my dear wife and children, and feeling reconciled to God and no enmity toward any human being, I am very happy." Resting his statements on widely held beliefs concerning the allegedly different natures of women and men, Garrison's perception of the domestic sphere as a place where he could recuperate from the pressures of public life was evident in an 1838 letter to his sister-in-law. Implicitly depicting the contrast between the private and public spheres in terms of a dichotomy between the intellect and emotion, he noted that while his "poor brain . . . reels under the pressure," his "heart" was "as tranquil as a summer's sea, and happier than any bird that ever warbled forth a song." Garrison used metaphors of slavery and imprisonment to describe his relationship with Helen. His intention, however, was ironic, and served to highlight the contrast between the intimacy enjoyed by abolitionists, and the destruction of family life that occurred under slavery:

"You perceive that I make a very submissive and even loyal prisoner, and am well pleased with my captivity, I am not anxious to have my fetters broken; for to serve and obey you is henceforth to be the pleasing duty of my life." Writing to Lucy Stone in March 1858, Henry Blackwell betrayed an optimism similar to Garrison's. Admitting that he would "doubtless make many mistakes & commit many errors," he expressed guilt at having kept her "in so *unsatisfied* a condition" since their wedding. Yet he remained confident that their marriage would succeed, and begged her forgiveness: "you must forgive them [his errors] for *I love you very dearly.*"[13]

The case of Abby Kelley and Stephen Foster casts further doubt upon the validity of Lawrence Friedman's thesis concerning the early stages of abolitionist marriages. His claim that the Kelley-Foster marriage commenced on a "fragile and worrisome basis" underestimated the elation they felt during the early part of their married life. There were questions to be resolved, as there are in every relationship. But the affection between Kelley and Foster, complementing their shared commitment to the slaves, played an important role in the resolution of those questions. Nearly a year after her marriage, Kelley revealed that her joy was undiminished. Declaring that "Stephen is mine and I am Stephen's," she claimed that if she had "known how much holier and happier and more useful married life was than single," she would not have "tarried so long in the outer walls of marriage—engagement."[14] For Kelley, there was no contradiction between marriage as a means of living a more complete existence, and her desire to retain her individuality. Rather, marriage could facilitate a sense of individuality. The attachment between Kelley and Foster remained powerful. And while Kelley was away lecturing on behalf of the slaves, Foster expressed his strong attachment to the domestic ideal. "Our house is no *home* to me," he lamented in 1851, "*in your absence.*"[15]

Abolitionists viewed love as an enduring emotion. Aware of the heady feelings of the early period of love, they were determined that their relationships would not only survive, but should improve over time. That optimism contrasted with their perception of the slaves' long-term romantic and domestic prospects. "Dear Lucy—we shall soon get over the *intoxication* of love," wrote Henry Blackwell in February 1855, "but then we shall have the better delight of intimate & calm communion & be thereby perpetually refreshed & revived." Blackwell's metaphoric reference to intoxication implied an ambivalence toward the passions aroused during the early stages of his relationship with Stone. His excitement was accompanied by an implicit distaste for the urges he experienced at that time. Yet his tempered criticism of those urges was not a rejection of specifically masculine desires; he inferred that Stone's feelings paralleled his. Concerning his domestic aspirations, Blackwell echoed William L. Garrison's views. "I want to be *quiet* dear Lucy," he wrote in 1856, "& to get time to *breathe* & *think* for the first time, since I was 14 years old."[16]

An obvious indication of the affection between abolitionist husbands and wives was their manner of addressing each other. Abby Kelley's reference to "My very dear Stephen," and James Mott's description of Lucretia Mott as "my dearly beloved," were typical. Conforming to a wider pattern, abolitionists frequently used affectionate nicknames.[17] These romantic sentiments were more than tokens. David Lee Child's love for Maria, along with his awareness of the difficulties he had imposed upon her, were apparent in an 1830 letter from the Vermont town of Williamstown: "My heart has got very homesick. It seems as if I were in a new state of existence. I had need to be absent to learn how necessary you are to me. I have passed thru many grand & beautiful natural scenes, but without you I lacked sense and enthusiasm to enjoy them. I live with the hope that the time will come when I shall have leisure and other means to indulge my strong desire to carry you to such places and to select such a residence as will gratify our taste. You cannot imagine how often I have thought of your bright and affectionate face looking up so kindly and confidently in mine. It makes my heart melt & the tears come to think how [sweetly] you have borne yourself to me in the severe trials which I have brought upon you." Despite the difficulties they encountered in the course of their marriage, David Lee Child's affection for his wife did not diminish; writing to Maria twenty-six years later, he exclaimed: "How I do miss my mate."[18]

Child's statement raised the issue of the separations endured by abolitionists. Responding to these separations—which were tangible manifestations of the tension between public obligations and individual, private desires and responsibilities—radical abolitionists affirmed the significance of their marital bonds. In the process they explicitly contrasted their own feelings with those of the slaves, whose family lives were so devastated by slavery. William L. Garrison, connecting his familial attachments with his sense of sacrifice on the slaves' behalf, commented on the pain of his separation from his family: "how grateful am I to God, that he has given me a free wife, and free children! I shall not be tortured with the apprehension, that you may be sold to some hyena-spirited slave-speculator, or that George or Willie may be kidnapped and reduced to slavery. Nor will your bosom be torn with anguish at the thought that I may be claimed and hurried off as the property of another." During one of Helen's rare absences from home, Garrison evinced his loneliness, as he frequently did when he was away. Noting in 1865 that "every day lessens the time of our separation," he added "We shall all rejoice when August arrives that we may have you once more with us."[19]

Henry Stanton also missed his family when he was away from home. "I saw you felt very sad when I left," he wrote to Elizabeth soon after the birth of their first child, "But, you did not feel worse than I did. To leave 'the kid and his mother,' was very trying. I assure you, I felt sad, solemn, & disconsolate." Stanton's statement offers a range of insights into his marriage. In the first instance, it was an unambiguous exclamation of his love for Elizabeth and the young child. His effusive statement might also indicate that he felt it necessary to reassure Elizabeth that his absence did not mean his love was abating. Stanton's extended absences from Seneca Falls did not detract from what remained a strong attachment to his family. Elizabeth Cady Stanton became increasingly independent, but Henry continued to miss his family. His exasperated pleas to his wife to correspond more frequently, continuing through the 1850s and 1860s, perhaps signified unrequited love. For Henry Stanton, these domestic attachments were particularly evident during periods of crisis; in accordance with domestic ideology, the private sphere was seen as a refuge from public concerns. As he remarked following the outbreak of the Civil War, a "sense of danger" turned his thoughts toward home.[20]

Abolitionists of both sexes, conforming to a wider pattern detailed by Karen Lystra, valued letters from loved ones. Suffering from an unspecified ailment in December 1851, Stephen Foster's expectations of enduring "a long Winter of the most *intense suffering,*" were eased by a letter from Abby Kelley. "The very sight of it," he explained joyously, "thrilled me with emotion." Indeed, he credited her letter with awakening "feelings" that he had "never experienced before," and "which only the most peculiar circumstances" could "ever awaken again." Foster described his sense of liberation upon receiving her letter. "I feel so free," he exclaimed, "the sight of your letter reminding me of the past & the deep sympathy & devotion which it creates, deeply affected me." Abolitionist women also welcomed letters from their loved ones. Those who remained at home urged their husbands to correspond frequently. Wendell Phillips was always tentative about leaving Ann, but when he did he wrote often, and while many of his letters were only a few lines in length, assuring her that he was in good health and inquiring of her well-being, they did signify the intimacy between himself and Ann. Not all abolitionist husbands, however, responded to their wives' calls for frequent correspondence and news. Following a visit from her husband in 1847, L. Maria Child rued that despite promising "faithfully" that he would inform her of "all particulars about his health," she had not heard from him in five weeks. After twenty years of marriage, and all too aware that David was "so very *apt* to be dilatory about writing," she "merely concluded that he was too busy to write." Nonetheless, she was concerned enough to ask a friend whether she knew if he had arrived safely back in Northampton. Complementing the significance attached to receiving letters from loved ones, abolitionists considered the process of letter *writing* as important. Again, L. Maria Child's comments are instructive. "It has been a great comfort to me to write them," she told David in 1836, "and perhaps it has been *some* comfort to you to receive them."[21]

The complex link between public and private obligations and reform, and the attachment between spouses, was evident in an 1846 exchange of letters between Helen Garrison and Ann and Wendell Phillips. Noting that it "was a severe trial to think of parting with" her husband "for so long," Helen told Ann that "for a time I could not think of it with the least composure." Four days later, Wendell responded, indicating that he and Ann had conferred over Helen's loneliness. Connecting the domestic sphere with public reform, Phillips referred to the sacrifice Helen was making for the abolitionist cause, in allowing her husband to travel to England. Through this exchange, Helen's attachment to her husband was evident, and her statement of the following month that she was "perfectly happy" because she was "so near [her] dear husband" confirmed the significance she placed on her marriage. Offering an insight into their domestic life, Helen presented an alternative view to the common representation of abolitionists as being sternly preoccupied with their reformism. Lamenting the absence of Garrison's "cheerful countenance," she missed "his pleasant voice which was always music to my soul." Helen Garrison was not a radical advocate of women's rights, but her attachment to her husband, and her loneliness during his absence, was not unusual. Lucy Stone's determination to retain her individuality did not preclude feelings of loneliness during Henry Blackwell's absences. "Now that your exile is nearly over, dear Harry," she wrote in June 1858, "I want to tell you, that in no other absence have I ever felt your loss so much, never longed so for you, never needed you, as I have during these 4 weary months. I was glad that constant change saved you from the gnawing hunger that I felt. *I hope* that we may not need to be so separated again."[22]

Alongside these expressions of loneliness, however, abolitionist women also valued their independence.[23] Angelina Grimké summed up the tensions within some women's minds between a desire for independence, and their love for their husbands. Grimké's concerns regarding Theodore Weld's response to coming home "to an empty house" typified abolitionists' sorrow at their separations from loved ones. It was possible, of course, that Grimké was concerned that Weld *would* be able to cope in her absence. But such an interpretation is dependent upon the notion that abolitionist women continued to believe that they were indispensable in the domestic sphere. Most of the women under review here, having moved successfully into the world of public reform, were not so insecure; they had secured a place in the world beyond the home, and did not need to defend the domestic realm as their only domain of expertise and authority. Supporting this interpretation was Grimké's recognition that separations from Weld were sometimes necessary. She sought to reassure him that he could continue in his public reformism, confident in the knowledge that affairs at home were progressing smoothly. Grimké told Weld that she missed him "more than I can tell," but she urged him not to "let home cares" interfere with his work. And, paralleling Ann Phillips's efforts to reassure Wendell of her ability to cope in his absence, Grimké did not want Weld to return home on account of her ill health. Similarly, abolitionist women's sorrow at their husbands' absences was mitigated by an awareness that there was a positive aspect to their separation. Noting that while she and Sarah thought they "should be uneasy at missing" Theodore "so little," Angelina remarked that their disappointment was alleviated by the belief that they were "rightly separated." Consequently, "vacuums" were "wonderfully filled up." Yet despite her resolution not to allow domestic concerns and loneliness to interfere with Weld's public abolitionism, and notwithstanding her determination not to appear dependent on Weld, Grimké's resolution soon weakened. Just nine days after writing the letter cited above, she told Weld: "we begin to miss you now *very much* and want you at home again."[24]

We have seen that while the Phillipses' marriage was affected by Ann's illness, they maintained a close and affectionate relationship. One of the ways by which radical abolitionist men manifested their intimate attachments to their wives was by caring for them in times of sickness. By assuming a nurturing role, these men were illustrating the depth of their challenge to prescribed gender roles; while such demands interfered with their public reformism, they generally accepted such responsibilities with stoicism.[25] Wendell Phillips's response to Ann's illness is revealing. Lawrence Friedman has noted that Phillips "initially reacted to this unanticipated state of affairs with thinly veiled resentment." But Phillips did not permit his wife's condition to detract from the intimacy of their relationship. Nor did he allow the inevitable interruptions to his public reformism caused by Ann's illness to lapse into bitterness or resentment, a considerable achievement considering that Phillips, more than any other abolitionist, had earned his public reputation on the basis of his oratorical skills, rather than as an editor or pamphleteer. Even a cursory examination of the correspondence between Wendell and Ann attests to their abiding affection. Along with their array of tender and playful nicknames, there was a mutual dependence that was certainly not weakened, but quite possibly strengthened, by Ann's illness. The physical support Wendell provided to Ann complemented the emotional encouragement she provided to him. Phillips professed the depth of these feelings: "I tell her [Ann]," he remarked to Elizabeth Pease in 1854, "that if I ever should lose her, there is to be nothing of me left you worth loving."[26]

The emotional attachment between abolitionist husbands and wives was linked to their ideas regarding sexuality. The issue of sexuality has been a major concern to historians interested in the women's rights movement, and more generally, women's condition. Abolitionists' attitudes toward sexuality—placed in the context of the society of which they were a part—were essential components of their wider ideology of gender, marriage, and the family. Nineteenth-century marriage, according to a recent survey of sexuality in the United States, was characterized by "a romantic, intimate, yet conflicted sexuality." Sexuality is difficult to define, and there are inherent problems in seeking to analyze that most private and inaccessible aspect of human relationships. Ellen K. Rothman has offered one guide to understanding and using the word "sexual." In addition to "any physical intimacy between a man and a woman," Rothman also referred to "the feelings and fantasies aroused by that intimacy."[27] While Rothman's definition is not without problems—not the least of which is that it excludes any possibility of sexual attraction between individuals of the same sex—it does encompass much of what constituted nineteenth-century sexuality.

For radical abolitionists, sexual expression was an issue requiring careful judgement. There were several conflicting imperatives. What was considered unrestrained or wasteful masculine sexuality was perceived as a threat to both the individual and the nation; aside from the procreative function, however, abolitionists sought to express their physical feelings for their spouses. Although the tensions between sexual desire, emotional intimacy, and the determination not to engage in practices that radical abolitionists considered as sexually aggressive are often not immediately apparent, they demand investigation. Since sexuality was also an essential element of the abolitionists' understanding of the evil of slavery, there was a relationship between the rhetoric and practice of their public reformism and their private behavior. While the abolitionists' discussions of sexuality were couched in the euphemistic language characteristic of the period, they regarded the question of sexuality as critical, and a close reading of their public and private utterances suggests that they were not devoid of passion. More specifically, radical abolitionists' determination to accord women an active role in all facets of the marriage relationship was problematic: while the sexual oppression of women lay at the heart of these abolitionists' perception and representation of slavery and marriage, they have also left hints that female abolitionists were prepared to acknowledge their physical desires. In the context of the nineteenth century, when women's sexuality was not only often denied, but feared, female abolitionists' acknowledgment of sexual feelings is further evidence of the depth of the abolitionist challenge to prevailing sexual mores. Because women's sexuality was closely tied to their moralizing function, the Garrisonians' interest in female sexuality challenged the assignment of women to the domestic sphere, where the prevailing ideology demanded they should exercise their moralizing influence.[28]

Given the strength of such assumptions, it is perhaps not surprising that the nineteenth century has often been regarded as a period of sexual prudery. Yet while it has been argued that it "is difficult to overstate the extent and intensity of prudery in America in 1840," the popular image of nineteenth-century repression of sexuality becomes less clear when exposed to closer analysis. "The society that emerged in the nineteenth century," observed Michel Foucault, "did not confront sex with a fundamental refusal of recognition." Rather, "it put into operation an entire machinery for producing true discourses concerning it [sex]." As Ronald Walters has noted, Americans were engaged in "public discourse" about sexuality, although their discussions and exchanges were frequently clouded by a "maddening delicacy and romantic vagueness."[29] Sexuality had not always been a subject that was considered a taboo, and radical abolitionists understood that evading the issue was no way to resolve the contentious issues arising from the sexual politics in which they were so interested. Discussing sexuality is always fraught with peril, but the tendency to view the nineteenth century as a period of sexual prudery complicates any analysis of Victorian sexuality. Much of the difficulty in assessing nineteenth-century sexuality lies in unraveling language from contemporary connotations, attitudes, and usage. Mindful of the possible disjunction between didactic literature and individual behavior, historians have suggested that women were more sexually independent than might otherwise be assumed. Disentangling the voluminous public prescriptive literature on sexuality from private behavior and individual attitudes is never easy, but abolitionists have left clues to their sexual values.[30]

The inherently controversial nature of sexuality, and its pivotal role in the delineation and exercise of power, shaped the public response to the abolitionist movement. In this regard, radical abolitionism seemed to strike at the very core of prevailing values and practices. Although there was a range of factors behind the vitriolic condemnation of Garrisonian abolitionists, the widespread perception of their radicalism led to their being associated in the public mind with free lovers, and other similar groups. "Free love" defies precise definition, but as John D'Emilio and Estelle Freedman have noted, during the nineteenth century the term did not refer to promiscuity, nor to sexual relations with multiple partners. While free lovers encompassed a range of views, they generally believed that "love, rather than marriage," should be that basis for sexual relations.[31] Many Americans denounced free love as a serious challenge to marriage and the family. Indeed, the amorphousness of free love made it easier for critics to associate it with abolitionism, to the detriment of both reforms. Abolitionists knew that many Americans looked askance at free love, and the connections between the two movements were, at best, tenuous. Although radical abolitionists were keenly interested in encouraging individuals to express their emotions more freely, they were guided by prevailing standards, and their constructions of sexuality were always a delicate balance between private desires and public obligations and expectations. In many ways they sought to project the same images that were being presented in domestic and other didactic literature, which unequivocally rejected free love.

There were common threads to abolitionism and free love, and several abolitionists—including Frances Wright—also proposed free love. More telling, however, is the evidence of considerable abolitionist hostility to the free love movement. Despite John C. Spurlock's admission that "free lovers distinguished themselves from feminists and abolitionists by their attitude toward marriage," he has inferred connections between free love and abolitionism. Spurlock referred to the case of the antislavery advocate Austin Kent, who advocated free love during the 1850s. Spurlock's evidence, however, is open to a different interpretation. Although he pointed out that Kent was a proponent of antislavery during the 1830s, Spurlock did not emphasize that it was not until the 1850s that Kent expressed interest in free love. Further evidence of the abolitionists' opposition to free love can be found in Stephen Foster's comments to the Free Convention, held in Rutland, Vermont, in 1858. While Foster's presence at Rutland would imply an interest in free love, the amendment he proposed to one resolution presented there indicated that he was more concerned with the rights of women in marriage than with the principles of free love. Marriage, Foster declared, should be based upon complete equality. Moreover, the Free Convention was concerned with far more than free love, and George Sennet, a speaker at Rutland, denied that those present advocated free love. Rather, Sennet stressed in the *Liberator,* the delegates were keenly interested in the question of "true marriage." Indeed, Sennet cited a resolution of the Rutland Convention to demonstrate his point: "Resolved, That the only true and natural marriage is an exclusive conjugal love between one man and one woman."[32]

There is further evidence of radical abolitionists' hostility to free love. Writing in 1855, Henry Blackwell hoped "that those 'free lovers' " would "not thrust their immoralities before the public in the 'Woman's Rights' disguise—which they are trying to assume." "It would be an infinite shame & pity," he told Lucy Stone, "to allow the just claims of woman to liberty of person, to rights of property, to industrial, social & political equality, to be associated with a conspiracy against purity & virtue & all the highest relations of Life." The Free Love movement survived into the postbellum period, and L. Maria Child, having earlier referred to the "mischief" she believed Ezra Heywood, a co-founder of the New England Free Love League, had inflicted upon abolitionism, expressed her continuing opposition to free love. Child acknowledged that she felt pessimistic concerning "the present diseased state of society." Yet she emphatically rejected free love as a means of reform. "I do not know what Mr. Heywood has really been doing," she told William L. Garrison in 1878, "I only know that the papers accuse him of advocating unlimited 'free love.' If so, he proposes a remedy worse than the disease; malignant as the disease is." Child condemned "the strange system that prevails at Oneida Institute" in terms of its specific effect upon women. Referring to an unnamed writer who "seems to know about these things," Child suggested the women at Oneida were "pale, care-worn, and discontented." Returning to the domestic theme, Child reasoned: "How can it be otherwise, when they live under a system, which renders domestic affection impossible[?]"[33]

The free love movement was just one expression of the contested sexuality of the nineteenth century. In the context of separate gender spheres, concepts of feminine delicacy and purity included the idealization of women as less physically expressive than men. That ideal translated, at least theoretically, into the assumption that women were less "sexual" than men. Such conclusions were both ironical and contradictory, given that women were largely defined, and constrained, by their gender. The very means of defining women were used to draw the boundaries of their sphere. Historians have offered an alternative perspective on the construction of nineteenth-century sexuality. Moving beyond the characterization of women as victims, and adopting a position that bore parallels to the views of recent scholars of African Americans, feminist scholars have contended that women were able to contribute to sexual ideology to shape their lives. In so doing these writers have denied that nineteenth-century women were powerless victims of male oppression. Nancy Cott has postulated that women influenced the ideology of sexuality. Rejecting suggestions that Victorian sexual ideology resulted solely from men's determination to repress women through control of their sexuality, Cott emphasized the benefits women derived from their alleged "passionlessness." "The positive contribution of passionlessness," she reasoned, "was to replace the sexual/carnal characterization of women with a spiritual/moral one" that allowed "women to develop their human faculties and self-esteem." Accordingly, the widely accepted perception that women "lacked carnal motivation" was "the cornerstone" of their supposed "moral superiority" over men. Cott contended that besides elevating women's status, and broadening their opportunities, an acceptance of the notion of passionlessness "created sexual solidarity among women." By excluding the carnal passion that was inevitably associated with males, women's relationships with each other were not only more spiritual, but were of a "higher character." During a period of unreliable contraception, passionlessness was an obvious means of limiting the frequency of sexual intercourse, thereby making it easier for women to exercise some control over the size of their families. Referring to the earlier work of Daniel Scott Smith and Linda Gordon, Cott concurred that women's ability to exercise such power within the family was an indication of their power.[34]

Analysis of radical abolitionists' attitudes toward sexuality must assess the extent to which they conformed to the model of "passionlessness" described by Cott. Drawing attention to an 1838 letter from Angelina Grimké to Theodore Weld, Cott has argued that Grimké's "passionless attitude was a feminist affirmation of woman's dignity in revulsion from male sexual domination." Grimké's comments are revealing, and corroborate Cott's thesis: "Instead of the higher, nobler sentiments being first aroused, and leading on the lower passions *captive* to their will, the *latter* seemed to be *lords* over the *former.* Well I am convinced that men in general, the vast majority, believe most seriously that women were made to gratify their animal appetites, *expressly* to minister to *their* pleasure—yea christian men too. My soul abhors such a base letting down of the high dignity of my nature as a woman. How I have feared the possibility of ever being married to one who regarded *this* as the *end*—the great design of marriage."[35] Implying that prevailing patterns of masculine behavior were at odds with women's elevated nature, and predicating her argument on the assumption that men and women were endowed with different natures, Grimké's statement supports Cott's argument that there were significant differences between Victorian women and men toward sexuality. Yet the fact that some abolitionist women were so determined to reform sexual attitudes and practices means that Cott's thesis concerning passionlessness as an effective force for the empowerment of women must be examined carefully. Abolitionists vigorously condemned the sexual abuses endemic to slave society, but reforming women's distaste for prevailing patterns of sexual power transcended the injustices of the slave states. Elizabeth Cady Stanton's 1853 assertion that "man in his lust has regulated this whole question of sexual intercourse long enough" expressed her dissatisfaction with the prevailing balance of sexual power, as well as her own marital experiences. As Sarah Grimké noted when she described the way in which men viewed women "as a mere instrument to be used for the gratification of passion," other female reformers also denounced the objectification of women.[36]

Typically, some abolitionists sought to effect reform by providing a proper example. This necessarily required the cooperation of abolitionist husbands. Theodore Weld's self-conscious respect for Angelina Grimké was evident in a letter written two months before their marriage. Weld alluded to his sexual desires, but—reaffirming that love between a man and a woman was the deepest expression of human affection—he connected those physical pleasures to higher, spiritual, objectives: "We marry Angelina not *merely* nor *mainly* nor *at all comparatively* to ENJOY, but together to do and to dare, together to toil and testify and suffer, together to crucify the flesh, with its affections and lusts and to keep ourselves and each other unspotted from the world, to live a life of faith in the son of God." For her part, Grimké attested to her faith in Weld. Having long thought that "marriage was *sinful,* because of what appeared to me almost invariably to prompt and lead to it," she expressed satisfaction that Weld's views corresponded to hers. "Beloved," she wrote in 1838, "your views of *courtship* are just like mine."[37]

Theodore Weld was not the only male abolitionist who was conscious of the dangers of what David Lee Child euphemistically described as men's "sensuality." Although he was referring primarily to the oppression of women outside the United States, Child's assertion that women in France were "more than almost any other the victims of men" revealed an awareness of the factors underpinning women's plight. William L. Garrison's concern that he conduct himself with appropriate propriety led him to exercise restraint during his courtship with Helen Benson. Characteristically, abolitionist men sought to balance conflicting imperatives. Henry Clarke Wright's *Unwelcome Child* captured radical abolitionists' determination to balance masculine physical desires with the need for self-control, and respect for women's feelings. Wright wrote that "his physical manhood, as well as his soul, is dear to the heart of his wife, because through this he can give the fullest expression to his manly power. But if such manifestations are made when the wife is not prepared to receive them, and when she repels them and dreads the consequences, his physical nature becomes associated, not with the pure joy of a longed for maternity, but with a deep sense of shame and degradation, with an outrage on her nature."[38]

There were other imperatives concerning the abolitionists' determination to express their feelings, which also contributed to their attitude toward sexuality. While conceding that abolitionist women referred to their sexual feelings, Blanche Hersh has argued that "the feminist-abolitionists" considered "female emancipation meant freedom *from* sex, not *for* it." But her implicit contrast between the women reformers of the nineteenth century and the ascendant sexual mores of the 1960s and 1970s—resting on a narrow definition of sexuality—fails to acknowledge the complexities and subtleties of nineteenth-century sexuality. Female abolitionists were appalled by what they considered the results of excessive sexuality, particularly in the slave states. Yet they also valued physical intimacy, which was in some respects more "sexual" than a late twentieth-century perspective might assume. Here, Carroll Smith-Rosenberg's theory that the twentieth-century "tendency to view human love and sexuality within a dichotomized universe of deviance and normality, genitality and platonic love," was "alien to the nineteenth century," helps us assess abolitionist constructions of sexuality. Abolitionists had to be careful not to behave in a manner considered improper. Angelina Grimké revealed the impact of the expectation that husbands and wives should exercise restraint in public. Following a reunion with her husband, she noted that she "would have given anything" to have thrown her arms around him and wept, if their "precious little children had been away." Grimké's disappointment was partly mitigated by her belief that "all things are rightly ordered." But evidently she would have preferred to have been able to express herself more freely. Whether Grimké's reference to the correct ordering of society concerned the necessity of people restraining themselves in order to suppress their emotiveness in favor of rationality, or a belief that God determined what was appropriate behavior, her belief in restraint was obvious.[39]

This matter of privacy was deeply important to abolitionists. Helen Garrison commented on the difficulties endured in the period preceding her husband's departure for Europe in 1846. Describing the tedium associated with hosting a continuous stream of guests, she made it clear that she and Lloyd sought, at least temporarily, solitude: "how did we long for a quiet retreat for a few hours to be by ourselves for thought and reflection." Foreshadowing the greater emphasis on private domestic space, other abolitionists also valued familial privacy. Angelina Grimké, lamenting an "incessant run of company," plaintively expressed her desire in 1840: "O how I *long* to have our little family *alone,* to sit down without any stranger."[40] These pleas for privacy suggest how the family, and the home, were perceived as barriers from the demands of the outside world.

Physical intimacy can be expressed in a variety of ways. The bedroom was a location of emotional as well as physical intimacy. After James Mott's death, Lucretia refused to sleep in the bed she and James had shared during their marriage. This suggested that regardless of the abolitionists' sexual practices, they found intimacy and companionship in their bedroom. Keeping in mind the social nature of many abolitionist households, and the fact that nineteenth-century dwellings offered limited private space, the opportunities for private conversations were probably limited. Accordingly, Henry Blackwell's request to Lucy Stone that she forgive his inability to adequately express himself in his correspondence, and not judge his comments "till we next are in our quiet bed *together,*" when he would have the chance to "explain" what he "really wanted to say," should not be construed as a solely sexual overture.[41]

These matters had been raised before abolitionists married. Karen Lystra has demonstrated that sexuality was a subject discussed by courting couples, and Ellen Rothman has noted that mid-nineteenth-century "courtship had room for erotic play, both in fantasy and in reality."[42] Two decades after William L. Garrison referred to the "the ice of my celibacy," Henry Blackwell broached the issue of sexuality with Lucy Stone. Reiterating that since she had not been married, Stone should not comment on marriage, Blackwell bluntly asserted: "Marriage is not a disease, but *celibacy* is." Enquiring whether Stone would "permit the injustice of the world to enforce upon you a life of celibacy?" Blackwell inferred that contrary to prevailing definitions of true womanhood, women were endowed with sexual desires and needs. Blackwell also pointed to his own physical desires: "Every night when I lie in bed I stretch out my arms for you in vain & all through the night even in my sleep I seem to feel lonely & comfortless without you." There are other references to sexual urges in Blackwell's correspondence with Stone. Seeking to convince her of the benefits of marriage, he revealed the conjunction of antislavery doctrine and personal concerns that characterized radical abolitionism. "Would it not be a *slavish* doctrine," he suggested in March 1854, "to preach that we *ought* to sentence ourselves to celibacy because men have enacted injustice with a statute[?]" Blackwell's plea revealed a mixture of guilt and responsibility, as he held men largely responsible for the iniquities of gender relations. Hoping that Stone would consider him in a different light to other men, Blackwell also sought to balance physical desires with a higher purpose and sentiment: "I think that you understand the force & virtue of *instinct* when guided by *affection* & *love.*"[43]

As Lewis Perry has demonstrated, a number of abolitionists were concerned with balancing "spontaneity" with the necessity for control. That determination was evident privately and publicly. Decrying the "icy frigidity" of some courtships, William L. Garrison expressed his disapproval "of an unseemly familiarity of conduct—a reckless disregard of all rules of propriety." There was a "happy medium," he assured Helen shortly before they wed, "between these extremes, which I think we have found." While abolitionists did not completely reject the need for social controls over individual behavior (which would have contradicted their sense of "civilization") they sought personal liberation, physically as well as spiritually. There were many elements to their vision of physical freedom, but their abhorrence of the physical cruelties of slavery was an important determinant of their personal concerns. Influenced also by the principles of individualism, radical abolitionists' perceptions of personal liberation included the rights of all to express themselves freely. In a letter wherein he expressed concern for Abby Kelley's health, Stephen Foster noted in 1844 that if it were not for his concern that she was "hastening to an untimely fate," he could "endure" their "separation for the present." Yet, echoing William L. Garrison's 1834 plea to Helen to "pardon the ardor of" his "love," Foster also revealed an unashamedly physical side to their relationship. Even though it was in the form of a denial, Foster's desires were evident. "I do not long," he ironically disclaimed, "*ardently long,* to *clasp you in my arms* & *press you* to my bosom to be torn from it *no more.*" The following year, alluding to Foster's impatience to marry, Kelley urged restraint, plainly telling him: "Don't pant so." Garrison, soon after his marriage, enthusiastically described how he had "thrown aside celibacy," and Henry Stanton's 1858 Valentine's Day message to Elizabeth evinces his enduring love and devotion, and suggests his physical desires. Referring to the "ardent attachment" he felt for Elizabeth, Stanton expressed the hope that soon he would be able to "rush into" her open arms "with all the impulse which love and longing can inspire."[44]

James Brewer Stewart has suggested that the affection Wendell and Ann Phillips maintained for each other served as a substitute for the sexual relations they were probably unable to enjoy. While there is merit in that notion, it must necessarily remain speculative. What can be said with certainty, however, is that Wendell Phillips assumed many of the responsibilities that normally devolved upon women, both in an affectionate sense, and with regard to the organization of the domestic sphere. Ann and Wendell did not allow their possible lack of sexual fulfillment to detract from what remained a loving relationship, and their marriage indicates that during the nineteenth century at least, nongenital physical expressions of affection were in some respects "sexual." Wendell Phillips's comment to Helen Garrison, "I bro^t^ Ann down in my arms," is suggestive of the conjunction between their physical intimacy and their emotional attachment. The physical affection between Ann and Wendell, coupled with a recognition of their mutual emotional intimacy, means that the claim that "restraint served as the key" to their marriage requires careful explanation. Beyond the obvious examples of emotional intimacy and attachment between Ann and Wendell, their expressions of physical intimacy should not be discounted on the assumption that sexual intercourse was a necessary precondition for, or the only determinant of, physical intimacy. The Phillipses' marriage serves as a good example of Lewis Perry's suggestion that one of the rewards of sexual "restraint was intimacy."[45]

Aspects of Angelina Grimké and Theodore Weld's marriage resembled that of Wendell and Ann Phillips. Grimké's health problems were not so long-standing as those of Ann Phillips, but they were significant. The miscarriage Grimké suffered between the birth of their second and third children, in conjunction with the pain she endured from a hernia and a prolapsed uterus, inevitably affected her marriage. Direct evidence is predictably elusive, but Grimké's ill-health must have restricted her sexual relationship with Weld, particularly during the early and mid-1840s. Yet, as Robert Abzug has implied, it was during that period that Theodore and Angelina "regained a caring attitude for each other."[46] Like Wendell and Ann Phillips, the emotional attachment between Weld and Grimké was apparently unhindered by an inability to express themselves sexually. To the contrary, ill-health probably contributed to greater understanding, and a higher degree of intimacy.

Alongside those measured suggestions that women could express themselves physically, some abolitionists believed that women could enjoy their sexuality. The subtleties of their language sometimes masked female abolitionists' real intention, but they did express physical desires. Citing a phrenological report that asserted that Elizabeth Cady Stanton was "capable of enjoying the connubial relation to a high degree," Elisabeth Griffith has noted that Stanton was "frank about her sexuality and objected to the Victorian view that women did not enjoy intercourse." Angelina Grimké, after a particularly candid meeting with Theodore Weld, acknowledged her awareness of his feelings: "Thou sayest, thou kept an extinguisher on thy spirit whilst thy wast at Brookline. I knew it, I *felt* it, and it *grieved* me because thou wouldst *leave* me when I tho't it would have been an inexpressible relief to thy full heart to have unburdened itself." Just three days later, Grimké expressed her own feelings rather less cryptically: "tho' Sister A[nna] thinks I take matters very cooly, and that my love is truly Platonic, yet *thou knowest* the weary longings of my hungering and thirsting spirit."[47] Other abolitionist women also betrayed sexual desires. "My arm of flesh is eager to follow the promptings of the spirit," Abby Kelley told Stephen Foster in July 1843, "and to encircle you." Lucy Stone, insisting that wives should not be the victims of their husbands' sexual urges, was cautious about consummating her marriage. Nevertheless, in her 1854 reference to "the barren desert of an unshared life," she had alluded to the importance of sexual expression. And the unmarried Sarah Grimké, who, like other reforming women, denounced unbridled masculine sexuality, also admitted that there could be a healthy expression of sexual feeling. Writing to black abolitionist Sarah Douglass in 1855, Grimké conceded that "sexual intercourse" within marriage was "as much the natural expression of affection as the warm embrace and ardent kiss."[48]

No abolitionist was more concerned with marital matters than L. Maria Child. Her marriage to David Lee Child, with its peculiar combination of intimacy and anxiety, provides a fascinating example of the tension between public and private life. As her domestic tracts revealed, Child placed great emphasis on the ideal of romantic love; while she encountered difficulties during her marriage, her affection for David remained strong. In what

Maria accurately described as "mediocrity of verse," the ambivalence, as well as the ongoing intimacy, of her relationship to David was evident: "*We've known the bond of grief / Through many a cloudy year— / But sorrow's power was ever brief / For it made thee doubly dear.*"[49] Although their marriage involved considerable difficulties, David and Maria maintained a deeply felt intimacy for each other. For at least a decade after their wedding, Maria tolerated her husband's "errors," describing them at one point as "entirely errors of judgement." Her belief that "this life" was "*only* a school for better existence" partly compensated for David's absences and his inability to provide a steady income. Yet as an 1836 letter attested, Maria sadly missed David: "How wearisome it is to be separated! A dozen times in the day some thought of my soul yearns for an answering voice from thine—and I feel as if I would travel ten miles if I could only sit and knit behind the wood pile, speaking to you now and then, while you were at work."[50] Child knew all too well that there were negative aspects to domesticity, but domestic life continued to exert a powerful appeal.

L. Maria Child's move to New York in 1841 brought deep loneliness and suffering, and despite the difficulties between herself and David, and his willingness to "part partnership, so far as *pecuniary* matters" were concerned, she continued to miss him intensely. Similarly, David continued to write reverentially of Maria.[51] Above all, Maria's correspondence evidences the depth of her attachment to David. Well aware of his shortcomings, and prepared to act independently when circumstances demanded, she nonetheless remained intimately connected to her husband. By the late 1840s she was contemplating a reunion. Although she feared that he would never change "in those points" that stood "in the way of his successful business," her aspirations remained constant. Generously praising his "noble kind heart," she hoped they would soon be able to "enjoy each other's society, without anything remaining of all our troubles and all our errors." More than anything, she desired a home, where he could be "contented," and where they could again enjoy each other's company. A visit from David in October 1849 further whet her desires. Likening his visit to "a second honeymoon," she affirmed that domestic love was "the best of earth's blessings." Nearly three decades after their marriage, Maria's love for David was undiminished. Anxious for her "dear absent mate" to return home, she was excited at the prospect of them having one of their "old cozy chats," reciting "the old prayer" together, before they went to sleep.[52]

Alongside that abiding commitment to her marriage, however, L. Maria Child found companionship with other men. Her condescension toward other women led her to consider herself implicitly a worthy companion of many men, but she sought more than intellectual companionship. Kirk Jeffrey has described the "curious attachment" between Child and Ole Bull, a Norwegian violinist visiting the United States. Child's interest in the arts, particularly her love of music, would have made Bull an attractive companion.[53] Child's distaste for the type of men with whom her husband was associating has been noted, but the contrast between those men and Bull's cultivated and cultured sophistication should not be underestimated. Writing to Anna Loring, Child revealed the impact of Bull and another male friend, John S. Dwight: "I have been enchanted with John Dwight's lectures. I have not been so taken off my feet with delight, since the first evening I heard Ole's violin; and when I say that, you know the imagination can no farther go. Dear Ole! God bless him! His romantic music, and his fresh character, have taken ten years off my weary life, and carried my soul back to the season of blossoms—fragrance and bird-singing. I did not think any thing would ever excite me much again; but John Dwight's two last lectures charmed me so much, that I wanted to catch him up and kiss him."[54] Beyond implying that on some matters at least, Loring was a confidante of Child's, this letter conveys a great deal. Child's attachment to what she regarded as refined culture was evident; besides demonstrating her love for the romantic and artistic aspect of her character, it evoked her joy at discovering that she could recapture sentiments she had long since given up as "youthful." Her references to excitement, and her desire to kiss Dwight, indicate that her sense of propriety did not mean she lacked passion.

Details are sketchy, but in the 1840s, during the period when she was "separated" from her husband, Child established a relationship with a younger man, John Hopper. Child's friendship with Hopper was an interesting mix, but the depth of her feelings for him was obvious. "I hardly care what happens to me," she told Ellis Gray Loring (who also supplied financial and emotional support to Child over a long period), "if I can only manage not to be separated from John." Child revealed the intensity of her feelings for Hopper: "my affections have got so entwined around him, that it would almost kill me to have to leave him." Regretting that she had "come to be *afraid* to lean upon David in all matters connected with *home* and *support,*" Child praised Hopper as "such a good hand to lean upon." By way of contrast to David's financial woes, and presenting Hopper's role in terms of traditional masculine functions, she remarked that he "manages all my affairs so well." Yet at the same time, Child's love for Hopper satisfied an unrequited maternal urge—as was the case in her friendship with Ole Bull. It is unclear why the Childs were unable to have children, but Maria's stoic acceptance of that fact did not mean she was happy about the situation. She noted that Hopper supplied "the place of a real son." Yet while Child drew a contrast between John's strengths and David's shortcomings, she maintained an attachment to her husband, and apparently did not consider the two men as alternatives, or competitors. Instead, she hoped that "things will so happen that David and he and I can live together, and bless each other." Furthermore, Child presented her ultimate ambition in terms congruent with domestic ideology. "It is my wish" she noted in 1843, "to do them both 'good and not evil all the days of my life.'"[55] Indeed, part of the attraction she felt for Hopper was the knowledge that she could "in many ways be useful to him."[56]

Child's perception of the two men's roles revealed her attachment to Hopper and confirmed that she saw her friendship with him as complementary to her marriage. Child may, as one of her biographers has suggested, felt guilt over the fact that she had not devoted the same attention to David as she had to those men with whom she established friendships.[57] But her friendship with Hopper helped her understand her own marriage, in both its limitations and its importance. Writing from New York in August 1841, she told Ellis Gray Loring that while she had "many a home-sick and husband-sick hour," the "ingenious kindness, and perpetual vicinity of John sometimes increases this sad feeling. His thousand little deliberate attentions remind me so much of Mr. Child, and yet are so insufficient for the cravings of a heart so fond of domestic life as mine."[58] Aside from her desire to provide a motherly role to Hopper and Bull, there were other similarities between the relationships Child forged with the younger men. In both cases she was motivated partly by a desire for companionship and support that was apparently lacking in her marriage. Yet despite the intimacy between Child and the younger men, there is no suggestion that she established sexual relations with either man. The satisfaction Child derived from her friendships with Bull and Hopper thus reinforces the contention that ideas of intimacy and sexuality were constructed very differently in the nineteenth century than they are in the late twentieth century.

It is for those reasons that Henry Blackwell's friendship with a certain "Mrs. P." must be assessed carefully. Andrea Moore Kerr has described Blackwell's 1869 relationship with "Mrs. P." (who was probably Abby Hutchinson Patton, reformer and member of the Singing Hutchinsons) as "an affair." Yet as Kerr implies, the phrase "affair" had different connotations during the nineteenth century than it has in subsequent eras. Blackwell's relationship with "Mrs. P.", notes Kerr, "may have been an unconsummated passion, a nineteenth-century romantic folly." Regardless of whether Blackwell's friendship with "Mrs. P." included a sexual relationship, it was significant in that it demonstrated the imperfections, and the resilience, of the Blackwell-Stone marriage. During the late 1860s, with Stone assiduously lobbying on behalf of woman's suffrage, the image of marital unity that she and Blackwell presented in public masked significant tensions in their relationship. Blackwell's friendship with "Mrs. P." was a manifestation of his domestic frustrations during that period. Despite his earlier assurances that he would not hinder Stone's public activities, by the postbellum period Blackwell was expressing discontent regarding the lengthy periods she spent away from home on lecturing tours. And as they had before their marriage, Stone and Blackwell differed over where they should reside; while he preferred to be close to New York, she favored Boston. As significant as these tensions were, however, the Stone-Blackwell marriage survived. In part, the survival of the marriage was a compromise: Stone continued to provide financial support to Blackwell, and he continued to involve himself in the women's rights movement.[59] Yet their marriage was based on something more—a deep and abiding love that not only helped them to overcome difficulties that emerged in their relationship, but that became more significant as time passed.

Writing to Stone in June 1853, the period in which Blackwell was earnestly wooing her, James Mott attested to the abolitionists' belief that marital love could increase over time. "I have lived in that state [marriage] for more than forty years," Mott told Stone, "and it has been one of harmony and love. As age advances, our love, if possible, increases." The abolitionists' response to old age affirms the intimacy between husband and wives. Writing in 1874, Wendell Phillips assured Ann that he loved "her more as time goes shorter." Characteristically, L. Maria Child juxtaposed her fears and her intimate attachment. "Day by day," she noted in 1862, "David and I rely more entirely upon each other for all our comfort. Sometimes it frightens me that we are becoming so very necessary to each other; for the time must come when one of us will be left; and then the loneliness! the loneliness!"[60]

Although abolitionists remained intellectually alert and active for as long as they could, advancing years brought ill health and incapacity. Yet such difficulties sometimes reinforced bonds between husbands and wives. Following David Lee Child's death, Maria told Thomas Wentworth Higginson that "life has been so unutterably lonely to me, since I have lost my kind old mate. The bond was greatly strengthened by his many years of feeble health, which made it necessary for me to care for him continually." Old age made less difference to Ann Phillips than it did to many of her abolitionist contemporaries, but Wendell's 1875 description confirms the intimacy between the two, and the extent to which he filled a nurturing role within their marriage. "Dear Helen," Phillips wrote to Helen Garrison, "Ann tells me to send you her kindest love & best thanks for the memory of her & the print you sent. The poor child has only memories to live on." Wendell's concern for Ann remained constant until his death in February 1884, and his final words were reputed to be "What will become of Ann?" Ironically, Ann outlived Wendell by fourteen months.[61]

This chapter has explored the value radical abolitionists attached to intimacy and affection within their own relationships, and offered insights into the ways in which they sought to express those emotions. On the physical level, radical abolitionists' marriages were a complex mix: they were determined, at all costs, not to replicate the injustices they believed were manifested most dreadfully in slave society; yet they also believed that in a true marriage, physical and emotional intimacy went hand in hand. Following the death of her husband, L. Maria Child affirmed the significance of the emotional aspect of abolitionists' marriages. "My dear, kind old mate passed away last night, at midnight," she told Sarah Shaw, "I am *so* thankful that my earnest prayer, to be able to take care of him to the last, has been answered!"[62] Child's comments reveal much about her own marriage, as well as the contrast between the abolitionists' vision of domestic love, and their understanding of slavery. The Childs' marriage was not without frustrations and tensions, but Maria's continuing affection for David was unmistakable, as was her ongoing desire to play the role of domestic nurse and carer. And again, because the domestic aspect of abolitionism reflected the imperatives of public reformism, Child's disappointments must be juxtaposed with the abolitionists' presentation of the horrors of slavery. Although abolitionists knew that marital affection should not be confused with equality, Maria's melancholy depiction of David's death stands as a poignant counterpoint to the abolitionists' descriptions of the violent separations of African American families that had taken place every day under slavery.

Conclusion

Conceived during a period of rapid population growth and geographical expansion, radical abolitionists' interest in domestic reform was contemporaneous with changes in family life and gender roles. The influence of radical abolitionism extended far beyond the issue of slavery, and much of the movement's notoriety derived from the way in which its proponents questioned the sexual and racial order in free as well as slave society. Predicated on the belief that women and men were endowed with different natures, the prevailing gender ideology suggested they also occupied separate spheres. Radical abolitionists challenged that gendered division of society, and, during a period in which the notions of "public" and "private" were in a state of transition, they questioned the very distinction between public and private. By engaging in activities that were clearly "political," abolitionist women played a significant part in forging a public political culture for American women. Yet while antislavery women established new relationships with public activities and institutions, radical abolitionists did not discard all the assumptions associated with domestic ideology. In many ways, Garrisonian abolitionism was an attempt to carry virtues widely associated with women—including purity, honesty, and a respect for domestic life—into the public realm. The Garrisonians' faith in these ideals was evident too in their private lives, where a radical belief that men and women should share household responsibilities was accompanied by an abiding adherence to certain values associated with domestic ideology. Among the most significant of these values was the elevation of motherhood, and the "maternalism" that was evident in radical abolitionism not only connected antislavery to the wider culture of nineteenth-century America, but also anticipated the reformism of subsequent generations of reformers.

Radical abolitionists' faith in maternal values also shaped their sororal relationships. Based on their shared domestic experiences, nineteenth-century women forged networks of supportive friendships. Abolitionist women, seeking to turn their exclusion from the public sphere to positive advantage, were no exception to that pattern. Sorority also influenced public reformism, and abolitionism was premised on the belief that alerting Northern women to the sufferings of slave women would prompt feelings of sympathy that would lead to opposition to slavery. Yet alongside these signs of the strength of antislavery sorority there were limits to the abolitionist sisterhood. In the first instance, their pronouncements on behalf of African American women under slavery did not translate into equitable treatment of black women in the North. Moreover, not only were friendships between white abolitionist women and their black counterparts relatively uncommon; they also lacked the intensity of friendships between white abolitionist women. Equally, female abolitionists' attitude toward, and treatment of, their domestic helpers indicates a belief in social hierarchy, based partly on notions of racial and ethnic difference, that was common among middle-class women during the nineteenth century. Institutionally, while women did establish their own antislavery societies, they also participated alongside men in the American Anti-Slavery Society, and in many of the local and state abolitionist organizations. Most important, sororal bonds between abolitionist women were subordinate to their marriages. The relationship between husband and wife, radical abolitionists believed, was the most significant of all human relationships.

Masculinity, like femininity, is a socially constructed phenomenon, and certain aspects of public and private life were common to nineteenth-century men. In the context of changing patterns of production, men were expected to provide for their families' material needs. Like their nonabolitionist contemporaries, antislavery men felt this responsibility, but they also believed they should contribute to their families' emotional well-being. While there were intimate friendships between abolitionist men, they regarded their marriages as the most important of their relationships. The belief that marriage was significant was not unusual among men in nineteenth-century America. But radical male abolitionists, paying particular attention to men's role within the private sphere, and endorsing—if not always practicing—a more equitable pattern of gender relations, moved between the private world of home and family, and the public sphere. In the process, they indicated, as their female coadjutors did, that the distinction between private and public was less rigid than the separate spheres ideology would suggest. Some abolitionist men encouraged their women companions to participate in public abolitionism. Distancing themselves from the patriarchy of slave society, and recognizing that the paternalism of the South rested on the physical coercion of slaves' labor, male abolitionists eschewed violence—the antislavery strategy of moral suasionism attested to their desire to effect peaceful emancipation. During the 1850s, however, when the conflict over slavery intensified and led ultimately to the Civil War, and when abolitionists were compelled to confront the question of violence, there was a reluctant and ambivalent "masculinization" of abolitionism.

Believing that the abuses of gender and family relations that were endemic to slave society were the antithesis of civilized values, radical abolitionists valued emotional and physical intimacy. They appreciated that affection within marriage did not necessarily lead to marital equality, and they did not succeed entirely in their attempts to create companionate marriages, but they were passionate in their expressions of love and affection for each other. That sense of emotional intimacy was paralleled by radical abolitionists' physical relationships. Female abolitionists expressed revulsion at what they regarded as the unrestrained sexuality of Southern society, but they nevertheless prized intimacy (which was in some senses more "sexual" than either a stereotype of Victorian morality, or a more recent perspective, might suggest). For their part, radical abolitionist men also condemned the sexual oppression of slave women, and were determined not to oppress their wives sexually. Yet they also believed that the proper channeling of sexual desires was an integral component of a healthy marriage. Convinced that slavery precluded any such equitable or healthy sexual expression, and decrying the fusion of economic, social, and sexual immoralities that occurred under slavery, abolitionists were horrified that slaves were used as virtual breeding stock. And the violent separation of parents from their slave offspring contrasted with radical abolitionists' efforts to create a peaceful domestic environment for their own children. All of this reinforces the contention that radical abolitionists were not an imbalanced or disturbed minority. It is important to distinguish deliberately chosen methods of agitation from real evidence of neuroses or psychotic disorders. Here, abolitionists' marriages are again illustrative: despite their deep-felt concerns over the injustices of gender relations as constructed in nineteenth-century America, and despite the tensions within their own marriages, there is compelling evidence that many abolitionists derived pleasure and satisfaction from their family lives.

The treatment and condition of women was at the center of the abolitionists' understanding of slavery. But radical abolitionists also perceived flaws in gender relations in the North that demanded attention. In articulating their antislavery ideology, they drew comparisons between the institutions of slavery and marriage. There were differences between the abolitionist and women's rights movements, the most significant being that while antislavery advocates sought the abolition of slavery, antebellum proponents of women's rights continued to believe in the ideal of marriage. Yet, agreeing that the question of marriage was a crucial one, abolitionists and women's rights advocates realized that the reality of marriage rarely corresponded to the idealized rhetoric attached to it. Given that many nineteenth-century supporters of women's rights first achieved public prominence in the abolitionist movement, it was perhaps only natural that they would apply their understanding of slavery, and their experiences within the antislavery movement, to their efforts to liberate women. But women's rights advocates' use of slavery to depict the injustices of women continued after the abolition of slavery, and rhetorically as well as ideologically, abolitionism was an important influence on the women's rights movement in the United States after 1865.

Opponents of abolitionism charged that the ultimate objective of the antislavery movement was not only the liberation of the slaves, but the complete *dismantling* (as opposed to the reform) of existing social relationships in the United States. Contrary to some interpretations, however, radical abolitionists did not seek to turn American society upside down. A central theme of this study has been that although abolitionists were widely denounced as radicals intent upon the destruction of the American social, political, and economic order, their reformism was largely shaped by the same forces and ideals that molded the society around them. True, radical abolitionists' prescription for the Southern states involved an enormous restructuring of social, political, and economic relations, and abolitionism was always based on the need for change in national values and institutions. But abolitionism was perceived and presented in terms of its effect on individual men and women. As with nineteenth-century marital practices, the inequalities of slavery precluded the establishment of human relationships based on respect for the individual. In addition to representing slavery in starkly personal terms, abolitionists explained their demands for emancipation in terms of the fulfillment of both American and modern ideals. Abolitionism thus reflected—and repudiated—the predominant culture. Even the most radical of the abolitionists did not reject all of the values around which prevailing attitudes and institutions were constructed. Indeed, they shared many of the premises and assumptions of their nonreformist contemporaries. The links between domesticity and abolitionism are indicative of the contradictions and ambiguities of antebellum middle-class reformism. At the heart of abolitionism, and the culture of nineteenth-century America, were certain assumptions, many of which revolved around gender and family. The belief in the family was thus an article of faith for all Americans. Encompassed within that ideology was an emphasis on women's role, and abolitionists—accepting on occasions the values inherent in prevailing notions of true womanhood—embraced the common view that women had a special part to play in society. Since American "development" was associated with the growth of "civilization," there were direct connections between women's role and American civilization.

Nonetheless, radical abolitionists' views conflicted with those of many Americans. Recognizing the divergence between the rhetoric and ideals of the American republic on the one hand, and the reality of race and gender relations on the other, the abolitionists' assault on racism and sexism was undeniably radical in the context of the nineteenth century. Indeed, because racism and sexism were so deeply embedded in American culture, any assault on them, even one as apparently conventional as the abolitionists' critique, was necessarily radical. The essential duality of abolitionism—a measured radicalism coexisting with an underlying faith in many aspects of American ideology and society—renders judgments about their success or failure difficult. Radical abolitionists' belief that marriage and family could accommodate the tension between individuality and collectivity sometimes appears naive. Equally, the broader problems arising from the presence of African Americans in the United States were not solved by the Civil War, and the questions of gender roles that were of concern to radical abolitionists remain largely unsolved.

Yet while the persistence of racial injustice and the continuing oppression of women denote the limitations of abolitionism, the movement remains of lasting significance. If nothing else, radical abolitionists recognized many of the problems that plagued human relationships, and they perceived the connections between economic and sexual exploitation. Radical abolitionists elaborated an agenda for subsequent debate, and their antislavery activities and ideologies contributed to the postbellum movements for purity, temperance, and women's rights. In so doing, they demonstrated an awareness of issues that have continued to interest subsequent generations of women and men. Perhaps most significant, by discussing these issues publicly, and by challenging prevailing gender codes and prescriptions, abolitionists introduced new matters into public discourse. In the process they tested the boundaries of what constituted "public" affairs. Radical abolitionists' heritage was evident in a way that succinctly signified their own emphasis on family reform. Fulfilling their parents' wishes, a number of abolitionists' children took an active interest in the reform issues of their day, involving themselves in the movements seeking women's rights and equality for African Americans.[1] With all that in mind, we should not dismiss the abolitionists too quickly; while they did not achieve all that they set out to accomplish, they left an indelible imprint on American society and on American reformism. Considering the hostile context in which they functioned, the abolitionists' achievements should not be slighted. In many ways, their failures—public and private—mirrored the shortcomings of the society they sought to reform.

NOTES

Introduction

1. See Lucretia Mott to Martha Wright, 22 May 1859, Lucretia Mott Papers, Friends Historical Library, Swarthmore College, Swarthmore, Pa. (hereafter cited as MP–FHL); Lillie B. Chace Wyman, "Reminiscences of Two Abolitionists," *New England Magazine* (January 1903): 550; George Lowell Austin, *The Life and Times of Wendell Phillips* (1884; reprint, n.p.: Afro-American Press, 1969), 86–87.

2. See Walters, *The Antislavery Appeal: American Abolitionism After 1830* (Baltimore: Johns Hopkins University Press, 1976), chap. 3. See also Blanche Hersh, *The Slavery of Sex: Feminist-Abolitionists in America* (Urbana: University of Illinois Press, 1978), chap. 7; Lawrence Friedman, *Gregarious Saints: Self and Community in American Abolitionism, 1830–1870* (Cambridge: Cambridge University Press, 1982), chap. 5; Dorothy Bass, "'The Best Hopes of the Sexes': The Woman Question in Garrisonian Abolitionism" (Ph.D. diss., Brown University, 1980); Donald Kennon, "'A Knit of Identity': Marriage and Reform in Mid-Victorian America" (Ph.D. diss., University of Maryland, 1981); Karen Sánchez-Eppler, *Touching Liberty: Abolition, Feminism, and the Politics of the Body* (Berkeley and Los Angeles: University of California Press, 1993); Debra Gold Hansen, *Strained Sisterhood: Gender and Class in the Boston Female Anti-Slavery Society* (Amherst: University of Massachusetts Press, 1993); Jean Fagan Yellin and John C. Van Horne, eds., *The Abolitionist Sisterhood: Women's Political Culture in Antebellum America* (Ithaca: Cornell University Press, 1994); Carolyn Luverne Williams, "Religion, Race, and Gender in Antebellum American Radicalism: The Philadelphia Female Anti-Slavery Society, 1833–1870" (Ph.D. diss., University of California, Los Angeles, 1991); Shirley J. Yee, *Black Women Abolitionists: A Study in Activism* (Knoxville: University of Tennessee Press, 1992); Deborah Bingham Van Broekhoven, "Needles, Pens and Petitions: Reading Women into Antislavery History," in *The North Looks at Slavery*, ed. Martin Blatt (Garland, forthcoming).

3. Dwight L. Dumond, *Antislavery: The Crusade for Freedom in America* (Ann Arbor: University of Michigan Press, 1961), 276; Stone to Samuel May, 14 August 1851, Anti-Slavery Collection, Boston Public Library (hereafter cited as ASC–BPL). On the "sisterhood of reforms," see Ronald Walters, *American Reformers, 1815–1860* (New York: Hill and Wang, 1978), ix.

4. "True marriage" was a recurrent phrase in abolitionist writings. See, for example, Henry C. Wright, *Marriage and Parentage; or, The Reproductive Element in Man, as a Means to His Elevation and Happiness*, 2d ed. (Boston: Bela Marsh, 1855), 157.

5. The best account of this process is Charles Sellers, *The Market Revolution: Jacksonian America, 1815–1846* (New York: Oxford University Press, 1991).

6. In 1790 the population of the United States was four million. By 1830, the year before William L. Garrison began publishing the *Liberator*, the population approached thirteen million, and on the eve of the Civil War there were more than thirty-one million people living in the United States. See Peter N. Carroll and David W. Noble, *The Free and the Unfree: A New History of the United States*, 2d ed. (New York: Penguin, 1988), 150.

7. See Tocqueville, *Democracy in America,* 2 vols. trans. Henry Reeve (1840; reprint, New York: Knopf, 1966) 2:193–97. On declining birth rates, see Sellers, *Market Revolution,* 240.

8. Jeanne Boydston, "The Pastoralization of Housework," in *Women's America: Refocusing the Past,* ed. Linda K. Kerber and Jane Sherron De Hart, 4th ed. (New York: Oxford University Press, 1995), 144; Nancy A. Hewitt, "Beyond the Search for Sisterhood: American Women's History in the 1980s," in *Unequal Sisters: A Multicultural Reader in U.S. Women's History,* ed. Ellen Carol DuBois and Vicki L. Ruiz (New York: Routledge, 1990), 8.

9. See Carl Degler, *At Odds: Women and the Family in America from the Revolution to the Present* (New York: Oxford University Press, 1980), vi; Motz, *True Sisterhood: Michigan Women and Their Kin, 1820–1920* (Albany: State University of New York Press, 1983), 8.

10. Linda Kerber, "Separate Spheres, Female Worlds, Women's Place: The Rhetoric of Women's History," *Journal of American History* 75 (1988): 10.

11. Cott, *The Grounding of Modern Feminism* (New Haven: Yale University Press, 1987), 5.

12. Bass, "Best Hopes of the Sexes," 275.

13. Kraditor, "American Radical Historians on Their Heritage," *Past and Present* 56 (1972): 138, 142–44, passim.

14. David Brion Davis, "The Nature and Limits of Dissent," in *The Great Republic: A History of the American People,* by Bernard Bailyn, et al., 1st ed., 2 vols. (Lexington, Mass.: Heath, 1977), 1:530.

15. Blackwell to Lucy Stone, 2 July 1853, Lucy Stone Papers (included in the Blackwell Family Papers), Manuscript Division, Library of Congress, Washington, D.C. (hereafter cited as LSP–LC); Weld to Angelina Grimké, 15 April 1838, in *Letters of Theodore Dwight Weld, Angelina Grimké Weld, and Sarah Grimké, 1822–1844,* ed. Gilbert H. Barnes and Dwight L. Dumond, 2 vols. (1934; reprint, New York: Da Capo, 1970), 2:637; *Una,* April 1854, 254. There were, of course, limitations to the marriage-slavery analogy. These limitations can be assessed in different ways. Karen Sánchez-Eppler, analyzing the "nature of" the "coincidence" between abolitionism and feminism, has used literary sources to argue that "the identifications of woman and slave, marriage and slavery" tended "toward asymmetry and exploitation." This depiction of the relationship between abolitionism and feminism as a "coincidence" is problematic, but Sánchez-Eppler is correct to suggest that the unequal relationship between slave women and abolitionist women could also be an "empowering political alliance." See Sánchez-Eppler, *Touching Liberty,* 10, 15, 17.

16. Cott, "Giving Character to Our Whole Civil Polity: Marriage and the Public Order in the Late Nineteenth Century," in *U.S. History as Women's History,* ed. Linda K. Kerber, Alice Kessler-Harris, and Kathryn Kish Sklar (Chapel Hill: University of North Carolina Press, 1995), 110; Blackwell to Lucy Stone, 12 July 1854, LSP–LC; Blackwell to Stone, [Summer 1855], in *Loving Warriors: Selected Letters of Lucy Stone and Henry B. Blackwell, 1853–1893,* ed. Leslie Wheeler (New York: Dial, 1981), 144. T. J. Jackson Lears has argued that the "boundaries" between "the spheres of social life" seem "discernible only in specific historical circumstances." See Lears, "The Concept of Cultural Hegemony: Problems and Possibilities," *American Historical Review* 90 (1985): 588.

17. The full text of the "Protest," "Published by LUCY STONE and HENRY B. BLACKWELL, on their Marriage, May 1st, 1855," is in the LSP–LC.

18. The best discussion of the 1840 split is Aileen Kraditor, *Means and Ends in American Abolitionism: Garrison and His Critics on Strategy and Tactics, 1834–1850* (New York: Pantheon Books, 1967).

19. See L. Maria Child to Angelina Grimké Weld, 26 December 1838, in *The Collected Correspondence of Lydia Maria Child,* ed. Patricia G. Holland and Milton Meltzer (Millwood,

N.Y.: Kraus Microform, 1979, microfiche), Card 5/Item 158 (hereafter cited as LMCP); the "Protest" published in the *Liberator*, 31 May 1839.

20. Sarah Grimké to Preston Day, 19 January 1869, Weld-Grimké Papers, William L. Clements Library, University of Michigan, Ann Arbor; Child to Francis Shaw, 15 February 1842, in *Lydia Maria Child: Selected Letters, 1817–1880*, ed. Milton Meltzer and Patricia G. Holland (Amherst: University of Massachusetts Press, 1982), 161; Lucretia Mott, "Signed Autograph Memo," 1873, MP–FHL. Child's full name was Lydia Maria Child, but as a young woman she dropped "Lydia," and began using "Maria." When signing her name she used "L. Maria" or "Maria." See also Eugene Genovese, *The World the Slaveholders Made: Two Essays in Interpretation* (New York: Pantheon Books, 1969), 158.

21. Thomas Haskell, "Convention and Hegemonic Interest in the Debate over Antislavery: A Reply to Davis and Ashworth," *American Historical Review* 92 (1987): 854 (my emphasis).

22. See Garrison to Ann Phillips, 1 January 1854, Crawford Blagden Collection of the Papers of Wendell Phillips, Houghton Library, Harvard University, Cambridge, Mass. On the relationship between antebellum religion and reform, see Robert H. Abzug, *Cosmos Crumbling: American Reform and the Religious Imagination* (New York: Oxford University Press, 1994).

23. On the abolitionists' constituency, see Edward Magdol, *The Antislavery Rank and File: A Social Profile of the Abolitionists' Constituency* (Westport, Conn.: Greenwood, 1986); Walters, "The Boundaries of Antislavery," in *Antislavery Reconsidered: New Perspectives on the Abolitionists*, ed. Lewis Perry and Michael Fellman (Baton Rouge: Louisiana State University Press, 1979), 19–22; John B. Jentz, "The Antislavery Constituency in Jacksonian New York City," *Civil War History* 27 (1981): 101–22. The terms "abolitionism" and "antislavery" are used herein to describe different phenomenon. Abolitionists were those people who formally belonged to an antislavery society or who were active in some way on behalf of the slaves. Alternatively, many more people came to hold "antislavery" opinions, but were not active members of antislavery societies. Another means of describing the difference between the two terms, is that whereas antislavery was an *attitude*, abolitionism entailed an *act*.

24. The task of assessing gender and family relations among black abolitionists is rendered more complex for the historian by the relative paucity of extant sources. Margot Melia's doctoral thesis provides the best analysis of gender relations and familial experiences amongst black Garrisonian women. On the difficulties involved in reconstructing the familial experiences of African-American reformers, see Melia, "The Role of Black Garrisonian Women in Antislavery and Other Reforms in the Antebellum North, 1830–1865" (Ph.D. diss., University of Western Australia, 1991), 14–15. On the role of African American families in antebellum reform, see James Oliver Horton, "Generations of Protest: Black Families and Social Reform in Ante-Bellum Boston," *New England Quarterly* 59 (1976): 242–56.

25. On Lucretia Mott, see Margaret Hope Bacon, *Valiant Friend: The Life of Lucretia Mott* (New York: Walker, 1980); Otelia Cromwell, *Lucretia Mott* (1958; reprint, New York: Russell and Russell, 1971); Lloyd C. M. Hare, *The Greatest American Woman: Lucretia Mott* (1937; reprint, New York: Negro Universities Press, 1970). There is no published biography of James Mott. Studies of the relationship between abolitionism and women's rights include Blanche Glassman Hersh, " 'Am I Not A Woman and A Sister?' Abolitionist Beginnings of Nineteenth-Century Feminism," in Perry and Fellman, *Antislavery Reconsidered*, 252–83; Ellen Carol DuBois, "Women's Rights and Abolition: The Nature of the Connection," in Perry and Fellman, *Antislavery Reconsidered*, 238–51.

26. The quotes are from Anne Warren Weston to Caroline and Deborah Weston, 3 June 1843, ASC–BPL; L. Maria Child to Lydia [Bigelow] Child, 2 April 1837, LMCP, 5/120. On Elizabeth Cady Stanton, see Elisabeth Griffith, *In Her Own Right: The Life of Elizabeth Cady Stanton* (New York: Oxford University Press, 1984); Alma Lutz, *Created Equal: A Biography*

of Elizabeth Cady Stanton, 1815–1902 (New York: John Day, 1940); Lois Banner, *Elizabeth Cady Stanton: A Radical for Women's Rights* (Boston: Little, Brown, 1980). On Henry Stanton, see Arthur H. Rice, "Henry B. Stanton As a Political Abolitionist," (Ed.D. diss., Columbia University, 1968). On the Lane Rebels, see Lawrence T. Lesick, *The Lane Rebels: Evangelicalism and Anti-Slavery in Antebellum America* (Metuchen, N.J.: Scarecrow, 1980).

27. Maria Stewart, an African American activist, had spoken publicly during 1832–33 on the problems facing free blacks. See Melia, "Black Garrisonian Women," 46–47.

28. Major biographies of the Grimké sisters include Katherine Du Pre Lumpkin, *The Emancipation of Angelina Grimké* (Chapel Hill: University of North Carolina Press, 1974); Gerda Lerner, *The Grimké Sisters from South Carolina: Pioneers for Woman's Rights and Abolition* (1967; reprint, New York: Schocken Books, 1971); Catherine Birney, *The Grimké Sisters: Sarah and Angelina Grimké: The First American Women Advocates of Abolition and Women's Rights* (1885; reprint, Westport, Conn.: Greenwood, 1977). On Theodore Weld, see Robert Abzug, *Passionate Liberator: Theodore Dwight Weld and the Dilemma of Reform* (New York: Oxford University Press, 1980); Benjamin P. Thomas, *Theodore Weld: Crusader for Freedom* (Brunswick, N.J.: Rutgers University Press, 1950).

29. Child, "Concerning Women," *The Independent,* 15 July 1869, LMCP, 71/1903. Biographies of L. Maria Child include Helene G. Baer, *The Heart is Like Heaven: The Life of Lydia Maria Child* (Philadelphia: University of Pennsylvania Press, 1964); Milton Meltzer, *Tongue of Flame: The Life of Lydia Maria Child* (New York: Cromwell, 1965); Deborah Pickman Clifford, *Crusader for Freedom: A Life of Lydia Maria Child* (Boston: Beacon, 1992); Carolyn L. Karcher, *The First Woman in the Republic: A Cultural Biography of Lydia Maria Child* (Durham, N.C.: Duke University Press, 1994). See also Kirk Jeffrey, "Marriage, Career, and Feminine Ideology in Nineteenth-Century America: Reconstructing the Marital Experience of Lydia Maria Child, 1828–1874," *Feminist Studies* 2 (1975): 113–30.There is no published biography of David Lee Child.

30. Foster, *The Brotherhood of Thieves; or, A True Picture of the American Church and Clergy: A Letter to Nathaniel Barney and Peter May of Nantucket* (New London, N.H.: W. Bolles, 1843), 9; "Letter from Boston," *Poetical Works,* 1:310, as quoted in Martin Duberman, *James Russell Lowell* (Boston: Houghton Mifflin, 1966), 114; David Lee Child to Maria Weston Chapman, 13 December 1843, ASC–BPL. L. Maria Child was one abolitionist who rejected Foster's brand of reformism. See Child to Ellis Gray Loring, 6 March 1843, LMCP, 16/463; Child to Maria Weston Chapman, 26 July 1857, ASC–BPL. Studies of Abby Kelley and Stephen Foster include Jane H. Pease, "The Freshness of Fanaticism: Abby Kelley Foster: An Essay in Reform" (Ph.D. diss., University of Rochester, 1969); Joel Bernard, "Authority, Autonomy, and Radical Commitment: Stephen and Abby Kelley Foster," *Proceedings of the American Antiquarian Society* 90 (1980); Dorothy Sterling, *Ahead of Her Time: Abby Kelley and the Politics of Antislavery* (New York: Norton, 1991); Troy Duncan, "Stephen Symonds Foster: Radical Abolitionist" (B.A. honors. diss., University of Newcastle, 1995); Jane H. Pease and William H. Pease, *Bound With Them in Chains: A Biographical History of the Antislavery Movement* (Westport, Conn.: Greenwood, 1972), 191–217.

31. The quote comes from John Rand to Samuel May, 16 February 1850, ASC–BPL. Information on Stone and Blackwell can be found in Elinor Rice Hays, *Those Extraordinary Blackwells: The Story of a Journey to a Better World* (New York: Harcourt, Brace and World, 1967); Elinor Rice Hays, *Morning Star: A Biography of Lucy Stone* (1961; reprint, New York: Octagon Books, 1978); Andrea Moore Kerr, *Lucy Stone: Speaking Out for Equality* (New Brunswick: Rutgers University Press, 1992); Alice Stone Blackwell, *Lucy Stone* (1930; reprint, New York: Kraus Reprint, 1971).

32. On Garrison, see John L. Thomas, *The Liberator: William Lloyd Garrison* (Boston: Little, Brown, 1963), 19; James B. Stewart, *William Lloyd Garrison and the Challenge of Emancipa-*

tion (Arlington Heights, Ill.: Harlan Davidson, 1992); Walter M. Merrill, *Against Wind and Tide: A Biography of Wm. Lloyd Garrison* (Cambridge: Harvard University Press, 1963).

33. Biographies of Wendell Phillips include James Brewer Stewart, *Wendell Phillips: Liberty's Hero* (Baton Rouge: Louisiana State University Press, 1986); Irving H. Bartlett, *Wendell Phillips: Brahmin Radical* (1961; reprint, Westport, Conn.: Greenwood, 1973); Oscar Sherwin, *Prophet of Liberty: The Life and Times of Wendell Phillips* (New York: Bookman Associates, 1958). On Maria Weston Chapman, see Pease and Pease, *Bound With Them in Chains*, 28–59.

34. Hersh examined fifty-one abolitionist women, whilst Kennon, more interested in marital relationships, based his findings on fifty-eight couples. See Hersh, *Slavery of Sex*, chaps. 4 and 7; Kennon, "Marriage and Reform," 9–42. There are common threads to these sample groups. Six of the eight women examined in this study were also included in Hersh's study. Excluded from Hersh's group were Helen Garrison and Ann Phillips, who did not fit into her category of "feminist-abolitionists." Kennon's sample group included several of the couples examined here; Abby Kelley and Stephen S. Foster; Henry and Elizabeth Cady Stanton; Lucretia and James Mott; Lucy Stone and Henry Blackwell; David and L. Maria Child; and Theodore and Angelina Grimké Weld. See also Nancy Hewitt, "The Social Origins of Women's Antislavery Politics in Western New York," in *Crusaders and Compromisers: Essays on the Relationship of the Antislavery Struggle to the Antebellum Party System* ed. Alan M. Kraut (Westport, Conn.: Greenwood, 1983), 209.

35. Hersh, *Slavery of Sex*, 120. See also Kennon, "Marriage and Reform," 22.

36. Theodore Weld and Elizabeth Cady Stanton are two such examples. Weld was converted to Presbyterianism by the evangelist Charles Grandison Finney in 1825. Stanton, raised as a Presbyterian, was profoundly affected by her exposure to Finney's preaching. That experience, and the subsequent influence of Theodore Parker, not only combined to make Stanton a thorough critic of many religious practices and principles, but also enabled her to perceive clearly their negative influence over women. See Abzug, *Passionate Liberator*, 28–51; Griffith, *In Her Own Right*, 19–21, 45–46.

37. See Sarah Grimké to Elizabeth Pease, 16 September 1848, Oswald G. Villard Papers, Houghton Library, Harvard University, Cambridge, Mass. See also Hersh, *Slavery of Sex*, 131–32, 142–47; Kennon, "Marriage and Reform," 13–18, 25–26. L. Maria Child and Lucy Stone both converted to Unitarianism; Lucretia Mott was a Quaker who sided with the Hicksite branch of the movement after the Great Separation of 1827; Abby Kelley left the Society of Friends in 1841. Sarah Grimké converted from Episcopalianism to the Society of Friends, only to incur the disapproval of the Philadelphia Quakers for her brand of reformism. Angelina Grimké's religious odyssey involved conversion from Episcopalianism to Presbyterianism to Quakerism. Like her elder sister, Angelina eventually alienated the Philadelphia Quakers by her abolitionist activities, and breached the rules of the Society of Friends by marrying Theodore Weld, who was a Presbyterian. Because she attended Angelina's wedding ceremony, Sarah was formally expelled from the Society. Angelina was further disillusioned by the Society of Friends' racist treatment of African Americans. See the entries for L. Maria Child, Abby Kelley Foster, Angelina and Sarah Grimké, Lucretia Mott, Lucy Stone, in *Notable American Women, 1607–1950: A Biographical Dictionary*, ed. Edward T. James, Janet Wilson James, Paul S. Boyer, 3 vols. (Cambridge: Belknap Press of Harvard University Press, 1971) 1:330, 648; 2:97–98, 592–93; 3:378–88; Angelina Grimké to Abby Kelley, 15 April 1837, Abigail Kelley Foster Papers, American Antiquarian Society, Worcester, Mass.; Lerner, *The Grimké Sisters from South Carolina*, 40–41, 50–51, 54–62, 67–75, 189–90; Keith Melder, "Abby Kelley and the Process of Liberation," in Yellin and Van Horne, *The Abolitionist Sisterhood*, 232–45.

38. Hersh, *Slavery of Sex*, 219; Kennon, "Marriage and Reform," 27. Lucretia Mott was born 3 January 1793, and married 10 April 1811; L. Maria Child was born 11 February 1802, and

married 19 October 1828; Angelina Grimké was born 20 February 1805, and married 14 May 1838; Abby Kelley was born 15 October 1810, and married 21 December 1845; Helen Garrison was born 23 February 1811, and married 4 September 1834; Ann Phillips was born 19 November 1813, and married 12 October 1837; Elizabeth Cady Stanton was born 12 November 1815, and married 11 May 1840; Lucy Stone was born 13 August 1818, and married 1 May 1855. See also Kennon, "Marriage and Reform," 27; Nancy Cott, *The Bonds of Womanhood: "Woman's Sphere" in New England, 1780–1835* (New Haven: Yale University Press, 1977), 13–14.

39. Hersh, *Slavery of Sex,* 219; Kennon, "Marriage and Reform," 29. Lucy Stone and Abby Kelley, who married later than the other women in this study (at ages 36 and 35 respectively), each bore one child; Angelina Grimké had three children; Lucretia Mott, six; and Elizabeth Cady Stanton and Helen Garrison both had seven children. For the national figures, see Sellers, *Market Revolution,* 240.

40. See *An Appeal to Females of the North, on the Subject of Slavery. By a Female of Vermont* (Philadelphia: John Thompson, 1838), 10; Samuel J. May, *Some Recollections of Our Antislavery Conflict* (1869; reprint, Miami, Fla.: Mnemosyne, 1969), 230.

41. See Cott, *Bonds of Womanhood,* 5.

Chapter 1. "The Dreadful Immorality"

1. George Fitzhugh, *Cannibals All! or Slaves Without Masters* (1857; reprint, Cambridge: Belknap Press of Harvard University Press, 1960), 36; Wendell Phillips, "Philosophy of the Abolition Movement," Address to the Massachusetts Anti-Slavery Society, 27 January 1853, in *The Abolitionists: A Collection of Their Writings,* ed. Louis Ruchames (New York: Putnam, Sons, 1963), 221. See also L. Maria Child, ed., *The Patriarchal Institution, as Described by Members of Its Own Family* (New York: American Anti-Slavery Society, 1860), 29. On the importance of the family to Southern ideology, see "A Treatise on the Patriarchal or Cooperative System of Society . . . Under the Name of Slavery," as quoted in James Oakes, *The Ruling Race: A History of American Slaveholders* (1982; reprint, New York: Vintage Books, 1983), 217–18; Eugene Genovese, " 'Our Family, White and Black': Family and Household in the Southern Slaveholders' World View," in *In Joy and In Sorrow: Women, Family, and Marriage in the Victorian South, 1830–1900,* ed. Carol Bleser (New York: Oxford University Press, 1991), 87. Ronald Walters has discussed the relationship between the themes of unrestrained power and sexuality in abolitionism. See Walters, "The Erotic South: Civilization and Sexuality in American Abolitionism," *American Quarterly* 25 (1973): 177–201.

2. Patterson, "Slavery and Social Death," in *Slavery in American Society,* ed. Lawrence B. Goodheart, Richard D. Brown, and Stephen G. Rabe, 3d ed. (Lexington, Mass.: Heath, 1993), 8; Angelina Grimké, *An Appeal to the Women of the Nominally Free States, Issued by an Anti-Slavery Convention of American Women* (New York: William S. Dorr, 1837), 14–15.

3. David Lee Child to Thomas S. Cavender, 12 November 1843, Child Papers, Anti-Slavery Collection, Boston Public Library (hereafter cited as ASC–BPL); L. Maria Child, *The Duty of Disobedience to the Fugitive Slave Act: An Appeal to the Legislators of Massachusetts* (Boston: American Anti-Slavery Society, 1860), 22; James A. Thome, "Speech of James A. Thome of Kentucky, delivered at the Annual Meeting of the American Anti-Slavery Society, May 6, 1834," in *The Antislavery Argument,* ed. William H. Pease and James H. Pease (Indianapolis: Bobbs-Merrill, 1965), 93; "Narrative of Mr. Caulkins," in *American Slavery As It Is: Testimony of a Thousand Witnesses,* by Theodore Weld (New York: American Anti-Slavery Society, 1839), 16.

4. Jean Fagan Yellin has argued that "the emblem of the female slave popularized by black and white 'female abolitionists' triggered the outrage of American women and moved them to unprecedented action: direct involvement in the slavery controversy." See Yellin, *Women*

and Sisters: The Antislavery Feminists in American Culture (New Haven: Yale University Press, 1989), 3. See also Phillip Lapsansky, "Graphic Discord: Abolitionist and Antiabolitionist Images," in *The Abolitionist Sisterhood: Women's Political Culture in Antebellum America,* ed. Jean Fagan Yellin and John C. Van Horne (Ithaca: Cornell University Press, 1994), 201–30; Elizabeth B. Clark, " 'The Sacred Rights of the Weak': Pain, Sympathy, and the Culture of Individual Rights in Antebellum America," *Journal of American History* 82 (1995): 481.

5. See Stowe, *Uncle Tom's Cabin or Life Among the Lowly* (1852; reprint, Middlesex: Penguin Books, 1986); Stowe, *The Key to Uncle Tom's Cabin: Presenting the Original Facts and Documents Upon Which the Story was Founded. Together With Corroborating Statements Verifying the Truth of the Work* (London: Clark, Beeton, 1853); see 32, 71–73, 75–78, 172–73. On the impact of *American Slavery As It Is* on Stowe, see Henry Blackwell to Lucy Stone, 13 June 1853, in *Loving Warriors: Selected Letters of Lucy Stone and Henry B. Blackwell, 1853 to 1893,* ed. Leslie Wheeler (New York: Dial, 1981), 37; Yellin, "Doing It Herself: *Uncle Tom's Cabin* and Woman's Role in the Slavery Crisis," in *New Essays on Uncle Tom's Cabin,* ed. Eric J. Sundquist (Cambridge: Cambridge University Press, 1986), 91.

6. See Sarah Grimké to Amos Phelps, 3 September 1837, ASC–BPL.

7. Grimké, *An Appeal to the Women of the Nominally Free States,* 17; Child, *Anti-Slavery Catechism* (Newburyport, Mass.: Charles Whipple, 1836), 13. Major studies of the slave family include John W. Blassingame, *The Slave Community: Plantation Life in the Antebellum South,* 2d ed. (New York: Oxford University Press, 1972), 149–91; Eugene Genovese, *Roll, Jordan, Roll: The World the Slaves Made* (London: Andre Deutsch, 1975), 450–57, 482–534; Herbert Gutman, *The Black Family in Slavery and Freedom* (New York: Pantheon Books, 1976).

8. Loguen, *The Rev. J. W. Loguen, as A Slave and As a Freeman. A Narrative of Real Life* (1859; reprint, New York: Negro Universities Press, 1968), 38; Bibb, *Narrative of the Life and Adventures of Henry Bibb, An American Slave, Written by Himself* (1850; reprint, New York: Negro Universities Press, 1969), 56–64, 74–83, 85–87, passim (quotations on 33, 79). The authors of slave narratives left no room for doubt that African Americans experienced as much anguish as whites when they were forced to leave their loved ones. In so doing, they reversed the claims of proslavery writers, who argued that African Americans were governed by brutal instincts, and hence incapable of forming stable, loving relationships. See Bibb, *Life and Adventures,* 80, 145–49; William Wells Brown, "The American Slave Trade," in the *Liberty Bell* (1848) reprinted in *Narrative of William W. Brown. A Fugitive Slave, Written By Himself,* 2d ed. (1848; reprint, Reading, Mass.: Addison-Wesley, 1969), 51–52; Marion Diedrich, " 'My Love Is Black As Yours Is Fair': Premarital Love and Sexuality in the Antebellum Slave Narrative," *Phylon* 47 (1986): 243.

9. Garrison to Helen E. Benson, 6 June 1834, in *The Letters of William Lloyd Garrison,* ed. Walter Merrill and Louis Ruchames 6 vols. (Cambridge: Belknap Press of Harvard University Press, 1971–81), 1:358 (hereafter cited as WLGL); Child, *The History of the Condition of Women, In Various Ages and Nations,* 2 vols. (Boston: John Allen, 1835), 2:268; Bibb, *Life and Adventures,* 38–39, 189.

10. Edmund Jackson, "The Effects of Slavery," *Liberator,* 21 January 1842; "Testimony of Angelina Grimké Weld," in Weld, *American Slavery,* 56.

11. Hildreth, *The Slave: or, Memoirs of Archy Moore,* 2 vols. (1836; reprint, Upper Saddle River, N.J.: Gregg, 1968), 1:1, 6, 43, 75, 2:114–17. Hildreth also wrote *Despotism in America: An Inquiry into the Nature, Results, and Legal Basis of Slave-Holding in the United States* (Boston: n.p., 1840). Antislavery articles by a person identified as "Hildreth" were published in the *National Anti-Slavery Standard.* See the editions for 16 July 1840 and 30 July 1840.

12. *Liberator,* 25 February, 9 June 1837; "Hampden," in the *Herald of Freedom,* as reprinted in the *Liberator,* 31 March 1837.
13. Child to Garrison, *Liberator,* 18 March 1837.
14. *Liberator,* 14 April 1837, 31 March 1837.
15. Holmes, "Uncle Tom's Cabin," *Southern Literary Messenger* 18 (December 1852), in *Slavery Defended: The Views of the Old South,* ed. Eric L. McKitrick (Englewood Cliffs, N.J.: Prentice-Hall, 1963), 101.
16. Brandstadter, "Uncle Tom and Archy Moore: The Antislavery Novel as Ideological Symbol," *American Quarterly* 26 (1974): 164–75; Child to Garrison, *Liberator,* 18 March 1837. Addressing the Massachusetts Anti-Slavery Society in 1853, Phillips argued that abolitionist sympathies had been aroused in the North prior to the publication of *Uncle Tom's Cabin. Archy Moore,* Phillips contended, was "a book of eminent ability," which "owed its want of success to no lack of genius, but only to the fact that it was born out of due time." See Phillips, "Philosophy of the Abolition Movement," in Ruchames, *The Abolitionists,* 236. On the role of domestic values in *Uncle Tom's Cabin,* see Gillian Brown, "Getting in the Kitchen with Dinah: Domestic Politics in *Uncle Tom's Cabin,*" *American Quarterly* 36 (1984): 503–23; Glenna Matthews, *"Just a Housewife": The Rise and Fall of Domesticity in America* (New York: Oxford University Press, 1987), 52–54.
17. Douglas, *The Feminization of American Culture* (New York: Knopf, 1978), 245; Gramsci, as quoted in James Joll, *Gramsci* (Glasgow: Fontana, 1977), 31.
18. Stowe to Frederick Douglass, 9 July 1851, in *Life and Letters of Harriet Beecher Stowe,* ed. Annie Fields (London: Sampson Low, Marston, 1897), 133–34. On the impact of Stowe's work, see Booker T. Washington, *Frederick Douglass* (1907; reprint, New York: Greenwood, 1969), 175. Stowe disagreed with much of what her elder sister had argued in her dispute with the Grimké sisters in the 1830s. Besides urging women to work actively against slavery, Stowe specifically disagreed with her sister's exhortations against petitioning. Women, she asserted, should petition the national government to end slavery. Jean Fagan Yellin has offered an alternative assessment of Harriet Beecher Stowe's position on abolitionism and women's role vis-à-vis Catharine Beecher. Whilst Yellin acknowledged that "on a spiritual level Stowe's attack on the patriarchal institution challenges all oppressive earthly authority," she concluded that "ultimately both the spiritual and the mundane dramas in *Uncle Tom's Cabin* counter the practical measures urged by the black and white activists following the Grimkés' lead." In essence, Yellin emphasized Beecher and Stowe's common perspective on women's role. The common appeal to domestic values is indisputable, but while literary critics of Stowe's work stress her conservatism, and point to the parallels with Beecher's ideology, the impact of *Uncle Tom's Cabin* in the 1850s must not be underestimated. The appeal of the novel was to widely held values, but it was perceived as an abolitionist document, and it aroused deep controversy. See Stowe, "Appeal to the Women of the Free States," in *Limits of Sisterhood: The Beecher Sisters on Women's Rights and Woman's Sphere,* ed. Jeanne Boydston, Mary Kelley, and Anne Margolis (Chapel Hill: University of North Carolina Press, 1988), 180–82; Yellin, "Doing It Herself," 102.
19. Phillips, as quoted in James Brewer Stewart, *Wendell Phillips: Liberty's Hero* (Baton Rouge: Louisiana State University Press, 1986), 105; *Liberator,* 26 March 1852, 17 December 1852.
20. See *Uncle Tom's Cabin,* chap. 10; Stanton to Elizabeth Smith Miller, 21 November 1852, in *Elizabeth Cady Stanton: As Revealed in Her Letters, Diary, and Reminiscences,* ed. Theodore Stanton and Harriot Stanton Blatch 2 vols. (1922; reprint, New York: Arno, 1969), 2:45–46. The importance of maternal values, and the importance of women in *Uncle Tom's Cabin* were discussed by Elizabeth Ammons, in "Heroines in *Uncle Tom's Cabin,*" *American Literature* 49 (1977): 161–79.

21. *Liberator,* 5 May 1832; William Wells Brown, *Lecture Before the Female Anti-Slavery Society of Salem, at Lyceum Hall, Nov. 14, 1847* (1847; reprint, Reading, Mass.: Addison-Wesley, 1969), 97.

22. *Liberator,* 30 April 1831; *Proceedings of the Anti-Slavery Convention of American Women, Held in the City of New York, May 9th, 10th, 11th, and 12th, 1837* (New York: William S. Dorr, 1837), 11.

23. Fitzhugh, *Sociology for the South,* in *Antebellum Writings of George Fitzhugh and Hinton Rowan Helper,* ed. Harvey Wish (New York: Capricorn Books, 1960), 70; Loguen, *A Slave and As a Freeman,* 26–27; Grimké, *Slavery in America: A Reprint of An Appeal to the Christian Women of the Slave States of America* (Edinburgh: William Oliphant and Son, 1837), 22; Stowe, "Appeal to the Women of the Free States," published in the *Independent,* 23 February 1854, in Boydston, Kelley, and Margolis, *Limits of Sisterhood,* 180. Michael P. Johnson has argued that the high incidence of infant deaths in the slave states stemmed in large measure from the overworking of pregnant women. See Johnson, "Smothered Slave Infants: Were Slave Mothers at Fault?" *Journal of Southern History* 47 (1981): 493–520.

24. See Stowe to Calvin Stowe, 26 July 1849, in Charles Edward Stowe, *Life of Harriet Beecher Stowe* (1889) in Boydston, Kelley, and Margolis, *Limits of Sisterhood,* 76; Stowe to Mrs. Fuller, February 1853, as quoted in *Harriet Beecher Stowe: The Story of Her Life,* by Charles Edward Stowe and Lyman Beecher Stowe (Boston: Houghton Mifflin, 1911), 154–55.

25. Mary Grew to Helen Garrison, 3 May [1848], ASC–BPL. See also Helen Garrison to Ann Phillips, n.d. (letter 20 in Helen Garrison to Ann Phillips Correspondence), Crawford-Blagden Collection of the Papers of Wendell Phillips, Houghton Library, Harvard University, Cambridge, Mass.

26. Child, *The Brother and Sister: and Other Stories* (Philadelphia: n.p., 1852), 90; Child, *On the Management and Education of Children. Being Mrs. Child's "Mother's Book," Revised and Adapted to the Use of English Parents and Teachers* (London: John W. Barber, 1835), 2–3. See also "Narrative and Testimony of Rev. Horace Moulton," in Weld, *American Slavery,* 18; "Juvenile Department" of the *Liberator,* 5 March 1831; Lawrence Levine, *Black Culture and Black Consciousness: Afro-American Folk Thought from Slavery to Freedom* (New York: Oxford University Press, 1977), 156.

27. *Proceedings of the Anti-Slavery Convention of American Women . . . 1837,* 17; Mary Grew to Lucretia Mott (n.d.), in *James and Lucretia Mott. Life and Letters,* ed. Anna Davis Hallowell (Boston: Houghton Mifflin, 1884), 127–29; Abby Kelley to Alla Foster, 17 April 1852, Abigail Kelley Foster Correspondence, Worcester Historical Museum, Worcester, Mass.; Leonard L. Richards, *"Gentlemen of Property and Standing": Anti-Abolition Mobs in Jacksonian America* (New York: Oxford University Press, 1970), 60; *Liberator,* 26 March 1852. See also J. R. Oldfield, "Anti-Slavery Sentiment in Children's Literature, 1750–1850," *Slavery and Abolition* 10 (1989): 44.

28. See *The Child's Book on Slavery; or, Slavery Made Plain* (Cincinnati: American Reform Tract and Book Society, 1857), 7, 17, 32; *Liberator,* 19 February 1831, 22 October 1831, 29 October 1831, 26 November 1831; John Neal, "The Instinct of Childhood," *National Anti-Slavery Standard; The Child's Anti-Slavery Book: Containing a Few Words About American Slave Children, and Stories of Slave Life* (New York: Carlston and Porter, n.d.). Assessing the response of British travelers to the United States, Richard Rapson has referred to the "blurring of the lines between young and old in the New World." That contention suggests that the abolitionists' enthusiasm for children's antislavery activities was an expression of wider societal trends. See Rapson, "The American Child as Seen By British Travellers," *American Quarterly* 17 (1965): 532.

29. See *Liberator,* 12 November 1831, for an example of the abolitionists' glorification of the home.

30. Child, *The Oasis,* viii. On the similar powers of women and girls as moralizing agents, see Glenda Gates Riley, "The Subtle Subversion: Changes in the Traditionalist Image of the American Woman," *The Historian* 32 (1970): 216.

31. Oliver Johnson, *William Lloyd Garrison and His Times; or, Sketches of the Anti-Slavery Movement in America, and of the Man who was its Founder and Leader,* rev. ed. (Boston: Houghton Mifflin, 1885), 331; *Seventh Annual Report of the Boston Female Anti-Slavery Society . . . 1840,* 31; Grimké, *An Appeal to the Women of the Nominally Free States,* 28, 34. For contrasting interpretations of the abolitionists' racialist attitudes, see Herbert Aptheker, *Abolitionism: A Revolutionary Movement* (Boston: Twayne, 1989), 69; George Fredrickson, *The Black Image in the White Mind: The Debate on Afro-American Character and Destiny, 1817–1914* (1971; reprint, New York: Harper Torchbooks, 1972), 107.

32. Child, *Anti-Slavery Catechism,* 28; Stowe, *Key to Uncle Tom's Cabin,* 41; Stone to Henry B. Blackwell, 21 June 1853, Lucy Stone Papers (included in the Blackwell Family Papers), Manuscript Division, Library of Congress, Washington, D.C. See also David W. Levy, "Racial Stereotypes in Antislavery Fiction," *Phylon* 31 (1970): 265–69.

33. See Jane H. Pease and William H. Pease, "Ends, Means, and Attitudes: Black-White Conflict in the Antislavery Movement," *Civil War History* 18 (1972): 117–28; Frederick Douglass, *My Bondage and My Freedom* (1855; reprint, New York: Arno, 1968), 361–62; Arno Bontemps, *Free at Last: The Life of Frederick Douglass* (New York: Dodd, Mead, 1971), 60–64; Wendell Phillips, *Speech of Wendell Phillips, Esq. at the Worcester Disunion Convention, January 15, 1857* (Boston: American Anti-Slavery Society, 1857), 13.

34. *The Child's Book on Slavery,* 29–31.

35. Child, "The African Race," *National Anti-Slavery Standard,* 27 April 1843.

36. Sarah Grimké to Catherine Brooks Yale, 13 July 1863, Weld-Grimké Papers, William L. Clements Library, University of Michigan, Ann Arbor (hereafter cited as WGP–UM). On Tilton's views, see Fredrickson, *Black Image in the White Mind,* 114–15.

37. Harriet Beecher Stowe to Henry Ward Beecher, 1 February 1851, Harriet Beecher Stowe Letters, Sterling Memorial Library, Yale University, New Haven, Conn.; Stowe, *Key to Uncle Tom's Cabin,* 25; Stowe, *Uncle Tom's Cabin,* 164.

38. Foster, *Revolution the Only Remedy for Slavery* (New York: American Anti-Slavery Society, 1855), 3. See also Jules Zanger, "The 'Tragic Octoroon' in Pre-Civil War Fiction," *American Quarterly* 18 (1966): 66; Child, *The Oasis,* ix; Yellin, *Women and Sisters,* 70–75.

39. Christine Stansell, *City of Women: Sex and Class in New York: 1789–1860* (New York: Knopf, 1986), 175; Sarah Grimké to Amos Phelps, 3 September 1837, ASC–BPL; Phillips, *Shall Women Have the Right to Vote? An Address by Wendell Phillips at Worcester, Mass. 1851* (n.p.: Equal Franchise Society of Pennsylvania, 1910), 26; Garrison to Helen Garrison, 11 August 1846, WLGL, 3:365; Frances Whipple, "Appeal to American Women," *Liberator,* 21 May 1836; Stephen Foster, in the *National Anti-Slavery Standard,* 7 March 1850. See also Catherine Clinton, "'Southern Dishonor': Flesh, Blood, Race, and Bondage," in Bleser, *In Joy and In Sorrow,* 57.

40. Child, *Anti-Slavery Catechism,* 15; Grimké to Gerrit Smith, 10 September 1839, Gerrit Smith Papers, Syracuse University Library, Department of Special Collections, Syracuse, N.Y.; Foster, *The Brotherhood of Thieves; or, A True Picture of the American Church and Clergy: Letter to Nathaniel Barney and Peter May of Nantucket* (Boston: n.p., 1844), 10; Phillips, "Philosophy of the Abolition Movement," in Ruchames, *The Abolitionists,* 221; Anthony, "What is American Slavery," Susan B. Anthony Papers, Manuscript Division, Library of Congress, Washington, D.C. The abolitionists' denunciations of Southern sexuality, viewed alongside their own measured behavior, affirms Michel Foucault's thesis that sexuality was

regarded as "the point of weakness where evil portents reach through to us; the fragment of darkness that we each carry within us." See Foucault, *The History of Sexuality,* 3 vols. trans. Robert Hurley (New York: Pantheon Books, 1978), 1:69. See also Loguen, *A Slave and As a Freeman,* 12; Walters, "The Erotic South," 177–201.

41. Anne Warren Weston to the New York Female Anti-Slavery Society, 21 July 1835, in the Boston Female Anti-Slavery Society Letterbook, 9 April 1834–6 January 1838, Massachusetts Historical Society, Boston (hereafter cited as BFASSL–MHS); Roper, *A Narrative of the Adventures and Escape of Moses Roper, From American Slavery; With a Preface by the Rev. T. Price, D.D.* (1838; reprint, New York: Negro Universities Press, 1970), 44; Grimké, *An Appeal to the Women of the Nominally Free States,* 21; "Testimony of Angelina Grimké Weld," in Weld, *American Slavery,* 53. On abolitionist women's sororal feelings to white southern women, see Anne Warren Weston to the New York Female Anti-Slavery Society, 21 July 1835, BFASSL–MHS. See also L. Maria Child, *An Appeal in Favor of that Class of Americans Called Africans* (1836; reprint, New York: Arno, 1968), 28–29; William Wells Brown, *Narrative,* 6; Anne Firor Scott, *The Southern Lady: From Pedestal to Politics, 1830–1930* (Chicago: University of Chicago Press, 1970), 46–52; Elizabeth Fox-Genovese, *Within the Plantation Household: Black and White Women in the Old South* (Chapel Hill: University of North Carolina Press, 1988), 243.

42. Brown, *Narrative,* 22–23, 42.

43. For references to the "family altar" see Angelina Grimké to Jane Smith, 19 October 1840, WGP–UM; *Proceedings of the Anti-Slavery Convention of American Women . . . 1837,* 17.

44. Foster, *Revolution the Only Remedy,* 3; Brown, *Narrative,* 13; Grimké, *An Appeal to the Women of the Nominally Free States,* 15. On the slaves' religion, see Albert J. Raboteau, *Slave Religion: The "Invisible Institution" in the Antebellum South* (Oxford: Oxford University Press, 1978).

45. *Liberator,* 7 May 1831. See also Child, *An Appeal,* 196.

46. "Refuge of Oppression" column of the *Liberator,* 20 February 1836; Fitzhugh, *Cannibals All,* 194–98. See also Linda Kerber, "Abolitionists and Amalgamators: The New York City Race Riots of 1834," *New York History* 48 (1967), 30. See also Richards, "*Gentlemen of Property and Standing,*" 16–17, 30–36; Lorman Ratner, "Northern Concern for Social Order as Cause for Rejecting Anti-Slavery, 1831–1840," *The Historian* 28 (1965): 1–18; Lorman Ratner, *Powder Keg: Northern Opposition to the Antislavery Movement, 1831–1840* (New York: Basic Books, 1968), 78.

47. Ruggles, "The 'Extinguisher' Extinguished! or David M. Reese, M.D. 'Used Up,'" in Ruchames, *The Abolitionists,* 84–85; Child, *The Oasis,* ix, xi; Garrison to Hannah Webb, 1 March 1843, WLGL, 3:131.

48. Whipple, *The Family Relation as Affected by Slavery* (Cincinnati: American Reform and Tract Society, n.d.) 12; Child to Louisa Loring, 15 January 1847, in *The Collected Correspondence of Lydia Maria Child,* ed. Patricia G. Holland and Milton Meltzer (Millwood, N.Y.: Kraus Microform, 1979, microfiche) Card 24/Item 691; "Narrative of Mr. Caulkins," in Weld, *American Slavery,* 15–16. On the question of the slaves' fertility, see Deborah Gray White, *Ar'n't I A Woman? Female Slaves in the Plantation South* (New York: Norton, 1985), 69; Robert Fogel and Stanley Engerman, *Time on the Cross: The Economics of American Negro Slavery,* 2 vols. (London: Wildwood, 1974), 1:78–86, 137.

49. Hildreth, *Archy Moore,* 1:3, 40; Grimké, *Slavery in America,* 11–12; Stanton, *The Slave's Appeal* (New York: Weed, Parsons, 1860), 5. On incest, see Peter Bardaglio, "'An Outrage upon Nature': Incest and the Law in the Nineteenth-Century South," in Bleser, *In Joy and In Sorrow,* 33. See also Brown, *Narrative,* 18; Elizabeth Buffum Chace, *Anti-Slavery Reminiscences* (Central Falls, R.I.: E.L. Freeman and Son, 1891), 36–37.

50. Abby Kelley recounted that she was accused of having relationships with African Americans. See Kelley to Samuel May, 9 November 1853, ASC–BPL. For abolitionist calls to end public expressions of prejudice, see Angelina Grimké, *An Appeal to the Women of the Nominally Free States,* 59; *Proceedings of the Anti-Slavery Convention of American Women . . . 1837,* 13.
51. Child, *Anti-Slavery Catechism,* 32–33.

Chapter 2. From Private to Public

1. On this issue see Lori D. Ginzberg, *Women and the Work of Benevolence: Morality, Politics, and Class in the Nineteenth-Century United States* (New Haven: Yale University Press, 1990).
2. L. Linton, in the *Lily,* 15 June 1854, 87.
3. Joseph Richardson, *A Sermon on the Duty and Dignity of Woman, Delivered April 22, 1832* (Hingham, Mass.: Jedidiah Farmer, 1833), 1. See also Leonard L. Richards, *"Gentlemen of Property and Standing": Anti-Abolition Mobs in Jacksonian America* (New York: Oxford University Press, 1970), 62.
4. Linda K. Kerber, "A Constitutional Right to Be Treated Like American Ladies: Women and the Obligations of Citizenship," in *U.S. History as Women's History: New Essays,* ed. Linda K. Kerber, Alice Kessler-Harris, and Kathryn Kish Sklar (Chapel Hill: University of North Carolina Press, 1995), 25; Carroll Smith-Rosenberg, "Dis-Covering the Subject of the 'Great Constitutional Discussion,' 1786–1789," *Journal of American History* 79 (1992): 855. On gendered constructions of republicanism, see also Stephanie McCurry, "The Two Faces of Republicanism: Gender and Proslavery Politics in Antebellum South Carolina," *Journal of American History* 78 (1992): 1245–64. The most comprehensive analysis of the abolitionists' links to republican ideology is Daniel J. McInerney's, *The Fortunate Heirs of Freedom: Abolition and Republican Thought* (Lincoln: University of Nebraska Press, 1994). It is curious, however, given the recent historiographical emphasis on republican motherhood and women's roles in the Revolutionary period, that McInerney does not specifically address the connections between republicanism and abolitionism in terms of gender relations and ideals about the family.
5. Aileen Kraditor coined the phrase "cult of domesticity" in the introduction to *Up From the Pedestal: Selected Writings on the History of American Feminism* (New York: Quadrangle, 1968), 11. In her study of the Boston Female Anti-Slavery Society, Debra Gold Hansen has argued that the "separate-spheres ideology was essentially conservative." See Hansen, *Strained Sisterhood: Gender and Class in the Boston Female Anti-Slavery Society* (Amherst: University of Massachusetts Press, 1993), 155. On the changing interpretations of the effects of domesticity, and for differing interpretations of the role of domestic ideology in women's search for autonomy, see Nancy Cott, *The Bonds of Womanhood: "Woman's Sphere" in New England, 1780–1835* (New Haven: Yale University Press, 1977), 197–201; Daniel Scott Smith, "Family Limitation, Sexual Control, and Domestic Feminism in Victorian America," *Feminist Studies* 1 (1972): 40–57; Gerda Lerner, "Just a Housewife," in Lerner, *The Majority Finds Its Past* (New York: Oxford University Press, 1979), 141.
6. Scott, "Gender: A Useful Category of Historical Analysis," *American Historical Review* 91 (1986): 1068; Gisela Bock, "Challenging Dichotomies: Perspectives on Women's History," in *Writing Women's History: International Perspectives,* ed. Karen Offen, Ruth Roach Pierson and Jane Rendall (Basingstoke: Macmillan, 1991), 5; Baker, *The Moral Frameworks of Public Life: Gender, Politics, and the State in Rural New York, 1870–1930* (New York: Oxford University Press, 1991). See also Michelle Zimbalist Rosaldo, "Women, Culture, and Society: A Theoretical Overview," in *Women, Culture, and Society,* ed. Michelle Zimbalist Rosaldo and Louise Lamphere (Stanford: Stanford University Press, 1974), 17–42; Janet Siltanen and Michelle Stanworth, "The Politics of Private Woman and Public Man," in

Women and the Public Sphere: A Critique of Sociology and Politics, ed. Janet Siltanen and Michelle Stanworth (London: Hutchinson, 1984), 186; Mary P. Ryan, *Women in Public: Between Banners and Ballots, 1825–1880* (Baltimore: Johns Hopkins University Press, 1990), 3–18, passim; Seth Koven and Sonya Michel, "Womanly Duties: Maternalist Politics and the Origins of Welfare States in France, Great Britain, and the United States, 1880–1920," *American Historical Review* 95 (1990): 1079. It is not only feminist scholars who have taken an interest in the public/private dichotomy. See, for example, Jürgen Habermas, *The Structural Transformation of the Public Sphere: An Inquiry into a Category of Bourgeois Society,* trans. Thomas Burger (Cambridge: MIT Press, 1989).

7. Skocpol, *Protecting Soldiers and Mothers: The Political Origins of Social Policy in the United States* (Cambridge: Belknap Press of Harvard University Press, 1992). Ronald Walters has argued that abolitionists stood "midway along" the "continuum from romantic reform" to the "middle-class moralists" of the late-nineteenth century. See Walters, "The Erotic South: Civilization and Sexuality in American Abolitionism," *American Quarterly* 25 (1973): 200. On the differences between antebellum and postbellum reformers, see Ginzberg, *Women and the Work of Benevolence,* 5.
8. Stanton, *Eighty Years and More: Reminiscences, 1815–1897* (1898; reprint, New York: Schocken Books, 1971), 20–21. See also Carl Degler, *At Odds: Women and the Family in America from the Revolution to the Present* (New York: Oxford University Press, 1980), 28; Ginzberg, *Women and the Work of Benevolence,* 3 n. 5.
9. See Merton L. Dillon, *The Abolitionists: The Growth of a Dissenting Minority* (DeKalb: Northern Illinois University Press, 1974).
10. Elizabeth Fox-Genovese and Eugene D. Genovese, *Fruits of Merchant Capital: Slavery and Bourgeois Property in the Rise and Expansion of Capitalism* (New York: Oxford University Press, 1983), 302; Grimké, *Letters to Catherine E. Beecher, In Reply to An Essay on Slavery and Abolitionism, Addressed to A. E. Grimké. Revised by the Author* (1838; reprint, Freeport, N.Y.: Books for Libraries Press, 1971), 119; Ann Phillips, introduction to *Feminism and Equality,* ed. Ann Phillips (Oxford: Basil Blackwell, 1987), 3.
11. See Hansen, *Strained Sisterhood,* 149, 156, 160; *National Anti-Slavery Standard,* 16 February 1842. Hansen's analysis is based also on her division of the women of the BFASS into "affluent Unitarians and Quakers" on the one hand and "middle-class Baptists and Congregationalists on the other." There is merit in that analysis but the categories are not so clear-cut as Hansen suggests. Again, the case of Lydia Maria Child is instructive. Child was a Unitarian, and she achieved a measure of financial independence from the proceeds of her prolific writings. Nevertheless, for many years she was certainly not affluent. See Hansen, *Strained Sisterhood,* 92. On "true womanhood," see Barbara Welter, "The Cult of True Womanhood: 1820–1860," *American Quarterly* 18 (1966): 151–74. On the importance of the Enlightenment as a source of women's increasing sense of individuality, see Degler, *At Odds,* 191; Marguerite Fisher, "Eighteenth-Century Theorists of Women's Liberation," in *"Remember the Ladies": New Perspectives on Women in America,* ed. Carol V. R. George (Syracuse: Syracuse University Press, 1975), 39–47; Richard J. Evans, *The Feminists: Women's Emancipation Movements in Europe, America and Australasia 1840–1920,* rev. ed. (London: Croom Helm, 1979), 13. On black women, see Anne M. Boylan, "Benevolence and Antislavery Activity among African American Women in New York and Boston, 1820–1840," in *The Abolitionist Sisterhood: Women's Political Culture in Antebellum America* ed. Jean Fagan Yellin and John C. Van Horne (Ithaca: Cornell University Press, 1994), 120, 123–25, 132.
12. See John Todd, *Woman's Rights* (1867; reprint, New York: Arno, 1972), 8; Stanton, "Report on Educating the Sexes Together" (delivered by Susan B. Anthony, at the New York State Teachers Convention, Troy, N.Y., 1856), Susan B. Anthony Papers, Manuscript Division, Library of Congress, Washington, D.C. (hereafter cited as SBA–LC). See also Nancy

Hewitt, *Women's Activism and Social Change: Rochester, New York, 1822–1872* (Ithaca: Cornell University Press, 1984), 215.

13. Child to Lucy Osgood and Mary Osgood, 11 May 1856, in *The Collected Correspondence of Lydia Maria Child,* ed. Patricia G. Holland and Milton Meltzer (Millwood, N.Y.: Kraus Microform, 1979, microfiche), Card 33/Item 915 (hereafter cited as LMCP). Beecher's *Treatise* was reprinted nearly every year from 1841 to 1856, while *The Frugal Housewife* was republished fourteen times within five years of its initial publication. See Kathryn Kish Sklar, *Catharine Beecher: A Study in American Domesticity* (New Haven: Yale University Press, 1973), 151; Herbert Edwards, "Lydia Maria Child's *The Frugal Housewife,*" *New England Quarterly* 26 (1953): 243.

14. Beecher, *A Treatise on Domestic Economy, For the Use of Young Ladies at Home, and at School* (1841; reprint, New York: Source Book Press, 1970), chap. 18; Child, *The American Frugal Housewife: Dedicated to Those Who Are Not Ashamed of Economy,* 16th ed. (Boston: Carter, Hendee, 1835), 6; Sklar, *Beecher,* 154; Stephanie Coontz, *The Social Origins of Private Life: A History of American Families, 1600–1900* (London: Verso, 1988), 212.

15. Douglas, *The Feminization of American Culture* (New York: Knopf, 1978), 56; Leonore Davidoff and Catherine Hall, *Family Fortunes: Men and Women of the English Middle Class, 1780–1850* (London: Hutchinson, 1987), 25; Stuart Blumin, *The Emergence of the Middle Class: Social Experience in the American City, 1760–1900* (New York: Cambridge University Press, 1989), 215; Charles Sellers, *The Market Revolution: Jacksonian America, 1815–1846* (New York: Oxford University Press, 1991), 242–43; Beecher, *Treatise,* passim; Child, *Frugal Housewife,* passim; Nathaniel W. Chittendon, *The Influence of Woman Upon the Destinies of a People; Being an Oration, with Salutatory Addresses Delivered at the Annual Commencement of Columbia College, October 3d, 1837* (New York: n.p., 1837), 16. See also Cott, *Bonds of Womanhood,* 15, 58–59; Linda Kerber, *Women of the Republic: Intellect and Ideology in Revolutionary America* (Chapel Hill: University of North Carolina Press, 1980), 7; Alexis de Tocqueville, *Democracy in America,* 2 vols., trans. Henry Reeve (1840; reprint, New York: Knopf, 1966), 2:212; Joel Perlmann and Dennis Shirley, "When Did New England Women Acquire Literacy?" *William and Mary Quarterly* 48 (1991): 51. On the preindustrial division of men and women into separate "worlds," see Linda K. Kerber, "Separate Spheres, Female Worlds, Women's Place: The Rhetoric of Women's History," *Journal of American History* 75 (1988): 18–19; Gerda Lerner, *The Creation of Patriarchy* (New York: Oxford University Press, 1986), 27–28, 212–13, 217–18.

16. Beecher, *Treatise,* 14; Child, *Frugal Housewife,* 91; Hannah Mather Crocker, *Observations on the Real Rights of Women, with Their Appropriate Duties, Agreeable to Scripture, Reason and Common Sense* (Boston: n.p., 1818), in Kraditor, *Up From the Pedestal,* 43; Jonathan F. Stearns, *Female Influence, and the True Christian Mode of its Exercise: A Discourse Delivered in the First Presbyterian Church in Newburyport, July 30, 1837* (Newburyport, Mass.: n.p., 1837), in Kraditor, *Up From the Pedestal,* 50; Sarah Baker to Abby Kelley, 31 May 1838, Abigail Kelley Foster Papers, American Antiquarian Society, Worcester, Mass.

17. See Sarah Grimké to Sarah Wattles, 12 August 1855, Weld-Grimké Papers, William L. Clements Library, University of Michigan, Ann Arbor (hereafter cited as WGP–UM); Henry Clarke Wright, *Marriage and Parentage: or, The Reproductive Element in Man, as a Means to His Elevation and Happiness,* 2d ed. (Boston: Bela Marsh, 1855), 291.

18. Henry Blackwell related the notion of efficiency within marriage to the attainment of private and public goals. "I quite agree with you," Blackwell told Lucy Stone in 1853, "that a connection which would be inconsistent with the most efficient prosecution of our highest aims ought never to be framed." See Blackwell to Stone, 2 July 1853, Lucy Stone Papers (included in the Blackwell Family Papers), Manuscript Division, Library of Congress, Washington, D.C., (hereafter cited as LSP–LC).

19. Stanton, *Eighty Years,* 137; Otelia Cromwell, *Lucretia Mott* (1958; reprint, New York: Russell and Russell, 1971), 7; Robert H. Abzug, *Passionate Liberator: Theodore Dwight Weld and the Dilemma of Reform* (New York: Oxford University Press, 1980), 206–7; Grimké to Sarah Wattles, 12 August 1855, WGP–UM. Note also that to support the case for women's education, Lucretia Mott stated that the "appeal of Catharine Beecher to woman, some years ago, urging her to aim at higher pursuits, was greatly encouraging." Also, Beecher visited the Motts in April 1856, and Lucretia agreed to stay on the platform during an address by Beecher. See Mott, *Discourse on Woman, delivered at the Assembly Buildings, December 17, 1849* (Philadelphia: W. P. Kildare, 1869), 9; Margaret Hope Bacon, *Valiant Friend: The Life of Lucretia Mott* (New York: Walker and Company, 1980), 135, 159–60.

20. See Garrison to Harriet Farnham Horton, 12 May 1830 in *The Letters of William Lloyd Garrison,* ed. Walter M. Merrill and Louis Ruchames, 6 vols. (Cambridge: Belknap Press of Harvard University Press, 1971–81), 1:92 (hereafter cited as WLGL). See also John Greenleaf Whittier, "Justice and Expediency," (1853), in *The Abolitionists: A Collection of Their Writings,* ed. Louis Ruchames (New York: Putnam 1963), 54.

21. See Foster to Wendell Phillips [24 July 1854], Crawford Blagden Collection of the Papers of Wendell Phillips, Houghton Library, Harvard University, Cambridge, Mass. (hereafter cited as CBC–HL); *Una,* 1 February 1853, 12. See also Foster to Wendell Phillips, 7 February 1844, CBC–HL; *Right and Wrong in Boston. Report of the Boston Female Anti-Slavery Society; With a Concise Statement of Events, Previous and Subsequent to the Annual Meeting of 1835* (Boston: Boston Female Anti-Slavery Society, 1836), 41. Further evidence of the abolitionists' faith in organization was the growth in the number of antislavery societies, which increased from 200 in 1835, to 527 in 1836. See David Brion Davis, "The Nature and Limits of Dissent," in *The Great Republic: A History of the American People,* by Bernard Bailyn, et al., 1st ed. 2 vols. (Lexington, Mass.: Heath, 1977), 1:554. See also Elkins, *Slavery: A Problem in American Institutional and Intellectual Life,* 2d ed. (Chicago: University of Chicago Press, 1968), 175; Aileen Kraditor, *Means and Ends in American Abolitionism: Garrison and His Critics on Tactics and Strategy* (New York: Pantheon Books, 1967), 12–17; James L. Huston, "The Experiential Basis of the Northern Antislavery Impulse," *Journal of Southern History* 56 (1990): 638–39.

22. See "Influence of America upon Europe," *Liberator,* 5 February 1831. See also L. Maria Child, *The Little Girl's Own Book, with Additional Sports and Games by Miss Leslie,* new ed. (Glasgow: John Reid, 1837), vi; Child, *The History of the Condition of Women, In Various Ages and Nations,* 2 vols. (Boston: John Allen, 1835), 2:265.

23. S. Flint, Jr., "Abolition is Democracy," *National Anti-Slavery Standard,* 13 May 1841; *Declaration of Sentiments of the American Anti-Slavery Society. Adopted at the Formation of said Society, in Philadelphia, on the 4th day of December, 1833* (New York: American Anti-Slavery Society, 1833), 1; Angelina Grimké, *An Appeal to the Women of the Nominally Free States, Issued by an Anti-Slavery Convention of American Women* (New York: William S. Dorr, 1837), 18; Child, ed., *The Oasis* (Boston: Benjamin C. Bacon, 1834), viii; Child, *The Evils of Slavery, and the Cure of Slavery. The First Proved by the Opinions of Southerners Themselves, and the Last Shown by Historical Evidence* (Newburyport, Mass.: Charles Whipple, 1836), 3–4. Abolitionists were accused of abrogating their patriotic responsibilities. See the comments by "A Slaveholder," *Liberator,* 28 January 1832.

24. Brown, *A Lecture Before the Female Anti-Slavery Society of Salem, At Lyceum Hall, Nov. 14, 1847* (1847; reprint, Reading, Mass.: Addison-Wesley, 1969), 95.

25. Beecher, *Treatise,* 3–9, 16–17, 23–24; *Proceedings of the Anti-Slavery Convention of American Women, Held in the City of New York, May 9th, 10th, 11th, and 12th, 1837* (New York: William S. Dorr, 1837), 8.

26. On "republican motherhood," see Kerber, *Women of the Republic,* chap. 9. See also Cott, *Bonds of Womanhood,* 104–5. Margot Melia has noted that the "strength of the free black Garrisonian commitment owed much to the influence of women who were its lynch pins." See Melia, "The Role of Black Garrisonian Women in Antislavery and Other Reforms in the Antebellum North, 1830–1865" (Ph.D. diss., University of Western Australia, 1991), 69.

27. Lucy Stone, "Address" reprinted in *The Proceedings of the Woman's Rights Convention, Held at Worcester, October 15th and 16th, 1851* (New York: Fowler and Wells, 1852), 27. See also Mott, *Discourse on Women,* 15–16; Gerrit Smith, *Woman Suffrage Above the Law. Letter from Gerrit Smith.* (Peterboro, N.Y.: n.p., 1873), 2.

28. Child, *Condition of Women,* 2:265; Grimké to Harriot Kezia Hunt, 31 May 1854, WGP–UM; Stanton, *Eighty Years,* 115.

29. See *Seventh Annual Report of the Boston Female Anti-Slavery Society. Presented October 14, 1840* (Boston: Boston Female Anti-Slavery Society, 1840), 21; *An Appeal to the Women of the North, on the Subject of Slavery. By a Female of Vermont* (Philadelphia: John Thompson, 1838), 3.

30. Garrison to Dr. John Browning, 1840, Alma Lutz Collection, Arthur and Elizabeth Schlesinger Library, on the History of Women in America, Radcliffe College, Cambridge, Mass.; Garrison to Helen Garrison, 11 August 1846, WLGL, 3:364. Garrison journeyed to Europe five times. See Walter M. Merrill, *Against Wind and Tide: A Biography of Wm. Lloyd Garrison* (Cambridge: Harvard University Press, 1963), 66–73, 164–70, 189–95, 317–19, 328–29. Catharine Beecher, claiming British abolitionists rested on higher moral ground than their American counterparts, lauded British abolitionists for their peaceful methods. See Beecher, *An Essay on Slavery and Abolitionism, with Reference to the Duty of American Females* (Philadelphia: Henry Perkins, 1837), 17–22, 35–36.

31. L. Maria Child's rejection of the French Revolution, wherein she specifically referred to the institution of marriage, connected principles close to the heart of the abolitionist ideology. The French Revolution, she pointed out, had not only torn "down Churches, and voted that there was no God," but has also "annulled marriage." See Child, "Letters from New-York–No. 51," *National Anti-Slavery Standard,* 23 February 1843. See also Sarah Grimké to Elizabeth [Pease] Nichol, 18 April 1848, Oswald G. Villard Papers, Houghton Library, Harvard University, Cambridge, Mass.

32. Mott to Phillips, 9 August 1841, CBC–HL; *Third Annual Report of the Board of Managers of the New England Anti-Slavery Society, Presented Jan. 21, 1835* (1835; reprint, Westport, Conn.: Negro Universities Press, 1970), 14; Child, *The Oasis,* 214; Child, *Condition of Women,* 2:147. In criticizing those Americans who emulated the habits of Europeans, L. Maria Child argued that extravagance was "the prevailing evil of the day." Note also Lucretia Mott's critique of the way in which "well-dressed" British "gentlemen" lived "in idleness on the labor of others." See Child, *Frugal Housewife,* 89; Mott, diary entry for 1 June 1840, in *Slavery and the "Woman Question": Lucretia Mott's Diary of Her Visit to Great Britain to Attend the World's Anti-Slavery Convention of 1840,* ed. Frederick B. Tolles (Haverford, Pa.: Friends Historical Association, 1952).

33. Black abolitionists were no exception to this trend. See Melia, "Black Garrisonian Women," 90–97.

34. Child, *Frugal Housewife,* 91, 103; Child, *The Girl's Own Book* (New York: Clark, Austin, 1833), iv; Child, *Celebrated Women; or, Biographies of Good Wives* (Boston: Higgins, Bradley and Dayton, 1858), 13; Beecher, *Treatise,* 1–25, 30; Sarah Grimké to Lucy Stone, 13 July [1850], LSP–LC. After the Civil War, Child criticized the practice of sending American children to Europe for their education. See Child to Theodore Tilton, in *The Independent,* 28 June 1866, in LMCP, 65/1727.

35. Beecher, *Treatise,* 13; *Proceedings of the Anti-Slavery Convention of American Women, Held in Philadelphia, May 15th, 16th, 17th and 18th, 1838* (Philadelphia: Merrihew and Gunn, 1838), 6.

36. Beecher, *Treatise,* chap. 4; Child, *Frugal Housewife,* 91–92; Child, *The Mother's Book,* 6th ed. (New York: C. S. Francis, 1844), 146; "Speech of Abby Kelley Foster" (n.d.), in *Woman's Rights Commensurate with Her Capacities and Obligations. A Series of Tracts, Comprising Sixteen Articles, Essays, Addresses, or Letters of the Prominent Advocates of Woman's Larger Sphere of Action* (Syracuse: n.p., 1853), 24. See also "To Mothers," *National Anti-Slavery Standard,* 3 September 1840. On black women abolitionists' interest in domestic education, see Melia, "Black Garrisonian Women," 72.

37. Gerda Lerner, *The Creation of Feminist Consciousness: From the Middle Ages to Eighteen-seventy* (New York: Oxford University Press, 1993), 277.

38. Beecher, *Essay on Slavery and Abolition,* 107–8; Child, *Anti-Slavery Catechism* (Newburyport, Mass.: Charles Whipple, 1836), 11; Grimké, *Letters on the Equality of the Sexes and the Condition of Woman. Addressed to Mary S. Parker, President of the Boston Female Anti-Slavery Society* (1838; reprint, New York: Source Book Press, 1970), 49; Child to Theodore Tilton, 27 May 1866, LMCP, 65/1722; Child to Anna [Loring] Dresel, 15 February 1873, LMCP, 80/2088.

39. Child, *The Brother and Sister: and Other Stories* (Philadelphia: n.p., 1852), passim (quotations on 9, 19, 31, 35, 42).

40. Rosaldo, "Woman, Culture, and Society," 28; Stanton, *Eighty Years,* 112; Stanton, "Report on Educating the Sexes Together," SBA–LC; Grimké to Gerrit Smith, 10 June 1854, Gerrit Smith Papers, Syracuse University Library, Department of Special Collections, Syracuse, N.Y. (hereafter cited as SP–SU). See also Barbara Leslie Epstein, *The Politics of Domesticity: Women, Evangelism, and Temperance in Nineteenth-Century America* (Middletown, Conn.: Wesleyan University Press, 1981), 76.

41. Grimké to Weld, 2 August 1849, WGP–UM; Grimké, *Letters to Catherine E. Beecher,* 123. See also Sklar, *Beecher,* 91–94; Gerda Lerner, *The Grimké Sisters from South Carolina: Pioneers for Women's Rights and Abolition* (1967; reprint, New York: Schocken Books, 1971), 97–100; Katharine Du Pre Lumpkin, *The Emancipation of Angelina Grimké* (Chapel Hill: University of North Carolina Press, 1974), 62–64.

42. Beecher, *Slavery and Abolitionism,* 105–6; Sarah Grimké to Augustus Wattles, et al., n.d. [c. 1858], WGP–UM; Angelina Grimké, *Letters to Catherine E. Beecher,* 122; Blackwell to Stone, 25 March 1858, in *Loving Warriors: Selected Letters of Lucy Stone and Henry B. Blackwell, 1853 to 1893,* ed. Leslie Wheeler (New York: Dial, 1981), 177.

43. See Child, *Frugal Housewife,* 91–92; James Mott to "My dear children" (Edward and Maria), 19 February 1838, Lucretia Mott Papers, Friends Historical Library, Swarthmore College, Swarthmore, Pa. Cf. Debra Gold Hansen, "Bluestockings and Bluenoses: Gender, Class, and Conflict in the Boston Female Anti-Slavery Society, 1833–1840" (Ph.D. diss., University of California at Irvine, 1988), 150.

44. Grimké, "Condition of Women," in Bartlett, *Letters on the Equality of the Sexes,* 129; Garrison to Benson, 24 April 1834, WLGL, 1:329. See also Theodore Weld to Angelina Grimké, 8 April 1838, in *Letters of Theodore Dwight Weld, Angelina Grimké Weld and Sarah Grimké, 1822–1844,* ed. Gilbert H. Barnes and Dwight L. Dumond, 2 vols. (1934; reprint, New York: Da Capo, 1970), 2:630 (hereafter cited as WGL). On the condemnation of fashion by "America moralists," see Karen Halttunen, *Confidence Men and Painted Women: A Study of Middle-Class Culture in America, 1830–1870* (New Haven: Yale University Press, 1982), 63–70.

45. *Rev. Mr. Judson's Letter to the Female Members of the Christian Churches, in the United States of America* (Providence, R.I.: H. H. Brown, 1832), 3, 10; Child, *The Family Nurse; or Companion to the Frugal Housewife* (Boston: Charles C. Hendee, 1837), 36; "Letter from Mrs. L. Maria Child," *National Anti-Slavery Standard,* 5 December 1868; *Report of the Proceedings of the Twentieth Anniversary, and of the Reception Held at St. James Hotel,* reprinted in *A History of the National Woman's Rights Movement, for Twenty Years, With the Proceedings of the Decade Meeting Held at Apollo Hall, October 20, 1870, from 1850 to 1870, With an Appendix Containing the History of the Movement During the Winter of 1871, in the National Capitol,* comp. Paulina Wright Davis (New York: Journeymen Printers' Co-Operative Association, 1871), 33. On the connections between women's rights and dress reform, see Robert Riegal, "Women's Clothes and Women's Rights," *American Quarterly* 15 (1963): 390–401. Note, too, that Margot Melia has pointed out that black Garrisonian women were "conservative" in dress. See Melia, "Black Garrisonian Women," 72.

46. Grimké to Harriot Kezia Hunt, 23 May 1855, WGP–UM. See also Angelina Grimké to Theodore Weld, n.d. [c. 1849], WGP–UM. David Donald's controversial thesis that abolitionism was led by a displaced social elite was premised partly on assumptions regarding the abolitionists' alleged psychological instabilities. See Donald, "Toward a Reconsideration of the Abolitionists," in his *Lincoln Reconsidered: Essays on the Civil War Era,* 2d ed. (New York: Knopf, 1956), 19–36.

47. Weston to the New York Female Anti-Slavery Society, 21 July 1835, in the Boston Female Anti-Slavery Society Letterbook, 9 April 1834–6 January 1838, Massachusetts Historical Society, Boston (hereafter cited as BFASSL–MHS).

48. *Right and Wrong in Boston . . . 1835,* 41–42; Angelina Grimké, *Slavery in America. A Reprint of an Appeal to the Christian Women of the United States of America. Intro. by George Thompson* (Edinburgh: William Oliphant and Son, 1838), 37–38.

49. Grimké to Henry C. Wright, 29 March 1838, Anti-Slavery Collection, Boston Public Library (hereafter cited as ASC–BPL); Grimké to Gerrit Smith, 9 April 1837, WGL, 1:377. See also *Liberator,* 19 January 1838; John Demos, "The Antislavery Movement and the Problem of Violent Means," *New England Quarterly* 37 (1964): 501–26; Lewis Perry, *Radical Abolitionism: Anarchy and the Government of God in Antislavery Thought* (Ithaca: Cornell University Press, 1973), 79–80.

50. Radical abolitionists, and historians, expressed varying opinions over the precise meaning of demands for the immediate abolition of slavery. L. Maria Child offered this interpretation of the term "immediatism": "we mean the right to hold property in man should be immediately relinquished." As Jane H. Pease and William H. Pease have put it, the term could be interpreted to mean "gradual emancipation immediately begun," or perhaps, "immediate emancipation gradually achieved." The pertinent point, however, is that while abolitionists and historians could argue over the meaning of the phrase "immediate abolition," many nineteenth-century Americans perceived it as evidence of the abolitionists' uncompromising radicalism. See Child, *The Oasis,* xi–xii; Pease and Pease, "Antislavery Ambivalence: Immediatism, Expediency, Race," *American Quarterly* 17 (1965): 682. See also David Brion Davis, "The Emergence of Immediatism in British and American Antislavery Thought," *Mississippi Valley Historical Review* 49 (1962): 209–30.

51. During the early 1830s abolitionists were forced to confront the issue of the slaves' right to use violent means to achieve their freedom. The most famous slave revolt, led by Nat Turner, provoked great fears and recriminations in the South, where the uprising was viewed as proof of the abolitionists' determination to completely break down society. Garrisonians, however, distanced themselves from the revolutionary doctrines preached by Turner. Abolitionists did not universally accept that slavery had to be ended by peaceful means, but many continued to reject violence. Furthermore, with some reformers working

explicitly for peace as well as abolitionism, there were close links between the two movements. See Carleton Mabee, *Black Freedom: The Nonviolent Abolitionists from 1830 Through the Civil War* (London: Macmillan, 1970), 51–66. On black Garrisonians' attitude toward slave revolts, see James Oliver Horton and Lois E. Horton, "The Affirmation of Manhood: Black Garrisonians, in Antebellum Boston," in *Courage and Conscience: Black and White Abolitionists in Boston,* ed. Donald M. Jacobs (Bloomington: Indiana University Press, 1993), 127–53.

52. See Kraditor, *Means and Ends.*

53. The 1835 report of the Boston Female Anti-Slavery Society was largely a defense of the controversy surrounding their invitation to the British abolitionist George Thompson to address their meeting. Underpinning the report was the belief that it was not the members of the Boston Female Anti-Slavery Society who desired, or brought on, the controversy. Rather, it was the activities of the violently inclined, predominantly male, opponents of abolition who had provoked the altercation. See *Right and Wrong in Boston . . . 1835.*

54. On abolitionist women's petitioning, see Deborah Bingham Van Broekhoven, " 'Let Your Names Be Enrolled': Method and Ideology in Women's Antislavery Petitioning," in Yellin and Van Horne, *The Abolitionist Sisterhood,* 179–99; Gerda Lerner, "The Political Activities of Antislavery Women," in her *The Majority Finds Its Past: Placing Women in History* (New York: Oxford University Press, 1979), 112–28; Judith Wellman, "Women and Radical Reform in Antebellum New York: A Profile of Grassroots Female Abolitionists," in *Clio Was a Woman: Studies in the History of American Women,* ed. Mabel E. Deutrich and Virginia C. Purdy (Washington, D.C.: Howard University Press, 1980), 112–31. L. Maria Child, writing to Charles Sumner on the anniversary of the Declaration of Independence, expressed confidence that "sooner or later, you will see that the republican ideas you advocate so earnestly cannot be consistently carried out while women are excluded from a share in the government." See Child to Sumner, 4 July 1870, LMCP, 73/1951. Not all historians have accepted the traditional thesis regarding the Garrisonians' stance on politics. One of Garrison's co-workers in the antislavery movement, Thomas Wentworth Higginson, noted that while the Garrisonians abstained from voting, many who did choose to vote "drew strength from them." See Higginson, *Contemporaries* (Boston: Houghton Mifflin, 1900), 246–47. See also James B. Stewart, "The Aims and Impact of Garrisonian Abolitionism, 1840–1860," *Civil War History* 15 (1969): 200; Ronald Walters, *The Antislavery Appeal: American Abolitionism After 1830* (Baltimore: Johns Hopkins University Press, 1976), 17.

55. On this process of "domestication," see Paula Baker, "The Domestication of Politics: Women and American Political Society, 1780–1920," *American Historical Review* 89 (1984): 621.

56. Grimké to Gerrit Smith, 10 June 1854, SP–SU. See also Nancy Hewitt, *Women's Activism and Social Change,* 39.

57. On the Grimké-Beecher debate, see also Sklar, *Beecher,* 132–37; Lerner, *Grimké Sisters,* 184–87.

58. Grimké, *Appeal to the Women of the Nominally Free States,* 15.

59. Daniel A. Clark, *The Wise Builder. A Sermon, Delivered to the Females of the First Parish in Amherst, Massachusetts, on Wednesday, the Third Day of May, 1820* (Boston: Ezra Lincoln, 1820), 11; Walter Harris, *A Discourse Delivered to the Members of the Female Cent Society, in Bedford, New Hampshire, July 18, 1814* (Concord, N.H.: George Houch, 1814), 12; Welter, "The Feminization of American Religion," in *Clio's Consciousness Raised: New Essays on the History of Women,* ed. Mary S. Hartman and Lois Banner (1974; reprint, New York: Octagon Books, 1976), 137–57; Mary P. Ryan, *Womanhood in America: From Colonial Times to the Present Day,* 3d ed. (New York: Franklin Watts, 1983), 127. See also Nancy Cott, "Young

Women in the Second Great Awakening in New England," *Feminist Studies* 3 (1975): 15–29; Rosalind Rosenberg, "In Search of Women's Nature," *Feminist Studies* 3 (1975): 141.

60. Crocker, *Observations on the Real Rights of Women,* in Kraditor, *Up From the Pedestal,* 41–42; Harris, *Discourse,* 13; Nathan S. S. Beman, *Female Influence and Obligations* (New York: American Tract Society, 185[?]), 3; *Liberator,* 11 August 1837, 18 August 1837; Lerner, *Grimké Sisters,* 189–90. Historians have distinguished between "benevolence" and "reform." See Anne Boylan, "Women in Groups: An Analysis of Women's Benevolent Organizations in New York and Boston, 1797–1840," *Journal of American History* 71 (1984), 497–523; Keith Melder, *Beginnings of Sisterhood: The American Woman's Rights Movement, 1800–1850* (New York: Schocken Books, 1977), 50; Blanche Hersh, *The Slavery of Sex: Feminist-Abolitionists in America* (Urbana: University of Illinois Press, 1978), 4.

61. Angelina Grimké to Amos Phelps, 2 September 1837, ASC–BPL. See also Sarah Grimké to Elizabeth [Pease] Nichol, 18 December 1837, ASC–BPL; Sarah Grimké to Amos Phelps, 3 September 1837, ASC–BPL; Anne Summers, "A Home from Home—Women's Philanthropic Work in the Nineteenth Century," in *Fit Work for Women,* ed. Sandra Burman (London: Croom Helm, 1979), 33; Donald Scott, "Abolitionism as a Sacred Vocation," in *Antislavery Reconsidered: New Perspectives on the Abolitionists,* ed. Lewis Perry and Michael Fellman (Baton Rouge: Louisiana State University Press, 1979), 52. On the Grimkés' lecturing activities during that volatile period, see Keith Melder, "Forerunners of Freedom: The Grimké Sisters in Massachusetts, 1837–38," *Essex Institute Historical Collections* 3 (1967): 223–49. Abolitionists quickly recognized the propaganda value that could be derived from the Grimkés' firsthand acquaintance with slavery. See Mary Grew to Melania Ammidon, 18 November 1836, ASC–BPL; Theodore Weld to Sarah and Angelina Grimké, 15 August 1837, WGL, 1:426.

62. Grimké, *Appeal to the Christian Women of the South,* 3d ed. (n.p.: n.p., 1836), 17, 26; Melania Ammidon to the Portland Female Anti-Slavery Society, 14 July 1835, BFASSL–MHS. See also Wright, *Marriage and Parentage,* 144–45; Henry Blackwell to Lucy Stone, 7 October 1853, LSP–LC.

63. Beecher, *Slavery and Abolitionism,* 56, 99–103. See also Lerner, *Creation of Feminist Consciousness,* 216.

64. Ginzberg, *Women and the Work of Benevolence,* 69.

65. Grimké, *Letters to Catherine E. Beecher,* 13, 36, 128; *Proceedings of the Third Anti-Slavery Convention of American Women, Held in Philadelphia, May 1st, 2nd and 3d, 1839* (Philadelphia: Merrihew and Thompson, 1839), 5; *Right and Wrong in Boston . . . 1835,* 5. See also Grimké, *Appeal to the Christian Women of the South,* 26.

66. "Address of the Boston Female Anti-Slavery Society to the Women of Massachusetts," *Liberator,* 13 August 1836; Grimké, *Letters to Catherine Beecher,* 29. See also Beecher, *Slavery and Abolitionism,* 17.

67. Beecher, *Slavery and Abolitionism,* 98–99; Grimké, *Letters to Catherine E. Beecher,* 114. See also Kerber, "Separate Spheres, Female Worlds, Woman's Place," 11.

68. Grimké, *Letters on the Equality of the Sexes,* 4–5 (my emphasis), 10; Grimké to Mary S. Parker, 11 July 1837, ASC–BPL.

69. *Proceedings of the Anti-Slavery Convention of American Women . . . 1837,* 9; Angelina Grimké, *Letters to Catherine E. Beecher,* 103, 108. See also Grimké, *Letter from Angelina Grimké Weld, to the Woman's Rights Convention, Held at Syracuse, Sept., 1852* (New York: n.p., 1852), 5.

70. Stanton to George C. Cole, as quoted in Alma Lutz, *Created Equal: A Biography of Elizabeth Cady Stanton, 1815–1902* (New York: John Day, 1940), 53; Grimké, *Letters to Catherine E. Beecher,* 117. See also Lucy Stone's "Address before the Friends Moral Reform Society of Gardner, Massachusetts," LSP–LC.

71. *Letter from Mrs. Elizabeth C. Stanton, to the Woman's Rights Convention, Held at Worcester, Oct., 1850,* in *Woman's Rights Commensurate with Her Capacities,* 2.

72. Grimké, *Letters to Catherine Beecher,* 110–12, 119; *Proceedings of the Anti-Slavery Convention of American Women . . . 1837,* 8.

73. *Appeal to the Females of the North,* 3.

74. Holmes, review of *Uncle Tom's Cabin,* in the *Southern Literary Messenger,* 18 (December 1852), 721–31, in *Slavery Defended: The Views of the Old South,* ed. Eric L. McKitrick (Englewood Cliffs, N.J.: Prentice-Hall, 1963), 100.

75. Tyler, cited in Richards, "*Gentlemen of Property and Standing,*" 57.

76. Helen Garrison to Caroline Weston, 31 October 1835, ASC–BPL; undated entry in *Letters and Journals of Thomas Wentworth Higginson,* ed. Mary Thatcher Higginson (1921; reprint, New York: Da Capo, 1969), 82. See also Anne Warren Weston to Mary Anne Estlin, 30 July 1854, ASC–BPL. On anti-abolition riots, refer to Richards, "*Gentlemen of Property and Standing*"; Lorman Ratner, *Powder Keg: Northern Opposition to the Antislavery Movement, 1831–1840* (New York: Basic Books, 1968).

77. Samuel Clemens, *The Adventures of Tom Sawyer* (1875; reprint, New York: Modern Library, 1940), 243.

78. See Keith Thomas, *Man and Nature: Changing Attitudes in England, 1500–1800* (London: Allen Lane, 1980), 25.

79. Sumner's speech, as quoted in David Donald, *Charles Sumner and the Coming of the Civil War* (New York: Knopf, 1960), 283, 285. Note Harriet Beecher Stowe's 1852 reference to the "civilized world." See Stowe to Gerrit Smith, 25 October 1852, SP–SU. Three days after having delivered the aforementioned speech in the Senate, Sumner was beaten by Preston Brooks, whose cousin, Senator Andrew Butler of South Carolina, had been at the receiving end of Sumner's invective. To the abolitionists, the brutality of Brooks's assault on Sumner, whose injuries precluded his returning to the Senate for over three years, coupled with the admiration heaped upon the assailant in the Southern states, further evinced slavery's pernicious influence on the entire nation. See Donald, *Charles Sumner and the Coming of the Civil War,* 289–347.

80. Blackwell to Stone, 3 January 1854, 22 January 1854, LSP–LC; *Liberator,* 7 May 1831.

81. Stanton to Susan B. Anthony, 1 March 1853, Elizabeth Cady Stanton Papers, Manuscript Division, Library of Congress, Washington, D.C. (hereafter cited as ECSP–LC). See also L. Maria Child, *On the Management and Education of Children; being Mrs. Child's "Mother's Book," Revised, and Adapted to the Use of English Teachers* (London: John W. Parker, 1835), 2–3, 46. On the emphasis on "Peace as a Way of Life" among the members of the Woman's Christian Temperance Union, see Ian Tyrrell, *Woman's World/Woman's Empire: The Woman's Christian Temperance Union in International Perspective, 1880–1930* (Chapel Hill: University of North Carolina Press, 1991), chap. 8.

82. Child, *Frugal Housewife,* 91; Grimké, "The Education of Women," in *Letters on the Equality of the Sexes and Other Essays,* ed. Elizabeth Ann Bartlett (New Haven: Yale University Press, 1988), 114; "Lynn Pioneer," *Lily,* 1 February 1849, 10. See also Elizabeth Cady Stanton to Gerrit Smith, 5 January 1851, ECSP–LC; Elizabeth Oakes Smith, "Sanctity of Marriage" (Syracuse: n.p., n.d.), 5, in *Woman's Rights Commensurate with Her Capacities.*

Chapter 3. The Practice of Domesticity

1. Mary P. Ryan, *Cradle of the Middle Class: The Family in Oneida County, New York, 1790–1865* (Cambridge: Cambridge University Press, 1981), 234; Stanton to George C. Cole, as quoted in *Created Equal: A Biography of Elizabeth Cady Stanton, 1815–1902,* by Alma Lutz (New York: John Day, 1940), 53.

2. The domestic characteristics lauded by black Garrisonians paralleled those valued by their white coadjutors. See Margot Melia, "The Role of Black Garrisonian Women in Antislavery and Other Reforms in the Antebellum North, 1830–1865" (Ph.D. diss., University of Western Australia, 1991), 72.

3. Sallie Holley to Stephen Foster and Abby Kelley, 15 November 1852, Abigail Kelley Foster Correspondence, Worcester Historical Museum, Worcester, Mass. (hereafter cited as KFC–WHM); Garrison to Lucretia Mott, 8 April 1867, Lucretia Mott Papers, Friends Historical Library, Swarthmore College, Swarthmore, Pa. (hereafter cited as MP–FHL); Blackwell to Lucy Stone [Summer 1855], in *Loving Warriors: Selected Letters of Lucy Stone and Henry B. Blackwell, 1853 to 1893,* ed. Leslie Wheeler (New York: Dial, 1981), 144. See also Anne Warren Weston to Mary Weston, 6 May 1839, Anti-Slavery Collection, Boston Public Library (hereafter cited as ASC–BPL); the *Una,* May 1855, 72. Lawrence Friedman's depiction of Maria Weston Chapman's Boston household parallels my description of Mott's home. See Friedman, *Gregarious Saints: Self and Community in American Abolitionism, 1830–1870* (Cambridge: Cambridge University Press, 1982), 55–57.

4. As quoted in Anna Davis Hallowell, ed., *James and Lucretia Mott: Life and Letters* (Boston: Houghton Mifflin, 1884), 126; Mott to Phebe Post Willis, 10 March 1835, MP–FHL.

5. Lucretia Mott to Anne Mott, 28 December 1828, in Hallowell, *James and Lucretia Mott,* 104–6; Mott to "Richard Webb and Others," 10 September 1848, ibid., 304.

6. Mott to Martha C. Wright, [December] 1848, in Hallowell, *James and Lucretia Mott,* 309; Mott to Martha C. Wright, 22 May 1859, MP–FHL. See also Lucretia Mott to Elizabeth Cady Stanton, 16 March 1855, Elizabeth Cady Stanton Papers, Manuscript Division, Library of Congress, Washington, D.C. (hereafter cited as ECSP–LC).

7. Cromwell, *Lucretia Mott* (1958; reprint, New York: Russell and Russell, 1971), 7; Rosenberger, "Montgomery County's Greatest Lady: Lucretia Mott," *Bulletin of the Historical Society of Pennsylvania* 6 (1948): 156; Bacon, *Valiant Friend: The Life of Lucretia Mott* (New York: Walker, 1980), 6, 68; Friedan, *The Feminine Mystique* (1963; reprint, New York: Dell, 1967), 244. See also Lloyd C. M. Hare, *The Greatest American Woman: Lucretia Mott* (1937; reprint, New York: Negro Universities Press, 1970), 175; Ethel K. Ware, "Lydia Maria Child and Anti-Slavery (Part 1)," *Boston Public Library Quarterly* 3 (1951): 252.

8. Lucretia and James Mott to Phebe Post Willis, 6 September 1838, MP–FHL; Hallowell, *James and Lucretia Mott,* 89.

9. "Address by Mrs. Lucy Stone Blackwell," in the *Boston Woman's Rights Convention, 1855. Reports on the Laws of New England, Presented to the New England Meeting. Convened at the Meionan, Sept. 19 and 20, 1855* (Boston: n.p., 1855), 21. For an example of Grimké referring to herself as Angelina Grimké Weld, see her letter to Mary Horner and Edith Kite, 7 July 1838, in *Letters of Theodore Dwight Weld, Angelina Grimké and Sarah Grimké,* ed. Gilbert H. Barnes and Dwight L. Dumond, 2 vols. (1934; reprint, New York: Da Capo, 1970), 2:685 (hereafter cited as WGL).

10. Stanton to Rebecca R. Eyster, 1 May 1847, in *Elizabeth Cady Stanton: As Revealed in Her Letters, Diary, and Reminiscences,* ed. Theodore Stanton and Harriot Stanton Blatch, 2 vols. (1922; reprint, New York: Arno, 1969), 2:16. See also Stanton, *Eighty Years and More: Reminiscences, 1815–1897* (1898; reprint, New York: Schocken Books, 1971), 72. At his wedding ceremony, Theodore Weld denounced the powers given to husbands over their wives. See Katharine Du Pre Lumpkin, *The Emancipation of Angelina Grimké* (Chapel Hill: University of North Carolina Press, 1974) 148; Robert Abzug, *Passionate Liberator: Theodore Dwight Weld and the Dilemma of Reform* (New York: Oxford University Press, 1980), 199.

11. Marilyn Ferris Motz, *True Sisterhood: Michigan Women and Their Kin, 1820–1920* (Albany: State University of New York Press, 1983), 7. See also Elisabeth Griffith, *In Her Own Right:*

The Life of Elizabeth Cady Stanton (New York: Oxford University Press, 1984), 44; Lutz, *Created Equal,* 20.

12. Lois Banner, *Elizabeth Cady Stanton: A Radical for Women's Rights* (Boston: Little, Brown, 1980), 18–22; Griffith, *In Her Own Right,* 26–34. On Henry Stanton's financial troubles in the period prior to his marriage, see Chapter 5.

13. Banner, *Elizabeth Cady Stanton,* 24–26.

14. Stanton, *Eighty Years,* 145; Stanton to Susan B. Anthony, 24 January 1856, 10 June 1856, n.d. [March 1859], ECSP–LC. Stanton expressed great pride in the fact that with the exception of her last child, the process of childbirth was far less debilitating for her than it was for many other women. See Griffith, *In Her Own Right,* 66, 70, 78, 97; Lutz, *Created Equal,* 106. On the reasons behind Henry Stanton's decision to move to Seneca Falls, see Banner, *Elizabeth Cady Stanton,* 30–31.

15. Mott to Stanton, 27 November 1852, ECSP–LC. See also Hallowell, *James and Lucretia Mott,* 58.

16. Henry Stanton to Elizabeth Cady Stanton, 19 October 1856, ECSP–LC.

17. Griffith, *In Her Own Right,* 80. On childbirth, and the increasing involvement of male doctors in birth procedures in the nineteenth century, see Carl Degler, *At Odds: Women and the Family in American from the Revolution to the Present* (New York: Oxford University Press, 1980), 56–60 (quotation on 56).

18. Stanton, *Eighty Years,* 145. See also Banner, *Elizabeth Cady Stanton,* 27; Griffith, *In Her Own Right,* 50.

19. Stanton, cited in a letter from Lucretia Mott to Richard and Hannah Webb, 25 February 1842, ASC–BPL; Stanton, *Eighty Years,* 112–26; Stephen Foster to Alla Foster, 5 October 1857, KFC–WHM; Beecher, *A Treatise on Domestic Economy, for the use of Young Ladies at Home, and at School* (1841; reprint, New York: Source Book, 1971), 49. See also Sarah Grimké to Theodore Grimké Weld, 26 November 1860, Weld-Grimké Papers, William L. Clements Library, University of Michigan, Ann Arbor (hereafter cited as WGP–UM).

20. See Stanton to Lucretia Mott, 22 October 1852, in Stanton and Blatch, *Elizabeth Cady Stanton,* 2:45; Stanton, "Our Young Girls," *Revolution,* 29 January 1868, 57; Grimké to Theodore Weld, n.d. [c. September 1859], WGP–UM. See also Lucretia Mott, "The Truth of God . . . The Righteousness of God," *Liberator,* 15 October 1841.

21. Lumpkin, *Angelina Grimké.* See also John Thomas, *The Liberator: William Lloyd Garrison* (Boston: Little, Brown, 1963), 254; Ellen Carol DuBois, "Struggling Into Existence: The Feminism of Sarah and Angelina Grimké," *Women: A Journal of Liberation* 1 (1970): 11.

22. Sarah Grimké to Anne Warren Weston, 1 December 1837, ASC–BPL; Angelina Grimké to Anne Warren Weston, 15 July 1838, ASC–BPL; Angelina Grimké to Theodore Weld, 2 May 1838, 28 March 1838, WGL, 2:653, 611. See also James Mott to Anne Warren Weston, 8 December 1837, ASC–BPL.

23. Grimké to Anne Warren Weston, 15 July 1838, ASC–BPL; Kelley to Stephen Foster, 30 July 1843, Abby Kelley Foster Papers, American Antiquarian Society, Worcester, Mass. (hereafter cited as KFP–AAS). See also Theodore Weld to Angelina Grimké, 15 April 1838, WGL, 2:638.

24. Angelina Grimké to Anne Warren Weston, 14 October 1838, ASC–BPL; Blackwell to Lucy Stone, 13 April 1855, Lucy Stone Papers (included in the Blackwell Family Papers), Manuscript Division, Library of Congress, Washington, D.C. (hereafter cited as LSP–LC). The Weld-Grimké courtship was covered by Abzug in *Passionate Liberator,* chap. 9.

25. Grimké to Anne Warren Weston, 14 October 1838, 15 July 1838, ASC–BPL. See also Catherine Birney, *The Grimké Sisters: Sarah and Angelina Grimké. The First American Women Advo-*

cates of Abolition and Women's Rights (1885; reprint, Westport, Conn.: Greenwood, 1977), 252; Theodore Weld to Sarah Grimké, 8 February 1838, WGL, 2:531; *Liberator,* 11 March 1837. Evidence of the abolitionists' personal interest in good health was the adoption of a strict vegetarian diet in the dining room of Oberlin College in 1835, and the abolitionists' preference to lodge at health reform boarding houses when they were absent from home on lecturing tours. See "Autobiographical Sketch of Henry B. Blackwell" [1894], Henry B. Blackwell Papers (included in the Blackwell Family Papers), Library of Congress, Washington, D.C. (hereafter cited as BP–LC); Regina Morantz, "Making Women Modern: Middle Class Women and Health Reform in 19th Century America," *Journal of Social History* 10 (1977): 490–91.

26. Henry Stanton to Theodore Weld, 22 September 1848, WGP–UM; Stanton to Mott, n.d. [1848], ASC–BPL; Elizabeth Cady Stanton to Angelina Grimké and Sarah Grimké, 25 June 1840, WGL, 2:847; Benjamin P. Thomas, *Theodore Weld: Crusader for Freedom* (New Brunswick: Rutgers University Press, 1950), 117, 120–21. Weld's loss of voice may have had psychological origins. See Abzug, *Passionate Liberator,* 152–54.

27. See Lumpkin, *Angelina Grimké,* 176–78; Abzug, *Passionate Liberator,* 217; Thomas, *Theodore Weld,* 189–90.

28. Grimké to Henry Clarke Wright, 19 November 1838, ASC–BPL; Grimké to Elizabeth Pease, 16 November 1840, ASC–BPL. See also Sarah Grimké to Abby Kelley, n.d. [April 1838], KFP–AAS.

29. *American Slavery As It Is: Testimony of a Thousand Witnesses* (New York: American Anti-Slavery Society, 1839).

30. Phillips, *Speech of Wendell Phillips, Esq. at the Worcester Disunion Convention, January 15, 1857* (Boston: American Anti-Slavery Society, 1857), 13; *Second Annual Report of the Board of Managers of the New-England Anti-Slavery Society, Presented January 15, 1834. With an Appendix* (1834; reprint, Westport, Conn.: Negro Universities Press, 1970), 26; *Liberator,* 29 October 1831; *Proceedings of the Third Anti-Slavery Convention of American Women, Held in Philadelphia, May 1st, 2d and 3d, 1839* (Philadelphia: Merrihew and Thompson, 1839), 7. On the free produce movement, see David Brion Davis, *The Problem of Slavery in Western Culture* (Ithaca: Cornell University Press, 1966), chap. 10; Ruth K. Neurmberger, *The Free Produce Movement: A Quaker Protest Against Slavery* (Durham: Duke University Press, 1942); Norman P. Wilkinson, "The Philadelphia Free Produce Attack Upon Slavery," *Pennsylvania Magazine of History and Biography* 6 (1942): 294–313; Margaret Hope Bacon, "By Moral Force Alone: The Antislavery Women and Nonresistance," in *The Abolitionist Sisterhood: Women's Political Culture in Antebellum America,* ed. Jean Fagan Yellin and John C. Van Horne (Ithaca: Cornell University Press, 1994), 276–81.

31. Phillida Bunkle, "The Origins of the Women's Movement in New Zealand: The Women's Christian Temperance Union, 1885–1895," in *Women in New Zealand Society,* ed. Bunkle and Beryl Hughes (Sydney: Allen and Unwin, 1980), 74.

32. Child to Ellis Gray Loring, 13 December 1841, in *The Collected Correspondence of Lydia Maria Child,* ed. Patricia G. Holland and Milton Meltzer (Millwood, N.Y.: Kraus Microform, 1979, microfiche), Card 12/Item 299 (hereafter cited as LMCP).

33. See Stuart M. Blumin, *The Emergence of the Middle Class: Social Experience in the American City, 1760–1900* (Cambridge: Cambridge University Press, 1989), 185; Nancy Cott, *The Bonds of Womanhood: "Woman's Sphere" in New England, 1780–1835* (New Haven: Yale University Press, 1977), 45.

34. Beecher, *Treatise,* 175–86. See also Daniel Clark, *The Wise Builder. A Sermon, Delivered to the Females of the First Parish in Amherst, Massachusetts, on Wednesday, the Third Day of May,*

1820 (Boston: Ezra Lincoln, 1820), 4; Child, *The American Frugal Housewife, Dedicated to Those Who are Not Ashamed of Economy,* 16th ed. (Boston: Carter, Hendee, 1835), 4.

35. Grimké, *An Appeal to the Women of the Nominally Free States: Issued by an Anti-Slavery Convention of American Women* (New York: William S. Dorr, 1837), 24; Grimké to Elizabeth Pease, 14 May 1839, ASC–BPL. See also Angelina Grimké Weld to Elizabeth Pease, 14 August 1839, ASC–BPL; William L. Garrison to Joseph Pease, 3 August 1840, ASC–BPL; Thomas Sturge to Henry G. and Maria Weston Chapman, 5 April 1841, ASC–BPL; Hallowell, *James and Lucretia Mott,* 86–87; Bacon, *Valiant Friend,* 41–42; Carolyn Luverne Williams, "Religion, Race, and Gender in Antebellum American Radicalism: The Philadelphia Female Anti-Slavery Society, 1833–1870" (Ph.D. diss., University of California, Los Angeles, 1991), 148–49, 368; Oscar Sherwin, *Prophet of Liberty: The Life and Times of Wendell Phillips* (New York: Bookman Associates, 1958), 305.

36. Howard Temperley has summarized the relationship between the meaning and use of the term "capitalism," and slavery. See Temperley, "Capitalism, Slavery and Ideology," *Past and Present* 75 (1977): 105–6.

37. Not all postbellum reformers maintained their faith in the marketplace as an agent of positive change or reform, and there is evidence that women's domestic experiences were behind criticisms of the free market. In contending that women's "specific cultural experience" shaped their "political activities through the Gilded Age into the first decade of the twentieth century," Mary Jo Buhle has traced the origins of women's interest in socialism to their separate cultural experience. Even there, however, domestic values such as harmony and cooperation were reflected in the particular form of socialism that was advocated by some of the leadership of the Woman's Christian Temperance Union (WCTU). In drawing attention to the "Socialist Alternative" within the WCTU, Ian Tyrrell has noted that they did not "treat economic and class conflict as central to socialist analysis." Rather, the objective was "to bring the classes together in cooperation." See Buhle, *Women and American Socialism, 1870–1920* (Urbana: University of Illinois Press, 1981), xv; Tyrrell, *Woman's World/Woman's Empire: The Woman's Christian Temperance Union in International Perspective, 1880–1930* (Chapel Hill: University of North Carolina Press, 1991), chap. 11 (quotation on 245). Henry Blackwell continued to advocate free produce as a means of abolishing slavery outside the United States in the postbellum period. See Blackwell to Lucy Stone, 30 April 1878, 28 October 1878, 12 April 1880, in Wheeler, *Loving Warriors,* 267–69, 278.

38. On black Garrisonian women's work outside the home, see Melia, "Black Garrisonian Women," 77–78.

39. The Philadelphia Female Anti-Slavery Society, for example, held annual sales from 1836 to 1861. See Ira V. Brown, "Cradle of Feminism: The Philadelphia Female Anti-Slavery Society, 1833–1840," *Pennsylvania Magazine of History and Biography* 2 (1978): 153. On the importance of the female antislavery societies' fairs as a source of income to the abolitionist movement, see Wendell Phillips to Helen Garrison, 26 September 1852, ASC–BPL; Catherine Clinton, "Maria Weston Chapman," in *Portraits of American Women: From Settlement to the Present,* ed. G. J. Barker-Benfield and Catherine Clinton (New York: St. Martin's, 1991), 151; Deborah Bingham Van Broekhoven, " 'A Determination to Labor . . .': Female Antislavery Activity in Rhode Island," *Rhode Island History* 44 (1985): 41. See also Jean R. Soderlund, "Priorities and Power: The Philadelphia Female Anti-Slavery Society," in Yellin and Van Horne, *The Abolitionist Sisterhood,* 82; Deborah Bingham Van Broekhoven, " 'Better Than A Clay Club': The Organization of Antislavery Fairs, 1835–1860" (forthcoming).

40. Grimké, *An Appeal to the Women of the Nominally Free States,* 59. On the free produce efforts of British abolitionist women, see Louis Billington and Rosamund Billington, " 'A Burning Zeal for Righteousness': Women in the British Anti-Slavery Movement, 1820–1860," in

Equal or Different: Women's Politics, 1800–1914, ed. Jane Rendall (Oxford: Basil Blackwell, 1987), 87–88; Clare Midgley, *Women Against Slavery: The British Campaigns, 1780–1870* (London: Routledge, 1992), 137–39. See also Leonore Davidoff and Catherine Hall, *Family Fortunes: Men and Women of the English Middle Class, 1780–1850* (London: Hutchinson, 1987), 433.

41. See Lori D. Ginzberg, *Women and the Work of Benevolence: Morality, Politics, and Class in the Nineteenth-Century United States* (New Haven: Yale University Press, 1990), 46–47; Nancy Hewitt, "The Social Origins of Women's Antislavery Politics in Western New York," in *Crusaders and Compromisers: Essays on the Relationship of the Antislavery Struggle to the Antebellum Party System,* ed. Alan M. Kraut (Westport, Conn.: Greenwood, 1983), 205.

42. Kelley to Maria Weston Chapman, 18 July 185[?], ASC–BPL.

43. Lee Chambers-Schiller, " 'A Good Work among the People': The Political Culture of the Boston Antislavery Fair," in Yellin and Van Horne, *The Abolitionist Sisterhood,* 265–67.

44. See Angelina Grimké to Theodore Weld, 27 May 1846, 1 July 1849, WGP–UM; Abzug, *Passionate Liberator,* 255–76.

45. See Grimké to Mary Grimké, n.d. [c. 1853], WGP–UM.

46. Grimké to Anne Warren Weston, 17 July 1838, ASC–BPL.

47. Angelina Grimké to Jane Smith, n.d. [1857], WGP–UM. See also Sarah Grimké to Augustus Wattles, et al., n.d. [c. 1854], WGP–UM.

48. Lumpkin, *Angelina Grimké,* 191–93, 195, 201; Angelina Grimké to Jane Smith, n.d. [1857?], WGP–UM. On Grimké's uncertainties, see Angelina Grimké to Theodore Weld, n.d. [c. 1849], WGP–UM.

49. Grimké to Weld, 2 August 1849, 8 September 1852, WGP–UM. See also Abzug, *Passionate Liberator,* 226–30, 246–47.

50. Angelina Grimké to Sarah Grimké, 26 March 1854, n.d. [c. 1854], WGP–UM. See also Lumpkin, *Angelina Grimké,* 199–203.

51. Grimké to Wright, 19 November 1838, ASC–BPL; Grimké to Sarah Wattles, 12 August 1855, WGP–UM. See also Lumpkin, *Angelina Grimké,* 187–88.

52. Joel Bernard, "Authority, Autonomy, and Radical Commitment: Stephen and Abby Kelley Foster," *Proceedings of the American Antiquarian Society* 90 (1980): 348–49. See also Henry C. Wright to Abby Kelley, 25 February 1839, KFP–AAS.

53. See Abby Kelley to Samuel May, 9 November 1853, ASC–BPL; Dorothy Sterling, *Ahead of Her Time: Abby Kelley and the Politics of Antislavery* (New York: Norton, 1991), 13–14; Oliver Johnson, *William Lloyd Garrison and His Times; or, Sketches of the Anti-Slavery Movement in America, and of the Man who was its Founder and Leader,* rev. ed. (Boston: Houghton Mifflin, 1885), 303; Elizabeth Cady Stanton, Susan B. Anthony, Matilda Joslyn Gage, et al., *History of Woman Suffrage,* 6 vols. (1881–1922; reprint, New York: Source Book, 1970), 1:40; *Seventh Annual Report of the Boston Female Anti-Slavery Society. Presented October 14, 1840* (Boston: Boston Female Anti-Slavery Society, 1840), 28.

54. Mott to Richard and Hannah Webb, 14 May 1849, ASC–BPL; Thompson to Anne Warren Weston, 17 March 1851, in *British and American Abolitionists: An Episode in Transatlantic Understanding,* ed. Clare Taylor (Edinburgh: Edinburgh University Press, 1974), 374; an unattributed letter, quoted in *Woman in the Nineteenth Century, and Kindred Papers Relating to the Sphere, Condition and Duties, of Woman,* by Margaret Fuller Ossoli (1855; reprint, New York: Norton, 1971), 111.

55. Alice Stone Blackwell, *Lucy Stone* (1930; reprint, New York: Kraus Reprint, 1971), 233–35; Sterling, *Ahead of Her Time,* 138.

56. Jane H. Pease, "The Freshness of Fanaticism: Abby Kelley Foster: An Essay in Reform" (Ph.D. diss., University of Rochester, 1969), 76; Bernard, "Authority, Autonomy, and Radical Commitment," 364; Sterling, *Ahead of Her Time,* 132, 162–63, 203–12, 221–21.

57. Kelley to Anne Warren Weston, 25 May 1839, ASC–BPL. See also Angelina Grimké to Theodore Weld, 5 September 1852, WGP–UM; Bernard, "Authority, Autonomy, and Radical Commitment," 367.

58. On this issue see Janet Farrell Brodie, *Contraception and Abortion in Nineteenth-Century America* (Ithaca: Cornell University Press, 1995).

59. Sterling, *Ahead of Her Time,* 238; Kelley to Sydney Howard Gay, 19 September 1847, Sydney Howard Gay Papers, Rare Book and Manuscript Library, Columbia University, New York City, (hereafter cited as SHGP-CU). Foster was absent from home when Alla was born. See Alma Lutz, *Crusade for Freedom: Women of the Antislavery Movement* (Boston: Beacon, 1968), 230.

60. Kelley to Foster, 22 November 1843, KFP–AAS. Jane and William Pease have pointed out that among the radical New Hampshire abolitionists, Foster was considered a moderate. See Pease and Pease, *Bound With Them in Chains: A Biographical History of the Antislavery Movement* (Westport, Conn.: Greenwood, 1972), 194–95.

61. Kelley to Gay, 19 September 1847, SHGP–CU.

62. Kelley to Maria Weston Chapman, 17 December 1847, ASC–BPL; Kelley to Sydney Howard Gay, 24 May 1849, SHGP–CU.

63. Kelley Foster to Sydney Howard Gay, 15 July 1849, SHGP–CU.

64. Kelley to Alla Foster, 6 January 1854, KFC–WHM. See also Abby Kelley to Stephen S. Foster, 21 July 185[?], KFP–AAS; Abby Kelley to Wendell Phillips, 20 August [18??], Crawford Blagden Collection of the Papers of Wendell Phillips, Houghton Library, Harvard University, Cambridge, Mass. (hereafter cited as CBC–HL).

65. Mott to Richard and Hannah Webb, 14 May 1849, ASC–BPL. See also Helen Garrison to Ann Phillips, 2 August 1851, CBC–HL.

66. Jones to Kelley, 23 January 1848, KFP–AAS. Jones subsequently established a career as a health reform lecturer. See Brodie, *Contraception and Abortion in Nineteenth-Century America,* 129–30.

67. Grimké to Pease, 11 February 1842, WGL, 2:918. See also Stone to Henry Blackwell, 9 May 1858, in Wheeler, *Loving Warriors,* 181.

68. Sterling, *Ahead of Her Time,* 257–58; Bernard, "Authority, Autonomy, and Radical Commitment," 370.

69. For a fresh analysis of Foster's abolitionism, see Troy Duncan, "Stephen Symonds Foster: Radical Abolitionist," (B.A. honors diss., University of Newcastle, 1995).

70. Foster to Kelley, 2 March 1855, KFP–AAS. Foster was not oblivious to the response his actions and pamphlets would provoke. Moreover, Foster did have his defenders in the abolition movement. See Foster to Abby Kelley, 12 February 1855, KFP–AAS; David Lee Child to Maria Weston Chapman, 13 December 1843, ASC–BPL; Anne Warren Weston to Caroline and Deborah Weston, 29 May 1843, ASC–BPL. Garrison published the results of an examination of Foster's skull by the well-known phrenologist Orson B. Fowler that purported to demonstrate Foster's sanity. See Russel Nye, *William Lloyd Garrison and the Humanitarian Reformers* (Boston: Little, Brown, 1955), 79. The common depiction of Foster as an unhinged or erratic character must be balanced against Abby's description of her husband. He "is never disturbed or anxious, on any occasion," she assured Sydney Howard Gay in 1849. See Kelley to Sydney Howard Gay, 17 August 1849, SHGP–CU.

71. Blackwell to Lucy Stone, 28 August 1853, 13 June 1853, LSP–LC.

72. Blackwell to Stone, 2 July 1853, LSP–LC.

73. Stone to Blackwell, 21 June 1853, LSP–LC; Stone Blackwell, *Lucy Stone,* 161. Stone had earlier expressed her desires regarding their wedding ceremony: "We will have no strangers—no formality of joining hands, but in a quiet, home-like way assume the life to which our love prompts." See Stone to Blackwell, 8 April 1855, LSP–LC.

74. Stone to Blackwell, 26 April 1856, LSP–LC.

75. Stone Blackwell, *Lucy Stone,* 193.

76. "Autobiographical Sketch by Henry B. Blackwell," BP–LC; Elinor Rice Hays, *Those Extraordinary Blackwells: The Story of a Journey to a Better World* (New York: Harcourt, Brace and World, 1967), 139–40.

77. Stone Blackwell, *Lucy Stone,* 199; Stone to Antoinette Brown Blackwell, 20 February 1859, as quoted in Wheeler, *Loving Warriors,* 185. See also Hays, *Extraordinary Blackwells,* 140–141; Hays, *Morning Star,* 155–59; Stone to Henry Blackwell, 9 May 1858, in Wheeler, *Loving Warriors,* 181.

78. Stone to Henry Blackwell, 22–23 July [1864], 4 September 1864, in Wheeler, *Loving Warriors,* 196, 199.

79. Stone to Margaret Campbell, 12 April 1877, in Wheeler, *Loving Warriors,* 265–66.

80. *National Anti-Slavery Standard,* 25 June 1840.

81. John White Chadwick, "The Anti-Slavery Women," in *A Life for Liberty: Anti-Slavery and other Letters of Sallie Holley,* ed. Chadwick (New York: Putnam, 1899), 4 (my emphasis); Stanton to Wendell Phillips, 16 January [1869], CBC–HL; Higginson, *Wendell Phillips* (Boston: Lee and Shepard, 1884), viii. See also James Brewer Stewart, *Wendell Phillips: Liberty's Hero* (Baton Rouge: Louisiana State University Press, 1986), 48, 76; Irving H. Bartlett, *Wendell Phillips: Brahmin Radical* (1961; reprint, Westport, Conn.: Greenwood, 1973), 35.

82. Lucretia Mott to Maria Weston Chapman, 29 July 1840, ASC–BPL; Ann Phillips to Maria Weston Chapman, 30 July 1839, in Taylor, *British and American Abolitionists,* 77; Ann Phillips to Anne and Deborah Weston, 25 May 1854, ASC–BPL.

83. Ann Phillips to Maria Weston Chapman, 30 July 1939, in Taylor, *British and American Abolitionists,* 77; Ann Phillips to Wendell Phillips, n.d. [c. 1854–55], 11 December 1856, 6 August 1858, CBC–HL. While it is impossible to be certain about the nature of Ann's illness, it might have been the result of rheumatic fever or rheumatism. See Irving Bartlett, ed., "New Light on Wendell Phillips: The Community of Reform 1840–1880," *Perspectives in American History* 12 (1979): 37; Stewart, *Liberty's Hero,* 85–86.

84. Phillips to May, 6 July 1846, 7 September 1852, Anti Slavery Papers, Division of Rare and Manuscript Collections, Cornell University Library, Ithaca, (hereafter cited as ASP–CUL). On their efforts to find a cure for Ann, see Stewart, *Liberty's Hero,* 82–86, 164–65, 175.

85. See William Lloyd Garrison, *Helen Eliza Garrison: A Memorial* (Cambridge, Mass.: n.p., 1876); Wendell Phillips, "Remarks at the funeral service of Mrs. Garrison, 125 Highland Street, Roxbury, Thursday, January 27, 1876," in his *Speeches, Lectures, and Letters. Second Series* (1891; reprint New York: Arno, 1969), 454–56; Helen Garrison to Mary May, 20 November 1862, ASC–BPL. See also Ralph Korngold, *Two Friends of Man: The Story of William Lloyd Garrison and Wendell Phillips and Their Relationship with Abraham Lincoln* (Boston: Little, Brown, 1950), 83; Nye, *William Lloyd Garrison,* 150. Debra Gold Hansen has noted that Helen Garrison "was a regular at the" Boston Female Anti-Slavery Society's meetings. But while Garrison was a member of some antislavery societies, her role in those societies was limited to the more traditional female activities, such as organizing social and

fundraising gatherings. It is not being suggested here that such activities should be slighted, but rather that her major contribution to abolitionism was made within the context of the domestic environment she sought to create. See Hansen, "Bluestockings and Bluenoses: Gender, Class, and Conflict in the Boston Female Anti-Slavery Society, 1833–1840" (Ph.D. diss., University of California at Irvine, 1988), 108.

86. Helen E. Benson to William L. Garrison, 19 July 1834, Oswald G. Villard Papers, Houghton Library, Harvard University, Cambridge, Mass., (hereafter cited as VP–HL); Helen Garrison to William L. Garrison, 10 December 1861, ASC–BPL; William L. Garrison to Helen Garrison, 2 February 1861, in *The Letters of William Lloyd Garrison,* ed. Walter M. Merrill and Louis Ruchames, 6 vols. (Cambridge: Belknap Press of Harvard University Press, 1971–81), 5:8 (hereafter cited as WLGL).

87. Garrison to Sarah T. Benson, 8 April 1837, WLGL, 2:255; William L. Garrison to Helen Garrison, 26 July 1846, WLGL, 3:354.

88. Phoebe Jackson to Helen Garrison, 24 April 1842, ASC–BPL; Helen Garrison to Sallie Holley, 14 December 1862, VP–HL. On the Garrisons' black houseguests, see James Oliver Horton and Lois E. Horton, *Black Bostonians: Family Life and Community Struggle in the Antebellum North* (New York: Holmes and Meier, 1979), 84–85. See also Abby Kelley to William and Helen Garrison, 12 September 1854, ASC–BPL; Helen Garrison to Mary May, 20 November 1862, ASC–BPL; Friedman, *Gregarious Saints,* 149.

89. Carolyn L. Karcher, *The First Woman in the Republic: A Cultural Biography of Lydia Maria Child* (Durham: Duke University Press, 1994), 197.

90. Child to Francis George Shaw, 2 August 1846, LMCP, 23/664; Child to Ellis Gray Loring, 9 May 1850, LMCP, 28/780. See also Child, "Concerning Women," in *The Independent,* 15 July 1869, in LMCP, 71/1903.

91. See David Lee Child to James Miller McKim, 5 November 1855, ASP–CUL; Kirk Jeffrey, "Marriage, Career, and Feminine Ideology in Nineteenth-Century America: Reconstructing the Marital Experience of Lydia Maria Child, 1828–1874," *Feminist Studies* 2 (1975): 115.

92. L. Maria Child to Lydia [Bigelow] Child, 2 August 1831, 23 June 1831, LMCP, 2/50, 2/48; L. Maria Child to David L. Child, 22 May 1835, LMCP, 3/72.

93. Stewart, *Liberty's Hero,* 320–21; Foster to Kelley, 17 August 1851, KFC–WHM. See also L. Maria Child to David L. Child, 28 July 1836, LMCP, 4/102. Many abolitionists borrowed money, and Gerrit Smith and Lewis Tappan proved generous to their fellow reformers. L. Maria Child received financial assistance from Ellis Gray Loring. See Thomas, *Theodore Weld,* 177; Child to Loring, 13 April 1851, 31 August 1851, 9 September 1856, LMCP, 28/804, 29/811, 39/940.

94. Child to Kelley, 1 October 1838, KFP–AAS; Jeffrey, "Marital Experience of Lydia Maria Child," 115.

95. Milton Meltzer, *Tongue of Flame: The Life of Lydia Maria Child* (New York: Cromwell, 1965), 16–21; Jeffrey, "Marital Experience of Lydia Maria Child," 117.

96. See *An Appeal in Favor of That Class of Americans Called Africans* (1836 ed.; reprint, New York: Arno, 1968); Mott to Anne Warren Weston, 8 July 1841, ASC–BPL; *Report of the Proceedings of the Twentieth Anniversary, and of the Reception Held at St. James Hotel,* reprinted in *A History of the National Woman's Rights Movement, for Twenty Years, With the Proceedings of the Decade Meeting Held at Apollo Hall, October 20, 1870, from 1850 to 1870, With an Appendix Containing the History of the Movement During the Winter of 1871, in the National Capitol,* comp. Paulina Wright Davis (New York: Journeymen Printers' Co-Operative Association, 1871), 12. See also Deborah Pickman Clifford, *Crusader for Freedom: A Life of Lydia Maria Child* (Boston: Beacon, 1992), 159.

97. *National Anti-Slavery Standard,* 20 May 1841; Child to Ellis Gray Loring, 11 August 1841, LMCP, 10/246.

98. Child to Loring, 25 January 1842, LMCP, 13/372; Child to Smith, 28 September 1841, Gerrit Smith Papers, Syracuse University Library, Department of Special Collections, Syracuse, N.Y.

99. Jeffrey, "Marital Experience of Lydia Maria Child," 117. On Maria's decision to separate her financial affairs, see her letters to Ellis Gray Loring, 21 March 1843, 12 June 1843, 16 June 1843, LMCP, 17/470, 17/498, 17/499.

100. Child to Louisa [Gilman] Loring, 28 February 1843, LMCP, 16/459.

101. Child to Francis George Shaw, 2 August 1846, LMCP, 23/664; Child to Louisa [Gilman] Loring, 29 April 1847, LMCP, 25/708.

Chapter 4. Antislavery Sisters

1. "In the recent flowering of women's history," Ian Tyrrell has written, "no issue has had so much written about it as this theme of sisterhood." See Tyrrell, *Woman's World/Woman's Empire: The Woman's Christian Temperance Union in International Perspective, 1880–1930* (Chapel Hill: University of North Carolina Press, 1991), 114. See also Carroll Smith-Rosenberg, "The Female World of Love and Ritual: Relations between Women in Nineteenth Century America," *Signs: Journal of Women in Culture and Society* 1 (1975): 21; William R. Taylor and Christopher Lasch, "Two 'Kindred Spirits': Sorority and Family in New England," *New England Quarterly* 36 (1963): 23–41; Nancy Cott, *The Bonds of Womanhood: "Woman's Sphere" in New England, 1780–1835* (New Haven: Yale University Press, 1977), 160, 177; Mary P. Ryan, "The Power of Women's Networks: A Case Study of Female Moral Reform in Antebellum America," *Feminist Studies* 5 (1979): 83. See also Jean Fagan Yellin, *Women and Sisters: The Antislavery Feminists in American Culture* (New Haven: Yale University Press, 1989), 10; Gisela Bock, "Challenging Dichotomies: Perspectives on Women's History," in *Writing Women's History: International Perspectives,* ed. Karen Offen, Ruth Roach Pierson, and Jane Rendall (Basingstoke: Macmillan, 1991), 5; Anne M. Boylan, "Women and Politics in the Era before Seneca Falls," *Journal of the Early Republic* 10 (1990): 363–82. The most recent synthesis of the role of women's organizations in the United States is Anne Firor Scott's *Natural Allies: Women's Associations in American History* (Urbana: University of Illinois Press, 1991).

2. Female abolitionists frequently used affectionate and sisterly terms. See, for example, Elizabeth Pease to Ann Phillips, 1 June 1844, Anti-Slavery Collection, Boston Public Library (hereafter cited as ASC–BPL); Abby Kelley to "Dear Sister" [Maria Weston Chapman], 19 December 1837, ASC–BPL; Helen Garrison to Ann Phillips, 2 August 1851, Crawford-Blagden Collection of the Papers of Wendell Phillips, Houghton Library, Harvard University, Cambridge, Mass., (hereafter cited as CBC–HL); Sarah Grimké, "Condition of Women," n.d., in *Letters on the Equality of the Sexes and Other Essays,* ed. Elizabeth Ann Bartlett (New Haven: Yale University Press, 1988), 130.

3. On the significance of women's social space, see Gerda Lerner, *The Creation of Feminist Consciousness: From the Middle Ages to Eighteen-Seventy* (New York: Oxford University Press, 1993), 279–80.

4. For a discussion of this theme, see Elizabeth Fox-Genovese, *Feminism Without Illusions: A Critique of Individualism* (Chapel Hill: University of North Carolina Press, 1991), chap. 1. See also Nancy Cott, *The Grounding of Modern Feminism* (New Haven: Yale University Press, 1987), 6–8, 201–2, 280–82.

5. Angelina Grimké and Sarah Grimké to Queen Victoria, 26 October 1839, ASC–BPL. On Sarah Grimké's praise for the French Revolution, see Grimké to Elizabeth [Pease] Nichol,

18 April 1848, Oswald G. Villard Papers, Houghton Library, Harvard University, Cambridge, Mass. (hereafter cited as VP–HL).

6. See Weld to Weston, 23 March 1836, 1 May 1837, ASC–BPL. See also Gerrit Smith, *Woman Suffrage Above Human Law. Letter from Gerrit Smith* (Peterboro, N.Y.: n.p., 1873), 2; Samuel J. May to Lucretia Mott, 25 June 1834, in the Incoming Correspondence of the Philadelphia Female Anti-Slavery Society, Historical Society of Pennsylvania, Philadelphia (hereafter cited as HSP). On the postbellum "sisterhood" see Tyrrell, *Woman's World/Woman's Empire,* chap. 6; Estelle Freedman, "Separatism as Strategy: Female Institution Building and American Feminism, 1870–1930," *Feminist Studies* 5 (1979): 517.

7. Hersh, *The Slavery of Sex: Feminist-Abolitionists in Antebellum America* (Urbana: University of Illinois Press, 1978), 219. Debra Gold Hansen has found that at "their time of involvement in the antislavery movement, 62% of the women" of the Boston Female Anti-Slavery Society "were married or widowed." Considering that the membership rolls of the Boston society included girls as young as thirteen or fourteen—hence too young to marry—Hansen's figures suggest the numerical preponderance of married women amongst Boston's women abolitionists. Jean R. Soderlund has noted that in 1838, some 45 percent of the participants in the Philadelphia Female Anti-Slavery Society were married. A decade later, however, the figure had risen to 62 percent. See Hansen, "Bluestockings and Bluenoses: Gender, Class, and Conflict in the Boston Female Anti-Slavery Society, 1833–1840" (Ph.D. diss., University of California at Irvine, 1988), 108; Hansen, *Strained Sisterhood: Gender and Class in the Boston Female Anti-Slavery Society* (Amherst: University of Massachusetts Press, 1993), 69; Soderlund, "Priorities and Power: The Philadelphia Female Anti-Slavery Society," in *The Abolitionist Sisterhood: Women's Political Culture in Antebellum America,* ed. Jean Fagan Yellin and John C. Van Horne (Ithaca: Cornell University Press, 1994), 75.

8. Stone to Blackwell, 3 September 1854, Lucy Stone Papers (included in the Blackwell Family Papers), Manuscript Division, Library of Congress, Washington, D.C. (hereafter cited as LSP–LC); Grimké to Sarah Wattles, 12 August 1855, Weld-Grimké papers, William L. Clements Library, University of Michigan, Ann Arbor (hereafter cited as WGP–UM). Carroll Smith-Rosenberg's emphasis on the complementary nature of heterosocial and homosocial worlds among females is helpful when analyzing abolitionist sorority. See Smith-Rosenberg, "Female World of Love and Ritual," 8. See also Lillian Faderman, *Surpassing the Love of Men: Romantic Friendship Between Women from the Renaissance to the Present Day* (New York: William Morrow, 1981), 172–77; E. Anthony Rotundo, "Romantic Friendship: Male Intimacy and Middle-Class Youth in the Northern United States, 1800–1900," *Journal of Social History* 23 (1989): 10.

9. See Jane H. Pease and William H. Pease, *They Who Would Be Free: Blacks' Search for Freedom, 1830–1861* (New York: Atheneum, 1974), 3–16. Leon Litwack's pioneering study of African Americans in the Northern states can be supplemented by a number of more recent studies. See Litwack, *North of Slavery: The Negro in the Free States, 1790–1860* (Chicago: University of Chicago Press, 1961); Julie Winch, *Philadelphia's Black Elite: Activism, Accommodation, and the Struggle for Autonomy, 1787–1848* (Philadelphia: Temple University Press, 1988); James Oliver Horton and Lois E. Horton, *Black Bostonians: Family Life and Community Struggle in the Antebellum North* (New York: Holmes and Meier, 1979); James O. Horton, *Free People of Color: Inside the African American Community* (Washington, D.C.: Smithsonian Institution Press, 1993); Leonard P. Curry, *The Free Black in Urban America, 1800–1850: The Shadow of the Dream* (Chicago: University of Chicago Press, 1981).

10. Child, introduction, to Harriet Jacobs, *Incidents in the Life of a Slave Girl. Written by Herself* (1861; reprint, Miami, Fla.: Mnemosyne, 1969), 7–8; Child to Gerrit Smith, 22 April 1864, Gerrit Smith Papers, Syracuse University Library, Department of Special Collections, Syracuse, N.Y. (hereafter cited as SP–SU).

11. Melia, "The Role of Black Garrisonian Women in Antislavery and Other Reforms, 1830–1865" (Ph.D. diss., University of Western Australia, 1991), 169. An exception was the friendships between Sarah and Angelina Grimké on the one hand, and Sarah Douglass on the other. See Katherine Du Pre Lumpkin, *The Emancipation of Angelina Grimké* (Chapel Hill: University of North Carolina Press, 1974), 75; Melia, "Black Garrisonian Women," 172–87. Note also Shirley J. Yee, *Black Women Abolitionists: A Study in Activism* (Knoxville: University of Tennessee Press, 1992), 90–96.

12. Winch, *Philadelphia's Black Elite,* 87; Hansen, "The Boston Female Anti-Slavery Society and the Limits of Gender Politics," in Yellin and Van Horne, *The Abolitionist Sisterhood,* 47, 58.

13. Garrison to the Boston Female Anti-Slavery Society, 9 April 1834, in the Boston Female Anti-Slavery Society Letterbook, Massachusetts Historical Society, Boston (hereafter cited as BFASSL–MHS); Mary Grew to Garrison, 11 April 1834, BFASSL–MHS.

14. Soderlund, "Priorities and Power," in Yellin and Van Horne, *The Abolitionist Sisterhood,* 68; Melia, "Black Garrisonian Women," 104–23 (quote on 116). See also Carolyn Luverne Williams, "Religion, Race, and Gender in Antebellum American Reform: The Philadelphia Female Anti-Slavery Society, 1833–1870" (Ph.D. diss., University of California, Los Angeles, 1991), 420, 469–80; Carolyn Luverne Williams, "The Female Antislavery Movement: Fighting against Racial Prejudice and Promoting Women's Rights in Antebellum America," in Yellin and Van Horne, *The Abolitionist Sisterhood,* 163–65.

15. Hansen, "The Boston Female Anti-Slavery Society," in Yellin and Van Horne, *The Abolitionist Sisterhood,* 57–58; Soderlund, "Priorities and Power," in ibid., 74. On the hierarchies within black women's reformism, see also Anne M. Boylan, "Benevolence and Antislavery Activity among African American Women in New York and Boston, 1820–1840," in ibid., 130.

16. Friedman, *Gregarious Saints: Self and Community in American Abolitionism, 1830–1870* (Cambridge: Cambridge University Press, 1982), 134–40 (quotations on 140).

17. See, for example, Sarah Grimké to Elizabeth Pease, 16 November 1838, ASC–BPL.

18. Holley to Kelley, 14 February 1853, Abby Kelley Foster Papers, American Antiquarian Society, Worcester, Mass. (hereafter cited as KFP–AAS); Grimké to Garrison, 16 June 1872, ASC–BPL; Grimké to Daniels, 5 November 1873, WGP–UM.

19. Mary Grew to Mrs. Howarth (President of the Amesbury Female Anti-Slavery Society), 17 May 1834, BFASSL–MHS; Kelley to Chapman, 11 February 18[??], ASC–BPL.

20. See the "Annual Report of the Philadelphia Female Anti-Slavery Society, for 1836," cited in Ira V. Brown, "Cradle of Feminism: The Philadelphia Female Anti-Slavery Society, 1833–1840," *Pennsylvania Magazine of History* 102 (1978): 151; "Annual Report of the Philadelphia Female Anti-Slavery Society, 1837," included in the *Philadelphia Female Anti-Slavery Society Minute Book, 1833–38,* HSP. See also Williams, "Philadelphia Female Anti-Slavery Society," 331.

21. Angelina Grimké to Sarah Grimké, n.d. [c. 1854], WGP–UM. See also Sarah Grimké to Angelina Grimké, 20 May 1846, WGP–UM; Angelina Grimké to Jane Smith, n.d. [1857?], WGP–UM; Angelina Grimké to Theodore Weld, 21 January 1838, in *Letters of Theodore Dwight Weld, Angelina Grimké Weld, and Sarah Grimké, 1822–1844,* ed. Gilbert H. Barnes and Dwight L. Dumond 2 vols. (1934; reprint, New York: Da Capo, 1970), 2:520 (hereafter cited as WGL); Lerner, *Grimké Sisters,* 322–25; Lumpkin, *Angelina Grimké,* 146, 163, 186–90.

22. Grimké to Kelley, 24 February [1838], Abigail Kelley Foster Correspondence, Worcester Historical Museum, Worcester, Mass. (hereafter cited as KFC–WHM); Weston to Lucia Weston, 21 September 1840, ASC–BPL. See also L. Maria Child to Louisa [Gilman] Loring,

31 May 1846, reprinted in *The Collected Correspondence of Lydia Maria Child*, ed. Patricia G. Holland and Milton Meltzer (Millwood, N.Y.: Kraus Microform, 1979, microfiche), Card 23/Item 659 (hereafter cited as LMCP).

23. Kelley to Chapman, 2 November 1843, ASC–BPL. See also Kelley to Foster, 22 November 1843, KFP–AAS. On the importance of the female kin network in the nineteenth century, see Marilyn Ferris Motz, *True Sisterhood: Michigan Women and Their Kin, 1820–1920* (Albany: State University of New York Press, 1983), 1–8.

24. Stanton, *Eighty Years and More: Reminiscences, 1815–1897* (1898; reprint, New York: Source Book, 1970), 83. See also Stanton to Angelina Grimké and Sarah Grimké, 25 June 1840, WGL, 2:847; Donald R. Kennon, "'An Apple of Discord'? The Woman Question at the World's Anti-Slavery Convention of 1840," *Slavery and Abolition: A Journal of Comparative Studies* 5 (1984): 255–57; Stanton to [Mott's children], 14 November 1880, Lucretia Mott Papers, Friends Historical Library, Swarthmore College, Swarthmore, Pa. (hereafter cited as MP–FHL); Frederick B. Tolles, ed., *Slavery and "The Woman Question": Lucretia Mott's Diary of Her Visit to Great Britain to Attend the World's Anti-Slavery Convention of 1840* (Haverford, Pa.: Friends' Historical Association, 1952), 41.

25. Ann Phillips to Elizabeth Pease, 3 July 1841, ASC–BPL. See also Helen Garrison to Ann Phillips, 30 September 1850, CBC–HL; Anne Warren Weston to Ann Phillips, 2 July 1843, CBC–HL.

26. Ann Phillips to Elizabeth Pease, 17 September 1841, ASC–BPL; Ann and Wendell Phillips to Elizabeth Pease, 3 July 1841, ASC–BPL.

27. See Carroll Smith-Rosenberg, "The Hysterical Woman: Sex Roles and Role Conflict in 19th Century America," *Social Research* 39 (1972): 668.

28. Lucy Stone to "dear Friend [Samuel] May," 23 September 1852, Alma Lutz Collection, Arthur and Elizabeth Schlesinger Library on the History of Women in America, Radcliffe College, Cambridge, Mass.; Stanton, *Eighty Years*, 118–19. Lucretia and James Mott lost their child, Thomas, in 1817; William and Helen Garrison lost a son in 1849; Sydney Howard and Elizabeth Gay lost a child in 1850. See Mary Grew to Helen Garrison, 3 May 1849, ASC–BPL; Ann Phillips to Sydney Howard Gay, 27 August [1850], Sydney Howard Gay Papers, Rare Books and Manuscript Library, Columbia University, New York City (hereafter cited as SHGP–CU); Lucretia Mott to Sydney Howard Gay, 13 April 1850, SHGP–CU; Lucretia Mott to Sydney Howard Gay and Elizabeth [Neall] Gay, 27 November 1850, SHGP–CU; Lucretia Mott to Phebe Post Willis, 1 November 1838, MP–FHL; Otelia Cromwell, *Lucretia Mott* (1958; reprint, New York: Russell and Russell, 1971), 27; Walter M. Merrill, *Against Wind and Tide: A Biography of Wm. Lloyd Garrison* (Cambridge: Harvard University Press, 1963), 251; Raimund E. Goerler, "Family, Self, and Anti-Slavery: Sydney Howard Gay and the Abolitionist Community" (Ph.D. diss., Case Western Reserve University, 1975), 255–57.

29. Ronald T. Takaki, *Iron Cages: Race and Culture in Nineteenth-Century America* (London: Athlone, 1980), 137–40; Grimké to Hunt, n.d. [1853], WGP–UM. For an example of the praise accorded Elizabeth Blackwell, see *Proceedings of the Woman's Rights Convention, Held at the Unitarian Church, Rochester, N. Y. August 2, 1848, to Consider the Rights of Woman, Politically, Religiously and Industrially. Revised by Mrs. Amy Post* (New York: Robert J. Johnson, 1870), 15. On the connections between women's reproductive function and their alleged frailties, see Frederick Holloway, *The Marriage Guide or Natural History of Generation; A Private Instructor for Married Persons and Those About to Marry Both Male and Female, In Everything Concerning the Physiology and Relations of the Sexual System and the Production or Prevention of Offspring—Including all the New Discoveries, Never Before Given in the English Language* (1860; reprint, New York: Arno, 1974), 25, 95.

30. Grimké to Hunt, 23 May 1855, WGP–UM; Grimké to Augustus Wattles, 1 June 1856, WGP–UM.

31. See Smith-Rosenberg, "Female World of Love and Ritual," 17–20; Carrol Lasser, "'Let Us Be Sisters Forever': The Sororal Model of Nineteenth-Century Female Friendship," *Signs: Journal of Women in Culture and Society* 14 (1988): 161. See also Andrew Sinclair, *The Better Half: The Emancipation of the American Woman* (1965; reprint, New York: Harper and Row, 1966), 155. On the ideology and treatment of women students at Oberlin College, see Ronald W. Hogeland, "Coeducation of the Sexes at Oberlin College: A Study of Social Ideas in Mid-Nineteenth-Century America," *Journal of Social History* 6 (1972–73): 160–76; Lori D. Ginzberg, "The 'Joint Education of the Sexes': Oberlin College's Original Vision," in *Educating Men and Women Together: Coeducation in a Changing World,* ed. Carol Lasser (Urbana: University of Illinois Press, 1987), 67–80.

32. See Elinor Rice Hays, *Morning Star: A Biography of Lucy Stone* (1961; reprint, New York: Octagon Books, 1978), 53. Kelley was herself a graduate of Oberlin, and her lectures there were also an important influence on Sallie Holley. See John White Chadwick, ed., *A Life for Liberty: Anti-Slavery and Other Letters of Sallie Holley* (New York: Putnam, 1899), 59.

33. *Report of the Proceedings of the Twentieth Anniversary, and of the Reception held at St. James' Hotel,* in *A History of the National Woman's Rights Movement, for Twenty Years, With the Proceedings of the Decade Meeting held at Apollo Hall, October 20, 1870, from 1850 to 1870, With an Appendix Containing the History of the Movement During the Winter of 1871, in the National Capitol,* comp. Paulina W. Davis (New York: Journeymen Printers' Co-Operative Society, 1871), 2; Mabel Collins Donnelly, *The American Victorian Woman: The Myth and the Reality* (Westport, Conn.: Greenwood, 1986), 23; Lucretia Mott to Sarah H. Speakman, 12 April 1838, MP–FHL.

34. Stanton to Anthony, 10 September 1855, in *Elizabeth Cady Stanton, Susan B. Anthony: Correspondence, Writings, Speeches,* ed. Ellen Carol DuBois (New York: Schocken Books, 1981), 59. See also Stanton, *Eighty Years,* 193–94; Elisabeth Griffith, *In Her Own Right: The Life of Elizabeth Cady Stanton* (New York: Oxford University Press, 1984), 74; Sarah Grimké to Abby Kelley, 24 February [1838], KFC–WHM.

35. Barry, *Susan B. Anthony: A Biography of a Singular Feminist* (New York: New York University Press, 1988), 65; Stanton, *Eighty Years,* 166; Mott to Stanton, 3 October 1848, Elizabeth Cady Stanton Papers, Manuscript Division, Library of Congress, Washington, D.C. (hereafter cited as ECSP–LC). See also Lois Banner, *Elizabeth Cady Stanton: A Radical For Women's Rights* (Boston: Little, Brown, 1980), 60; Griffith, *In Her Own Right,* 74, 96; Elizabeth Cady Stanton, Susan B. Anthony, Matilda Joslyn Gage, et al., *History of Woman Suffrage,* 6 vols. (1881–1922; reprint, New York: Source Book, 1970), 1:460 (hereafter cited as HWS); Rheta Childe Dorr, *Susan B. Anthony: The Woman Who Changed the Mind of a Nation* (1928; reprint, New York: AMS Press, 1970), 80; Sarah Grimké to Stanton, 29 March 1854, ECSP–LC.

36. Stanton, *Eighty Years,* 166. See also Antoinette Brown to Lucy Stone, [late February 1850], in *Friends and Sisters: Letters between Lucy Stone and Antoinette Brown Blackwell, 1846–93,* ed. Carol Lasser and Marlene Deahl Merrill (Urbana: University of Illinois Press, 1987), 70; Abby Kelley to Sydney Howard Gay, 9 December 1851, SHGP–CU.

37. See Anthony to Lydia Mott, n.d., in *Life and Work of Susan B. Anthony,* ed. Ida Husted Harper 3 vols. (1898; reprint, Salem, N.H.: Ayer, 1983), 1:170; Anthony, "Homes of Single Women," speech delivered in 1877, Susan B. Anthony Papers, Manuscript Division, Library of Congress, Washington, D.C. (hereafter cited as SBA–LC). On Antoinette Brown's determination not to marry, see her letters to Lucy Stone, 22 September 1847, [December 1848], [August 1849], in Lasser and Merrill, *Friends and Sisters,* 31, 46, 56.

38. Harper, *Susan B. Anthony,* 1:128–29; Stone to Anthony, n.d., ibid., 1:139; Mott to Anthony, n.d., ibid., 1:170.

39. Grimké to Anne Warren Weston, 15 July 1838, ASC–BPL; Grew to Helen Garrison, 23 July 1846, ASC–BPL. See also Antoinette Brown to Lucy Stone, [early September 1847], in Lasser and Merrill, *Friends and Sisters,* 26–27.

40. Kelley to Gay, 19 September 1847, SHGP–CU. On abolitionist women's interest in each other's domestic arrangements, see, for example, Sallie Holley to Abby Kelley, 13 September 1853, KFC–WHM; Abby Kelley to Sydney Howard Gay, 19 September 1847, SHGP–CU.

41. Helen Garrison to Caroline Weston, 31 October 1835, ASC–BPL; Herbert Aptheker, *Abolitionism: A Revolutionary Movement* (Boston: Twayne, 1989), 41. See also Eric Foner, "Abolitionism and the Labor Movement in Ante-bellum America," in *Anti-Slavery, Religion, and Reform: Essays in Memory of Roger Anstey,* ed. Christine Bolt and Seymour Drescher (Hamden, Conn.: Dawson, 1980), 254–71; Carl J. Guarneri, *The Utopian Alternative: Fourierism in Nineteenth-Century America* (Ithaca: Cornell University Press, 1991), 252–57; George Fitzhugh, *Cannibals All! or Slaves Without Masters* (1857; reprint Cambridge: Belknap Press of Harvard University Press, 1960), 18; Jonathan A. Glickstein, "'Poverty is Not Slavery': American Abolitionists and the Competitive Labor Market," in *Antislavery Reconsidered: New Perspectives on the Abolitionists,* ed. Lewis Perry and Michael Fellman (Baton Rouge: Louisiana State University Press, 1979), 195–218. Not all abolitionists were reticent about addressing questions of class oppression. Wendell Phillips, for example, eventually advocated on behalf of the working class. See James Brewer Stewart, *Wendell Phillips: Liberty's Hero* (Baton Rouge: Louisiana State University Press, 1986), 258–59, 261–63.

42. Grimké, *Letters to Catherine E. Beecher,* 116; "Report on Educating the Sexes Together," written by Elizabeth Cady Stanton, delivered by Susan B. Anthony, to the New York State Teachers Convention, Troy, N.Y., 1856, SBA–LC; Stanton to Gerrit Smith, 5 January [1851], ECSP–LC; *The Proceedings of the Woman's Rights Convention Held at Syracuse, September 8th, 9th and 10th, 1852* (Syracuse, N.Y.: n.p., 1852), 64; HWS, 1:28; *The Proceedings of the Woman's Rights Convention, Held at Worcester, October 15th and 16th, 1851* (New York: Fowler and Wells, 1852), 18.

43. Stone to Henry Blackwell, 4 June 1857, LSP–LC; Child to Lucy Osgood, 4 February 1869, LMCP, 70/1878; Child, *The American Frugal Housewife, Dedicated to Those Who are Not Ashamed of Economy,* 16th ed. (Boston: Carter, Hendee, 1835), 106; Child to Sarah Shaw, 31 July 1877, 25 August 1877, LMCP, 88/2335, 88/2338.

44. Beecher, *A Treatise on Domestic Economy, for the use of Young Ladies at Home, and at School* (1841; reprint, New York: Source Book, 1971), chap. 18. On domestic service, see David Katzman, *Seven Days a Week: Women and Domestic Service in Industrializing America* (New York: Oxford University Press, 1980); Faye E. Dudden, *Serving Women: Household Service in Nineteenth-Century America* (Middletown, Conn.: Wesleyan University Press, 1983); Hansen, *Strained Sisterhood,* 50–52.

45. See L. Maria Child to Angelina Grimké to 4 February 1874, WGP–UM; L. Maria Child to Elizabeth Cady Stanton, 24 May 1863, ECSP–LC.

46. Garrison to Holley, 14 December 1862, VP–HL; Grimké to Anne Warren Weston, 15 July 1838, ASC–BPL; Grimké to Jane Smith, n.d. [1857], WGP–UM. See also Ann Phillips to Wendell Phillips, 16 March 1866, CBC–HL; Anna Davis Hallowell, ed., *James and Lucretia Mott. Life and Letters* (Boston: Houghton Mifflin, 1884), 257, 331; L. Maria Child to Louisa [Gilman] Loring, 12 December 1840, LMCP, 9/219; Henry Blackwell to Lucy Stone, 3 March 1858, LSP–LC.

47. Sarah Grimké to Julia Tappan, 10 November 1868, WGP–UM; Stanton to Smith Miller, n.d. [November 1852], ECSP–LC. See also Helen Garrison to Caroline Weston, 31 October

1835, ASC–BPL. On Willard's presence in Stanton's home, see Griffith, *In Her Own Right,* 70; Mary B. Oakley, *Elizabeth Cady Stanton* (New York: Feminist Press, 1972), 58; Alma Lutz, *Created Equal: A Biography of Elizabeth Cady Stanton, 1815–1902* (New York: John Day, 1940), 61. On the shortage of domestic helpers, see Nancy Cott, *Bonds of Womanhood,* 48; Gail Hamilton [Mary A. Dodge], *Woman's Wrongs: A Counter Irritant* (1868; reprint, New York: Arno, 1972), 123.

48. *Proceedings of the Woman's Rights Convention . . . 1848,* 11, 15; *Correspondence Between Lydia Maria Child, Gov. Wise and Mrs. Mason, of Virginia* (Boston: American Anti-Slavery Society, 1860), 26. See also *Liberator,* 31 December 1859.

49. Garrison to Helen Garrison, 25 June 1865, ASC–BPL; Helen Garrison to Ann Phillips, 24 August [1847], 22 July 1850, CBC–HL.

50. Stone to Stanton, 14 August 1853, ECSP–LC; Mott to Abby Kelley, 18 March 1839, KFP–AAS; Child to Lucy Osgood, 4 February 1869, in *Lydia Maria Child: Selected Letters, 1817–1880,* ed. Milton Meltzer and Patricia G. Holland (Amherst: University of Massachusetts Press, 1982), 485; Child to "the Advocates of Woman Suffrage in Iowa," 30 May 1870, LMCP, 73/1947; Child to Sarah Parsons, 10 February 1877, LMCP, 87/2304.

51. Child, *The History of the Condition of Women, in Various Ages and Nations* (Boston: John Allen, 1835), 266–67; Child to Louisa [Gilman] Loring, 12 December 1840, LMCP, 9/219.

52. Kelley to Foster, 14 March 1845, KFP–AAS; Sallie Holley to "Miss [Caroline?] Putnam," 22 March 1853, in Chadwick, *Life for Liberty,* 117.

53. "Mrs. Elizabeth Cady Stanton's Address at the Decade Meeting, on Marriage and Divorce," in *Report of the Proceedings of the Twentieth Anniversary and of the Reception Held at the St. James Hotel, (19 & 20 October, 1870)* (New York: Journeyman's Printers' Co-Operative, 1871), 71 (my emphasis).

54. Phillips to Garrison, 19 July 1852, ASC–BPL; Blackwell, "Objections to Woman Suffrage Answered," in the *Woman's Journal,* "Special Edition," November 1884, in the Blackwell Family Papers, Arthur and Elizabeth Schlesinger Library on the History of Women in America, Radcliffe College, Cambridge, Mass. (hereafter cited as BFP–SLRC); Blackwell, incomplete letter of protest to "Mr. President" (n.d.), BFP–SLRC. See also Henry Ward Beecher, *Women's Influence in Politics, an Address Delivered by Henry Ward Beecher at the Cooper Institute, New York, Thursday Evening, Feb. 2, 1860* (Boston: C. K. Whipple, 1870), 6. Writing in 1870, L. Maria Child was emphatic in her feelings toward nativism: "I dislike and despise this petty 'Native American' feeling." See Child to John Greenleaf Whittier, 31 July 1870, in Meltzer and Holland, *Lydia Maria Child,* 497.

55. Child to Sarah Blake [Sturgis] Shaw, 27 October 1856, LMCP, 34/952.

56. Child, preface to *The Oasis* (Boston: Benjamin C. Bacon, 1834), ix; Child to Sarah Shaw, 25 August 1877, LMCP, 88/2338; Ann Phillips to Wendell Phillips, n.d. [1874], CBC–HL; Angelina Grimké to Theodore Weld, 7 August 1853, WGP–UM; Sarah Grimké to Mary [?], 7 April 1869, WGP–UM; Kelley to Foster, 14 March 1845, KFP–AAS, (my emphasis in Kelley quote).

57. *National Anti-Slavery Standard,* 9 December 1841. Writing to Thomas Wentworth Higginson, Child later criticized the female author Gail Hamilton: "The cause of woman suffers from the flippant and conceited utterances of such writers as Gail Hamilton. She is a sample of a real female mind, as that phrase has been applied by satirists; smart, self-conscious, unaffecting and untrained. She attracts a large class of minds similar to her own in superficiality." See Child to Higginson, 24 June 1877, LMCP, 88/2328.

58. Blackwell to Stone, 13 June 1853, LSP–LC; Stone to Blackwell, 21 June 1853, LSP–LC; Blackwell to Stone, 18 March 1855, LSP–LC; Garrison to Helen Garrison, 29 July 1869,

ASC–BPL. See also R. Jackson Wilson, *Figures of Speech: American Writers and the Literary Marketplace, from Benjamin Franklin to Emily Dickinson* (New York: Knopf, 1989), 148.

59. Child to Francis George Shaw, 2 August 1846, LMCP, 23/664; Child to Anna Loring, 13–14 October 1844, in Meltzer and Holland, *Lydia Maria Child,* 213; Child to Gerrit Smith, 23 July 1864, SP–SU; Child to Theodore Tilton, 27 May 1866, LMCP, 65/1722; Blackwell to Lucy Stone, 13 October 1855, LSP–LC. See also Samuel J. May, *The Rights and Condition of Women; A Sermon Preached in Syracuse, Nov., 1845,* 3d ed., in *Woman's Rights Commensurate with Her Capacities and Obligations. A Series of Tracts, Comprising Sixteen Articles, Essays, Addresses, or Letters of the Dominant Advocates of Woman's Larger Sphere of Action* (Syracuse, N.Y.: n.p., 1853), 10.

60. Child to Samuel Joseph May, 5 January 1865, LMCP, 61/1611; Child to Francis George Shaw, 27 May 1841, LMCP, 10/233.

61. Mott to James Miller McKim, 22 July 1838, MP–FHL; Garrison to Phillips, 18 July 1846, CBC–HL.

Chapter 5. "A True Manly" Life

1. Exceptions are Blanche Glassman Hersh, who has briefly traced the background, attitudes, and behavior of several abolitionist husbands, and Donald Yacovone, who has noted abolitionist men's efforts to achieve intimacy with each other. See Hersh, "'A Partnership of Equals': Feminist Marriages in 19th-Century America," *University of Michigan Papers on Women's Studies* 2 (1977): 41–45; Hersh, *The Slavery of Sex: Feminist-Abolitionists in America* (Urbana: University of Illinois Press, 1978), chap. 7; Yacovone, "Abolitionists and the 'Language of Fraternal Love,'" in *Meanings for Manhood: Constructions of Masculinity in Victorian America,* ed. Mark C. Carnes and Clyde Griffen (Chicago: University of Chicago Press, 1990), 85–95.

2. Rotundo, *American Manhood: Transformations in Masculinity from the Revolution to the Modern Era* (New York: Basic Books, 1993), 1; Lori D. Ginzberg, *Women and the Work of Benevolence: Morality, Politics, and Class in the Nineteenth-Century United States* (New Haven: Yale University Press, 1990), 20; Grimké to Amos Phelps, 2 September 1837, Anti-Slavery Collection, Boston Public Library (hereafter cited as ASC–BPL). The first generation of scholars of the antislavery movement—some of whom were friends of certain abolitionists—were also interested in establishing the abolitionists' masculine credentials. See Lillie Buffum Chace Wyman, *American Chivalry* (Boston: W. B. Clarke, 1913), 1–31, 69–92. Bertram Wyatt-Brown, focusing on the events at the 1850 Convention of the American Anti-Slavery Society (AASS), has revealed that abolitionist men were not averse to disparaging their opponents' masculinity. In so doing they suggested that they were concerned with such attributes. See Wyatt-Brown, "The Abolitionist Controversy: Men of Blood, Men of God," in *Men, Women, and Issues in American History,* ed. Howard H. Quint and Milton Cantor, 2 vols. (Homewood, Ill.: Dorsey Press, 1975), 1:225–29.

3. E. Anthony Rotundo, "Learning about Manhood: Gender Ideals and the Middle-Class Family in Nineteenth-Century America," in *Manliness and Morality: Middle-Class Masculinity in Britain and America, 1800–1940,* ed. J. A. Mangan and James Walvin (Manchester: Manchester University Press, 1987), 37–40; Marsh, "Suburban Men and Masculine Domesticity, 1870–1915," *American Quarterly* 40 (1988): 165–86; Marsh, "From Separation to Togetherness: The Social Construction of Domestic Space in American Suburbs, 1840–1915," *Journal of American History* 76 (1989): 513–14. Abolitionist men also presaged the "Knights of the New Chivalry" described by the prominent postbellum temperance advocate Frances Willard. See Ian Tyrrell, *Woman's World/Woman's Empire: The Woman's Christian Temperance Union in International Perspective, 1880–1930* (Chapel Hill: University of

North Carolina Press, 1991), 134. See also Charles E. Rosenberg, "Sexuality, Class and Role in 19th-Century America," *American Quarterly* 25 (1973): 131–53.

4. *Report of the Proceedings of the Twentieth Anniversary and of the Reception Held at St. James' Hotel,* reprinted in *A History of the National Woman's Rights Movement, for Twenty Years, With the Proceedings of the Decade Meeting held at Apollo Hall, October 20, 1870, from 1850 to 1870, With an Appendix Containing the History of the Movement During the Winter of 1871 in the National Capital,* comp. Paulina W. Davis (New York: Journeyman's Printers' Co-Operative, 1871), 8. See also Francesca M. Cancian, *Love in America: Gender and Self-Development* (Cambridge: Cambridge University Press, 1987), 22.

5. Henry Blackwell to Lucy Stone, 13 June 1853, Lucy Stone Papers, included in the Blackwell Family Papers, Manuscript Division, Library of Congress, Washington, D.C. (hereafter cited as LSP–LC).

6. Lawrence Friedman, noting the differences between the "men of the Boston clique" and "Tappan circle stewards," has distinguished the former group's "more liberalized and appreciative perception of Woman's Sphere," from the more "recalcitrant" response of the latter. See Friedman, *Gregarious Saints: Self and Community in American Abolitionism, 1830–1870* (Cambridge: Cambridge University Press, 1982), 144. With regard to the electoral process, Lori D. Ginzberg has noted that by the 1850s "the belief in a peculiarly female form of social change—moral suasion—had lost much of its credibility, or at least its universality." See Ginzberg, *Women and the Work of Benevolence,* 215.

7. Garrison to May, 19 December 1846, in *The Letters of William Lloyd Garrison* ed. Walter M. Merrill and Louis Ruchames, 6 vols. (Cambridge: Belknap Press of Harvard University Press, 1971–81), 3:462, (hereafter cited as WLGL); Garrison to Helen Garrison, 26 July 1846, WLGL, 3:354; Garrison to Ann Phillips, 10 September 1848, Crawford-Blagden Collection of the Papers of Wendell Phillips, Houghton Library, Harvard University, Cambridge, Mass. (hereafter cited as CBC–HL); Child to Sarah Parsons, 10 February 1877, in *The Collected Correspondence of Lydia Maria Child,* ed. Patricia G. Holland and Milton Meltzer (Millwood, N.Y.: Kraus Microform, 1979, microfiche), Card 87/Item 2304 (hereafter cited as LMCP).

8. Coontz, *The Social Origins of Private Life: A History of American Families, 1600–1900* (London: Verso, 1988), 181–82. See also David Pugh, *Sons of Liberty: The Masculine Mind in Nineteenth-Century America* (Westport, Conn.: Greenwood, 1983), 3; Peter Stearns, *Be A Man! Males in Modern Society* (New York: Holmes and Meier, 1979), 83, 209.

9. *Liberator,* 24 January 1851; Abzug, *Passionate Liberator: Theodore Dwight Weld and the Dilemma of Reform* (New York: Oxford University Press, 1980), 168; Emerson, as quoted in *American Transcendentalism, 1830–1860: An Intellectual Inquiry,* by Paul F. Boller Jr. (New York: Putnam, 1974), 90. On the prevalence of the imagery of individualistic frontiersmen and explorers, see Mark Carnes, introduction to *Meanings for Manhood,* ed. Carnes and Griffen 2; E. Anthony Rotundo, "Body and Soul: Changing Ideals of American Middle-Class Manhood, 1770–1920," *Journal of Social History* 16 (1983): 26; Richard Slotkin, *Regeneration Through Violence: The Mythology of the American Frontier, 1600–1860* (Middletown, Conn.: Wesleyan University Press, 1973), 21.

10. Thomson, *Great Auction Sale of Slaves, at Savannah, Georgia, March 2d and 3d, 1859. Reported for the Tribune* (New York: American Anti-Slavery Society, 1859), 4; Weld to Anne Warren Weston, 23 March 1836, ASC–BPL; Carroll Smith-Rosenberg, "Davy Crockett as Trickster: Pornography, Liminality, and Symbolic Inversion in Victorian America," in Smith-Rosenberg, *Disorderly Conduct: Visions of Gender in Victorian America* (New York: Oxford University Press, 1985), 91–98; Child to Eliza Scudder, 6 February 1870, LMCP, 71/1926. See also Abzug, *Passionate Liberator,* 124; Stearns, *Be A Man!* 51–52.

11. Weld to Grimké, 2 May 1838, in *Letters of Theodore Dwight Weld, Angelina Grimké Weld, and Sarah Grimké 1822–1844,* ed. Gilbert H. Barnes and Dwight L. Dumond, 2 vols. (1934; reprint, New York: Da Capo, 1970), 2:659 (hereafter cited as WGL).

12. Rotundo, *American Manhood,* 135; Blackwell to Lucy Stone, 27 February 1855, 16 January 1856, 12 May 1856, LSP–LC; Leslie Wheeler, ed., *Loving Warriors: Selected Letters of Lucy Stone and Henry B. Blackwell, 1853–1893* (New York: Dial, 1981), 169; Kelley to Samuel May, 15 September 1853, ASC–BPL. Garrisonians found their strongest support in New England, but they worked to promote their brand of antislavery in the West. See Douglas A. Gamble, "Garrisonian Abolitionists in the West: Some Suggestions for Study," *Civil War History* 23 (1977): 58–59.

13. For examples of male abolitionists referring to each other as "brother," see Henry B. Stanton to Theodore Weld, 4 August 1832, WGL, 1:87; Elizur Wright to Weld, 5 September 1833, 2 November 1833, WGL, 1:114, 119; Weld to Lewis Tappan, 18 March 1834, WGL, 1:132; Lewis Tappan to Weld, 10 July 1834, WGL, 1:153.

14. Anthony Rotundo, "Romantic Friendship: Male Intimacy and Middle-Class Youth in the Northern United States, 1800–1900," *Journal of Social History* 23 (1989): 1–21. See also Friedman, *Gregarious Saints,* 137–40.

15. Stuart to Weld, 2 November 1845, 17 April 1853, 11 April 1846, Weld-Grimké Papers, William L. Clements Library, University of Michigan, Ann Arbor (hereafter cited as WGP–UM). Weld's most recent biographer, Robert H. Abzug, has noted that "in all but the sexual sense, Theodore and Charles became lovers." An earlier biographer of Weld, Benjamin P. Thomas, remarked that Stuart "was as tender-hearted as a woman." See Abzug, *Passionate Liberator,* 31; Thomas, *Theodore Weld: Crusader for Freedom* (New Brunswick, N.J.: Rutgers University Press, 1950), 17.

16. Weld to Grimké, December 28, 1837, WGL, 1:509.

17. Yacovone, "'Language of Fraternal Love,'" 94; Barker, *Captain Charles Stuart, Anglo-American Abolitionist* (Baton Rouge: Louisiana State University Press, 1986), 35; Weld to Grimké, 16 February 1838, 28 December 1837, WGL, 2:557, 509; Grimké to Weld, 21 January 1838, WGL, 2:520.

18. Yacovone, "'Language of Fraternal Love,'" 91–92; Abzug, *Passionate Liberator,* 168–69.

19. Barker, *Charles Stuart,* 152.

20. Rotundo, "Romantic Friendship," 14–18 (quotation on 14); Weld to Grimké, 18 February 1838, WGL, 2:562. Whilst he quoted an excerpt of that letter from Weld to Grimké ("wept on his neck from *very love to him*") Lawrence Friedman did not emphasize the second part of the longer quotation I have used. Friedman, of course, was more interested in contrasting abolitionist fraternity with abolitionist sorority. Nonetheless, Weld's determination to prove to Grimké that his love for her filled a gap that his relationship with Stuart could not fulfill was also significant. See Friedman, *Gregarious Saints,* 139. See also Abzug, *Passionate Liberator,* 190; Weld to Angelina Grimké, 1 March 1838, WGL, 2:581–83; Barker, *Charles Stuart,* 252–53, 264–66, 283–87, 295–98.

21. Trollope, *Domestic Manners of the Americans* (1832; reprint, Gloucester: Alan Sutton, 1984), 110; Garrison to Helen E. Benson, 12 April 1834, WLGL, 1:316; Garrison to Helen Garrison, 9 November 1835, ASC–BPL.

22. Garrison to Elizabeth Pease, 15 May 1842, WLGL, 3:76; Friedman, *Gregarious Saints,* 49–50, 71–75; Garrison to Chapman, 19 July 1848, WLGL, 3:367; Garrison to Ann Phillips, 1 January 1854, CBC–HL. Note also Garrison's letters to Rogers, which he signed "Yours Lovingly." See Garrison to Rogers, 21 May 1839, 24 April 1840, WLGL, 1:461, 589. See also

Walter Merrill, *Against Wind and Tide: A Biography of Wm. Lloyd Garrison* (Cambridge: Harvard University Press, 1963), 169.

23. See Mark C. Carnes, *Secret Ritual and Manhood in Victorian America* (New Haven: Yale University Press, 1989), 79; Mary Ann Clawson, *Constructing Brotherhood: Class, Gender and Fraternalism* (Princeton: Princeton University Press, 1989), 178–79; Rotundo, *American Manhood,* 200–202.

24. Child to Maria Weston Chapman, 12 December 1842, 11 January 1843, 18 June 1843, 4 September 1843, 15 September 1843, ASC–BPL.

25. Friedman, *Gregarious Saints,* 59–62.

26. See Marilyn Motz, *True Sisterhood: Michigan Women and Their Kin, 1820–1920* (Albany: State University of New York Press, 1983), 21; Joe Dubbert, *A Man's Place* (Englewood Cliffs, N.J.: Prentice-Hall, 1979), 20–21. On the values deemed desirable in men, and in marriage, see Michael Gordon, "The Ideal Husband as Depicted in the Nineteenth-Century Marriage Manual," in *The American Man,* ed. Elizabeth Pleck and Joseph Pleck (Englewood Cliffs, N.J.: Prentice-Hall, 1980), 150–56.

27. Stanton to Phelps, 17 April 1840, ASC–BPL; Stanton to Smith, 17 April 1840, 10 May 1840, Gerrit Smith Papers, Syracuse University Library, Department of Special Collections, Syracuse, N.Y.; Stanton to Elizabeth Cady Stanton, n.d. [autumn 1843], Elizabeth Cady Stanton Papers, Manuscript Division, Library of Congress, Washington, D.C. (hereafter cited as ECSP—LC). There is historiographical debate regarding the extent to which women replaced their family of origin with a family of procreation. See Carl Degler, *At Odds: Women and the Family in America from the Revolution to the Present* (New York: Oxford University Press, 1980), 106–9; Motz, *True Sisterhood,* 5.

28. Stearns, *Be a Man!* 9.

29. Foster to Kelley, 10 August 1843, Abby Kelley Foster Papers, American Antiquarian Society, Worcester, Mass. (hereafter cited as KFP—AAS). See also Joel Bernard, "Authority, Autonomy, and Radical Commitment: Stephen and Abby Kelley Foster," *Proceedings of the American Antiquarian Society* 90 (1980): 348–49.

30. Blackwell to Stone, 2 May 1854, 12 July 1854, LSP–LC; Foster to Abby Kelley, 10 August 1843, KFP–AAS; Blackwell to Stone, 2 July 1853, LSP–LC.

31. Wendell Phillips to Ann Phillips, 1 April 1867, 5 March 1873, CBC–HL.

32. Garrison to Helen Garrison, 31 May 1871, ASC–BPL; Abzug, *Passionate Liberator,* 225–28 (quotation on 228). See also Charles C. Burleigh to Lucretia Mott, 4 July 1841, ASC–BPL; Wendell Phillips to Ann Phillips, 1 April 1867, CBC–HL; David Lee Child to L. Maria Child, 17 March 1859, LMCP, 40/1104.

33. John L. Thomas, *The Liberator: William Lloyd Garrison* (Boston: Little, Brown, 1963), 19; James B. Stewart, *William Lloyd Garrison and the Challenge of Emancipation* (Arlington Heights, Ill.: Harlan Davidson, 1992), 3.

34. Foster to Kelley, 17 August 1851, Abigail Kelley Foster Correspondence, Worcester Historical Museum, Worcester, Mass. (hereafter cited as KFC—WHM); Stephen Foster to Lysander Spooner, 8 January 1859, ASC–BPL. See also Angelina Grimké and Sarah Grimké to Jane Smith, 6 December 1849, WGP–UM; Weld to Garrison, 28 April 1863, ASC–BPL; James Mott to Phebe Post Willis, 23 April 1834, Lucretia Mott Papers, Friends Historical Library, Swarthmore College, Swarthmore, Pa. (hereafter cited as MP–FHL).

35. *National Anti-Slavery Standard,* 1 December 1866; quote from *Walker's Appeal* in James O. Horton and Lois E. Horton, "Violence, Protest, and Identity: Black Manhood in Antebellum America," in James O. Horton, *Free People of Color: Inside the African-American*

Community (Washington, D.C.: Smithsonian Institution Press, 1993), 83; Leverenz, *Manhood and the American Renaissance* (Ithaca: Cornell University Press, 1989), 108–20; Horton and Horton, "The Affirmation of Manhood: Black Garrisonians in Antebellum Boston," in *Courage and Conscience: Black and White Abolitionists in Boston,* ed. Donald M. Jacobs (Bloomington: Indiana University Press, 1993), 127–53.

36. Bibb, *Narrative of the Life and Adventures of Henry Bibb, An American Slave, Written by Himself* (1850; reprint, New York: Negro Universities Press, 1969), 2, 35, 83, 105, 177–78; Loguen, *The Rev. J. W. Loguen, as A Slave and As a Freeman. A Narrative of a Real Life* (1859; reprint, New York: Negro Universities Press, 1968), 33, 41. See also Willie Lee Rose, *Slavery and Freedom* (New York: Oxford University Press, 1982), 29; Donald C. Matthews, "The Abolitionists on Slavery: The Critique Behind the Social Movement," *Journal of Southern History* 33 (1967): 177.

37. F. H. Green, "The Slave Wife," *National Anti-Slavery Standard,* 4 June 1846. See also John Thompson, *The Life of John Thompson. A Fugitive Slave. Containing the History of 25 Years in Bondage, and His Providential Escape* (1856; reprint, New York: Negro Universities Press, 1968), 30–31.

38. Stewart, "An Address Delivered At The African Masonic Hall," Boston, 17 February 1833, in *Maria Stewart, America's First Black Woman Political Writer,* ed. Marilyn Richardson (Bloomington: Indiana University Press, 1987), 59–60.

39. "Particular Instructions to AASS Lecturers," in the Maloney Collection of McKim-Garrison Papers, Rare Books and Manuscript Division, New York Public Library, New York City (hereafter cited as MGP–NYPL).

40. Cott, "Eighteenth-Century Family and Social Life Revealed in Massachusetts Divorce Records," *Journal of Social History* 10 (1976): 30; Jennings, *The Married Lady's Companion, or Poor Man's Friend* (1808) in *Roots of Bitterness: Documents of the Social History of American Women,* ed. Nancy Cott (New York: Dutton, 1972), 115. On "Masculine Achievers," see Rotundo, "Learning about Manhood," 36–37.

41. Blackwell to Lucy Stone, 25 April 1858, in Wheeler, *Loving Warriors,* 179–80; Blackwell to Stone, 24 August 1853, LSP–LC. See also Lawrence Goodheart, *Abolitionist, Actuary, Atheist: Elizur Wright and the Reform Impulse* (Kent, Ohio: Kent State University Press, 1990), 118.

42. See, for example, James Mott to Adam and Ann Mott, 23 February 1811, 20 July 1811, 1 October 1811, in Hallowell, *James and Lucretia Mott,* 42–43, 44.

43. Mott, *Brief Hints to Parents, on the Subject of Education* (Philadelphia: n.p., 1824); Stanton to Mott, n.d. [1848], ASC–BPL; Abzug, *Passionate Liberator,* 283–85. See also James Mott to Sydney Howard Gay, 22 July 1847, Sydney Howard Gay Papers, Rare Books and Manuscript Library, Columbia University, New York City (hereafter cited as SHGP–CU).

44. Theodore Weld to Charles Stuart Weld and Theodore Grimké Weld, n.d. [August 1851], WGP–UM. See also Henry Blackwell to Lucy Stone, 12 July 1854, LSP–LC; Richard O. Curry and Lawrence B. Goodheart, " 'Knives in Their Heads': Passionate Self-Analysis and the Search for Identity in American Abolitionism," *Canadian Review of American Studies* 14 (1983): 405.

45. See Abzug, *Passionate Liberator,* 259–60. In practice, the Weld-Grimké schools proved a constant drain on the family's finances.

46. Blackwell to Lucy Stone, 11 February 1857, 24 August 1853, [November–December 1856], LSP–LC. See also Dorothy Sterling, *Ahead of Her Time: Abby Kelley and the Politics of Antislavery* (New York: Norton, 1991), 242.

47. James Mott to Anne Mott, 2 February 1820, in Hallowell, *James and Lucretia Mott,* 72.

48. See Ginzberg, *Women and the Work of Benevolence,* 25.

49. Carolyn L. Karcher, *The First Woman in the Republic: A Cultural Biography of Lydia Maria Child* (Durham, N.C.: Duke University Press, 1994), 242; Otelia Cromwell, *Lucretia Mott* (1958; reprint, New York: Russell and Russell, 1971), 45.

50. Garrison to George W. Benson, 17 December 1847, WLGL, 3:539; Garrison to Wendell Phillips Garrison, 10 September 1868, ASC–BPL. See also Thomas, *William Lloyd Garrison,* 91.

51. Stanton to Phelps, 4 January 1840 [incorrectly dated 1839], 17 April 1840, 11 April 1840, [April 1840], ASC–BPL. See also Stanton to John Greenleaf Whittier, 18 April 1840, G. W. Pickard Papers, Houghton Library, Harvard University, Cambridge, Mass. On Judge Cady's opposition to Elizabeth's plans to marry Stanton, see Alma Lutz, *Created Equal: A Biography of Elizabeth Cady Stanton 1815–1902* (New York: John Day, 1940), 20.

52. Lutz, *Created Equal,* 40. It should be noted that even better-off male abolitionists were prepared to take advantage of the largesse of their parents-in-law. Wendell and Ann Phillips's home was an inheritance from Ann's father. See James B. Stewart, *Wendell Phillips: Liberty's Hero* (Baton Rouge: Louisiana State University Press, 1986) 83.

53. Henry Stanton to Elizabeth Cady Stanton, n.d. [Autumn 1843], 20 February 1851, ECSP–LC.

54. Hopper, "Tales of Oppression," in the *National Anti-Slavery Standard,* 5 November 1840; Grimké, *An Epistle to the Clergy of the Southern States* (New York: n.p., 1836), 13.

55. Friedman, *Gregarious Saints,* 50–54 (quotation on 50). See also 100–102 for a description of Gerrit Smith's role in maintaining harmony within the group described by Friedman as the "voluntarists of the burned-over-district."

56. Kelley to Stephen Foster, 13 August 1843, KFP–AAS; Kelley to Samuel May, 9 November 1853, ASC–BPL.

57. See Child's diary entries, reprinted in *Lydia Maria Child: Selected Letters, 1817–1880,* ed. Milton Meltzer and Patricia G. Holland (Amherst: University of Massachusetts Press, 1982), 5. See also Robert Abzug, *Cosmos Crumbling: American Reform and the Religious Imagination* (New York: Oxford University Press, 1994), 196.

58. *National Anti-Slavery Standard,* 16 February 1843; *Liberator,* 26 April 1839; Garrison to Hannah Webb, 1 March 1842, WLGL, 3:129; Child to Sumner, 17 June 1860, LMCP, 45/1227.

59. Rotundo, *American Manhood,* 135; Andrea Moore Kerr, *Lucy Stone: Speaking Out for Equality* (New Brunswick, N.J.: Rutgers University Press, 1992), 143; Elinor Rice Hays, *Those Extraordinary Blackwells: The Story of a Journey to a Better World* (New York: Harcourt, Brace and World, 1967), 126; Blackwell to Stone, n.d. [summer 1855], in Wheeler, *Loving Warriors,* 144.

60. Blackwell to Stone, 7 February 1856, LSP–LC; Stone to Blackwell, 9 August [1864], in Wheeler, *Loving Warriors,* 198.

61. Kelley to Stephen Foster, 2 February 1845, KFP–AAS; Kelley to Chapman, 18 February 1846, ASC–BPL; Kelley to Chapman, 17 July 1845, ASC–BPL; Kelley to Gay, 11 November 1845, SHGP–CU.

62. Foster to Kelley, [August 1851], KFC–WHM; Bernard, "Authority, Autonomy, and Radical Commitment," 373–75; Foster to Phillips, [24 July 1857], CBC–HL.

63. Blackwell to Lucy Stone, 3 January 1854, LSP–LC; Parker, *A Sermon on the Public Function of Woman, Preached at the Music Hall, March 27, 1853* (Boston: Robert F. Wallcut, 1853), 5; May, *The Rights and Condition of Women; A Sermon Preached in Syracuse, Nov., 1845,* 3d ed.

reprinted in *Woman's Rights Commensurate with Her Capacities and Obligations. A Series of Tracts, Comprising Sixteen Articles, Essays, Addresses, or Letters of the Dominant Advocates of Woman's Larger Sphere of Action* (Syracuse, N.Y.: n.p., 1853), 3–4.

64. Sarah Grimké and Angelina Grimké to Henry Clarke Wright, 27 August 1837, ASC–BPL; Wright to Kelley, 25 February 1839, KFP–AAS; Stearns, *Jealousy: The Evolution of an Emotion in American History* (New York: Oxford University Press, 1989), 23; Lewis Perry, *Childhood, Marriage, and Reform: Henry Clarke Wright, 1797–1870* (Chicago: University of Chicago Press, 1980), 183. See also *Liberator*, 6 March 1840; Theodore Weld to Lewis Tappan, 23 January 1843, WGL, 2:966; Theodore Weld to Angelina Grimké, 9 May 1838, WGL, 2:673; Lewis Perry, *Radical Abolitionism: Anarchy and the Government of God in Antislavery Thought* (Ithaca: Cornell University Press, 1973), 52; Abzug, *Passionate Liberator*, 180–84, 199; Alma Lutz, *Crusade for Freedom: Women of the Antislavery Movement* (Boston: Beacon, 1968), 121; Gerda Lerner, *The Grimké Sisters from South Carolina: Pioneers for Woman's Rights and Abolition* (1967; reprint, New York: Schocken Books, 1971), 176–78.

65. See William S. McFeely, *Frederick Douglass* (New York: Norton, 1991), 156; Douglass, "Let Woman Take Her Rights," An Address Delivered in Worcester, Mass., on 24 October 1850, in *The Frederick Douglass Papers. Series One: Speeches, Debates, and Interviews*, vol. 2: *1847–54*, ed. John W. Blassingame (New Haven: Yale University Press, 1982), 249.

66. McFeely, *Frederick Douglass*, 154; Rosetta Douglass, as quoted in *We Are Your Sisters: Black Women in the Nineteenth Century*, ed. Dorothy Sterling (New York: Norton, 1984), 134. See also James O. Horton, "Freedom's Yoke: Gender Conventions Amongst Antebellum Free Blacks," *Feminist Studies* 12 (1986): 66, 71; Philip S. Foner, ed., *Frederick Douglass on Women's Rights* (1976; reprint, New York: Da Capo, 1992).

67. *Liberator*, 15 December 1837; statement by Garrison, 4 October 1846, MGP–NYPL.

68. Garrison to Henry Ward Beecher, 10 May 1870, ASC–BPL; Stone to Frank Garrison, [March] 1889, ASC–BPL. See also Louis Filler, *The Crusade Against Slavery, 1830–1861* (1960; reprint, New York: Harper and Row, 1963), 129; Thomas, *William Lloyd Garrison*, 372.

69. Garrison to Pease, 6 November 1837, in *British and American Abolitionists: An Episode in Transatlantic Understanding*, ed. Clare Taylor (Edinburgh: Edinburgh University Press, 1974), 62; Garrison to May, 15 September 1834, ASC–BPL; Garrison to George W. Benson, 4 September 1835, ASC–BPL.

70. Garrison to the Editor of the Boston *Courier*, 16 December 1828, WLGL, 1:71; *Liberator*, 6 September 1834; Garrison to Lucretia Mott, 28 April 1840, in Hallowell, *James and Lucretia Mott*, 139.

71. Blackwell to Lucy Stone, 7 October 1853, LSP–LC; Blackwell to Stone, 9 September 1853, LSP–LC.

72. *National Reformer*, December 1838, 59, as quoted in Margot Melia, "The Role of Black Garrisonian Women in Antislavery and Other Reforms in the Antebellum North, 1830–1865" (Ph.D. diss., University of Western Australia, 1991), 321; Bibb, *Narrative of the Life and Adventures*, 34.

73. Friedman, *Gregarious Saints*, 141–42, 149; Garrison to McKim, 31 December 1866, MGP–NYPL; Garrison to Wendell Phillips Garrison, 17 October 1869, ASC–BPL; Garrison, *Helen Eliza Garrison: A Memorial* (Cambridge, Mass.: Riverside, 1876), 5, 25–26.

74. Garrison to Dr. John Browning, 1840, Alma Lutz Collection, Arthur and Elizabeth Schlesinger Library on the History of Women in America, Radcliffe College, Cambridge, Mass. With reference to Garrison's actions in London, Elizabeth Cady Stanton later admitted: "At that time I did not fully appreciate the sacrifice he made." The more she considered his actions there, however, the greater her respect for him. With characteristic immodesty,

Garrison claimed in a letter to his wife that if he had arrived in London earlier "we would have carried our point triumphantly." See Stanton to Elizabeth Pease, 12 February 1842, ASC–BPL; Garrison to Helen Garrison, 29 June 1840, in Taylor, *British and American Abolitionists,* 92.

75. Mott to Maria Weston Chapman, 29 July 1840, ASC–BPL. See also Donald R. Kennon, " 'An Apple of Discord'? The Woman Question at the World's Anti-Slavery Convention of 1840," *Slavery and Abolition: A Journal of Comparative Studies* 5 (1984): 260; Kathryn Kish Sklar, " 'Women Who Speak for an Entire Nation': American and British Women Compared at the World Anti-Slavery Convention, London, 1840," *Pacific Historical Review* 59 (1990): 467–68; George Lowell Austin, *The Life and Times of Wendell Phillips* (1884; reprint, New York: Afro American Press, 1969), 101, 151; Douglas H. Maynard, "The World's Anti-Slavery Convention of 1840," *Mississippi Valley Historical Review* 67 (1960): 459–60; Ira V. Brown, *Mary Grew: Abolitionist and Feminist, 1813–1896* (Selinsgrove, Pa.: Susquehanna University Press, 1991), 27, 29.

76. Wendell Phillips Garrison and Francis Jackson Garrison, *William Lloyd Garrison, 1805–1879: The Story of His Life Told by His Children,* 4 vols. (New York: Century, 1885), 2:83; William L. Garrison to Helen E. Garrison, 29 June 1840, WLGL, 2:655; Stanton, *Eighty Years and More: Reminiscences, 1815–1897* (1898; reprint, New York: Schocken Books, 1971), 79; Elizabeth Cady Stanton, Susan B. Anthony, Matilda Joslyn Gage, et al., *History of Woman Suffrage,* 6 vols. (1889–1922; reprint, New York: Source Book, 1970), 1:61 (hereafter cited as HWS). See also *Report of the Proceedings of the Twentieth Anniversary,* in Davis, *History of the National Woman's Rights Movement,* 12; Lutz, *Created Equal,* 28–29. Reports of Henry Stanton's denials can be found in the *Liberator,* 4 December 1840 and the *National Anti-Slavery Standard,* 22 October 1840. James Gillespie Birney explained to Lewis Tappan that Stanton had denied reports that he had voted in "favor of the admission of the women as delegates to the Conference." Stanton also suggested that it was Wendell Phillips who claimed that he [Stanton] had voted on the women's behalf. See James Gillespie Birney to Lewis Tappan, 29 August 1840, in *Letters of James Gillespie Birney, 1831–1857,* ed. Dwight L. Dumond, 2 vols. (New York: D. Appleton-Century, 1938), 2:596. It was ironical that Henry Stanton unwittingly played a role in determining the course of Angelina Grimké's public abolitionism. Gerda Lerner has pointed out that "half in jest," Stanton suggested that Grimké address the legislative committee of the Massachusetts State Legislature "on behalf of the anti-slavery petitions presented by women." Stanton, according to Lerner, was astonished when Grimké decided to do so. Dwight Dumond has offered a different interpretation of those events. As well as claiming that Stanton (along with Weld) "steadfastly encouraged Angelina during the first trying months of her agency," he also asserted that Stanton "insisted that she should appear before the legislative committee on petitions and other antislavery activities." Dumond's revisionist account of the antislavery movement, like that of Gilbert H. Barnes before him, generally sought to establish and affirm the importance of the non-Garrisonian abolitionists, and it seems that general ideological framework shaped his interpretation of the events just described. See Lerner, *The Grimké Sisters,* 218; Dumond, *Antislavery: The Crusade for Freedom in America* (Ann Arbor: University of Michigan Press, 1961), 196.

77. Stanton, *Eighty Years,* 104; Elisabeth Griffith, *In Her Own Right: The Life of Elizabeth Cady Stanton* (New York: Oxford University Press, 1984), 39–40.

78. Hersh, *Slavery of Sex,* 97. Note Stanton's comments to Elizabeth Neall Gay. "Are you among those who rejoice at the success of the 'liberty party'[?] I do very much. . . . Slavery is a political question created and sustained by laws & must be put down by law." Claiming "the right to look at" William L. Garrison's "actions & opinions with the same freedom & impartiality that I do of every other man," Stanton remarked to Elizabeth Pease that she was "not fully converted to the doctrine of no human government." Noting that she was "in

favor of political action & the organization of a third party as the most efficient way of calling forth & directing action," Stanton also asserted that "many of the Garrison party are in favor of political action, but not of the third party." See Stanton to Gay, 26 November 18[??], SHGP–CU; Stanton to Pease, 12 February 1842, ASC–BPL. See also Ginzberg, *Women and the Work of Benevolence,* 89–90. For evidence of Stanton's support of the Garrisonians, see Wendell Phillips to Ann Phillips, n.d. [1859], CBC–HL.

79. Henry Stanton to Elizabeth Cady Stanton, 15 February 1851, ECSP–LC; Lutz, *Created Equal,* 66; Blackwell to Lucy Stone, 7 February 1856, LSP–LC; Gerrit Smith to Stanton, 6 January 1856, ECSP–LC. On Stanton's refusal to attend the Seneca Falls convention, see Judith Wellman, "The Seneca Falls Women's Rights Convention: A Case Study of Social Networks," in *Women's America: Refocusing the Past,* ed. Linda K. Kerber and Jane Sherron De Hart, 4th ed. (New York: Oxford University Press, 1995), 207. For varying interpretations of Henry Stanton's response to women's attempts to improve their lot, see Arthur H. Rice, "Henry B. Stanton as a Political Abolitionist" (Ed.D. diss., Columbia University, 1968), 143; Donald R. Kennon, "'A Knit of Identity': Marriage and Reform in Mid-Victorian America" (Ph.D. diss., University of Maryland, 1981), 31; Lutz, *Created Equal,* 46; Andrew Sinclair, *The Better Half: The Emancipation of the American Woman* (1965; reprint, New York: Harper and Row, 1966), 61. For Henry Blackwell's support of the Bloomer costume, see also *Proceedings of the National Women's Rights Convention, Held at Cleveland, Ohio, on Wednesday, Thursday, and Friday, October 5th, 6th, and 7th, 1853* (Cleveland: Gray, Beardsley, Spear, 1854), 49–50; Henry Blackwell to Lucy Stone, 7 February 1856, in Wheeler, *Loving Warriors,* 156.

80. James Mott to Adam Mott and Anne Mott, 18 June 1840, in Hallowell, *James and Lucretia Mott,* 73–74; HWS, 1:69; *Report of the Proceedings of the Twentieth Anniversary,* in Davis, *History of the National Woman's Rights Movement,* 8. See also *Proceedings of the Woman's Rights Convention, Held at the Unitarian Church, Rochester, N.Y., August 2, 1848, To Consider the Rights of Women, Politically, Religiously and Industrially. Revised by Mrs. Amy Post* (New York: Robert J. Johnston, 1870), 3.

81. Hundley, *Social Relations in Our Southern States* (New York: Henry B. Price, 1860). 7. See also Peter Filene, *Him/Her/Self: Sex Roles in Modern America* (New York: Harcourt Brace Jovanovich, 1974), 104.

82. See the letter from the Church Committee of Dartmouth College to Stephen Foster, 4 October 1841, KFP–AAS; E. D. Sanborn to Stephen Foster, 7 April 1842, KFP–AAS.

83. Bertram Wyatt-Brown, *Southern Honor: Ethics and Behavior in the Old South* (New York: Oxford University Press, 1982), 294–98 ("natural impulse" quotation on 295); Charles E. Rosenberg, "Sexuality, Class and Role in 19th-Century America," *American Quarterly* 25 (1973): 139. See also Dubbert, *Man's Place,* 41–44; Catherine Clinton, *The Plantation Mistress: Woman's World in the Old South* (New York: Pantheon Books, 1982), 72; Steven M. Stowe, *Intimacy and Power in the Old South: Ritual in the Lives of the Planters* (Baltimore: Johns Hopkins University Press, 1987), 81–82.

84. Kellogg, as quoted in *Primers for Prudery: Sexual Advice to Victorian America,* ed. Ronald Walters (Englewood Cliffs, N.J.: Prentice-Hall, 1974), 39; *Liberator,* 16 January 1846; Tappan, *The Life of Arthur Tappan* (New York: Hurd and Houghton, 1870), 121, as quoted in "The Erotic South: Civilization and Sexuality in American Abolitionism," by Ronald Walters, *American Quarterly* 25 (1973): 195; an undated quote by Weld and Grimké, as quoted in Lerner, *The Grimké Sisters,* 347; Abzug, *Passionate Liberator,* 283. On the warnings against the alleged dangers of masturbation, see Ben Barker-Benfield, "The Spermatic Economy: A Nineteenth Century View of Sexuality," *Feminist Studies* 1 (1972): 48–49. James Brewer Stewart has depicted Wendell Phillips as "the picture of masculine vitality—extremely handsome, popular, a vigorous boxer and wrestler." See Stewart, "Heroes, Vil-

lains, Liberty, and License: The Abolitionist Vision of Wendell Phillips," in *Antislavery Reconsidered: New Perspectives on the Abolitionists,* ed. Lewis Perry and Michael Fellman (Baton Rouge: Louisiana State University Press, 1979), 180. On the connections between masculinity and sport, see Eric Dunning, "Sport as a Male Preserve: Notes on the Social Sources of Masculine Identity and its Transformations," in *Quest for Excitement: Sport and Leisure in the Civilizing Process,* ed. Dunning and Norbert Elias (New York: B. Blackwell, 1986), 267–83; Steven A. Riess, "Sport and the Redefinition of American Middle-class Masculinity," *International Journal of the History of Sport* 8 (1991): 5–27.

85. Garnet, "Address to the Slaves of the United States of America," 16 August 1843, in *The Black Abolitionist Papers,* vol. 3: *The United States, 1830–1846,* ed. C. Peter Ripley (Chapel Hill: University of North Carolina Press, 1991), 408–10; *North Star,* 26 January 1849. See also Jane H. Pease and William H. Pease, *They Who Would Be Free: Blacks' Search for Freedom, 1830–1861* (New York: Atheneum, 1974), chap. 11; Howard H. Bell, "National Negro Conventions of the Middle 1840s: Moral Suasion vs. Political Action," *Journal of Negro History* 42 (1957): 251–56.

86. See the proceedings of the "Anti-Slavery Convention at Valley Falls, R.I.," *Liberator,* 27 September 1850. See also Carleton Mabee, *Black Freedom: The Nonviolent Abolitionists from 1830 Through the Civil War* (London: Macmillan, 1970), 295, 318; Ronald Walters, *The Antislavery Appeal: American Abolitionism After 1830* (Baltimore: Johns Hopkins University Press, 1976), 32. John Demos has overstated the shift in abolitionist sensibilities when he argued that the "decline of non-violent abolitionism in the 1850s was nothing short of a total collapse." See Demos, "The Antislavery Movement and the Problem of Violent 'Means,'" *New England Quarterly* 37 (1964): 522.

87. Michael Fellman, "Rehearsal for Civil War: Antislavery and Proslavery at the Fighting Point in Kansas, 1854–1856," in Perry and Fellman, *Antislavery Reconsidered,* 297–98; Child to J. Peter Lesley, 1 January 1855, LMCP, 31/877; Child, "To the Women of Kansas," *National Anti-Slavery Standard,* 2 January 1857; Child to Sarah Shaw, 9 November 1856, LMCP, 34/956.

88. "Of the male sex who attend these [women's rights] Conventions," they noted, "for the purpose of taking a part in them, the majority are hen-pecked husbands, and all of them ought to wear petticoats." See the *New York Herald,* 12 September 1852, in HWS, 1:854.

89. Probably referring to William L. Garrison, the author continued by suggesting that Phillips's "co-laborer in the cause might perhaps sell a file of old newspapers to aid in the firing of the Capitol, but would scarcely march upon a war of invasion. Men who hold the great bonds of society, the honor of the country, and the lives of other people so very 'cheap,' have always been, according to our observations, particularly economical of their own carcasses." See the Baltimore *Patriot,* reprinted in the *Liberator,* 2 June 1854. See also *Right and Wrong in Boston. Report of the Boston Female Anti-Slavery Society; With a Concise Statements of Events Previous and Subsequent to the Annual Meeting of 1835* (Boston: Boston Female Anti-Slavery Society, 1836), 12; *Liberator,* 9 May 1851; Louis Filler, "Nonviolence and Abolition," *University Review* 30 (1964): 174.

90. Fellman, "Theodore Parker and the Abolitionist Role in the 1850s," *Journal of American History* 61 (1974): 672–76. See also George Fredrickson, *The Inner Civil War: Northern Intellectuals and the Crisis of the Union* (New York: Harper Torchbooks, 1965), 36; Tilden G. Edelstein, *Strange Enthusiasm: A Life of Thomas Wentworth Higginson* (New Haven: Yale University Press, 1968), 117–18.

91. Mott's comments to the "Twenty-Fourth Annual Meeting of the Pennsylvania Anti-Slavery Society, October 25–26, 1860," in the *National Anti-Slavery Standard,* 3 November 1860. See also L. Maria Child to John Brown, 26 October 1859, LMCP, 41/1123; William L. Garrison to Oliver Johnson, 1 November 1859, WLGL, 4:661; Fredrickson, *Inner Civil War,* 41.

92. Wyatt-Brown, *Yankee Saints and Southern Sinners* (Baton Rouge: Louisiana State University Press, 1985), 124; Phillips, as quoted by David B. Davis in *Slavery and Human Progress* (New York: Oxford University Press, 1984), 265; *Liberator,* 3 February 1860; Foster, *Revolution the Only Remedy for Slavery* (New York: American Anti-Slavery Society, 1855), 16; *Liberator,* 19 January 1859; Foster to Lysander Spooner, 8 January 1859, ASC–BPL. Garrison noted that "John Brown executed will do more for our good cause, incomparably, than John Brown pardoned." Note also Garrison's comments on the evening of Brown's hanging (2 December 1859): "I thank God when men who believe in the right and duty of wielding carnal weapons, are so far advanced that they will take those weapons out of the scale of despotism, and throw them into the scale of freedom." See Garrison to "An Unknown Correspondent," 18 December 1859, WLGL, 4:665; Garrison's comments in Garrison and Garrison, *William Lloyd Garrison,* 2:491–92. On the wider response to Brown's conviction and execution, see Fredrickson, *Inner Civil War,* 38–48.

93. Child to Shaw, 3 August 1856, LMCP, 33/933; Child, *The Right Way the Safe Way, Proved by Emancipation in the British West Indies, and Elsewhere* (1860; reprint, New York: Arno, 1969), 96; *Liberator,* 13 February 1857.

94. Stewart, *Liberty's Hero,* 214–15, 104–5, 184; Stewart, "Heroes, Villains, Liberty, and License," 187–88; Phillips, *Speech of Wendell Phillips, Esq. at the Worcester Disunion Convention, January 15, 1857* (Boston: American Anti-Slavery Society, 1857), 13; Phillips, "Crispus Attucks," Speech Delivered at the Festival Commemorative of the British Massacre, in Faneuil Hall, 5 March 1858, reprinted in *Speeches, Lectures, and Letters. Second Series,* by Wendell Phillips (1891; reprint, New York: Arno, 1969), 69; Stowe, *Dred, A Tale of the Great Dismal Swamp* (1856), in *Abolition and Social Justice in the Era of Reform,* ed. Louis Filler (New York: Harper & Row, 1972), 341.

95. Pease and Pease, "Confrontation and Abolition in the 1850's," *Journal of American History* 58 (1972): 930; *National Anti-Slavery Standard,* 3 June 1854; *Liberator,* 9 June 1854.

96. Blackwell to Stone, 1 September 1854, LSP–LC. Note also Thomas Wentworth Higginson's involvement in a slave rescue where a courthouse guard was killed. See Edelstein, *Strange Enthusiasm,* 155–61.

97. See Foster to Kelley, 31 October 1854, KFP–AAS; Bernard, "Authority, Autonomy, and Radical Commitment," 376–77; Jane H. Pease and William H. Pease, *Bound With Them in Chains: A Biographical History of the Antislavery Movement* (Westport, Conn.: Greenwood, 1972), 204–5.

98. Wheeler, *Loving Warriors,* 187; Hays, *Those Extraordinary Blackwells,* 151. David Lee Child was involved in the 1820s Franco-Spanish war. L. Maria Child claimed in December 1862 that her husband has "all along been anxious to go to the war." "But his health," she explained, "is so very precarious that one day's march would break him down." See Milton Meltzer, *Tongue of Flame: The Life of Lydia Maria Child* (New York: Cromwell, 1965), 22–23; Child to William Lloyd Garrison Haskins, 28 December 1862, in Meltzer and Holland, *Lydia Maria Child,* 423–24.

99. Grimké to William L. Garrison, 30 November 1863, ASC–BPL. Note also Thomas Wentworth Higginson's comment that although the Garrisonians "took little part in raising troops for war," the "tradition of their influence did much to impel the army." See Higginson, *Contemporaries* (Boston: Houghton Mifflin, 1900), 247.

Chapter 6. "My Heart's Dearest Idol"

1. For examples of abolitionists marking letters "private," see Theodore Weld to Angelina Grimké, 8 February 1838, in *Letters of Theodore Dwight Weld, Angelina Grimké Weld, and Sarah Grimké, 1822–1844,* ed. Gilbert H. Barnes and Dwight L. Dumond, 2 vols. (1934; reprint, New York: Da Capo, 1970), 2:532 (hereafter cited as WGL); William L. Garrison to

Helen E. Benson, 26 March 1834, in *The Letters of William Lloyd Garrison,* ed. Walter Merrill and Louis Ruchames, 6 vols. (Cambridge: Belknap Press of Harvard University Press, 1971–81), 1:305 (hereafter cited as WLGL).

2. The quote is from Linda K. Kerber and Jane Sherron De Hart, "Gender and the New Women's History" in *Women's America: Refocusing the Past,* ed. Linda K. Kerber and Jane Sherron De Hart, 4th ed. (New York: Oxford University Press, 1995), 11.

3. Lystra, *Searching the Heart: Women, Men, and Romantic Love in Nineteenth-Century America* (New York: Oxford University Press, 1989), 192; Foster to Abigail Kelley, 17 August 1851, Abigail Kelley Foster Correspondence, Worcester Historical Museum, Worcester, Mass. (hereafter cited as KFC–WHM); Stanton, *Address at the Decade Meeting,* in *Report of the Proceedings of the Twentieth Anniversary and of the Reception Held at the St. James Hotel, (19 & 20 October, 1870)* (New York: Journeyman's Printers' Co-Operative, 1871), 71; Weld to Angelina Grimké, 1 March 1838, in WGL 2:582; L. Maria Child to David Lee Child, 28 July 1836, in *The Collected Correspondence of Lydia Maria Child,* ed. Patricia G. Holland and Milton Meltzer (Millwood, N.Y.: Kraus Microform, 1979, microfiche), Card 4/Item 102 (hereafter cited as LMCP). See also John Demos, *A Little Commonwealth: Family Life in Plymouth Colony* (New York: Oxford University Press, 1970); Edward Shorter, *The Making of the Modern Family* (1975; reprint, London: Collins, 1976), 15.

4. Lystra, *Searching the Heart,* 208; Ann Terry Green to Wendell Phillips, n.d. [1836], Crawford-Blagden Collection of the Papers of Wendell Phillips, Houghton Library, Harvard University, Cambridge, Mass. (hereafter cited as CBC–HL); Blackwell to Stone, 18 March 1855, 6 March 1855, in the Lucy Stone Papers, (included in the Blackwell Family Papers), Manuscript Division, Library of Congress, Washington, D.C. (hereafter cited as LSP–LC).

5. Garrison to George W. Benson, 29 March 1834, WLGL, 1:306; Elizabeth Cady Stanton, *Eighty Years and More: Reminiscences, 1815–1897* (1898; reprint, New York: Schocken Books, 1971), 60–61; Elisabeth Griffith, *In Her Own Right: The Life of Elizabeth Cady Stanton* (New York: Oxford University Press, 1984), 30–31; James B. Stewart, *Wendell Phillips: Liberty's Hero* (Baton Rouge: Louisiana State University Press, 1986), 44, 48–49; Weld to Grimké, 16 February 1838, WGL, 2:557. See also Daniel Scott Smith, "Parental Power and Marriage Patterns—An Analysis of Historical Trends in Hingham, Massachusetts," *Journal of Marriage and the Family* 35 (1973): 426; Nancy Cott, "Passionlessness: An Interpretation of Victorian Sexual Ideology, 1790–1850," *Signs: Journal of Women in Culture and Society* 4 (1978): 228; Ellen K. Rothman, *Hands and Hearts: A History of Courtship in America* (New York: Basic Books, 1984), 28–29. Glenda Gates Riley has noted that as female morals became increasingly important, they naturally came to be stressed as a desirable quality in a mate. Consequently, young men were encouraged to seek a mate who was "morally suitable." See Riley, "The Subtle Subversion: Changes in the Traditionalist Image of the American Woman," *The Historian* 32 (1970): 217.

6. Joel Bernard, "Authority, Autonomy, and Radical Commitment: Stephen and Abby Kelley Foster," *Proceedings of the American Antiquarian Society* 90 (1980): 364; Robert Abzug, *Passionate Liberator: Theodore Dwight Weld and the Dilemma of Reform* (New York: Oxford University Press, 1980), 166–67; Grimké to Theodore Weld, n.d. [1849], Weld-Grimké Papers, William L. Clements Library, University of Michigan, Ann Arbor (hereafter cited as WGP–UM); Blackwell to Stone, 6 February 1855, LSP–LC.

7. Kelley to Foster, 14 March 1845, 22 March 1845, Abby Kelley Foster Papers, American Antiquarian Society, Worcester, Mass. (hereafter cited as KFP–AAS); Abby Kelley to Sydney Howard Gay, 22 January 1846, Sydney Howard Gay Papers, Rare Books and Manuscript Library, Columbia University, New York City (hereafter as SHGP–CU).

8. Mott to Richard and Hannah Webb, 2 April 1841, Anti-Slavery Collection, Boston Public Library (hereafter cited as ASC–BPL); Foster to Phillips, 24 July [1857], CBC–HL; Elizabeth Cady Stanton, Susan B. Anthony, and Matilda Joslyn Gage, et al., *History of Woman*

Suffrage, 6 vols. (1881–1922, reprint, New York: Source Book, 1970), 2:175; Jane H. Pease, "The Freshness of Fanaticism: Abby Kelley Foster: An Essay in Reform" (Ph.D. diss., University of Rochester, 1969), 232–34.

9. Writing to Theodore Weld in 1848, Stanton discussed the educational requirements of her son Daniel, and noted that "Henry & I talked the matter all over." Appending a note to his wife's letter, Stanton pointed out that he would have liked adequate time to have his son properly prepared for Weld's "moulding hand," and expressed regret that they had not been forewarned of his plans to establish a school. See Elizabeth Cady Stanton and Henry Stanton to Theodore Weld, 22 September 1848, WGP–UM.

10. Stanton, *Eighty Years,* 58; Lystra, *Searching the Heart,* 38; Stone to Blackwell, 10 October 1854, LSP–LC.

11. Grimké to Weld, 21 January 1838, WGL, 2:520; Kelley to Garrison, 22 July 1859, Alma Lutz Collection, Arthur and Elizabeth Schlesinger Library on the History of Women in America, Radcliffe College, Cambridge, Mass. See also Henry Blackwell to Lucy Stone, 18 March 1855, LSP–LC; William L. Garrison to Helen E. Benson, 6 June 1834, WLGL, 1:358; Theodore Weld to Angelina Grimké, 15 April 1838, WGL, 2:635; Angelina Grimké to Weld, 29 April 1838, WGL, 2:648; Abby Kelley to Wendell Phillips, 24 July 1859, CBC–HL.

12. Friedman, *Gregarious Saints: Self and Community in American Abolitionism, 1830–1870* (Cambridge: Cambridge University Press, 1982), 146–47; Garrison to George W. Benson, 12 September 1834, ASC–BPL. See also Lystra, *Searching the Heart,* 200. Friedman's argument was similar to that of Carroll Smith-Rosenberg, who has emphasized the initial trauma of marriage. See Smith-Rosenberg, "The Female World of Love and Ritual: Relations between Women in Nineteenth-Century America," *Signs: Journal of Women in Culture and Society* 1 (1975): 22. In his editorial comment on Garrison's first published letter, which was signed "An Old Bachelor," Walter Merrill has suggested that Garrison's father might have been the real author. Notwithstanding that speculative suggestion, there was no doubting that Garrison used "An Old Bachelor," and the abbreviation "A. O. B." to sign a number of letters. See "An Old Bachelor" to the editor of the Newburyport *Herald,* 21 May 1822, WLGL, 1:5–6. See also Merrill, "A Passionate Attachment: William Lloyd Garrison's Courtship of Helen Eliza Benson," *New England Quarterly* 29 (1956): 182–84.

13. Garrison to George W. Benson, 12 September 1834, ASC–BPL; Garrison to Phoebe Jackson, 19 September 1840, Maloney Collection of McKim-Garrison Papers, Rare Books and Manuscript Division, New York Public Library, New York City; Garrison to Sarah T. Benson, 24 September 1838, ASC–BPL; Garrison to Helen Benson, 6 June 1834, WLGL, 1:358; Blackwell to Stone, 25 March 1858, in *Loving Warriors: Selected Letters of Lucy Stone and Henry B. Blackwell, 1853–1893,* ed. Leslie Wheeler (New York: Dial, 1981), 176–77.

14. Friedman, *Gregarious Saints,* 147; Kelley to Sydney Howard Gay, 28 November 1846, SHGP–CU. L. Maria Child regretted that she and David had not married sooner. See L. Maria Child to David Lee Child, 8 August 1830, LMCP, 2/44. See also Kelley to Gay, 1 April 1846, SHGP–CU; Kelley to Phillips, 11 April 1846, CBC–HL.

15. Foster to Kelley, 17 August 1851, KFC–WHM. See also David Lee Child to L. Maria Child, 17 March 1859, Anti Slavery Papers, Division of Rare and Manuscript Collection, Cornell University Library, Ithaca, N.Y. (hereafter cited as ASP–CUL).

16. Blackwell to Stone, 13 February 1855, 26 January 1856, LSP–LC. See also William L. Garrison to Helen Garrison, 31 July 1835, WLGL, 1:482.

17. Kelley to Stephen Foster, [1 April] 1844, KFC–WHM; James Mott to Lucretia Mott, 30 May 1855, Lucretia Mott Papers, Friends Historical Library, Swarthmore College, Swarthmore, Pa. (hereafter cited as MP–FHL); Lystra, *Searching the Heart,* 19. Wendell Phillips typically described Ann as "Dear little precious soul, my own sweet Andy Tandy." See Wendell Phillips to Ann Phillips, 14 April 1867, CBC–HL. See also Henry Blackwell to Lucy Stone,

12 May 1866, in Wheeler, *Loving Warriors,* 215; Lucy Stone to Henry Blackwell, 11 April 1872, in Wheeler, *Loving Warriors,* 243; David Lee Child to L. Maria Child, 5 March 1843, LMCP, 16/462; L. Maria Child to David Lee Child, 27 October 1856, LMCP, 34/951.

18. David Lee Child to L. Maria Child, 3 October 1830, 18 October 1856, ASP–CUL.

19. William L. Garrison to Helen Garrison, 20 May 1840, WLGL, 2:620; William L. Garrison to Helen Garrison, 25 June 1865, ASC–BPL. Henry Blackwell commented to Lucy Stone: "how I *count the days,* till we shall again be in each other's arms." See Blackwell to Stone, 11 February 1857, in Wheeler, *Loving Warriors,* 166. See also Stephen Foster to Abby Kelley, 14 February [1853], KFP–AAS; James Mott to Phebe Post Willis, 23 April 1834, MP–FHL; James Mott to Sydney Howard Gay, 22 July 1847, SHGP–CU; Wendell Phillips to Ann Phillips, 26 February 1868, CBC–HL.

20. Henry Stanton to Elizabeth Cady Stanton, n.d. [autumn 1843], 18 April 1861, Elizabeth Cady Stanton Papers, Manuscript Division, Library of Congress, Washington, D.C. (hereafter cited as ECSP–LC).

21. Lystra, *Searching the Heart,* chap. 1; Foster to Kelley, 2 December 1851, KFC–WHM; Ann Phillips to Wendell Phillips, 24 November 1855, 29 March 1862, CBC–HL; Wendell Phillips to Ann Phillips, 25 December 1868, CBC–HL; L. Maria Child to Susan Lyman, 8 August 1847, LMCP, 25/712; L. Maria Child to David Lee Child, 31 July 1836, LMCP, 4/103. See also Lucretia Mott to "All at Home," 27 October 1858, MP–FHL.

22. Garrison to Ann Phillips, 18 July 1846, CBC–HL; Phillips to Helen Garrison, 22 July 1846, ASC–BPL; Garrison to Ann Phillips, 18 August 1846, CBC–HL; Stone to Blackwell, 2 June 1858, in Wheeler, *Loving Warriors,* 184.

23. On husbands' absences, see Marilyn Ferris Motz, *True Sisterhood: Michigan Women and Their Kin, 1820–1920* (Albany: State University of New York Press, 1983), 25.

24. Grimké to Weld, 5 September 1852, 15 April 1841, 22 January 1843, 13 September 1848, 22 September 1848, WGP–UM. See also Helen Garrison to Ann Phillips, 9 July 1854, CBC–HL.

25. See David Lee Child to Sydney Howard Gay, 4 August 1846, SHGP–CU; Angelina Grimké to Theodore Weld, n.d. [1849], WGP–UM.

26. Friedman, *Gregarious Saints,* 147; Phillips to Pease, 7 August 1854, ASC–BPL. See also Helen Garrison to Ann Phillips, 22 July 1850, CBC–HL; Stewart, *Liberty's Hero,* 86; Thomas Wentworth Higginson, *Contemporaries* (Boston: Houghton Mifflin, 1900), 264.

27. John D'Emilio and Estelle Freedman, *Intimate Matters: A History of Sexuality in America* (New York: Harper and Row, 1988), xi; Rothman, "Sex and Self-Control: Middle Class Courtship in America, 1770–1870," *Journal of Social History* 15 (1982): 410. On the changing interpretations of Victorian sexuality, see Carol Zisowitz Stearns and Peter N. Stearns, "Victorian Sexuality: Can Historians Do It Better?" *Journal of Social History* 18 (1985): 625–34.

28. Frederick Holloway argued in 1860 that when the clitoris "is unduly developed or excitable, the sexual propensity often becomes irresistible, causing *Nymphomania* or *Furor Uterinus,* and leading to moral delinquency." See Holloway, *The Marriage Guide or Natural History of Generation; A Private Instructor for Married Persons and Those About to Marry Both Male and Female, In Everything Concerning the Physiology and Relations of the Sexual System and the Production or Prevention of Offspring—Including all the New Discoveries, Never Before Given in the English Language* (1860; reprint, New York: Arno, 1974), 39.

29. The first quote is from Milton Rugoff, *Prudery and Passion: Sexuality in Victorian America* (New York: Putnam, 1971), 46; Foucault, *The History of Sexuality,* 3 vols, trans. Robert Hurley (New York: Pantheon Books, 1978), 1:69; Walters, introduction to *Primers for Prudery: Sexual Advice to Victorian America,* ed. Ronald G. Walters (Englewood Cliffs, N.J.:

Prentice-Hall, 1974), 2. Emily Hahn has noted that from the time of white settlement of North America in the early seventeenth century, through the second half of the eighteenth century, women were unprudish and matter-of-fact about sex. See Hahn, *One Upon a Pedestal* (New York: Cromwell, 1974), 24. See also Edmund Morgan, "The Puritans and Sex," *New England Quarterly* 25 (1942): 591–607.

30. See Carl Degler, "What Ought To Be and What Was: Women's Sexuality in the Nineteenth Century," *American Historical Review* 79 (1974): 1467–90; Estelle Freedman, "Sexuality in Nineteenth-Century America: Behavior, Ideology, and Politics," *Reviews in American History* 10 (1982): 196–97; Charles Rosenberg, "Sexuality, Class and Role in 19th-Century America," *American Quarterly* 25 (1973): 149.

31. D'Emilio and Freedman, *Intimate Matters,* 113.

32. Spurlock, *Free Love: Marriage and Middle-Class Radicalism in America, 1825–1860* (New York: New York University Press, 1988), 140, 166; Bernard, "Authority, Autonomy, and Radical Commitment," 382–83; *Liberator,* 9 July 1858. See also D'Emilio and Freedman, *Intimate Matters,* 113; Lewis Perry, *Childhood, Marriage, and Reform: Henry Clarke Wright, 1797–1870* (Chicago: University of Chicago Press, 1980), 251–52.

33. Blackwell to Stone, 17 September 1855, LSP–LC; Child to Maria Weston Chapman, [26 July 1857], LMCP, 36/1014; Child to Garrison, 14 August 1878, LMCP, 90/2405. Note also Child's 1872 comment that "a misguided and mischievous set of women are doing their utmost to mix up 'Free Love,' with the [women's rights] movement." See Child to Anna [Loring] Dresel, 1 March 1872, LMCP, 78/2041. On Heywood, see Spurlock, *Free Love,* 218–19; D'Emilio and Freedman, *Intimate Matters,* 163–64. On the Oneida venture, see Ronald Walters, *American Reformers, 1815–1860* (New York: Hill and Wang, 1978), 54–60.

34. Cott, "Passionlessness," 233–34. See also Smith, "Family Limitation, Sexual Control, and Domestic Feminism in Victorian America," *Feminist Studies* 1 (1972): 40–57; Linda Gordon, *Woman's Body, Woman's Right: A Social History of Birth Control in America* (1976; reprint, Middlesex: Penguin Books, 1977), 103.

35. Cott, "Passionlessness," 234–35; Grimké to Weld, 4 March 1838, WGL, 2:587.

36. Stanton to Susan B. Anthony, 1 March 1853, ECSP–LC; Grimké, "The Education of Woman," n.d., in *Letters on the Equality of the Sexes and Other Essays,* ed. Elizabeth Ann Bartlett (New Haven: Yale University Press, 1988), 116. See also Lois Banner, *Elizabeth Cady Stanton: A Radical for Woman's Rights* (Boston: Little, Brown, 1980), 35.

37. Weld to Grimké, 12 March 1838, WGL, 2:601; Grimké to Weld, 4 March 1838, WGL, 2:587. Note also Weld's comment: "How panteth my heart after thee my beloved." See Weld to Angelina Grimké, 8 April 1838, WGL, 2:628. Ronald Walters has described the Weld-Grimké courtship as "a veritable orgy of restraint." See Walters, "The Erotic South: Civilization and Sexuality in American Abolitionism," *American Quarterly* 25 (1973): 189.

38. David Lee Child to L. Maria Child, 20 February 1837, ASP–CUL; Merrill, "A Passionate Attachment," 187; Wright, *The Unwelcome Child* (1860), as quoted in Perry, *Henry Clarke Wright,* 243.

39. Hersh, *The Slavery of Sex: Feminist-Abolitionists in America* (Urbana: University of Illinois Press, 1978), 210, 244–47 (quotations on 210); Smith-Rosenberg, "The Female World of Love and Ritual," 8; Grimké to Weld, n.d. [September 1849], WGP–UM.

40. Garrison to Ann Phillips, 18 July 1846, CBC–HL; Grimké to Jane Smith, 19 October 1840, WGP–UM.

41. Anna Davis Hallowell, ed., *James and Lucretia Mott: Life and Letters* (Boston: Houghton Mifflin, 1884), 440; Margaret Hope Bacon, *Valiant Friend: The Life of Lucretia Mott* (New York: Walker, 1980), 30, 200; Blackwell to Stone, 12 September 1855, in Wheeler, *Loving Warriors,* 145.

42. Lystra, *Searching the Heart,* chap. 3; Rothman, *Hands and Hearts,* 122. See also Perry, *Henry Clarke Wright,* 244.

43. Garrison to Samuel J. May, 15 September 1834, ASC–BPL; Blackwell to Stone, 5 May 1854, 12 July 1854, 10 January 1855, 1 March 1854, 2 April 1855, LSP–LC.

44. Perry, "'We Have Had Conversations in the World': The Abolitionists and Spontaneity," *Canadian Review of American Studies* 6 (1975): 3–26; Garrison to Helen E. Benson, 6 June 1834, WLGL, 1:358; Foster to Kelley, 18 March 1844, KFP–AAS; Kelley to Foster, 2 February 1845, KFP–AAS; Garrison to Helen E. Benson, 24 April 1834, WLGL, 1:328; Garrison to George W. Benson, 12 September 1834, ASC–BPL; Henry Stanton to Elizabeth Cady Stanton, 14 February 1858, ECSP–LC.

45. Stewart, *Liberty's Hero,* 86–90; Phillips to Garrison, 19 July 1852, ASC–BPL; Perry, "'Progress, Not Pleasure, Is Our Aim': The Sexual Advice of an Antebellum Radical," *Journal of Social History* 12 (1979): 358. See also James B. Stewart, "Heroes, Villains, Liberty and License: The Abolitionist Vision of Wendell Phillips," in *Antislavery Reconsidered: New Essays on the Abolitionists,* ed. Lewis Perry and Michael Fellman (Baton Rouge: Louisiana State University Press, 1979), 178.

46. Abzug was imprecise regarding the timing of what he rightly perceived as the renewed intimacy between Weld and Grimké. While he asserted that "it is clear from later events that Theodore and Angelina regained a caring understanding of each other," he did not directly claim that their restored intimacy actually occurred during the period of Angelina's illness. See Abzug, *Passionate Liberator,* 246. See also Lerner, *The Grimké Sisters from South Carolina: Pioneers for Woman's Rights and Abolition* (1967; reprint, New York: Schocken Books, 1971), 288–92; Katharine Du Pre Lumpkin, *The Emancipation of Angelina Grimké* (Chapel Hill: University of North Carolina Press, 1974), 245–46.

47. Griffith, *In Her Own Right,* 96–97; Grimké to Weld, 29 April 1838, 2 May 1838, WGL, 2:647, 653. The "Sister Anna" Grimké referred to was Anna R. Frost of Philadelphia.

48. Kelley to Foster, 30 July 1843, KFP–AAS; Andrew Moore Kerr, *Lucy Stone: Speaking Out for Equality* (New Brunswick: Rutgers University Press, 1992), 77–78, 91–92; Stone to Henry Blackwell, 3 September 1854, LSP–LC; Sarah Grimké to Sarah Douglass, 19 June 1855, as quoted in Margot Melia, "The Role of Black Garrisonian Women in Antislavery and Other Reforms in the Antebellum North, 1830–1865" (Ph.D. diss., University of Western Australia, 1991), 185.

49. L. Maria Child to David Lee Child, 31 July 1836, LMCP, 4/103. Other abolitionists also quoted poets, or wrote poems of their own, expressing their affection for their loved ones. Little of what they wrote was good poetry, but it did convey their intimate attachments. See William L. Garrison to Helen E. Benson, 26 March 1834, WLGL, 1:303–4; William L. Garrison to Helen Garrison, 28 May 1840, WLGL, 2:630.

50. L. Maria Child to David Lee Child, 28 July 1836, 22 May 1835, 24 July 1836, LMCP, 4/102, 3/72, 4/101. There is implicit evidence of the Childs' hardships during the early years of their marriage. Writing to her mother-in-law, Maria noted that they had two boarders staying with them all winter. It was not uncommon for middle-class people to take in boarders during the nineteenth century, usually in an effort to supplement the household income. See L. Maria Child to Lydia [Bigelow] Child, [February 1830], LMCP, 2/24.

51. Child to Ellis Gray Loring, 21 March 1843, LMCP, 17/470. "I am *minus* the best wife," wrote David, "that God ever gave to a man. . . . I do love you. Will you write me soon?" See David Lee Child to L. Maria Child, 16 March 1846, LMCP, 21/608.

52. L. Maria Child to Lydia [Bigelow] Child, 16 February 1849, LMCP, 26/747; L. Maria Child to Francis George Shaw, 2 August 1846, LMCP, 23/664; L. Maria Child to David Lee Child,

31 August 1849, LMCP, 27/758; L. Maria Child to Marianne Cabot Silsbee, 29 October 1849, LMCP, 27/762; L. Maria Child to David Lee Child, 27 October 1856, LMCP, 34/951.

53. Kirk Jeffrey, "Marriage, Career, and Feminine Ideology in Nineteenth-Century America: Reconstructing the Marital Experience of Lydia Maria Child, 1828–1874," *Feminist Studies* 2 (1975): 118. On Bull, see Milton Meltzer and Patricia Holland's editorial note in *Lydia Maria Child: Selected Letters, 1817–1880* (Amherst: University of Massachusetts Press, 1982), 213.

54. Child to Anna Loring, 23 March 1846, LMCP, 23/655.

55. Child to Ellis Gray Loring, 6 March 1843, LMCP, 16/463. Child also described Hopper as an "adopted son" who was "the greatest comfort that ever the Lord did raise up to bless a forlorn individual." See Child to Louisa Loring, 28 February 1843, LMCP, 16/459. Note also Child's 1831 comment to her mother-in-law: "I do wish I could be a mother—and that even more for my husband's sake, than for my own. But God's will be done. I am certain that Divine Providence orders all things for our good." See also Child's 1853 remark: "I so need a loving daughter." See Child to Lydia [Bigelow] Child, 23 June 1831, LMCP, 2/48; Child to Ellis Gray Loring, 1 September 1853, LMCP, 30/849. Child's description of Bull as being "like a child" was a hint of her maternal urge. See L. Maria Child to John S. Dwight, 23 October 1844, in Meltzer and Holland, *Lydia Maria Child,* 215. See also Jeffrey, "Marital Experience of Lydia Maria Child," 118.

56. Child also noted that "John Hopper is very dear to me, for we have been together in many dark hours." As well as noting that Hopper was "unceasingly kind" to her, Child also claimed he was "the *only* bond strong enough to bind me to N. York for a single month, if other circumstances did not combine to make it advantageous to be here." See Child to Louisa Loring, 31 May 1846, LMCP, 23/659. With regard to children, Child claimed later: "If I had had children to provide for, it is highly probable I should have been more ambitious myself." See Child to [Sarah] Maria Parsons, 29 December 1850, LMCP, 28/798.

57. Helene G. Baer, *The Heart is Like Heaven: The Life of Lydia Maria Child* (Philadelphia: University of Pennsylvania Press, 1964), 203.

58. Child to Ellis Gray Loring, 11 August 1841, LMCP, 10/246.

59. Kerr, *Lucy Stone,* 144–45, 148–52, 205 (quotations on 144).

60. Mott to Stone, 29 June 1853, LSP–LC; Wendell Phillips to Ann Phillips, [March] 1874, as quoted in Stewart, *Liberty's Hero,* 313; L. Maria Child to Lucy Osgood, 3 May 1862, LMCP, 52/1408. See also Child to John Greenleaf Whittier, 8 November 1864, LMCP, 60/1588.

61. Child to Higginson, 9 September 1877, LMCP, 88/2340; Phillips to Garrison, [December 1875], ASC–BPL; Phillips, as quoted in Stewart, *Liberty's Hero,* 334. See also Lloyd C. M. Hare, *The Greatest American Woman: Lucretia Mott* (1937; reprint, New York: Negro Universities Press, 1970), 295; Stewart, *Liberty's Hero,* 311.

62. Child to Shaw, 18 September 1874, LMCP, 83/2178. See also Lucretia Mott to "Cousin Mary," 25 January 1868, MP–FHL.

Conclusion

1. Any reading of Wendell Phillips Garrison and Francis Jackson Garrison's four-volume account of their father's reform activities, or of the other works compiled by abolitionists' children, reveals the extent to which they accepted many of their parents' values. See *William Lloyd Garrison, 1805–1879: The Story of His Life. Told by His Children,* 4 vols. (New York: Century, 1885). See also Theodore Stanton Blatch and Harriot Stanton Blatch, *Elizabeth Cady Stanton: As Revealed in Her Letters, Diary, and Reminiscences,* 2 vols. (1922; reprint, New York: Arno, 1969).

BIBLIOGRAPHY

PRIMARY SOURCES

Manuscript Collections

American Antiquarian Society, Worcester, Massachusetts
Abby Kelley Foster Papers
Boston Public Library, Boston, Massachusetts
Anti-Slavery Collection:
Child Papers
Garrison Papers
May Correspondence
Phelps Papers
Spooner Papers
Weston Family Papers
Wright Papers
William L. Clements Library, University of Michigan, Ann Arbor, Michigan
Weld-Grimké Papers
Division of Rare and Manuscript Collection, Cornell University Library, Ithaca, New York
Anti Slavery Papers:
David Lee Child Correspondence
Wendell Phillips Correspondence
Friends Historical Library, Swarthmore College, Swarthmore, Pennsylvania
Lucretia Mott Papers
Historical Society of Pennsylvania, Philadelphia
Papers of the Philadelphia Female Anti-Slavery Society
Houghton Library, Harvard University, Cambridge, Massachusetts
Crawford-Blagden Collection of Wendell Phillips Papers
Mrs. Horatio A. Lamb Papers
G. W. Pickard Papers
Oswald G. Villard Papers
Library of Congress (Manuscript Division), Washington, D.C.
Susan B. Anthony Papers
Blackwell Family Papers (including Henry B. Blackwell Papers and Lucy Stone Papers)
Elizabeth Cady Stanton Papers
Massachusetts Historical Society, Boston, Massachusetts
Boston Female Anti-Slavery Society. Letterbook, 9 April 1834–6 January 1838
New York Public Library (Rare Books and Manuscript Division), New York City
Sydney Howard Gay Papers
Maloney Collection of McKim-Garrison Papers
Smith Family Papers
Rare Book and Manuscript Library, Columbia University, New York City
Sydney Howard Gay Papers

Schlesinger Library, Radcliffe College, Cambridge, Massachusetts
Susan B. Anthony Papers
Blackwell Family Papers
Alma Lutz Collection
Harriet Jane (Hanson) Robinson Papers
Sterling Memorial Library, Yale University, New Haven, Connecticut
Stowe Family Papers
Harriet Beecher Stowe Papers
Syracuse University Library, Department of Special Collections, Syracuse, New York
Gerrit Smith Papers
Worcester Historical Museum, Worcester, Massachusetts
Abigail Kelley Foster Correspondence

Published Material

Abel, Annie Heloise, and Frank J. Klingberg, eds. *A Side-Light on Anglo-American Relations, 1839–1858.* 1927; reprint, New York: Augustus M. Kelley, 1970.

An Appeal to the Females of the North, on the Subject of Slavery. By a Female of Vermont. Philadelphia: John Thompson, 1838.

Ball, Charles. *Slavery in the United States: A Narrative of the Life and Adventures of Charles Ball, A Black Man, Who Lived Forty Years in Maryland, South Carolina and Georgia, Under Various Masters, And was One Year in the Navy with Commodore Barney, During the Late Year, Containing an Account of the Manners and Usages of the Planters and Slaveholders of the South—A Description of the Condition and Treatment of the Slaves, With Observations Upon the State of Morals Amongst the Cotton Planters, And the Perils and Sufferings of a Fugitive Slave, Who Twice Escaped From the Cotton Country.* 1837; reprint, New York: Negro Universities Press, 1969.

Bartlett, Elizabeth Ann, ed. *Letters on the Equality of the Sexes and Other Essays.* New Haven: Yale University Press, 1988.

Bartlett, Irving H., ed. "New Light on Wendell Phillips: The Community of Reform, 1840–1880." *Perspectives in American History* 12 (1979): 3–251.

Barnes, Gilbert H., and Dwight L. Dumond, eds. *Letters of Theodore Dwight Weld, Angelina Grimké Weld and Sarah Grimké, 1822–1844.* 2 vols. 1934; reprint, New York: Da Capo, 1970.

Beecher, Catharine E. *An Essay on Slavery and Abolitionism, with Reference to the Duty of American Females.* Philadelphia: Henry Perkins, 1837.

——. *A Treatise on Domestic Economy, for the use of Young Ladies at Home, and at School.* 1841; reprint, New York: Source Book, 1971.

Beecher, Henry Ward. *Women's Influence in Politics, an Address Delivered at the Cooper Institute, New York, Thursday Evening, Feb. 2, 1860.* Boston: C. K. Whipple, 1870.

Beman, Rev. Nathan S. S. *Female Influence and Obligations.* New York: American Tract Society, 185[?]

Bibb, Henry. *Narrative of the Life and Adventures of Henry Bibb, An American Slave, Written by Himself.* 1850; reprint, New York: Negro Universities Press, 1969.

Blassingame, John W., ed. *The Frederick Douglass Papers. Series One: Speeches, Debates, and Interviews.* Vol. 2, *1847–54.* New Haven: Yale University Press, 1982.

Boston Woman's Rights Convention, 1855. Reports on the Laws of New England, Presented to the New England Meeting. Convened at the Meionan, Sept. 19 and 20, 1855. Boston: n.p. 1855.

Boydston, Jeanne, Mary Kelley, and Anne Margolis, eds. *The Limits of Sisterhood: The Beecher Sisters on Women's Rights and Women's Sphere.* Chapel Hill: University of North Carolina Press, 1988.

Brown, William Wells. *A Lecture Delivered Before the Female Anti-Slavery Society of Salem, At Lyceum Hall, Nov. 14, 1847.* 1847; reprint, Reading, Mass.: Addison-Wesley, 1969.

——. *Narrative of William W. Brown. A Fugitive Slave, Written by Himself.* 2d ed., 1848; reprint, Reading, Mass.: Addison-Wesley, 1969.

Cabot, Susan C. *What Have We, as Individuals, to do with Slavery?* New York: American Anti-Slavery Society, 1855.

Ceplair, Larry, ed. *The Public Years of Sarah and Angelina Grimké: Selected Writings, 1835–1839.* New York: Columbia University Press, 1989.

Chace, Elizabeth Buffum. *Anti-Slavery Reminiscences.* Central Falls, R.I.: R. L. Freeman and Sons, 1891.

Chadwick, John White, ed. *A Life for Liberty: Anti-Slavery and other Letters of Sallie Holley.* New York: Putnam, 1899.

Chapman, Maria Weston. *Right and Wrong in Boston. No.3.* Boston: Isaac Knapp, 1837.

——. *Right and Wrong in Massachusetts.* 1839; reprint, New York: Negro Universities Press, 1969.

——. *"How Can I Help to Abolish Slavery?" or, Councils to the Newly Converted.* New York: American Anti-Slavery Society, 1855.

Child, David Lee. *The Despotism of Freedom; or the Tyranny and Cruelty of American Republican Slave Masters, Shown to be the Worst in the World; in a Speech Delivered at the First Anniversary of the New England Anti-Slavery Society, 1833.* Boston: Boston Young Men's Anti-Slavery Society, 1833.

Child, Lydia Maria. *The Girl's Own Book.* New York: Clark Austin, 1833.

——. *Good Wives.* Boston: Carter, Hendee, 1833.

——, ed. *The Oasis.* Boston: Benjamin C. Bacon, 1834.

——. *The American Frugal Housewife, Dedicated to Those Who are Not Ashamed of Economy.* 16th ed. Boston: Carter, Hendee, 1835.

——. *The History of the Condition of Women, In Various Ages and Nations.* 2 vols. Boston: John Allen, 1835.

——. *On the Management and Education of Children; being Mrs Child's "Mother's Book," Revised, and Adapted to the Use of English Parents and Teachers.* London: John W. Parker, 1835.

——. *Anti-Slavery Catechism.* Newburyport, Mass.: Charles Whipple, 1836.

——. *An Appeal in Favor of That Class of Americans Called Africans.* 1836; reprint, New York: Arno, 1968.

——. *The Evils of Slavery, and the Cure of Slavery. The First Proved by the Opinions of Southerners Themselves, and the Last Shown by Historical Evidence.* Newburyport, Mass.: Charles Whipple, 1836.

——. *Philothea, a Romance.* Boston: Otis, Broader, 1836.

——. *The Family Nurse; or, Companion of The Frugal Housewife.* Boston: Charles J. Hendee, 1837.

——. *The Little Girl's Own Book, with Additional Sports and Games, by Miss Leslie.* Glasgow: John Reid, 1837.

——. *The Mother's Book.* 6th ed. New York: C. S. Francis, 1844.

——. *Letters from New York.* 10th ed. New York: C. S. Francis, 1849.

——. *The Brother and Sister: and Other Stories.* Philadelphia: n.p., 1852.

——. *Celebrated Women; or, Biographies of Good Wives.* Boston: Higgins, Bradley and Dayton, 1858.

——. *Correspondence Between Lydia Maria Child, Gov. Wise and Mrs. Mason, of Virginia.* Boston: American Anti-Slavery Society, 1860.

——. *The Duty of Disobedience to the Fugitive Slave Act: An Appeal to the Legislators of Massachusetts.* Boston: American Anti-Slavery Society, 1860.

——, ed. *The Patriarchal Institution, as Described by Members of Its Own Family.* New York: American Anti-Slavery Society, 1860.

——. *The Right Way the Safe Way, Proved by Emancipation in the British West Indies, and Elsewhere.* 1860; reprint, New York: Arno, 1969.

The Child's Anti-Slavery Book: Containing a Few Words About American Slave Children, and Stories of Slave Life. New York: Carlston and Porter, n.d.

The Child's Book on Slavery; or, Slavery Made Plain. Cincinatti: American Reform Tract and Book Society, 1857.

Chittendon, Nathaniel W. *The Influence of Woman Upon the Destinies of a People; Being an Oration, with Salutatory Addresses, Delivered at the Annual Commencement of Columbia College, October 3d, 1837.* New York: n.p., 1837.

Clark, Daniel A. *The Wide Builder. A Sermon, Delivered to the Females of the First Parish in Amherst, Massachusetts, on Wednesday, the Third Day of May, 1820.* Boston: Ezra Lincoln, 1820.

Clemens, Samuel. *The Adventures of Tom Sawyer.* 1875; reprint, New York: Modern Library, 1940.

Cott, Nancy, ed. *Roots of Bitterness: Documents of the Social History of American Women.* New York: Dutton, 1972.

Davis, Paulina W., comp. *A History of the National Woman's Rights Movement, for Twenty Years, With the Proceedings of the Decade Meeting held at Apollo Hall, October 20, 1870, from 1850 to 1870, With an Appendix Containing the History of the Movement During the Winter of 1871, in the National Capitol.* New York: Journeyman's Printers' Co-Operative, 1871.

Declaration of Sentiments of the American Anti-Slavery Society. Adopted at the Formation of said Society, in Philadelphia, on the 4th day of December, 1833. New York: American Anti-Slavery Society, n.d.

Dodge, Mary A. [Gail Hamilton]. *Woman's Wrongs: A Counter Irritant.* 1868; reprint, New York: Arno, 1972.

Douglass, Frederick. *My Bondage and My Freedom.* 1855; reprint, New York: Arno, 1968.

DuBois, Ellen, ed. *Elizabeth Cady Stanton, Susan B. Anthony: Correspondence, Writings, Speeches.* New York: Schocken Books, 1981.

Dumond, Dwight L., ed. *Letters of James Gillespie Birney, 1831–1857.* 2 vols. New York: Appleton-Century, 1938.

Fields, Annie, ed. *Life and Letters of Harriet Beecher Stowe.* London: Sampson Low, Marston, 1897.

Filler, Louis, ed. *Abolition and Social Justice in the Era of Reform.* New York: Harper and Row, 1972.

First Annual Report of the Board of Managers of the New-England Anti-Slavery Society, Presented Jan. 9, 1833. With an Appendix. 1833; reprint, Westport, Conn.: Negro Universities Press, 1970.

Fitzhugh, George. *Cannibals All! or, Slaves Without Masters.* Edited by C. Vann Woodward. 1857; reprint, Cambridge: Belknap Press of Harvard University Press, 1960.

Foner, Philip S., ed. *Frederick Douglass on Women's Rights.* 1976; reprint, New York: Da Capo, 1992.

Foster, Stephen Symonds. *The Brotherhood of Thieves; or, A True Picture of the American Church and Clergy: A Letter to Nathaniel Barney and Peter May of Nantucket.* New London, N.H.: W. Bolles, 1843.

——. *Revolution the Only Remedy for Slavery.* New York: American Anti-Slavery Society, 1855.

Fredrickson, George, ed. *William Lloyd Garrison.* Englewood Cliffs, N.J.: Prentice-Hall, 1968.

Garrison, Wendell Phillips, and Francis Jackson Garrison. *William Lloyd Garrison, 1805–1879: The Story of His Life. Told by His Children.* 4 vols. New York: Century, 1885.

Garrison, William Lloyd. *Helen Eliza Garrison: A Memorial.* Cambridge, Mass.: Riverside, 1876.

Greene, Dana, ed. *Lucretia Mott: Her Complete Speeches and Sermons.* New York: Edwin Mellin, 1980.

Grimké, Angelina E. *Appeal to the Christian Women of the South.* 3d ed. N.p.: n.p., 1836.

——. *An Appeal to the Women of the Nominally Free States, Issued by an Anti-Slavery Convention of American Women.* New York: William S. Dorr, 1837.

——. *Slavery in America. A Reprint of An Appeal to the Christian Women of the Slave States of America.* Edinburgh: William Oliphant and Son, 1837.

——. *Letters to Catherine E. Beecher, In Reply to An Essay on Slavery and Abolitionism, Addressed to A. E. Grimké. Revised by the Author.* 1838; reprint, Freeport, N.Y.: Books for Libraries, 1971.

——. *Letter from Angelina Grimké Weld, to the Women's Rights Convention, Held at Syracuse, Sept., 1852.* New York: n.p., 1852.

Grimké Weld, Angelina. *In Memory of Sarah Moore Grimké. Born in Charleston, South Carolina, November 26, 1792. Died in Hyde Park, Massachusetts, December 23, 1873.* N.p.: n.d., n.d.

Grimké, Sarah M. *An Epistle to the Clergy of the Southern States.* New York: n.p., 1836.

——. *Letters on the Equality of the Sexes and the Condition of Women. Addressed to Mary S. Parker, President of the Boston Female Anti-Slavery Society.* 1838; reprint, New York: Source Book, 1970.

Hallowell, Anna Davis, ed. *James and Lucretia Mott. Life and Letters.* Boston: Houghton Mifflin, 1884.

Harper, Ida Husted, ed. *Life and Works of Susan B. Anthony.* 3 vols. 1898; reprint, Salem, N.H.: Ayer, 1983.

Harris, Walter. *A Discourse Delivered to the Members of the Female Cent Society, in Bedford, New Hampshire, July 18, 1814.* Concord, N.H.: George Houch, 1814.

Higginson, Mary Thatcher, ed. *Letters and Journals of Thomas Wentworth Higginson, 1846–1906.* 1921; reprint, New York: Da Capo, 1969.

Higginson, Thomas Wentworth. *Wendell Phillips.* Boston: Lee and Shepard, 1884.

——. *Contemporaries.* Boston: Houghton, Mifflin, 1900.

Hildreth, Richard. *The Slave: or Memoirs of Archy Moore* 2 vols. 1836; reprint, Upper Saddle River, N.J.: Gregg, 1968.

Holland, Patricia G., and Milton Meltzer, eds. *The Collected Correspondence of Lydia Maria Child.* Microfiche. Millwood, N.Y.: Kraus Microform, 1979.

Holloway, Frederick. *The Marriage Guide or Natural History of Generation; A Private Instructor for Married Persons and Those About to Marry Both Male and Female, In Everything Concerning the Physiology and Relations of the Sexual System and the Production or Prevention of Offspring—Including all the New Discoveries, Never Before Given in the English Language.* 1860; reprint, New York: Arno, 1974.

Hundley, Daniel R. *Social Relations in Our Southern States.* New York: Henry B. Price, 1860.

Jacobs, Harriet. *Incidents in the Life of a Slave Girl. Written by Herself.* Edited by Lydia Maria Child. 1861; reprint, Miami, Fla.: Mnemosyne, 1969.

Johnson, Oliver. *William Lloyd Garrison and His Times; or, Sketches of the Anti-Slavery Movement, and of the Man who was Its Founder, and Leader.* Rev. ed. Boston: Houghton Mifflin, 1885.

Judson, Adoniram. *Rev. Mr. Judson's Letter, to the Female Members of Christian Churches, in the United States of America.* Providence, R.I.: H. H. Brown, 1832.

Kraditor, Aileen S., ed. *Up From the Pedestal: Selected Writings in the History of American Feminism.* New York: Quadrangle, 1968.

Lasser, Carol, and Marlene Deahl Merrill, eds. *Friends and Sisters: Letters Between Lucy Stone and Antoinette Brown Blackwell, 1846–93.* Urbana: University of Illinois Press, 1987.

Loguen, Rev. J. W. *The Rev. J. W. Loguen, as A Slave and as a Freeman. A Narrative of a Real Life.* 1859; reprint, New York: Negro Universities Press, 1968.

McKitrick, Eric L., ed. *Slavery Defended: The Views of the Old South.* Englewood Cliffs, N.J.: Prentice-Hall, 1963.

May, Samuel J. *The Rights and Conditions of Women; A Sermon, Preached in Syracuse, Nov., 1854.* 3d ed. N.p.: n.p., 1854.

——. *Some Recollections of Our Antislavery Conflict.* 1869; reprint, Miami, Fla.: Mnemosyne, 1969.

Meltzer, Milton, and Patricia G. Holland, eds. *Lydia Maria Child: Selected Letters, 1817–1880.* Amherst: University of Massachusetts Press, 1982.

Merrill, Walter M., and Louis Ruchames, eds. *The Letters of William Lloyd Garrison.* 6 vols. Cambridge: Belknap Press of Harvard University Press, 1971–81.

Moral Condition of Slaves. New York: Published by R. G. Williams for the American Anti-Slavery Society, 1839.

Mott, James. *Brief Hints to Parents, on the Subject of Education.* Philadelphia: n.p., 1824.

Mott, Lucretia. *Discourse on Women, Delivered at The Assembly Buildings, December 17, 1849.* Philadelphia: W. P. Kildare, 1869.

Ossoli, Margaret Fuller. *Woman in the Nineteenth Century, and Kindred Papers Relating to the Sphere, Condition and Duties, of Woman.* 1855; reprint, New York: Norton, 1971.

Parker, Theodore. *A Sermon on the Public Function of Women, Preached at the Music Hall, March 27, 1853.* Boston: Robert F. Wallcut, 1853.

Pease, William H., and Jane H. Pease, eds. *The Antislavery Argument.* Indianapolis: Bobbs-Merrill, 1965.

Phillips, Wendell. *Speech of Wendell Phillips, Esquire, at the Worcester Disunion Convention, January 15, 1857.* Boston: American Anti-Slavery Society, 1857.

——. *Speeches, Lectures, and Letters. Second Series.* 1891; reprint, New York: Arno, 1968.

——. *Shall Women Have the Right to Vote? Address by Wendell Phillips at Worcester, Mass. 1851.* N.p.: Republished by the Equal Franchise Society of Pennsylvania, 1910.

Proceedings of the Anti-Slavery Convention of American Women, Held in the City of New York, May 9th, 10th, 11th, and 12th, 1837. New York: William S. Dorr, 1837.

Proceedings of the Anti-Slavery Convention of American Women, Held in Philadelphia, May 15th, 16th, 17th and 18th, 1838. Philadelphia: Merrihew and Gunn, 1838.

Proceedings of the National Women's Rights Convention, Held at Cleveland, Ohio, on Wednesday, Thursday, and Friday, October 5th, 6th, and 7th, 1853. Cleveland: Gray, Beardsley, Spear, 1854.

Proceedings of the Third Anti-Slavery Convention of American Women, Held in Philadelphia, May 1st, 2d, and 3d, 1839. Philadelphia: Merrihew and Thompson, 1839.

Proceedings of the Woman's Rights Convention, Held at The Broadway Tabernacle, in the City of New York, on Tuesday and Wednesday, Sept. 6th and 7th, 1853. New York: Fowler and Wells, 1853.

Proceedings of the Woman's Rights Convention, Held at the Unitarian Church, Rochester, N.Y. August 2, 1848, To Consider the Rights of Woman, Politically, Religiously and Industrially. Revised by Mrs. Amy Post. New York: Robert J. Johnson, 1870.

The Proceedings of the Woman's Rights Convention, Held at Worcester, October 23d & 24th, 1850. Boston: Prentiss and Sawyer, 1851.

The Proceedings of the Woman's Rights Convention, Held at Worcester, October 15th and 16th, 1851. New York: Fowler and Wells, 1852.

Report of the Proceedings of the Twentieth Anniversary and of the Reception Held at the St. James Hotel, (19 & 20 October, 1870). New York: Journeyman's Printers' Co-Operative, 1871.

Richardson, Joseph. *A Sermon on the Duty and Dignity of Woman, Delivered April 22, 1832.* Hingham, Mass.: Jedidiah Farmer, 1833.

Richardson, Marilyn, ed. *Maria Stewart, America's First Black Woman Political Writer.* Bloomington: Indiana University Press, 1987.

Right and Wrong in Boston. Report of the Boston Female Anti-Slavery Society; With a Concise Statement of Events Previous and Subsequent to the Annual Meeting of 1835. Boston: Boston Female Anti-Slavery Society, 1836.

Ripley, C. Peter, ed. *The Black Abolitionist Papers.* Vol. 3, *The United States,* 1830–1846. Chapel Hill: University of North Carolina Press, 1991.

Roper, Moses. *A Narrative of the Adventures and Escape of Moses Roper, From American Slavery: With a Preface by the Rev. T. Price, D.D.* 1838; reprint, New York: Negro Universities Press, 1970.

Ruchames, Louis, ed. *The Abolitionists: A Collection of Their Writings.* New York: Putnam, 1963.

Second Annual Report of the Board of Managers of the New England Anti-Slavery Society, Presented January 15, 1834. With an Appendix. 1834; reprint, Westport, Conn.: Negro Universities Press, 1970.

Seventh Annual Report of the Boston Female Anti-Slavery Society. Presented October 14, 1840. Boston: Boston Female Anti-Slavery Society, 1840.

Smith, Gerrit. *Woman Suffrage Above the Law. Letter from Gerrit Smith.* Peterboro, N.Y.: n.p., 1873.

Stanton, Elizabeth Cady. *The Slave's Appeal.* Albany, N.Y.: Weed, Parsons, 1860.

——. *The Woman's Bible.* 1895; reprint, New York: Arno, 1972.

——. *Eighty Years and More: Reminiscences, 1815–1897.* 1898; reprint, New York: Schocken Books, 1971.

Stanton, Elizabeth Cady, Susan B. Anthony, and Matilda Joslyn Gage, et al. *History of Woman Suffrage.* 6 vols. 1881–1922; reprint, New York: Source Book, 1970.

Stanton, Henry B. *Random Recollections.* 3d ed. New York: Harper and Brothers, 1887.

Stanton, Theodore, and Harriot Stanton Blatch, eds. *Elizabeth Cady Stanton: As Revealed in Her Letters, Diary, and Reminiscences.* 2 vols. 1922; reprint, New York: Arno, 1969.

Sterling, Dorothy, ed. *We Are Your Sisters: Black Women in the Nineteenth Century.* New York: Norton, 1984.

Stowe, Harriet Beecher. *Uncle Tom's Cabin, or Life Among the Lonely.* Edited by Ann Douglas. 1852; reprint, Middlesex: Penguin Books, 1986.

——. *The Key to Uncle Tom's Cabin: Presenting the Original Facts and Documents Upon Which the Story was Founded. Together With Corroborating Statements Verifying the Truth of the Work.* London: Clark, Beeton, 1853.

Taylor, Clare, ed. *British and American Abolitionists: An Episode in Transatlantic Understanding.* Edinburgh: Edinburgh University Press, 1974.

Third Annual Report of the Board of Managers of the New England Anti-Slavery Society, Presented Jan. 21, 1835. 1835; reprint, Westport, Conn.: Negro Universities Press, 1970.

Thompson, John. *The Life of John Thompson, A Fugitive Slave; Containing His History of 25 Years in Bondage, and His Providential Escape.* 1856; reprint, New York: Negro Universities Press, 1968.

Thomson, Mortimer. *Great Auction Sale of Slaves, at Savannah, Georgia, March 2d and 3d, 1859. Reported for the Tribune.* New York: American Anti-Slavery Society, 1859.

Tocqueville, Alexis de. *Democracy in America.* Translated by Henry Reeve. 2 vols. New York: Knopf, 1966.

Tolles, Frederick B., ed. *Slavery and "The Woman Question": Lucretia Mott's Diary of Her Visit to Great Britain to Attend the World's Anti-Slavery Convention of 1840.* Haverford, Pa.: Friends' Historical Association, 1952.

Trollope, Fanny. *Domestic Manners of the Americans.* 1832; reprint, Gloucester: Alan Sutton, 1984.

Walters, Ronald G., ed. *Primers for Prudery: Sexual Advice to Victorian America.* Englewood Cliffs, N.J.: Prentice-Hall, 1974.

Weld, Theodore Dwight. *American Slavery As It Is: Testimony of a Thousand Witnesses.* New York: American Anti-Slavery Society, 1839.

——. *In Memory of Angelina Grimké Weld. Born in Charleston, South Carolina, February 20, 1805. Died in Hyde Park, Massachusetts, October 26, 1879.* Boston: George H. Ellis, 1880.

Wheeler, Leslie, ed. *Loving Warriors: Selected Letters of Lucy Stone and Henry B. Blackwell, 1853 to 1893.* New York: Dial, 1981.

Whipple, Charles King. *The Family Relation as Affected by Slavery.* Cincinatti: American Reform and Tract Society, n.d.

Wish, Harvey, ed. *Antebellum Writings of George Fitzhugh and Hinton Rowan Helper on Slavery.* New York: Capricorn Books, 1960.

Woman's Rights Commensurate with Her Capacities and Obligations. A Series of Tracts Comprising Sixteen Articles, Essays, Addresses, or Letters of the Prominent Advocates Of Woman's Larger Sphere of Action. Syracuse, N.Y.: n.p., 1853.

Wright, Henry C. *Marriage and Parentage: or, The Reproductive Element in Man, as a Means to His Elevation and Happiness.* 2d ed. Boston: Bela Marsh, 1855.

Contemporary Newspapers and Magazines

Liberator. Boston, 1831–65.

Lily. Seneca Falls, N.Y., 1849–54.

National Anti-Slavery Standard. New York, 1840–70.

Revolution. New York, 1868–71.

Una. Providence, R.I., 1853–55.

SECONDARY SOURCES

Abbott, Richard H. *Cotton and Capital: Boston Businessmen and Antislavery Reform, 1854–1868.* Amherst: University of Massachusetts Press, 1991.

Abzug, Robert H. *Passionate Liberator: Theodore Dwight Weld and the Dilemma of Reform.* New York: Oxford University Press, 1980.

——. *Cosmos Crumbling: American Reform and the Religious Imagination.* New York: Oxford University Press, 1994.

Ammons, Elizabeth. "Heroines in *Uncle Tom's Cabin.*" *American Literature* 49 (1977): 161–79.

Andsell, Douglass B. A. "William Lloyd Garrison's Ambivalent Approach to Labour Reform." *Journal of American Studies* 24 (1990): 402–7.

Aptheker, Herbert. *Abolitionism: A Revolutionary Movement.* Boston: Twayne, 1989.

Ashworth, John. "The Relationship between Capitalism and Humanitarianism." *American Historical Review* 92 (1987): 813–28.

Austin, George Lowell. *The Life and Times of Wendell Phillips.* 1884; reprint, n.p. Afro-American Press, 1969.

Bacon, Margaret Hope. *Valiant Friend: The Life of Lucretia Mott.* New York: Walker, 1980.

Baer, Helene G. *The Heart is Like Heaven: The Life of Lydia Maria Child.* Philadelphia: University of Pennsylvania Press, 1964.

Bailyn, Bernard, et al. *The Great Republic: A History of the American People.* 1st ed. Lexington, Mass.: Heath, 1977.

Baker, Paula. "The Domestication of American Politics: Women and American Political Society, 1780–1920." *American Historical Review* 89 (1984): 620–47.

——. *The Moral Frameworks of Public Life: Gender, Politics, and the State in Rural New York, 1870–1930.* New York: Oxford University Press, 1991.

Banner, Lois W. *Elizabeth Cady Stanton: A Radical for Women's Rights.* Boston: Little, Brown, 1980.

Barker, Anthony J. *Captain Charles Stuart, Anglo-American Abolitionist.* Baton Rouge: Louisiana State University Press, 1986.

Barker-Benfield, Ben. "The Spermatic Economy: A Nineteenth Century View of Sexuality." *Feminist Studies* 1 (1972): 45–74.

Barker-Benfield, G.J., and Catherine Clinton, eds. *Portraits of American Women: From Settlement to the Present.* New York: St. Martin's, 1991.

Barnes, Gilbert H. *The Antislavery Impulse, 1830–1844.* 1933; reprint, New York: Harbinger Books, 1964.

Barry, Kathleen. *Susan B. Anthony: A Biography of a Singular Feminist.* New York: New York University Press, 1988.

Bartlett, Irving H. *Wendell Phillips: Brahmin Radical.* 1961; reprint, Westport, Conn.: Greenwood, 1973.

Basch, Françoise. "Women's Rights and the Wrongs of Marriage in Mid-Nineteenth-Century America." *History Workshop: A Journal of Socialist and Feminist Historians* 22 (1986): 18–40.

Bass, Dorothy Courtenay. " 'The Best Hopes of the Sexes': The Woman Question in Garrisonian Abolitionism." Ph.D. diss., Brown University, 1980.

Bell, Howard H. "National Negro Conventions of the Middle 1840s: Moral Suasion vs. Political Action." *Journal of Negro History* 42 (1957): 247–60.

Bernard, Joel. "Authority, Autonomy, and Radical Commitment: Stephen and Abby Kelley Foster." *Proceedings of the American Antiquarian Society* 90 (1980): 347–86.

Birney, Catherine H. *The Grimké Sisters: Sarah and Angelina Grimké. The First American Women Advocates of Abolition and Woman's Rights.* 1885; reprint, Westport, Conn.: Greenwood, 1977.

Blassingame, John W. *The Slave Community: Plantation Life in the Antebellum South.* 2d ed. New York: Oxford University Press, 1972.

Bleser, Carol, ed. *In Joy and In Sorrow: Women, Family, and Marriage in the Victorian South.* New York: Oxford University Press, 1991.

Blumin, Stuart. *The Emergence of the Middle Class: Social Experience in the American City, 1760–1900.* New York: Cambridge University Press, 1989.

Boller, Paul F. *American Transcendentalism, 1830–1860: An Intellectual Inquiry.* New York: Putnam, 1974.

Bolt, Christine, and Seymour Drescher. *Antislavery, Religion, and Reform: Essays in Memory of Roger Anstey.* Hamden, Conn.: Dawson, 1980.

Bontemps, Arna. *Free at Last: The Life of Frederick Douglass.* New York: Dodd, Mead, 1971.

Boylan, Anne M. "Women in Groups: An Analysis of Women's Benevolent Organizations in New York and Boston, 1797–1840." *Journal of American History* 71 (1984): 497–523.

——. "Women and Politics in the Era Before Seneca Falls." *Journal of the Early Republic* 10 (1990): 363–82.

Brandstadter, Evan. "Uncle Tom and Archy Moore: The Antislavery Novel as Ideological Symbol." *American Quarterly* 26 (1974): 164–75.

Brodie, Janet Farrell. *Contraception and Abortion in Nineteenth-Century America.* Ithaca: Cornell University Press, 1994.

Brown, Gillian. "Getting in the Kitchen with Dinah: Domestic Politics in *Uncle Tom's Cabin.*" *American Quarterly* 36 (1984): 503–23.

Brown, Ira V. "Cradle of Feminism: The Philadelphia Female Anti-Slavery Society, 1833–1840." *Pennsylvania Magazine of History and Biography* 102 (1978): 143–66.

——. *Mary Grew: Abolitionist and Feminist, 1813–1896.* Selinsgrove, Pa.: Susquehanna University Press, 1991.

Buhle, Mary Jo. *Women and American Socialism, 1870–1920.* Urbana: University of Illinois Press, 1981.

Bunkle, Phillida, and Beryl Hughes, eds. *Women in New Zealand Society.* Sydney: Allen and Unwin, 1980.

Burman, Sandra, ed. *Fit Work for Women.* London: Croom Helm, 1979.

Cancian, Francesca M. *Love in America: Gender and Self-Development.* Cambridge: Cambridge University Press, 1987.

Carnes, Mark C. *Secret Ritual and Manhood in Victorian America.* New Haven: Yale University Press, 1989.

Carnes, Mark C., and Clyde Griffen, eds. *Meanings for Manhood: Constructions of Masculinity in Victorian America.* Chicago: University of Chicago Press, 1990.

Carroll, Peter N., and David W. Noble. *The Free and the Unfree: A New History of the United States.* 2d ed. New York: Penguin, 1988.

Chapman, John Jay. *William Lloyd Garrison.* 2d ed. Boston: Atlantic Monthly, 1921.

Clark, Elizabeth B. "'The Sacred Rights of the Weak': Pain, Sympathy, and the Culture of Individual Rights in Antebellum America." *Journal of American History* 82 (1995): 463–93.

Clawson, Mary Ann. *Constructing Brotherhood: Class, Gender, and Fraternalism.* Princeton, N.J.: Princeton University Press, 1989.

Clifford, Deborah Pickman. *Crusader for Freedom: A Life of Lydia Maria Child.* Boston: Beacon, 1992.

Clinton, Catherine. *The Plantation Mistress: Woman's World in the Old South.* New York: Pantheon, 1982.

Coontz, Stephanie. *The Origins of Private Life: A History of American Families, 1600–1900.* London: Verso, 1988.

Cott, Nancy. "Young Women in the Second Great Awakening in New England." *Feminist Studies* 3 (1975): 15–29.

——. "Divorce and the Changing Status of Women in Eighteenth-Century Massachusetts." *William and Mary Quarterly* 33 (1976): 586–614.

——. "Eighteenth-Century Family and Social Life Revealed in Massachusetts Divorce Records." *Journal of Social History* 10 (1976): 20–43.

——. *The Bonds of Womanhood: "Woman's Sphere" in New England, 1780–1835.* New Haven: Yale University Press, 1977.

——. "Passionlessness: An Interpretation of Victorian Sexual Ideology, 1790–1850." *Signs: Journal of Women in Culture and Society* 4 (1978): 219–36.

——. *The Grounding of Modern Feminism.* New Haven: Yale University Press, 1987.

Cox, Stephen Lawrence. "Power, Oppression, and Liberation: New Hampshire Abolitionism and the Radical Critique of Slavery, 1825–1850." Ph.D. diss., University of New Hampshire, 1980.

Cromwell, Otelia. *Lucretia Mott.* 1958; reprint, New York: Russell and Russell, 1971.

Curry, Leonard P. *The Free Black in Urban America, 1800–1850: The Shadow of the Dream.* Chicago: University of Chicago Press, 1981.

Curry, Richard O., and Lawrence B. Goodheart. "'Knives in Their Heads': Passionate Self-Analysis and the Search for Identity in American Abolitionism." *Canadian Review of American Studies* 14 (1983): 401–14.

D'Emilio, John, and Estelle Freedman. *Intimate Matters: A History of Sexuality in America.* New York: Harper and Row, 1988.

Davidoff, Leonore, and Catherine Hall. *Family Fortunes: Men and Women of the English Middle Class, 1780–1850.* London: Hutchinson, 1987.

Davis, David B. "The Emergence of Immediatism in British and American Antislavery Thought." *Mississippi Valley Historical Review* 49 (1962): 209–30.

——. *The Problem of Slavery in Western Culture.* Ithaca: Cornell University Press, 1966.

——. *Slavery and Human Progress.* New York: Oxford University Press, 1984.

——. "Reflections on Abolitionism and Ideological Hegemony." *American Historical Review* 92 (1987): 797–812.

Davis, Hugh. *Joshua Leavitt: Evangelical Abolitionist.* Baton Rouge: Louisiana State University Press, 1990.

Degler, Carl N. "What Ought To Be and What Was: Women's Sexuality in the Nineteenth Century." *American Historical Review* 79 (1974): 1467–90.

——. *At Odds: Women and the Family in America From the Revolution to the Present.* New York: Oxford University Press, 1980.

Demos, John. "The Antislavery Movement and the Problem of Violent 'Means.'" *New England Quarterly* 37 (1964): 501–26.

——. *A Little Commonwealth: Family Life in Plymouth Colony.* New York: Oxford University Press, 1970.

Demos, John, and Sarane Spence Boocock. *Turning Points: Historical and Sociological Essays on the Family.* Chicago: University of Chicago Press, 1978.

Deutrich, Mabel E., and Virginia C. Purdy. *Clio Was a Woman: Studies in the History of American Women.* Washington, D.C.: Howard University Press, 1980.

Diedrich, Marion. "'My Love is Black as Yours is Fair': Premarital Love and Sexuality in the Antebellum Slave Narrative." *Phylon* 47 (1986): 238–47.

Dillon, Merton L. *The Abolitionists: The Growth of a Dissenting Minority.* DeKalb: Northern Illinois University Press, 1974.

Donald, David. *Lincoln Reconsidered: Essays on the Civil War Era.* 2d ed. New York: Knopf, 1956.

——. *Charles Sumner and the Coming of the Civil War.* New York: Knopf, 1960.

Donnelly, Mabel Collins. *The American Victorian Woman: The Myth and the Reality.* Westport, Conn. Greenwood, 1986.

Dorr, Rheta Childe. *Susan B. Anthony: The Woman Who Changed the Mind of a Nation.* 1928; reprint, New York: AMS Press, 1970.

Douglas, Ann. *The Feminization of American Culture.* New York: Knopf, 1978.

Dubbert, Joe. *A Man's Place.* Englewood Cliffs, N.J.: Prentice-Hall, 1979.

Duberman, Martin, ed. *The Antislavery Vanguard: New Essays on the Abolitionists.* Princeton: Princeton University Press, 1965.

——. *James Russell Lowell.* Boston: Houghton Mifflin, 1966.

DuBois, Ellen Carol. "Struggling Into Existence: The Feminism of Sarah and Angelina Grimké." *Women: A Journal of Liberation* 1 (1970): 4–11.

——. "The Radicalism of the Woman Suffrage Movement: Notes Toward the Reconstruction of Nineteenth-Century Feminism." *Feminist Studies* 3 (1975): 63–71.

——. *Feminism and Suffrage: The Emergence of an Independent Women's Movement in America, 1849–1869.* Ithaca: Cornell University Press, 1978.

DuBois, Ellen Carol, and Vicki L. Ruiz, eds. *Unequal Sisters: A Multicultural Reader in U.S. Women's History.* New York: Routledge, 1990.

Dudden, Faye E. *Serving Women: Household Service in the Nineteenth Century.* Middletown: Wesleyan University Press, 1983.

Dumond, Dwight L. *Antislavery: The Crusade for Freedom in America.* Ann Arbor: University of Michigan Press, 1961.

Duncan, Troy. "Stephen Symonds Foster: Radical Abolitionist." B. A. honors. diss., University of Newcastle, 1995.

Dunning, Eric, and Norbert Elias, eds. *Quest for Excitement: Sport and Leisure in the Civilizing Process.* New York: B. Blackwell, 1986.

Edelstein, Tildon G. *Strange Enthusiasm: A Life of Thomas Wentworth Higginson.* New Haven: Yale University Press, 1968.

Edwards, Herbert. "Lydia Maria Child's *The Frugal Housewife.*" *New England Quarterly* 26 (June 1953): 243–49.

Elkins, Stanley M. *Slavery: A Problem in American Institutional and Intellectual Life.* 2d ed. Chicago: University of Chicago Press, 1968.

Epstein, Barbara L. *The Politics of Domesticity: Women, Evangelism, and Temperance in Nineteenth-Century America.* Middletown: Wesleyan University Press, 1981.

Evans, Richard J. *The Feminists: Women's Emancipation Movements in Europe, America and Australasia, 1840–1920.* Rev. ed. London: Croon Helm, 1979.

Faderman, Lillian. *Surpassing the Love of Men: Romantic Friendship and Love Between Women from the Renaissance to the Present.* New York: William Morrow, 1981.

Fellman, Michael. "Theodore Parker and the Abolitionist Role in the 1850s." *Journal of American History* 61 (1974): 666–84.

Filene, Peter G. *Him/Her/Self: Sex Roles in Modern America.* New York: Harcourt Brace Jovanovich, 1974.

Filler, Louis. *The Crusade Against Slavery, 1830–1861.* 1960; reprint, New York: Harper and Row, 1963.

——. "Nonviolence and Abolition." *University Review* 30 (1964): 172–78.

Fogel, Robert, and Stanley Engerman. *Time on the Cross: The Economics of American Negro Slavery.* 2 vols. London: Wildwood, 1974.

Foucault, Michel. *The History of Sexuality.* Translated by Robert Hurley. 3 vols. New York: Pantheon Books, 1978.

Fox-Genovese, Elizabeth. *Within the Plantation Household: Black and White Women in the Old South.* Chapel Hill: University of North Carolina Press, 1988.

——. *Feminism Without Illusions: A Critique of Individualism.* Chapel Hill: University of North Carolina Press, 1991.

Fox-Genovese, Elizabeth, and Eugene D. Genovese. *Fruits of Merchant Capital: Slavery and Bourgeois Property in the Rise and Expansion of Capitalism.* New York: Oxford University Press, 1983.

Fredrickson, George, M. *The Inner Civil War: Northern Intellectuals and the Crisis of the Union.* New York: Harper and Row, 1968.

——. *The Black Image in the White Mind: The Debate on Afro-American Character and Destiny, 1817–1914.* New York: Harper and Row, 1971.

Freedman, Estelle. "Separatism as Strategy: Female Institution Building and American Feminism, 1870–1930." *Feminist Studies* 5 (1979): 512–29.

——. "Sexuality in Nineteenth-Century America: Behavior, Ideology, and Politics." *Reviews in American History* 10 (1982): 196–215.

Friedan, Betty. *The Feminine Mystique.* 1963; reprint, New York: Dell, 1967.

Friedman, Lawrence J. "The Gerrit Smith Circle: Abolitionism in the Burned-Over District." *Civil War History* 26 (1980): 18–38.

——. *Gregarious Saints: Self and Community in American Abolitionism, 1830–1870.* Cambridge: Cambridge University Press, 1982.

Gamble, Douglas A. "Garrisonian Abolitionists in the West: Some Suggestions for Study." *Civil War History* 23 (1977): 52–68.

Genovese, Eugene. *The World The Slaveholders Made: Two Essays in Interpretation.* New York: Pantheon Books, 1969.

——. *Roll, Jordan, Roll. The World the Slaves Made.* London: Andre Deutsch, 1975.

George, Carol V. R., ed. *"Remember The Ladies": New Perspectives on Women in American History.* Syracuse: Syracuse University Press, 1975.

Ginzberg, Lori D. *Women and the Work of Benevolence: Morality, Politics, and Class in the Nineteenth-Century United States.* New Haven: Yale University Press, 1990.

Goerler, Raimund E. "Family, Self, and Anti-Slavery: Sydney Howard Gay and the Abolitionist Community." Ph.D. diss., Case Western Reserve University, 1975.

Goodheart, Lawrence. *Abolitionist, Actuary, Atheist: Elizur Wright and the Reform Impulse.* Kent: Kent State University Press, 1990.

Goodheart, Lawrence, Richard D. Brown, and Stephen G. Rabe, eds. *Slavery in American Society.* 3rd ed. Lexington, Mass.: Heath, 1993.

Gordon, Linda. *Woman's Body, Woman's Right: A Social History of Birth Control in America.* 1976; reprint, Middlesex: Penguin, 1977.

Griffith, Elisabeth. *In Her Own Right: The Life of Elizabeth Cady Stanton.* New York: Oxford University Press, 1984.

Guarneri, Carl J. *The Utopian Alternative: Fourierism in Nineteenth-Century America.* Ithaca: Cornell University Press, 1991.

Gutman, Herbert. *The Black Family in Slavery and Freedom.* New York: Pantheon Books, 1976.

Habermas, Jürgen. *The Structural Transformation of the Public Sphere: An Inquiry into a Category of Bourgeois Society.* Translated by Thomas Burger. Cambridge: MIT Press, 1989.

Hahn, Emily. *Once Upon a Pedestal.* New York: Cromwell, 1974.

Halbersleben, Karen Irene. "'She Hath Done What She Could': Women's Participation in the British Antislavery Movement, 1825–1870." Ph.D. diss., State University of New York at Buffalo, 1987.

Halttunen, Karen. *Confidence Men and Painted Women: A Study of Middle-Class Culture in America, 1830–1870.* New Haven: Yale University Press, 1982.

Hansen, Debra Gold. "Bluestockings and Bluenoses: Gender, Class, and Conflict in the Boston Female Anti-Slavery Society, 1833–1840." Ph.D. diss., University of California at Irvine, 1988.

——. *Strained Sisterhood: Gender and Class in the Boston Female Anti-Slavery Society.* Amherst: University of Massachusetts Press, 1993.

Hare, Lloyd C. M. *The Greatest American Woman: Lucretia Mott.* 1937; reprint, New York: Negro Universities Press, 1970.

Hartman, Mary S., and Lois Banner, eds. *Clio's Consciousness Raised: New Perspectives on the History of Women.* 1974; reprint, New York: Octagon Books, 1976.

Haskell, Thomas L. "Capitalism and the Origins of Humanitarian Sensibility." *American Historical Review* 90 (1985): 339–61; (1985): 547–66.

——. "Convention and Hegemonic Interest in the Debate over Antislavery: A Reply to Davis and Ashworth." *American Historical Review* 92 (1987): 829–78.

Hawkins, Hugh, ed. *The Abolitionists: Means, Ends, and Motivations.* Lexington, Mass.: Heath, 1964.

Hays, Elinor Rice. *Those Extraordinary Blackwells: The Story of a Journey to a Better World.* New York: Harcourt, Brace and World, 1967.

——. *Morning Star: A Biography of Lucy Stone.* 1961; reprint, New York: Octagon Books, 1978.

Hersh, Blanche. "'A Partnership of Equals': Feminist Marriages in 19th-Century America." *University of Michigan Papers on Women's Studies* 3 (1977): 39–61.

——. *The Slavery of Sex: Feminist-Abolitionists in America.* Urbana: University of Illinois Press, 1978.

Hewitt, Nancy A. *Women's Activism and Social Change: Rochester, New York, 1822–1872.* Ithaca: Cornell University Press, 1984.

Hofstadter, Richard. *The American Political Tradition, And the Men Who Made It.* 1948; reprint, New York: Vintage Books, 1973.

Hoganson, Kristin. "Garrisonian Abolitionists and the Rhetoric of Gender, 1850–1860." *American Quarterly* 45 (1993): 556–95.

Hogeland, Ronald W. "'The Female Appendage': Feminine Life Styles in America, 1820–1860." *Civil War History* 17 (1971): 101–14.

——. "Coeducation of the Sexes at Oberlin College: A Study of Social Ideas in Mid-Nineteenth Century America." *Journal of Social History* 6 (1972–73): 160–76.

Horton, James Oliver. "Generations of Protest: Black Families and Social Reform in Ante-Bellum Boston." *New England Quarterly* 49 (1976): 242–56.

——. "Freedom's Yoke: Gender Conventions Among Antebellum Free Blacks." *Feminist Studies* 12 (1986): 51–76.

——. *Free People of Color: Inside the African American Community.* Washington, D.C.: Smithsonian Institution Press, 1993.

Horton, James Oliver, and Lois E. Horton. *Black Bostonians: Family Life and Community Struggle in the Antebellum North.* New York: Holmes and Meier, 1979.

Huston, James L. "The Experiential Basis of the Northern Antislavery Impulse." *Journal of Southern History* 56 (1990): 609–40.

Jackson, R. Wilson. *Figures of Speech: American Writers and the Literary Marketplace, from Benjamin Franklin to Emily Dickinson.* New York: Knopf, 1989.

Jacobs, Donald M. *Courage and Conscience: Black and White Abolitionists in Boston.* Bloomington: Indiana University Press, 1993.

James, Edward T., Janet Wilson James, and Paul S. Boyer, eds. *Notable American Women, 1607–*

1950: A Biographical Dictionary. 3 vols. Cambridge: Belknap Press of Harvard University Press, 1971.

Jeffrey, Kirk. "Marriage, Career, and Feminine Ideology in Nineteenth-Century America: Reconstructing the Marital Experience of Lydia Maria Child, 1828–1874." *Feminist Studies* 2 (1975): 113–30.

Jentz, John B. "The Antislavery Constituency in Jacksonian New York City." *Civil War History* 27 (1981): 101–22.

Johnson, Michael P. "Smothered Slave Infants: Were Slave Mothers at Fault?" *Journal of Southern History* 67 (1981): 493–520.

Joll, James. *Gramsci.* Glasgow: Fontana, 1977.

Karcher, Carolyn L. *The First Women in the Republic: A Cultural Biography of Lydia Maria Child.* Durham, N.C.: Duke University Press, 1994.

Katzman, David. *Seven Days a Week: Women and Domestic Service in Industrializing America.* New York: Oxford University Press, 1980.

Kennon, Donald R. " 'A Knit of Identity': Marriage and Reform in Mid-Victorian America." Ph.D. diss., University of Maryland, 1981.

——. " 'An Apple of Discord': The Woman Question at the World's Anti-Slavery Convention of 1840." *Slavery and Abolition: A Journal of Comparative Studies* 6 (1984): 244–66.

Kerber, Linda. "Abolitionists and Amalgamators: The New York City Race Riots of 1834." *New York History* 48 (1967): 28–39.

——. *Women of the Republic: Intellect and Ideology in Revolutionary America.* Chapel Hill: University of North Carolina Press, 1980.

——. "Separate Spheres, Female Worlds, Women's Place: The Rhetoric of Women's History." *Journal of American History* 75 (1988): 9–39.

Kerber, Linda K., and Jane Sherron De Hart, eds. *Women's America: Refocusing the Past.* 4th ed. New York: Oxford University Press, 1995.

Kerber, Linda K., Alice Kessler-Harris, and Kathryn Kish Sklar, eds. *U.S. History as Women's History: New Essays.* Chapel Hill: University of North Carolina Press, 1995.

Kerr, Andrea Moore. *Lucy Stone: Speaking Out for Equality.* New Brunswick: Rutgers University Press, 1992.

Korngold, Ralph. *Two Friends of Man: The Story of William Lloyd Garrison and Wendell Phillips and Their Relationship with Abraham Lincoln.* Boston: Little, Brown, 1950.

Koven, Seth, and Sonya Michel. "Womanly Duties: Maternalist Politics and the Origins of Welfare States in France, Germany, Great Britain, and the United States, 1880–1920." *American Historical Review* 95 (1990): 1076–1108.

Kraditor, Aileen S. *Means and Ends in American Abolitionism: Garrison and His Critics on Strategy and Tactics.* New York: Pantheon Books, 1967.

——. "American Radical Historians on Their Heritage." *Past and Present* 56 (1972): 136–53.

Kraut, Alan M., ed. *Crusaders and Compromisers: Essays on the Relationship of the Antislavery Struggle to the Antebellum Party System.* Westport, Conn.: Greenwood, 1983.

Lasser, Carol, ed. *Educating Men and Women Together: Coeducation in a Changing World.* Urbana: University of Illinois Press, 1987.

——. " 'Let Us Be Sisters Forever': The Sororal Model of Nineteenth-Century Female Friendship." *Signs: Journal of Women in Culture and Society* 14 (1988): 158–81.

Lears, T. J. Jackson. "The Concept of Cultural Hegemony: Problems and Possibilities." *American Historical Review* 90 (1985): 567–93.

Lerner, Gerda. *The Grimké Sisters from South Carolina: Pioneers for Woman's Rights and Abolition.* 1967; reprint, New York: Schocken Books, 1971.

——, ed. *The Majority Finds Its Past: Placing Women in History.* New York: Oxford University Press, 1979.

——. *The Creation of Patriarchy.* New York: Oxford University Press, 1986.

——. *The Creation of Feminist Consciousness: From the Middle Ages to Eighteen-Seventy.* New York: Oxford University Press, 1993.

Lesick, Lawrence. *The Lane Rebels: Evangelicalism and Anti-Slavery in Antebellum America.* Metuchen, N.J.: Scarecrow, 1980.

Leverenz, David. *Manhood and the American Renaissance.* Ithaca: Cornell University Press.

Levine, Lawrence. *Black Culture and Black Consciousness: Afro-American Folk Thought from Slavery to Freedom.* New York: Oxford University Press, 1977.

Levy, David W. "Radical Stereotypes in Antislavery Fiction." *Phylon* 31 (1970): 262–89.

Litwack, Leon. *North of Slavery: The Negro in the Free States, 1790–1860.* Chicago: University of Chicago Press, 1961.

Lumpkin, Katharine Du Pre. *The Emancipation of Angelina Grimké.* Chapel Hill: University of North Carolina Press, 1974.

Lutz, Alma. *Created Equal: A Biography of Elizabeth Cady Stanton, 1815–1902.* New York: John Day, 1940.

——. *Crusade for Freedom: Women of the Antislavery Movement.* Boston: Beacon, 1968.

Lystra, Karen. *Searching the Heart: Women, Men, and Love in Nineteenth-Century America.* New York: Oxford University Press, 1989.

Mabee, Carleton. *Black Freedom: The Nonviolent Abolitionists from 1830 Through the Civil War.* London: Macmillan, 1970.

Magdol, Edward. *The Antislavery Rank and File: A Social Profile of the Abolitionists' Constituency.* Westport, Conn.: Greenwood, 1986.

Mangan, J. A. and James Walvin. *Manliness and Morality: Middle-Class Masculinity in Britain and America, 1800–1940.* Manchester: Manchester University Press, 1987.

Marsh, Margaret. "Suburban Men and Masculine Domesticity, 1870–1915." *American Quarterly* 40 (1988): 165–86.

——. "From Separation to Togetherness: The Social Construction of Domestic Space in American Suburbs, 1840–1915." *Journal of American History* 76 (1989): 506–27.

Matthews, Donald C. "The Abolitionists on Slavery: The Critique Behind the Social Movement." *Journal of Southern History* 33 (1967): 163–82.

Matthews, Glenna. *"Just a Housewife": The Rise and Fall of Domesticity in America.* New York: Oxford University Press, 1987.

Maynard, Douglas H. "The World's Anti-Slavery Convention of 1840." *Mississippi Valley Historical Review* 47 (1960): 452–71.

McCurry, Stephanie. "The Two Faces of Republicanism: Gender and Proslavery Politics in Antebellum South Carolina." *Journal of American History* 78 (1992): 1245–64.

McFeely, William S. *Frederick Douglass.* New York: Norton, 1991.

McInerney, Daniel J. " 'A State of Commerce': Market Power and Slave Power in Abolitionist Political Economy." *Civil War History* 37 (1991): 101–19.

——. *The Fortunate Heirs of Freedom: Abolition and Republican Thought.* Lincoln: University of Nebraska Press, 1994.

Melder, Keith. "Forerunners of Freedom: The Grimké Sisters in Massachusetts, 1837–38." *Essex Institute Historical Collections* 3 (1967): 223–49.

——. *Beginnings of Sisterhood: The American Woman's Rights Movement, 1800–1850.* New York: Schocken Books, 1977.

Melia, Margot. "The Role of Black Garrisonian Women in Antislavery and Other Reforms in the Antebellum North, 1830–1865." Ph.D. diss., University of Western Australia, 1991.

Meltzer, Milton. *Tongue of Flame: The Life of Lydia Maria Child.* New York: Cromwell, 1965.

Merrill, Walter M. "A Passionate Attachment: William Lloyd Garrison's Courtship of Helen Eliza Benson." *New England Quarterly* 39 (1956): 182–203.

——. *Against Wind and Tide: A Biography of Wm. Lloyd Garrison.* Cambridge: Harvard University Press, 1963.

Midgley, Clare. *Women Against Slavery: The British Campaigns, 1780–1870.* London: Routledge, 1992.
Morantz, Regina Markell. "Making Women Modern: Middle-Class Women and Health Reform in 19th-Century America." *Journal of Social History* 10 (1977): 490–507.
Morgan, Edmund. "The Puritans and Sex." *New England Quarterly* 25 (1942): 591–607.
Motz, Marilyn Ferris. *True Sisterhood: Michigan Women and Their Kin, 1820–1920.* Albany: State University of New York Press, 1983.
Neurmberger, Ruth K. *The Free Produce Movement: A Quaker Protest Against Slavery.* Durham, N.C.: Duke University Press, 1942.
Norton, Mary Beth. *Liberty's Daughters: The Revolutionary Experience of American Women, 1750–1800.* Boston: Little, Brown, 1980.
Nye, Russel B. *William Lloyd Garrison and the Humanitarian Reformers.* Boston: Little, Brown, 1955.
Oakes, James. *The Ruling Race: A History of American Slaveholders.* 1982; reprint, New York: Vintage Books, 1983.
Oakley, Mary B. *Elizabeth Cady Stanton.* New York: Feminist Press, 1972.
Offen, Karen, Ruth Roach Pierson, and Jane Rendall, eds. *Writing Women's History: International Perspectives.* Basingstoke: Macmillan, 1991.
Oldfield, J. R. "Anti-Slavery Sentiment in Children's Literature, 1750–1850." *Slavery and Abolition* 10 (1989): 44–59.
Pease, Jane H. "The Freshness of Fanaticism: Abby Kelley Foster: An Essay in Reform." Ph.D. diss., University of Rochester, 1969.
Pease, Jane H., and William H. Pease. "Antislavery Ambivalence: Immediatism, Expediency, Race." *American Quarterly* 17 (1965): 682–95.
——. *Bound With Them in Chains: A Biographical History of the Antislavery Movement.* Westport, Conn.: Greenwood, 1972.
——. "Confrontation and Abolition in the 1850s." *Journal of American History* 58 (1972): 923–37.
——. "Ends, Means, and Attitudes: Black-White Conflict in the Antislavery Movement." *Civil War History* 18 (1972): 117–28.
——. *They Who Would Be Free: Blacks' Search for Freedom, 1830–1861.* New York: Atheneum, 1974.
Perlmann, Joel, and Dennis Shirley. "When Did New England Women Acquire Literacy?" *William and Mary Quarterly* 48 (1991): 50–67.
Perry, Lewis *Radical Abolitionism: Anarchy and the Government of God in Antislavery Thought.* Ithaca: Cornell University Press, 1973.
——. "'Progress, Not Pleasure, Is Our Aim': The Sexual Advice of an Antebellum Radical." *Journal of Social History* 12 (1979): 354–67.
——. *Childhood, Marriage, and Reform: Henry Clarke Wright, 1797–1870.* Chicago: University of Chicago Press, 1980.
Perry, Lewis, and Michael Fellman, eds. *Antislavery Reconsidered: New Perspectives on the Abolitionists.* Baton Rouge: Louisiana State University Press, 1979.
Phillips, Anne, ed. *Feminism and Equality.* Oxford: Basil Blackwell, 1987.
Pleck, Elizabeth, and Joseph Pleck, eds. *The American Man.* Englewood Cliffs, N.J.: Prentice-Hall, 1980.
Pugh, David G. *Sons of Liberty: The Masculine Mind in Nineteenth-Century America.* Westport, Conn.: Greenwood, 1983.
Quint, Howard H., and Milton Cantor, eds. *Men, Women, and Issues in American History.* Vol. 1. Homewood, Ill.: Dorsey, 1975.
Raboteau, Albert J. *Slave Religion: The "Invisible Institution" in the Antebellum South.* New York: Oxford University Press, 1978.
Rapson, Richard L. "The American Child as Seen by British Travellers, 1845–1935." *American Quarterly* 17 (1965): 520–34.

Ratner, Lorman. "Northern Concern for Social Order as a Cause for Rejecting Anti-Slavery, 1831–1840." *The Historian* 28 (1965): 1–18.

——. *Powder Keg: Northern Opposition to the Antislavery Movement, 1831–1840.* New York: Basic Books, 1968.

Rendall, Jane, ed. *Equal or Different: Women's Politics, 1800–1914.* Oxford: Basil Blackwell, 1987.

Rice, Arthur H. "Henry B. Stanton as a Political Abolitionist." Ed.D. diss., Columbia University, 1968.

Richards, Leonard. *"Gentlemen of Property and Standing": Anti-Abolition Mobs in Jacksonian America.* New York: Oxford University Press, 1970.

Riegal, Robert E. "Women's Clothes and Women's Rights." *American Quarterly* 15 (1963): 390–401.

Riess, Steven A. "Sport and the Redefinition of American Middle-Class Masculinity." *International Journal of the History of Sport* 8 (1991): 5–27.

Riley, Glenda Gates. "The Subtle Subversion: Changes in the Traditionalist Image of the American Woman." *The Historian* 32 (1970): 210–27.

Rosaldo, Michelle Zimbalist, and Louise Lamphere, eds. *Woman, Culture, and Society.* Stanford: Stanford University Press, 1974.

Rosenberg, Charles E. "Sexuality, Class and Role in 19th-Century America." *American Quarterly* 25 (1973): 131–53.

Rosenberg, Rosalind. "In Search of Woman's Nature." *Feminist Studies* 3 (1975): 141–54.

Rosenberger, Homer T. "Montgomery County's Greatest Lady: Lucretia Mott." *Bulletin of the Historical Society of Montgomery County* 6 (1948): 91–171.

Rothman, Ellen K. "Sex and Self-Control: Middle-Class Courtship in America, 1770–1870." *Journal of Social History* 15 (1982): 409–25.

——. *Hands and Hearts: A History of Courtship in America.* New York: Basic Books, 1984.

Rotundo, E. Anthony. "Body and Soul: Changing Ideals of American Middle-Class Manhood, 1770–1920." *Journal of Social History* 16 (1983): 23–38.

——. "Romantic Friendship: Male Intimacy and Middle-Class Youth in the Northern United States, 1800–1900." *Journal of Social History* 23 (1989): 1–25.

——. *American Manhood: Transformations in Masculinity from the Revolution to the Modern Era.* New York: Basic Books, 1993.

Rugoff, Milton. *Prudery and Passion: Sexuality in Victorian America.* New York: Putnam, 1971.

Ryan, Mary P. "The Power of Women's Networks: A Case Study of Female Moral Reform in Antebellum America." *Feminist Studies* 4 (1979): 66–85.

——. *Cradle of the Middle Class: The Family in Oneida County, New York, 1790–1865.* Cambridge: Cambridge University Press, 1981.

——. *The Empire of the Mother: American Writing about Domesticity, 1830–1860.* New York: Hamworth, 1982.

——. *Womanhood in America: From Colonial Times to the Present.* 3d ed. New York: Franklin Watts, 1983.

Sánchez-Eppler, Karen. "Bodily Bonds: The Intersecting Rhetorics of Feminism and Abolitionism." *Representations* 24 (1988): 28–59.

——. *Touching Liberty: Abolition, Feminism, and the Politics of the Body.* Berkeley and Los Angeles: University of California Press, 1993.

Scott, Anne Firor. *The Southern Lady: From Pedestal to Politics, 1830–1930.* Chicago: University of Chicago Press, 1970.

——. *Natural Allies. Women's Associations in American History.* Urbana: University of Illinois Press, 1991.

Scott, Joan W. "Gender: A Useful Category of Historical Analysis." *American Historical Review* 91 (1986): 1053–75.

Sellers, Charles. *The Market Revolution: Jacksonian America, 1815–1846.* New York: Oxford University Press, 1991.

Sherwin, Oscar. *Prophet of Liberty: The Life and Times of Wendell Phillips.* New York: Bookman Associates, 1958.

Shorter, Edward. *The Making of the Modern Family.* 1975; reprint, London: Collins, 1976.

Siltanen, Janet, and Michelle Stanworth. *Women and the Public Sphere: A Critique of Sociology and Politics.* London: Hutchinson, 1984.

Sinclair, Andrew. *The Emancipation of the American Woman.* 1965; reprint, New York: Harper and Row, 1966.

Sklar, Kathryn Kish. *Catharine Beecher: A Study in American Domesticity.* New Haven: Yale University Press, 1973.

——. "'Women Who Speak for an Entire Nation': American and British Women Compared at the World Anti-Slavery Convention, London, 1840." *Pacific Historical Review* 59 (1990): 453–99.

Skocpol, Theda. *Protecting Soldiers and Mothers: The Political Origins of Social Policy in the United States.* Cambridge: Belknap Press of Harvard University Press, 1992.

Slotkin, Richard. *Regeneration Through Violence: Mythology of the American Frontier, 1600–1860.* Middletown: Wesleyan University Press, 1973.

Smith, Daniel Scott. "Family Limitation, Sexual Control, and Domestic Feminism in Victorian America." *Feminist Studies* 1 (1972): 40–57.

——. "Parental Power and Marriage Patterns—An Analysis of Historical Trends in Hingham, Massachusetts." *Journal of Marriage and the Family* 35 (1973): 419–28.

Smith-Rosenberg, Carroll. "The Female World of Love and Ritual: Relations between Women in Nineteenth-Century America." *Signs: Journal of Women in Culture and Society* 1 (1975): 1–29.

——. *Disorderly Conduct: Visions of Gender in Victorian America.* New York: Oxford University Press, 1985.

——. "Dis-Covering the Subject of the 'Great Constitutional Discussion,' 1786–1789." *Journal of American History* 79 (1992): 841–73.

Spurlock, John C. *Free Love: Marriage and Middle-Class Radicalism in America, 1825–1860.* New York: New York University Press, 1988.

Stansell, Christine. *City of Women: Sex and Class in New York, 1789–1860.* New York: Knopf, 1986.

Stearns, Carol Zisowitz, and Peter N. Stearns. "Victorian Sexuality: Can Historians Do It Better?" *Journal of Social History* 18 (1985): 625–34.

——. *Anger: The Struggle for Emotional Control in America's History.* Chicago: University of Chicago Press, 1986.

Stearns, Peter N. *Be A Man! Males in Modern Society.* New York: Holmes and Meier, 1979.

——. *Jealousy: The Evolution of an Emotion in American History.* New York: Oxford University Press, 1989.

Sterling, Dorothy. *Ahead of Her Time: Abby Kelley and the Politics of Antislavery.* New York: Norton, 1991.

Stewart, James B. "The Aims and Impact of Garrisonian Abolitionism, 1840–1860." *Civil War History* 15 (1969): 197–209.

——. *Wendell Phillips: Liberty's Hero.* Baton Rouge: Louisiana State University Press, 1986.

——. *William Lloyd Garrison and the Challenge of Emancipation.* Arlington Heights, Ill.: Harlan Davidson, 1992.

Stone Blackwell, Alice. *Lucy Stone.* 1930; reprint, New York: Kraus Reprint, 1971.

Stowe, Charles Edward, and Lyman Beecher Stowe. *Harriet Beecher Stowe: The Story of Her Life.* Boston: Houghton Mifflin, 1911.

Stowe, Steven. *Intimacy and Power in the Old South: Ritual in the Lives of the Planters.* Baltimore: Johns Hopkins University Press, 1987.

Sundquist, Eric J., ed. *New Essays on Uncle Tom's Cabin.* Cambridge: Cambridge University Press, 1986.

Takaki, Ronald T. *Iron Cages: Race and Culture in Nineteenth-Century America.* New York: Knopf, 1979.

Taylor, William R., and Christopher Lasch. "Two 'Kindred Spirits': Sorority and Family in New England, 1839–1846." *New England Quarterly* 36 (1963): 23–41.

Temperley, Howard. "Capitalism, Slavery and Ideology." *Past and Present* 75 (1977): 94–118.

Thomas, Benjamin P. *Theodore Weld: Crusader for Freedom.* New Brunswick: Rutgers University Press, 1950.

Thomas, John L. *The Liberator: William Lloyd Garrison.* Boston: Little, Brown, 1963.

Thomas, Keith. *Man and Nature: Changing Attitudes in England, 1500–1800.* London: Allen Lane, 1980.

Tyrell, Ian. *Woman's World/Woman's Empire: The Woman's Christian Temperance Union in International Perspective, 1880–1930.* Chapel Hill: University of North Carolina Press, 1991.

Van Broekhoven, Deborah Bingham. "'A Determination to Labor . . . ': Female Antislavery Activity in Rhode Island." *Rhode Island History* 44 (1985): 35–44.

——. "'Better Than A Clay Club': The Organization of Antislavery Fairs, 1835–1860." Forthcoming.

——. "Needles, Pens and Petitions: Reading Women into Antislavery History." In *The North Looks at Slavery,* edited by Martin Blatt. Garland, forthcoming.

Walsh, Mary Roth. *"Doctors Wanted, No Women Need Apply": Sexual Barriers in the Medical Profession, 1835–1975.* New Haven: Yale University Press, 1977.

Walters Ronald G. "The Erotic South: Civilization and Sexuality in American Abolitionism." *American Quarterly* 25 (1973): 177–201.

——. *The Antislavery Appeal: American Abolitionism After 1830.* Baltimore: Johns Hopkins University Press, 1976.

——. *American Reformers.* New York: Hill and Wang, 1978.

Ware, Ethel K. "Lydia Maria Child and Anti-Slavery." *Boston Public Library Quarterly* 3 (1951): 251–75; 4 (1952): 34–49.

Washington, Booker T. *Frederick Douglass.* 1907; reprint, New York: Greenwood, 1969.

Welter, Barbara. "The Cult of True Womanhood: 1820–1860." *American Quarterly* 18 (1966): 151–74.

White, Deborah Gray. *Ar'n't I a Woman? Female Slaves in the Plantation South.* New York: Norton, 1985.

Wilkinson, Norman P. "The Philadelphia Free Produce Attack Upon Slavery." *Pennsylvania Magazine of History and Biography* 6 (1942): 294–313.

Williams, Carolyn Luverne. "Religion, Race, and Gender in Antebellum American Radicalism: The Philadelphia Female Anti-Slavery Society, 1833–1870." Ph.D. diss., University of California, Los Angeles, 1991.

Wilson, R. Jackson. *Figures of Speech: American Writers and the Literary Marketplace, from Benjamin Franklin to Emily Dickinson.* New York: Knopf, 1989.

Winch, Julie. *Philadelphia's Black Elite: Activism, Accommodation, and the Struggle for Autonomy, 1787–1848.* Philadelphia: Temple University Press, 1988.

Wyatt-Brown, Bertram. *Southern Honor: Ethics and Behavior in the Old South.* New York: Oxford University Press, 1982.

——. *Yankee Saints and Southern Sinners.* Baton Rouge: Louisiana State University Press, 1985.

Wyman, Lillie Buffum Chace. "Reminiscences of Two Abolitionists." *New England Magazine* (January 1903): 536–50.

——. *American Chivalry.* Boston: W. B. Clarke, 1913.

Yee, Shirley J. *Black Women Abolitionists: A Study in Activism.* Knoxville: University of Tennessee Press, 1992.

Yellin, Jean Fagan. *Women and Sisters: The Antislavery Feminists in American Culture* New Haven: Yale University Press, 1989.

Yellin, Jean Fagan, and John C. Van Horne, eds. *The Abolitionist Sisterhood: Women's Political Culture in Antebellum America.* Ithaca: Cornell University Press, 1994.

Zanger, Jules. "The Tragic Octoroon' in Pre-Civil War Fiction." *American Quarterly* 18 (1966): 63–70.

INDEX